Embodied Economies

Latinidad
TRANSNATIONAL CULTURES IN THE UNITED STATES

This series publishes books that deepen and expand our understanding of Latina/o populations, especially in the context of their transnational relationships within the Americas. Focusing on borders and boundary-crossings, broadly conceived, the series is committed to publishing scholarship in history, film and media, literary and cultural studies, public policy, economics, sociology, and anthropology. Inspired by interdisciplinary approaches, methods, and theories developed out of the study of transborder lives, cultures, and experiences, titles enrich our understanding of transnational dynamics.

Matt Garcia, Series Editor, Professor of Latin American,
Latino and Caribbean Studies, and History, Dartmouth College

For a list of titles in the series, see the last page of the book.

Embodied Economies

Diaspora and Transcultural Capital in Latinx Caribbean Fiction and Theater

ISRAEL REYES

RUTGERS UNIVERSITY PRESS

NEW BRUNSWICK, CAMDEN, AND NEWARK,

NEW JERSEY, AND LONDON

Library of Congress Cataloging-in-Publication Data

Names: Reyes, Israel, author.
Title: Embodied economies : diaspora and transcultural capital in Latinx Caribbean
    fiction and theater / Israel Reyes.
Description: New Brunswick : Rutgers University Press, [2022] | Series:
    Latinidad: transnational cultures in the United States | Includes
    bibliographical references and index.
Identifiers: LCCN 2021038287 | ISBN 9781978827851 (paperback ; alk. paper) |
    ISBN 9781978827868 (cloth ; alk. paper) | ISBN 9781978827875 (epub) |
    ISBN 9781978827882 (pdf)
Subjects: LCSH: American literature—Caribbean American authors—History
    and criticism. | American fiction—21st century—History and criticism. |
    Caribbean fiction (Spanish)—21st century—History and criticism. |
    Social mobility in literature. | Culture in literature. | Group identity
    in literature. | Emigration and immigration in literature. | LCGFT:
    Literary criticism.
Classification: LCC PS153.C27 E63 2022 | DDC 810.9/868729—dc23/eng/20211118
LC record available at https://lccn.loc.gov/2021038287

A British Cataloging-in-Publication record for this book is available from the British
Library.

References to internet websites (URLs) were accurate at the time of writing. Neither the author
nor Rutgers University Press is responsible for URLs that may have expired or changed since
the manuscript was prepared.

♾ The paper used in this publication meets the requirements of the American National Standard for Information Sciences—Permanence of Paper for Printed Library Materials, ANSI
Z39.48-1992.

www.rutgersuniversitypress.org

Manufactured in the United States of America

For my parents, Tacho y Margo Reyes

Contents

Contents

Note on Translations
and Terminology

When available, I cite published translations of Spanish-language texts by translator's name in the endnotes. All other translations are my own.

When deciding whether to use Latina, Latino, Latinx, or Hispanic, I chose Latinx as the gender-neutral adjective, while using Latina and Latino to describe gender-specific characters and identities. I also chose to use Latinx Caribbean rather than the more commonly used Hispanic Caribbean to gesture toward the diasporic imaginary and decolonial discourses articulated by the works of fiction and theater I analyze in the following chapters.

Embodied Economies

Introduction

Me es imposible describir esta "cierta manera." Sólo diré que había un polvillo dorado y antiguo entre sus piernas nudosas, un olor de albahaca y hierbabuena en sus vestidos, una sabiduría simbólica, ritual, en sus gestos y en su chachareo. Entonces supe de golpe que no ocurriría el apocalipsis.

—Antonio Benítez-Rojo, La isla que se repite: El Caribe y la perspectiva posmoderna

It's impossible for me to describe this "certain way"; I will only say that there was an ancient and golden dust between their knotted legs, a scent of basil and mint in their dresses, a symbolic, ritual wisdom in their gestures and their carefree chatter. I suddenly realized there would be no apocalypse.

—Antonio Benítez-Rojo, The Repeating Island: The Caribbean and the Postmodern Perspective

Cuban writer and intellectual Antonio Benítez-Rojo (1931–2005) witnesses this "certain way," or *cierta manera*," as a child living through the fear and foreboding during the Cuban Missile Crisis of October 1962. He focuses on the image of two Black Cuban women and the embodied practice of their carefree walking, while the rest of the nation is huddled in dread of the coming nuclear annihilation. His attention to "performance" and "rhythm" in this way of walking, as he later theorizes, marks the intersection between national identities, cultural imaginaries, and the material and bodily practices that situate and differentiate communities and societies in a global context. However, apocalypses in the Caribbean do happen, whether they be caused by natural or man-made disasters. When the Berlin Wall fell in 1989, it would be the Cuban economy that would crumble since its reliance on the Soviet Union was now at an end, launching the country into the more than decade-long malaise and era of extreme poverty known as the Special Period.[1] At the time I write this introduction, it has been over ten years since the deadly earthquake that leveled Haiti in 2010. And while a million or more displaced Haitians crossed the border to find refuge in the Dominican Republic and other countries across the Americas, only three years later would the courts strip the citizenship from tens of thousands of Dominicans of Haitian descent and deport them to a country they did not know.[2] In Puerto Rico, the last decades of economic, environmental, and political devastation have left the archipelago only further entrenched in the U.S. colonialist regime, while triggering one of the most significant outflows of Puerto Ricans to the United States since the days of Operation Bootstrap in the 1950s and 1960s.[3] As Sandra Ruiz argues, "September 2017's Hurricane Maria is a chief instance of how the Rican [sic] body, in particular, continuously enacts permanent endurance practices to cultivate an existence under colonial time."[4] Despite these natural and man-made catastrophes, the people of the Caribbean find ways to emerge from the rubble of their toppled cities, broken economies, and corrupt governments. Their *cierta manera* could not stave off these apocalypses, nevertheless, yet Caribbean peoples and nations have had to mobilize and make do—*hacer de tripas corazón*—through a combination of protest, art, and performance in order to resist the crushing effects of these near apocalyptic events and oppressive circumstances. Furthermore, when that *cierta manera* takes flight, as in the case of the multiple Caribbean histories of exile, migration, and diaspora, those ways of walking are often recalibrated and redirected, and those particular embodiments of race, gender, and sexuality confront new fields of social mobility where a Caribbean *cierta manera* is incongruous, devalued, and denigrated. The works of fiction and theater I compare and analyze in this book tell the familiar story of ambitious individuals who migrate to the United States and struggle to improve their lives, but they also question how these dreams stand to reproduce the logic of social domination and economic exploitation, redirecting their *cierta manera* to confront the contradictions of their newly accumulated economic and cultural capital.

For Benítez-Rojo, the embodied practices of the Caribbean *cierta manera* simultaneously invoke and stave off catastrophe and resist annihilation. Benítez-Rojo's concept imagines the ways Caribbean history and cultural production have resisted concepts of linear time, linguistic purity, and homogenous national identities. His argument attempts to establish "that the Caribbean is an important historico-economic sea and, further, a cultural meta-archipelago without center and without limits, a chaos within which there is an island that proliferates endlessly, each copy a different one, founding and refounding ethnological materials like a cloud will do with its vapor."[5] Benítez-Rojo's formulation offers great insight into how Latinx Caribbean cultures transform and reproduce through dispersal and displacement, as in the case of the multiple exiles, migrations, and diasporas that are narrated or dramatized in the literature I examine throughout this book. In particular, these works of fiction and theater explore the embodiment and mobility that constitute embedded strategies of survival and empowerment in the pursuit of economic upward mobility.

However, Benítez-Rojo's depiction of the two Black Cuban women and their way of walking invokes gender and racial essentialisms that undermine his overall analysis of the link between culture and the history of what he calls a "Caribbean machine" of the plantation economy. In her analysis of how Caribbean male writers like Paul Gilroy and Benítez-Rojo have characterized the female body through maritime metaphors, Omise'eke Natasha Tinsley writes, "Bleeding, orgasming, or both, Benítez-Rojo's cunnic Caribbean overexposes the sexualized bodies that Gilroy denies. Like the sea, the space between women's legs is at once insistently present and insistently ethereal; like the sea, the space between women's legs becomes a metaphor to mine."[6] Furthermore, the overarching frame Benítez-Rojo develops from postmodern chaos theory imagines an arbitrary and unmoored trajectory for Caribbean nations and communities, which ostensibly appears as liberatory but runs aground against the rigid, centralized controls of the contemporary neoliberal economy and continued U.S. domination over its colonized territories in the region.

One way to reorient Benítez-Rojo's notion of the Caribbean *cierta manera* is to place it in counterpoint with an earlier use of that phrase and concept in the 1974 film *De cierta manera / One Way or Another*, by Black Cuban filmmaker Sara Gómez (1943–1974). Gómez studied music at the Conservatorio de La Habana and worked as a student journalist before she began her filmmaking career at the Instituto Cubano del Arte e Industria Cinematográficos (ICAIC) in 1961 as a production assistant. She directed her first documentary, *Iré a Santiago / I Will Go to Santiago*, in 1964 and worked alongside other Cuban filmmakers such as Tomás Gutiérrez Alea and Julio García Espinoza. However, in 1974 she succumbed to an asthma attack before she could finish her first and only full-length feature film, *De cierta manera / One Way or Another*, which Gutiérrez Alea and García Espinoza then edited and brought to release in 1977.[7] The film is innovative for its combination of a fictional love story with documentary footage and omniscient voiceovers that convey the Revolutionary critique of false consciousness and push the Cuban nation toward a modern, progressive restructuring of society. In particular, the film explores the obstacles to overcoming the anachronistic social norms around race and gender, repeatedly symbolized through sequences showing a wrecking ball demolishing the slums of Las Yaguas and busy laborers building new, modern residences for the most marginal and impoverished members of Cuban society.

The fictional love story revolves around Yolanda—a light-skinned schoolteacher from a well-educated family who, prior to the Revolution, *tenía recursos* (had resources)—and Mario, a dark-skinned worker from the Las Yaguas community who—up until conscription in the Cuban military—was an aimless and delinquent youth who had no sense of purpose other than having a good time. The love story serves as a dialectical exchange between Yolanda's more progressive attitude toward gender equality and Mario's entrenched machismo, which places him in a compromising position with his male friends who cling to the regressive attitudes toward male privilege and a code of honor. Many of the film's criticisms are aimed at the Afro-Cuban secret male societies—the *ñáñigos*—in which myth and ritual serve to perpetuate misogyny and violence. The film's dismissive posture toward Santería, in general, reflects the contemporaneous cultural politics of the Cuban regime, which sought to suppress all forms of religious practice, including those associated with Afro-Cuban traditions.[8] And in spite of her more progressive gender politics, Yolanda clashes with the disenfranchised and impoverished members of the community where she has been assigned to teach. She, too, holds on to pre-Revolutionary norms around race and class, and she resents the criticisms of her colleagues who confront her about her high-handed treatment of her students and their families. The title of the film conveys how these social norms are uncritically accepted and reproduced (in a certain way), but also how these obstacles to progressive modernity must be overcome (one way or another).

Yet it is not only the title that serves as a counterpoint with which I attempt to reorient Benítez-Rojo's use of the phrase *cierta manera*. The film also includes several scenes in which walking a certain way reveals the embodied practices that can hinder or propel societal change. In an intimate bedroom scene, Yolanda, wearing only a shirt and underwear, teases Mario for the two different ways he walks: first, the macho swagger he uses to fit in with his male friends; and second, the more casual, less guarded way he walks when meeting with her. She stands up and imitates Mario's hypermasculine gait as a way to denaturalize the male privilege this certain way of walking reproduces in homosocial relations. However, in the final scene, we see a long shot of both Yolanda and Mario as they walk through the changing neighborhood of Las Yaguas. They argue animatedly as they move up the street, and the camera looks down from above to situate their lover's quarrel amid the promise of a newly restructured society. In his analysis of this film, Rafael Ocasio writes,

> As the end of the film stresses, Mario cannot explain or, at least, verbalize the reason for breaking away from what he labels "men's moral code." The last scene presents Mario and Yolanda, walking together, holding hands, as they head back to Las Yaguas's modern multi-leveled housing project, which the viewer assumes is the same witnessed by the documentary in its building stages. The visual references to a black culture (whether religious or social) are eliminated from the shot, which emphasizes the modernity of the construction. Modernism becomes, therefore, equated with revolutionary behavior; the Las Yaguas community will undergo a painful epiphany similar to that of Mario.[9]

The "visual references to a black culture" are not entirely absent, however, as Yolanda and Mario embody their mixed-raced heritage, although their path forward is redirected toward the Cuban regime's modernization project. Both Benítez-Rojo and Gómez link these certain ways of walking and moving to broader historico-political changes taking place in Revolutionary Cuban society. Whereas Benítez-Rojo extols an essentialist and enduring Caribbean *cierta manera* from the perspective of a white masculine gaze, Gómez mobilizes her characters dialogically and dialectically as agents of change and transformation, as much of their bodily practices as of the Cuban nation. Their new way of walking leaves unresolved their contentious bickering, but they stick together to move toward a community rebuilt through the collective effort of a multiracial, egalitarian society. Individual and collective mobility follow the intersecting paths of bodily practices and economic regimes.

The counterpoint I establish between Benítez-Rojo and Gómez owes its critical approach to another Cuban writer, anthropologist, and intellectual: Fernando Ortiz (1881–1969). Ortiz's seminal work, *Contrapunteo cubano del tabaco y el azúcar / Cuban Counterpoint: Tobacco and Sugar* (1940/1995), examines the material and bodily practices that are associated with these two agricultural products and how colonialism and capitalism transformed these crops into global commodities. Through this comparative approach, the indigenous tobacco and the imported sugar constitute the two crops most associated with Cuban national identity, yet their origins, cultivation, and methods of use and ingestion have widely different impacts on the land, the economy, and the bodies of those who consume them. Enrico Mario Santí explains, "Ortiz took the title from Cuban folk music. According to Pichardo, Cuban *contrapunteo* means 'dispute or saucy or colorful sayings exchanged by two or more people; and from this the vulgar reciprocal verb *contrapuntearse* (to counterpoint)."[10] The discursive battle between Don Tabaco and Doña Azúcar also invokes the medieval morality narrative by Juan Ruiz, Arcipreste de Hita, whose *Libro de buen* amor (1330) pits two allegorical characters—don Carnal and doña Cuaresma—in a discursive battle that satirizes medieval theological debates.[11] In spite of the palimpsests and parodies in Ortiz's Cuban counterpoint, his allegory essentializes race and gender in its analysis of Cuban and Caribbean societies, particularly its use of figurative tropes that characterize tobacco as indigenous and male and sugar as white and female.[12] My reimagining of counterpoint resists such essentializing figurations, yet it remains attentive to the ways economic and cultural capital are acquired and legitimized through embodied practices, which inevitably engage with the politics of racial, gender, and sexual identities.

Ortiz's counterpoint develops the concept of "transculturation" to more precisely identify how cultural contact, conflict, and transformation are generated through the production of tobacco and sugar as agricultural commodities. Ortiz coins this term as a corrective to the Anglo-American concept of acculturation, which assumes a complete assimilation from a marginal to a dominant culture. Ortiz examines the commodification of tobacco and sugar to understand the ways cultures in contact engage in a creative process of acquisition (acculturation), loss (deculturation), and change (neoculturation). Ortiz's definition, and its focus on Cuba, also considers transculturation through the force of state power, the exploitative and extractive practices of capitalist expansion under colonialism, and the commoditization of enslaved and subaltern subjects, whose racialized bodies have been and continue to be a primary resource, factor of production, and fetishized consumable good. The term "transculturation" has been debated, reconceptualized, and critiqued by a number of Latin American studies scholars, yet Ortiz's original coining of this term in 1940 remains relevant for its early analysis of the link between cultures in contact and economic systems.[13]

Latinx Caribbeans of the diaspora undergo multiple processes of transculturation through migration and in the cultural "contact zones," which Mary Louise Pratt defines as "social spaces where disparate cultures meet, clash, and grapple with each other, often in highly asymmetrical relations of domination and subordination—like colonialism, slavery, or their aftermaths as they are lived out across the globe today."[14] In the case of Puerto Rican, Dominican, and Cuban diasporic subjects, these contact zones are dispersed across multiple locations, both in U.S. ethnic enclaves and in the Caribbean basin. The literary texts, art, films, media, and cultural institutions that articulate this experience reflect the way transculturation can serve to destabilize the elitist hierarchies that a colonialist legacy has instituted in its imperative to legitimize and segregate nationalist literary traditions, languages, gender and sexual identities, racial communities, and social classes. The transcultural capital that these diasporic subjects use helps to navigate the multiple sites of conflict and trajectories of passage enacted in the specific transnational relations of the Latinx Caribbean, where cultures in contact construct and deconstruct values, ideologies, and subjectivities according and in opposition to the logic of capitalist expansion and the politics of globalization.

Transculturation allows for an alternate way to conceptualize what Ortiz identifies as the U.S. notion of "the melting pot," which emphasizes shedding the language and practices associated with a heritage culture and adopting the language and practices of a hegemonic culture. Ortiz argues that in Cuba, and more generally the Americas as a whole, the history of conquest, geographic displacements, and demographic shifts shows how transformation occurs in multiple directions, even as power structures establish themselves along lines of technological and economic dominance. Ortiz writes:

> en todo abrazo de culturas sucede lo que en la cópula genética de los individuos: la criatura siempre tiene algo de ambos progenitores, pero también siempre es distinta de cada uno de los dos.[15]

> the result of every union of cultures is similar to that of reproductive process between individuals: the offspring always has something of both parents but is always different from each of them.[16]

Once again, Ortiz's figurative language instills a biological essentialism in his theory, which reflects the organicist functionalism in anthropology that characterized the work of Bronislaw Malinowski, one of Ortiz's interlocutors and the author of a short introduction to the first edition of *Contrapunteo*. Nevertheless, the theory of transculturation does more than use gendered allegories or functionalist essentialisms to develop its intervention in Cuban and Latin American cultural debates; it establishes a compelling link between capitalist economic development and the habits of the mind and body. Unlike the notions of acculturation and the "melting pot," which reproduce and legitimize dominant forms of capital, transculturation allows for an analysis of Latinx Caribbean literature and theater as forms of decolonial discourse. Aníbal Quijano defines the coloniality of power as the logic of colonialism that continues to position non-European nations and former European colonies in a dominated and dependent relationship with Europe and the United States. This coloniality of power is also structured on a racial hierarchy in which the white male European occupies the highest position of privilege

in the socioeconomic pyramid that characterizes Western notions of modernization and progress. In this way, counterpoint as method and transculturation as
theory help understand how the embodied economies of the Latinx Caribbean
diaspora operate both within the matrices of the coloniality of power and at the
margins of U.S. hegemonic culture.[17]

What does Ortiz's counterpoint between tobacco and sugar and his theory of
transculturation have to do with Latinx Caribbean upward mobility in the diaspora? The theory of transculturation also encompasses the discursive, material, and
ideological dimensions of how colonized and diasporic subjects engage with economic upward mobility through cultural exchange and appropriation. Enrique S.
Pumar argues: "The reader of *Counterpoint* will be curious about the relationship
between transculturation and the promotion of entrepreneurship. Here Ortiz offers
an alternative to Schumpeter's view. Rather than emphasizing the functions of individual entrepreneurs in society, as Schumpeter does, Ortiz sees the process of
transculturation as one of the engines behind the diffusion of social initiatives and
innovations. This insight has been corroborated by the recent findings in the literature on enclave economies, which illustrates that the social capital that immigrants bring along often translates into economic resources and opportunities."[18]
The research of Alejandro Portes and Rubén G. Rumbaut has made similar claims
about the fungibility of Latinx heritage cultures in the pursuit of upward mobility.[19]
My analysis of Latinx Caribbean fiction and theater engages with the social and
economic dimensions of transculturation both in the context of the diaspora and
enclave communities as well as in the geopolitical coloniality of power that persists
in the Caribbean basin. Through a similar comparative approach and a reimagined
theory of transculturation, I develop my analysis of upward mobility in Latinx
Caribbean literature and theater through a counterpoint between those works that
reflect a diasporic experience and those that reflect the experiences and histories of
the Spanish-speaking Caribbean nations to which these far-flung communities and
ethnic enclaves can trace their linguistic and cultural heritage.

Circling back to the counterpoint between Benítez-Rojo and Gómez, I take into
account the fact that Benítez-Rojo experienced exile firsthand when he defected
from Cuba in 1980 after a long career in high-level ministerial positions.[20] Gómez,
on the other hand, remained in Cuba until her early demise in 1974, and although
I can only speculate what her trajectory as a filmmaker could have been, her collaborations with figures like Tomás Gutiérrez Alea suggest that she would have continued to depict the changes in Cuban society with a critical eye but within the
Revolution's ideological boundaries. In many ways, Benítez-Rojo's articulation of
the Caribbean *cierta maerna* reflects a nostalgia characteristic of the conservative
Cuban exile community, where memories of life before the Revolution are idealized and deployed as bulwarks against acknowledging societal change. Meanwhile,
Gómez's *de cierta manera* not only embraces change but imposes it so broadly that,
like the Castro regime's dictums on acceptable forms of literature, art, and cinema,
it pushes aside those embodied practices that do not conform to the parameters
of a Revolutionary cultural agenda. As the audience of her film watch Yolanda

and Mario walk toward the horizon of a modernized Cuba, we see the future is nevertheless imagined as a heteronormative trajectory. Transculturation is an unstable and indeterminate process, whether it characterizes the experience of diaspora for an individual or defines the historical and political circumstances under which cultures come into contact and conflict. Transculturation allows for a consideration of cultural change under hierarchies of power without falling into a historical determinism that preordains homogenizing outcomes.

My reimagining of Ortiz's counterpoint and transculturation also considers how racial and cultural hybridity have been conceptualized more predominately as mestizaje in the U.S. Latinx context. In particular, Gloria Anzaldúa's canonical theorization of mestizaje has had wide acknowledgment as a queering of race, gender, sex, and language, and while her notion of mestizaje destabilizes essentialized and overdetermined categories of identity, it remains geopolitically situated at the border between Mexico and the United States.[21] Border theory, as in the work of José David Saldívar, expands the reach of the borderlands to far-flung locations where cultures come into contact and conflict.[22] Yet his work reflects the literary and cultural production of Chicana/o/x writers and artists, which does not fully engage with the experiences and histories of the Latinx Caribbean and its multiple diasporas. Ortiz's formulation has to be reconsidered through these important contributions as well as through the pioneering work of Cuban American performance studies scholar and queer theorist José Esteban Muñoz, whose notion of disidentification has reshaped the way Latinx studies conceptualizes the hierarchies of power and legitimacy when minoritarian subjects appropriate and repurpose elements of majoritarian culture.[23]

Furthermore, as Alberto Sandoval-Sánchez and Nancy Saporta-Sternbach have shown, transculturation remains a viable and valuable term for describing and theorizing the transnational routes through which cultures come into contact, as well as how the emerging "transculturated" forms of literary and theatrical expression remain in dialogue with the contemporary cultures of the Latinx heritage homelands, whether these be south of the U.S.-Mexico border or spread out across the Caribbean basin.[24] Transculturation allows for a theorization of cultural hybridity that, as Ortiz originally showed, takes into account the material and embodied practices through which disparate and often hostile cultures encounter and transform one another. Ortiz's focus on the production of tobacco and sugar as global commodities, despite his racialized and heteronormative allegory, underscores how economics and Latinx Caribbean cultural imaginaries are co-constitutive and self-structuring. This focus also allows for an expanded analysis that considers how transculturation can create and provide access to different forms of capital, which is how I bring this term into yet another counterpoint with the critical terminology developed by French sociologist Pierre Bourdieu (1930–2002).

The mobility of Benítez-Rojo's and Gómez's *cierta manera* resonates with what Bourdieu has said about how we embody our class and constitute our epistemologies and identities. "We learn bodily," Bourdieu says; that is, our bodies are inscribed into a social order, and our attachments and senses of place and belonging reveal how our aspirations and desires can reproduce the exploitative and exclusionary social structures we often confront and fight to change.[25] Migrants from Puerto Rico, the Dominican Republic, and Cuba who have established enclaves in the United States bring that certain way of being and moving in their attempts to navigate their new terrain as economic agents. Through transculturation, they adopt new material and bodily practices that facilitate their upward mobility, yet their racial and linguistic difference often impedes their efforts in a climate of white nationalism, rigid class hierarchies, and cultural elitism. This constellation of material and cultural practices, social and cultural values, and forms of empowerment comprises what I call an "embodied economy," and it can align or come into conflict with state power, hegemonic discourses and institutions, and global markets. The values and practices Latinx Caribbean migrants do adopt from dominant Anglo-American culture can reproduce many of the structures of power that have been imposed on them through military intervention, colonialism, and economic exploitation. Nevertheless, they also search for ways to skirt destruction and regenerate the communitarian values that are part of the certain way that Benítez-Rojo and Gómez articulate in their works. The chapters in this book examine these constellations of embodiment through works of fiction and theater that show how this nonlinear and often contradictory pattern emerges as part of the diasporic experience, with its simultaneous assimilation to and resistance against instrumentalist neoliberal discourses of social and economic mobility.

In short, how can Latinx Caribbean cultures transgress and transform what is known as the American Dream? In the neoliberal economy of the United States, the discourse of white nationalism compels upwardly mobile immigrants to trade in their ties to ethnic and linguistic communities in order to assimilate to the dominant culture. As Leo R. Chávez argues, these Spanish-speaking immigrants, exiles, and refugees are perceived as a "Latino threat."[26] The comments sections of right-wing websites like Breitbart.com or the *Daily Caller* are littered with calls for legal immigrants to totally assimilate to white American values and follow the example of previous generations who immigrated "the right way" and supposedly abandoned all cultural ties to their homelands and uncritically adopted all aspects U.S. national identity. The acculturation model of the so-called melting pot expects immigrants to embrace the English language, acknowledge the superiority of Protestant self-reliance, and adopt the Anglo-American drive to pursue wealth accumulation as an unquestionable social good. Consequently, for Latinx Caribbean immigrants and exiles, this means abandoning Spanish, rejecting forms of communal interdependence, and adopting white, middle-class forms of embodiment in order to mitigate any ethnic and racial identity markers that might hinder their trajectory of upward mobility. However, many Latinx immigrants have challenged this model and have remained loyal to the cultural heritage of their home countries, even as they pursue the promise of a better life for themselves, their families, and their communities. This transactional process of acquiring and trading in various kinds of material and embodied practices across traditions is that phenomenon I call "transcultural capital," and it is that process I intend to explore in recent works of the Latinx Caribbean fiction and theater of the twentieth and twenty-first centuries. The term "transcultural capital" has been used in recent social science scholarship on diaspora and transnational migration to Europe. Ulrike Hanna Meinhof and Anna Triandafyllidou also draw from the work of Bourdieu and develop the term "transcultural capital" to describe the experience of migrant musicians in Europe:

> Through the concept of transcultural capital we will be able to describe in an interactive and mutually supporting way some of the everyday life practices of the migrant musicians we studied: for example the strategic possibilities of strong local and transnational ties within and across migrant communities (social capital), of widespread bi- or multilingualism, bi- or multiculturalism (cultural capital), of retaining vibrant artistic roots in originating cultures but blending these with new local and global influences. Migrants can strategically employ their transcultural capital to maximize rather than restrict their options, thus furthering their economic and professional development in their daily lives. Transcultural capital thus supersedes the oppositional discourses of "diasporic" communities on the one hand and "cosmopolitan" flows on the other by underlining the potential arising from a repertoire of options drawn from across the spectrum.[27]

In the case of Latinx and Hispanic Caribbean diasporic communities in the United States, transcultural capital describes how those elements of minoritarian heritage and cultural practices can accrue value in social and economic fields where acculturation and assimilation to the dominant norms have been naturalized as the legitimate means with which to attain upward mobility. In some of the literary and dramatic works that depict empowerment through transcultural capital, a decolonial strategy can emerge from radical embodiments of the diasporic experience, but this is not always the case. The analyses I develop in the chapters that follow compare different works by the same author or works by different authors to show how that decolonial discourse does or does not emerge from a text's formal elements, such as narrative and dramatic structures, figurative language, and metatextuality. While an accumulation of capital ostensibly gives agency to the diasporic subject, it can also reproduce the hegemonic structures of power in a neoliberal economy. Contemporary Latinx Caribbean literary and cultural production that represents the experiences and histories of the diaspora delineates the habitus of Latinx agents who attempt to transform transcultural capital into economic capital.

My focus in these debates is an analysis of the fiction and theater of the Latinx Caribbean diaspora that brings into dialogue Ortiz's notion of transculturation with Bourdieu's concept of capital, which is not only an economic measure of wealth and empowerment but also an embodied practice of cultural and social values. Bourdieu broadens Marx's theory of capital as a transformational process of money to commodities and back to money—MCM—in order to connect economic exchanges with cultural exchanges that accrue value and empower subjects in their social relations.[28] Marx's and Bourdieu's theories of capital conceptualize how surplus value must constantly project forward through recirculation and transformation in order to sustain its accumulative trajectory. However, Bourdieu also links capital to the schemes of perception—or habitus—that reflect economic actors' social formations and through which they comprehend new experiences, confront choices, and determine what actions are appropriate based not solely on rational choice but also on what they believe is reasonable. Both capital and habitus operate in social fields, in which economic actors position themselves according to preexisting class hierarchies but, as in a field of play, can engage in upward or downward mobility based on the value of their capital and on the adaptability of their habitus. Similar to Ortiz's counterpoint between tobacco and sugar, Bourdieu's contribution to the analysis of developing and advanced capitalist societies moves beyond the notion that culture is an epiphenomenon of modes of production and proposes a broader examination of how social relations are structured through material and bodily practices of labor, food, fashion, sports, religion, and sex. These practices and dispositions constitute the embodied economies of the diasporic subjects that appear in Latinx Caribbean fiction and theater, and while their transcultural capital facilitates their individual upward mobility, it can also serve to increase and transfer its value from one generation to the next, or from one person to the community and back again.

The relational dynamic among Bourdieu's key concepts—capital, habitus, and field—allows for an analysis that examines the way economic agency is articulated by literature and art. Bourdieu's "logic of practice" emphasizes a reflexive methodology that proposes transcending the binary oppositions of objectivism and subjectivism that have characterized transdisciplinary scholarship. Loïc J. D. Wacquant, sociologist and close collaborator with Bourdieu, describes how the "fuzzy logic of practical sense" in Bourdieu's scholarship proposes a break from Cartesian notions of rational subjectivity and objective materialism, a deconstructive turn that also appears in Aníbal Quijano's notion of the coloniality of power.[29] For Bourdieu, "The relation between the social agent and the world is not that between a subject (or consciousness) and an object, but a relation of 'ontological complicity'—or mutual 'possession' . . . —between habitus, as the socially constituted principle of perception and appreciation, and the world, which determines it. 'Practical sense' operates at the preobjective, non-thetic level; it expresses this social sensitivity which guides us prior to our positing objects as such."[30] Through such an optic, a literary and cultural studies analysis can discern the various social fields that characterize the Latinx Caribbean diasporic experience, while also delineating how the diasporic subject acts as an economic agent who "plays the field" as a means of attaining upward mobility through transcultural capital.

Bourdieu developed his key concepts through his sociological research on Algerian and French communities and institutions, and many of his contributions to theory and scholarship refer specifically to those social formations. He conducted his research through opinion surveys, quantitative demographic data, oral interviews, and discourse analysis of government and industry promotional literature.

Although he advocates for a pluralistic approach in the use of diverse methodologies, he emphasizes that the foremost concern is a sustained analysis of how the scientific object is constructed: "The long and short of it is, social research is something much too serious and too difficult for us to allow ourselves to mistake scientific *rigidity*, which is the nemesis of intelligence and invention, for scientific *rigor*, and thus to deprive ourselves of this or that resource available in the full panoply of intellectual traditions of our discipline and the sister disciplines of anthropology, economics, history, etc. In such matters I would say that only one rule applies: 'it is forbidden to forbid,' or, watch out for methodological watchdogs!"[31] Bourdieu combined diverse empiricist methods with a consistent engagement with European philosophy, further dismantling the artificial opposition between methodology and theory. Like Fernando Ortiz, whose early work on the Afro-Cuban secret societies has been criticized for characterizing these practices as forms of delinquency that lead to criminality, Bourdieu, too, has come under critical scrutiny for reproducing intellectual elitism and for foreclosing the potential of social and cultural transformation from below.[32] However, Bourdieu has called for a "reflexive sociology," or "sociology of sociology," in which researchers invest as much time and effort in the analysis of empirical data as in the elaboration of a metacritique of the academic field where knowledge production accrues value. This is the "radical doubt" he underscores as crucial for researchers who must "avoid becoming the object of the problems that you take as your object."[33]

This radical doubt allows for the scholar and critic to examine the positionality of their own discourse in relation to their objects of study, and it poses a question: what species of capital do the scholar and critic require to engage in these forms of knowledge production, and what forms of capital become available for acquisition and accumulation through this scholarly and critical engagement? That reflexivity includes an acknowledgment that, even as I adopt a critical stance in relation to the Latinx Caribbean culture and the experience of the diaspora I share, I also pursue this scholarly project as an embrace and defense of my Latinx heritage and identity. There is no doubt that this book constitutes an act of self-positioning in the academic field, and as such follows "the rules of the game" as a means of accumulating symbolic and economic capital. Nevertheless, as I hope to show throughout the book and especially in the conclusion, for this book there is more at stake than my standing in the profession. I propose a reflexive analysis of Latinx transcultural capital as part of a critical pedagogy that engages and empowers the diasporic community while remaining attentive to the pitfalls of reproducing symbolic violence and exploitative forms of social domination.

My objective as a literary scholar is to draw from Bourdieu's key concepts not in an attempt to produce a sociology of Latinx Caribbean literature, which would be a separate but worthwhile project, but rather as a reflexive analysis of the way fiction and theater articulate the discourses and material practices that enshrine conventional wisdom and common sense—doxify—and those that resist and deconstruct—dedoxify—the arbitrary dualisms that reproduce social hierarchies of exclusion and domination. Bourdieu's definition of *doxa* refers to the dominant, practical beliefs about cultural and social mores and how these accepted truths or discourses of conventional wisdom normalize and reproduce social structures of domination and exclusionary forms of cultural legitimacy. *Doxa* is "a set of fundamental beliefs which does not even need to be asserted in the form of an explicit, self-conscious dogma."[34] Furthermore, these sets of *doxa*, which establish social hierarchies and regulate the position takings of economic agents in social fields, are also reproduced by their embodiments in an individual or collective habitus. Whether in the *doxa* of race, ethnicity, gender, sexuality, or ableness, a person learns, inhabits, and performs the naturalized discourses that value some forms of embodiment over others, and these valued forms attain social and cultural legitimacy as those that all individuals and social formations should strive to reproduce. A *doxa* is "a state of the body" in which social values are naturalized and "converted to motor schemes and body automatisms." Bourdieu writes, "It is because agents never know completely what they are doing that what they do has more sense than they know."[35] These embodiments manifest in the norms for how a person presents himself or herself as a raced, gendered, and sexed subject who assumes an ethnic identity and belongs to a particular social and economic class. Deviations from the dominant norms devalue the types of cultural capital that facilitate access to dominant positionings in social and economic fields. Furthermore, those missteps become ever more contemptible in the eyes of those who take for granted the inherited legitimacy of their embodiments of race, ethnicity, gender, sexuality, and class.

In the chapters that follow, I define and adapt other key terms and concepts I draw from Bourdieu's reflexive sociology, such as misrecognition, symbolic violence, and hysteresis.[36] Placed in counterpoint with Ortiz's theory of transculturation, Bourdieu's critical toolkit provides the lexicon with which to analyze transcultural capital in Latinx Caribbean fiction and theater. The following chapters explicitly engage with the internal contradictions of Latinx transcultural capital through a decolonial critique of the neoliberal state, in which upward mobility and wealth accumulation are institutional mechanisms that perpetuate social and economic inequalities. The Latinx traditions of communitarian values that persist in diasporic ethnic enclaves become the collective means with which to mitigate the symbolic violence inflicted by neoliberal political economies that maintain Latinx Caribbeans in a constant state of displacement, second-class status, and colonialist exploitation. Communitarian values and collective action are not inherently Latinx, but they are part of the array of embodied practices—a bodily hexis—in which language, race, gender, and sexuality are the means by which the diasporic subject articulates and is articulated by the institutional fields of power that facilitate the disequilibrium in value between different forms of social and cultural capital. In some cases, the fiction and theater I examine in this book reproduce elements of the symbolic violence of Latinx transcultural capital, which appears as an uncritical embodiment of the logic of social domination and coloniality, whether in the discourses on upward mobility and wealth accumulation or in the exploitative material and cultural practices that form part of the diasporic experience. Through comparative analyses, these works of fiction and theater reveal the strategies that Latinxs as economic agents have engaged to mitigate the contradictory logic of their transcultural capital and, in some cases, imagine ways to dismantle the institutionalized systems of oppression that perpetuate state violence, economic inequality, and social and cultural disenfranchisement.

While transculturation has been theorized as an evolutionary process of societal change, these literary texts demonstrate how transculturation is a form of capital; it creates its own conditions for existence and recirculation and provides diasporic subjects with a logic of practice, a set of dispositions, an economic unconscious, a dialectic between the rational and the reasonable, and embodied knowledge—in other words, a habitus—all within an array of fields of structured and structuring action. Through this analysis we can discern the social conditions in which transculturation is generated and in which it is exchanged and circulated as capital, which allows us to understand the relation between social institutions and the diasporic subject in the context of cultures in contact and conflict. An analysis of transcultural capital foregrounds writing and performance as creative arts in the fields of cultural production, and through genres such as the novel, the short story, theater, and performance, these forms of cultural production articulate the economic imaginaries of diasporic subjects and their communities. This body of fiction and theater delineates the structuring structures of the fields of education, finance, family, religion, government, and civil institutions, while also accounting for the revolutionary imaginary that resists and decolonizes the doxa that situate the diasporic subject in conditions of social and economic marginalization and subaltern status.

The island nations of the Latinx Caribbean—Cuba, Puerto Rico, and the Dominican Republic—share linguistic, racial, and cultural histories while also presenting specific political and economic realities that have shaped the social relations of each national group. The trajectories of their diasporas, migrations, and exiles are also contingent on these specific political and economic realities. Nevertheless, the most enduring shared history among the islands of the Latinx Caribbean is that of colonialism, starting from the Spanish conquest and colonization to present-day U.S. military, economic, and cultural hegemony in the region. Antonio Benítez-Rojo characterizes that shared history of colonialism, the slave trade, and the plantation economy as a machine—a "repeating island" (*isla que se repite*)— that reproduces itself as variegated iterations across the Caribbean:

> . . . *¿cómo dejar establecido que el Caribe es un mar histórico-económico principal y, además, un meta-archipiélago cultural sin centro y sin límites, un caos dentro del cual hay una isla que se repite incesantemente—cada copia distinta—, fundiendo y refundiendo materiales etnológicos como lo hace una nube con el vapor de agua?*[37]

> . . . how to establish that the Caribbean is an important historico-economic sea and, further, a cultural meta-archipelago without center and without limits, a chaos within which there is an island that proliferates endlessly, each copy a

different one, founding and refounding ethnological materials like a cloud will do with its vapor?[38]

The driving force of that machine—the plantation economy—established the Caribbean's peripheral status through extractive colonialism and slave labor. Although Puerto Rico is the only one of the three Latinx Caribbean islands that still maintains a colonial status politically with the United States, Cuba and the Dominican Republic continue to contend with the military and economic dominance of U.S. interests in the Caribbean. This shared history has created the conditions for the multiple diasporas that have displaced and dislocated many Latinx Caribbeans across the Americas. The political intervention and economic dominance of the United States have led to waves of migration from the Caribbean to hegemonic centers, but also from one island nation to another. The fiction and theater I analyze in the following chapters, which I structure around a literary critical counterpoint, document these diasporic experiences and the strategies that Latinx Caribbean subjects have employed as forms of transcultural capital to mitigate the disruptive effects of their geopolitical and cultural dislocation.

In the first chapter, "A Future for Cuban Nostalgia in Plays by Nilo Cruz and Eduardo Machado," I examine how the plays' characters rely on their nostalgia while historical changes impose paradigm shifts in the way they are empowered as political and economic agents. Cuban American playwrights Nilo Cruz and Eduardo Machado chronicle the violent ruptures of history, and their plays confront the economic, political, and societal changes as Cuban and Cuban American melodramas. The Cuban family of cigar makers at the center of Cruz's *Anna in the Tropics* (2003), living in Ybor City, Florida, on the eve of the Great Depression, struggles to retain the revered artisanal practices that are part of the Cuban cigar industry, despite the economic and historical changes that make them incompatible with hypermodernization in the United States. In Machado's *The Cook* (2011), an Afro-Cuban woman obstinately preserves the objects and possessions of her wealthy, white former employers who fled Cuba after the Revolution, even if it means her own family's present needs suffer from neglect. Although situated in Cuba, Machado's play conveys the anxiety and estrangement of the playwright's own exile experience. Through dramatic structure, Cruz's and Machado's plays visualize economic and cultural futures for the characters who either resist or embrace historical change, which can hinder or facilitate the decommodification of their Cuban nostalgia.

Chapter 2, "Decolonizing Queer Camp in Novels by Edwin Sánchez and Ángel Lozada," the main characters desire a radical break with their cultural heritage, their families, and communities. The gay Latino men in the two novels I compare relocate to big cities, or move from their working-class, Latinx enclaves to the predominantly white, upwardly mobile "gayborhoods" of Manhattan, in order to live openly and reinvent themselves as members of a community of taste makers and conspicuous consumers. Sánchez and Lozada resituate their characters, moving them from a place of submissive dependency to a position that, while economically precarious, resists the symbolic violence that white, homonormative values impose on gay Latino men. Both Sánchez and Lozada write about the experiences of gay Puerto Rican men who dream of fame and fortune in the big city, and they portray the sexual excesses, rampant consumerism, and elitist standards of taste that qualify as signs of having "made it" in the exclusionary social cliques of the A-gay lifestyle. Although Sánchez and Lozada use queer camp to deconstruct the dominant cultural values that enshrine whiteness and wealth as the standards toward which all gay men must aspire, Lozada's fictional work portrays a grim descent into self-destructive narcissism, whereas Sánchez's novel imagines an affirmational embodiment of communitarian values. Lozada's *No quiero quedarme sola y vacía* (*I Don't Want to End Up Alone and Empty*, 2006) and Sánchez's *Diary of a Puerto Rican Demigod* (2015) show how transcultural capital can, on the one hand, lead to bankruptcy and an insolvent identity, while, on the other hand, reaffirm the value of honoring one's debt to family and community.

In chapter 3, "Zero-Sum Games in Fiction by Junot Díaz and Rita Indiana Hernández," I compare how Díaz's short-story collection, *This Is How You Lose Her* (2012), and Hernández's *Papi* (2005) use humor, irony, and textual and genre hybridity to articulate the self-aware pose of the postmodern *plátano*: the neoliberal Dominican subject who straddles multiple linguistic, cultural, and economic imaginaries. These fictional portrayals of the effects of the Latinx Caribbean diaspora—both in the United States and back in the Dominican Republic (the DR)—explore how the pursuit of upward mobility separates immigrant families and entrenches forms of social domination and symbolic violence. Díaz and Hernández depict the machismo that Dominican men claim not only as their paternalistic heritage and masculine privilege, but also as a sign of economic empowerment and accumulation of capital. In particular, the Dominican men in their fictions uphold their birthright to have sexual relations with multiple women, and they perceive the ability to financially support two or more families—in both the United States and the DR—as a virtue of masculine domination. The narrative voices and techniques each writer deploys are characterized by a dual register that, on the one hand, reproduces and celebrates a masculine identity associated with Dominican machismo while, on the other hand, undermines the exploitative values of this form of masculinity. Díaz's and Hernández's fictions reveal the symbolic violence that perpetuates forms of masculine domination in the diaspora, as well as undergirds the economic logic of coloniality in the context of global neoliberalism. Considering the recent controversies involving accusations of sexual abuse against Díaz and the revelations of abuse he suffered as a child, even though Díaz's fiction exposes the exploitative consequences of these games of masculine domination, the narrative voice in his work is also engaged in a playful and not entirely innocent game with the reader, who is seduced into taking pleasure in the textual performance that links sexual violence to economic agency. In contrast, Hernández's queer textual performance deconstructs the narratives that make economic agency contingent on masculine domination, and the games in which her narrative voice is engaged empower rather than seduce the reader, which helps to undermine the violent and exploitative legacy of Dominican machismo.

From melodrama to musical theater, chapter 4 looks at Lin-Manuel Miranda's most successful Broadway productions to date, *In the Heights* (2005) and *Hamilton* (2015). "The Gentrification of Our Dreams in Lin-Manuel Miranda's Musical Theater" shows how Miranda's musicals portray the struggles that immigrants and their children face when they lack the cultural and social capital that facilitates upward mobility through education. While *In the Heights* proposes collective agency through Latinx communitarian values, *Hamilton* stages a subversive form of race-conscious casting that puts Black and Brown faces on the foundational narratives of white nationalism, in particular the narratives of the exceptional individual and cultural assimilation. Miranda's successes on Broadway have provided him with great financial gains and media visibility, which he has used to promote political causes and campaigns, but which have also exposed him to criticism and protests from other Puerto Ricans. Considering Miranda's musicals side by side reveals how the same transcultural capital that empowers Latinx economic agents and creates wealth also recirculates in a field of power where positions of inequality constantly reconstitute themselves.

The contradictions of transcultural capital extend to those works that depict female empowerment and social justice. In chapter 5, "Race, Sex, and Enterprising Spirits in Works by Dolores Prida and Mayra Santos Febres," I compare the play *Botánica* (1991), by Cuban American playwright Dolores Prida, and the novel *Fe en disfraz* (*Fe in Disguise*, 2009), by Puerto Rican poet and fiction writer Mayra Santos Febres, to examine how their female characters face trade-offs that arise when their entrepreneurial spirits encourage them to turn their bodies into racialized commodities, to profit from their transgressive sexualities, or to use others to achieve their self-promoting ends. Prida's *Botánica* and Santos Febres's *Fe en disfraz* depict the experiences of U.S. Latinas and *afrolatinoamericanas* as economic agents who capitalize on their racial identities and commodified bodies. Prida, whose play represents Puerto Rican and multiethnic Latinx experiences in New York, offers a bilingual staging of an upwardly mobile Latina of mixed heritage. The protagonist desires to put her Spanish language skills and college education to use not only to pursue a professional career in international finance but also to escape from the obligations to her Latina family. By the end of the play, however, the main character turns to the Afro-Caribbean religious practices and solidarity of her female community to confront racism, discrimination, and the "whitening" of their urban enclaves due to gentrification. Santos Febres, whose novel depicts Latin American, Puerto Rican, and U.S. Latinx communities, explores the racial politics and embodied economies of knowledge production through the character of an empowered *afrovenezolana* academic whose scholarship gives voice to the unacknowledged histories and genealogies of Black women in Latin America. Unlike Prida's play, however, the communitarian bonds in this novel remain virtual and archival, while the legacy of slavery and sexual violence is reinscribed on the protagonist's body. Nevertheless, both Prida and Santos Febres are wary of how local knowledge and traditions can be appropriated in economic exchanges, and they acknowledge that using Latinx culture to engage with capital can lead to a gentrification of the body, mind, and spirit.

The final chapter and its analysis of educational capital brings my book full circle while also allowing for a critical reflection on the status of transcultural capital in Latinx and Latin American studies. The conclusion considers this scholarship not only as a body of knowledge but as forms of embodied knowledge that are practiced in the classroom, in our profession, and in our communities. In this way, I heed Bourdieu's call to engage in a reflexive analysis in order to remain attentive to the historical and material conditions that provide me the space to pursue this type of scholarship. In other words, much of what I explore in this book reflects my own experience as a Puerto Rican from a working-class background, which serves as my own form of transcultural capital. With *Embodied Economies*, I examine the uses of literary language, genre, narrative technique, and theatrical staging that contribute to a critical understanding of how upward mobility is fraught with contradictions and possibilities. I propose an analysis of transcultural capital to empower the people of the Latinx Caribbean diaspora while remaining attentive to the pitfalls of reproducing symbolic violence and social domination.

CHAPTER 1

A Future for Cuban Nostalgia in Plays by Nilo Cruz and Eduardo Machado

Nostalgia speaks in riddles and puzzles, so one must face them in order not to become its next victim—or its next victimizer.

—*Svetlana Boym*, The Future of Nostalgia

In Fernando Ortiz's allegorical debate or *contrapunteo* between tobacco and sugar, he claims: "*El tabaco y el azúcar son los personajes más importantes de la historia de Cuba*"[1] ("Tobacco and sugar are the two most important figures in Cuban history").[2] This structuring dichotomy has shaped not only Cuban history but also its political economy, the racial hierarchies of its social formations, as well as the material and bodily practices that are associated with *cubanía*. In numerous passages, Ortiz establishes a series of binary oppositions in which tobacco and sugar play out their antagonistic but mutually constitutive roles in Cuban history:

> *El tabaco nace, el azúcar se hace. El tabaco nace puro, como puro se fabrica y puro se fuma; para lograr la sacarosa, que es el azúcar puro, hay que recorrer un largo ciclo de complicadas operaciones fisioquímicas, sólo para eliminar impurezas de jugos, bagazos, cachazas, defecaciones y enturbamientos de la polarización.*[3]

> Tobacco is born, sugar is made. Tobacco is born pure, is processed pure and smoked pure. To secure saccharose, which is pure sugar, a long series of complicated physiochemical operations are required merely to eliminate impurities—bagasse, scum, sediment, and obstacles in the way of crystallization.[4]

As Ortiz traces this dichotomous history, he attributes cultural autochthony to tobacco, as its cultivation and use originated with the indigenous peoples of the Americas, and capitalist coloniality to sugar, as its importation and production required rapacious exploitation of the land and dehumanizing slave labor. However, Ortiz also contends that among the indigenous tribes of the Americas, where tobacco consumption originated, and among the Black Africans who later adopted its use, "*suele el tabaco ser propio de los hombres, ser masculino su espíritu y no poder plantarlo las mujeres*"[5] ("tobacco was a thing for men, masculine in its spirit, and could not be planted by women").[6] Sugar, however, "*ha sido siempre más golosina de mujeres que apetencia de hombres*"[7] ("has always been more of a woman's sweetmeat than a man's need").[8] Ortiz adopts this gendered characterization throughout his own counterpoint analysis, starting with the aforementioned allegory of Don Tabaco y Doña Azúcar and continuing throughout the text. Ortiz's analysis of the structural dichotomy between tobacco and sugar reflects a nostalgia for premodern and pre-Conquest forms of consumption, which are associated with a vigorous masculinity and racial purity, as well as a critique and condemnation of the capitalist expansion of sugar, which is associated with a debilitating femininity and a racial mestizaje. Ortiz's own binary oppositions contain within them contradictions that vacillate between preserving and protecting Cuban traditions, while also reproducing structural inequalities based on the conventional wisdom around gender and racial norms.

In this chapter, two Cuban American plays restage the tensions between nostalgia and history, purity and hybridity, and masculine and feminine forms of economic empowerment that Ortiz found in his counterpoint between tobacco and sugar. Contemporary Cuban American literature and theater have explored the tension and conflict that characterize portrayals of nostalgia in the cultural imaginary of the exile community, in particular the seemingly contradictory aspirations to forge autonomous, transcultural identities in exile yet also reclaim a heritage of *cubanía* through collective memory and a desire to return to the island, whether physically or symbolically. These tensions emerge as family melodramas in Nilo Cruz's *Anna in the Tropics* and Eduardo Machado's *The Cook*, two plays that chronicle the violent ruptures of Cuban history and the contradictions of transcultural capital in the experience of exile and diaspora. The plays depict two families—one in pre-Depression era Ybor City, Florida, and the other in post-Revolutionary Havana, Cuba—and how they confront the economic, political, and societal changes that occur at key moments in Cuban and Cuban American history. The families in these plays also represent the entrepreneurial spirit that is a doxic value in the logic of capitalist expansion and ownership of the means of production. The plays position the Cuban entrepreneur at moments of historical conflict and transition. In *Anna in the Tropics*, Cruz portrays the period immediately preceding the stock market crash of 1929 as well as the automation of the cigar industry and its demise in South Florida.[9] Machado's *The Cook* depicts the Cuban Revolution and subsequent socialization of the means of production, expropriation of private property, and the early waves of exiles to the United States.[10] *The Cook*'s plotline extends its historical scope and also explores the post-Soviet era and the Special Period of the 1990s. As forecasters of economic conditions, the entrepreneurial characters in these plays are oriented toward future outcomes, rational decision making, and competitive risk taking. Yet they are also bound to precedent to the point of inertia, and they reproduce the real and symbolic violence of authoritarianism and exploitation.

A comparison of these two works shows how the tension between historical change and nostalgia can constitute what Bourdieu calls the hysteresis effect. Hysteresis, a term most commonly associated with physics and mechanical science, describes how, like a rubber band, a morphological change occurs when an elastic material is stretched and returns to form, yet is reshaped in the process. The hysteresis effect occurs at moments of historical rupture that occasion a radical shift in the social relations that doxify symbolic violence.[11] In *Anna in the Tropics* and *The Cook*, that violence erupts politically and culturally and is inflicted on the bodies of the plays' characters. This time lag is articulated in these plays as nostalgia, either for the bodily and material practices of the Cuban homeland, or the hierarchical social relations of a pre-Revolutionary political economy. Cruz and Machado develop these entrepreneurial characters as conflicted figures that turn to nostalgia as a means to endure and overcome the vicissitudes of history. The climaxes and denouements of the plays position the entrepreneurs before uncertainty as empowered agents of change. The nostalgia in these plays emerges at the intersection of historical change, affect, and embodied practices, and it reveals the persistent practical habits that reproduce the social relations of capitalism, wealth accumulation, and upward mobility, even under predominantly socialist economic conditions. Through dramatic structure, the plays visualize economic and cultural futures for the characters who either resist or embrace historical change, which can hinder or facilitate the decommodification of their Cuban nostalgia, or what Svetlana Boym has called a reflective nostalgia. This chapter explores how nostalgia and the hysteresis effect have constituted the Cuban American embodied economy, in which raced, gendered, and sexed bodies accrue value as forms of transcultural capital through the material practices and labor that are situated in social fields of power.

Both Nilo Cruz (b. 1960) and Eduardo Machado (b. 1953) were born in Cuba and came to the United States as children—Cruz with his family in 1970 on one of the Freedom Flights (1965–1973), Machado and his younger brother as unaccompanied minors in 1961 during Operation Pedro Pan (1960–1963). These playwrights' works have addressed the exile experience as well as life in Cuba before and during the Castro regime from a variety of perspectives. Cruz's play *A Bicycle Country* (1999) portrays the experience of three *balseros* (refugee rafters) who exchange stories of their lives in Cuba and dream of what awaits them in the United States. In *Two Sisters and a Piano* (1999), Cruz dramatizes the lives of two political prisoners under house arrest for supporting *perestroika* reforms in Cuba during the 1990s. More recently, in *The Color of Desire* (2011), Cruz explores how the early years of the Cuban Revolution impact a family of theater performers, both those who wish to remain on the island and those who attempt to leave for the United States. José Esteban Muñoz writes, "Cruz's writing practice attempts to cast a picture of *cubanía*, of Cubanness as a way of being in the world; this picture not only helps us to begin to achieve a historical materialist understanding of Cuba, but it also encourages us to access *cubanía* as a structure of feeling that supercedes [sic] national boundaries and pedagogies."[12] The historical dimensions of this *cubanía* are clearly evident in *Anna in the Tropics*, for which Cruz was awarded the Pulitzer Prize in drama. The play is set in Ybor City, Florida, in 1929, just prior to the stock market crash and ensuing Great Depression. The family depicted in the play shares with later generations of exiles a longing for the cultural traditions of the homeland and feelings of estrangement in their adopted home in the United States, particularly as they confront changes in the cigar-making industry that affect their business as owners of a cigar factory. This nostalgia at a moment of impending historical change pervades the characters' cultural imaginaries as a hysteresis effect, in which a time lag in adapting to shifting economic and social fields drives the dramatic tensions and eruptions of violence in the play.

Eduardo Machado has also developed a prolific body of theatrical works and recently a culinary memoir of his experiences as an actor, playwright, Cuban exile, and Latino gay man. Machado depicts several generations of a Cuban family in a cycle of four plays, published together as *The Floating Island Plays* (1991), with a fifth, *Kissing Fidel*, published in 2011. Spanning the period from the late 1920s to the early 1990s, these plays portray how an entrepreneurial Cuban family weathers the historical changes and contradictions that modernization, revolution, and exile have brought about for the Cuban nation and the diaspora. Ricardo Ortiz studies extensively one of the plays in this cycle, *Fabiola* (1985), and has described its dramatic structure as an articulation of the "contretemps" of Cuban history, which "performs the tragic fallout of a missed historical rendezvous between the two chief forces, revolution and exile, marking Cuban time, and making (impossible) Cuban history, since 1959."[13] In Machado's later work, in particular his culinary memoir *Tastes Like Cuba: An Exile's Hunger for Home* (2007) and the play *Havana Is Waiting* (2011), the contretemps of Cuban history extends to include the experiences of exiles who return to Cuba and the conflict between their expectations of what that return trip will accomplish and the eventual embrace of the Cuban people who defend life under the Castro regime. The dramatic arc of Machado's play *The Cook* similarly engages the historical changes and their impact on the Cuban nation that occurred after the Revolution, and it also addresses the tensions that arise when Cuban exiles return to the island and impose anachronistic expectations of their place in contemporary Cuban society. As with Cruz's *Anna in the Tropics*, the characters depicted in *The Cook* struggle with the hysteresis effect that they experience as they confront economic and social changes, from the immediate aftermath of the Revolution, to the political and cultural persecutions of the 1970s, and finally to the hardships and economic reforms of the Special Period in the 1990s. What distinguishes the two plays is the kind and quantity of resources, or capital, to which the characters have access that empower them as change agents. Ultimately, the conditions in which the characters exercise their ability to confront change and adapt to it play a key role in constituting the value of their material and bodily practices.

As the citations from Muñoz and Ortiz show, Cuban American nostalgia emerges at the intersection of historical change, affect, and embodied practices; in other words, it has become part of the array of dispositions that constitute the habitus of the exile community. The characters in Cruz's and Machado's plays experience the hysteresis effect as they negotiate their nostalgic dispositions with the shifts in the social and economic fields that occur because of radical historical changes or because of the dislocations of exile and diaspora. The hysteresis effect tends to entrench existing hierarchies of privilege, and those agents with greater accumulations of economic, social, and cultural capital will be better positioned to overcome the disruptions and displacements that occur at pivotal moments of historical change and societal crisis. An inability to adapt one's bodily and material practices can lead to "negative sanctions when the environment with which they are actually confronted is too distant from that to which they are objectively fitted."[14] As the habitus of different agents call upon accumulated capital to overcome the disruptions and displacements of change, the embodied experience of these agents undergoes symbolic and physical violence, particularly those from marginal or subaltern social formations. That is, those at a disadvantage reembody their dominated social position through forms of racial, gender, and sexual oppression, that is, the "negative sanctions" that regulate doxa in material and bodily practices. In the theatrical works of Cruz and Machado, the hysteresis effect appears in the emotional and physical violence inflicted by the characters on each other, or by the state on the characters, as they long nostalgically for cultural traditions and social hierarchies that are no longer operative due to the diasporic experience, economic crisis, or political revolution.

THE FUTURE ANTERIOR OF CUBAN NOSTALGIA

In Nilo Cruz's Pulitzer Prize–winning play, *Anna in the Tropics*, a Cuban American family in Ybor City, Florida, struggles to maintain their cultural traditions as they also negotiate the industrial and economic changes that impact their cigar-making factory during the pre-Depression era. The play synthesizes a defense of art and literature with a critique of industrialization and the crises of capitalism. The Cuban family at the center of the play stands at a transitional moment in history, and the uncertainties they face not only will impact their business and the livelihood of the workers they employ but also reflect the way the Cuban American community has developed its identity and its strategies for cultural and material survival in the United States. The play shows that nostalgia has been and continues to be a way that Cuban Americans anticipate change and plan for the future. In particular, the play's intertextual elements articulate a future anterior of Cuban American identity by citing a literary heritage that serves to prefigure the history and experience of the Cuban Revolution, exile, and the fragmentation of the Cuban national family. Consequently, the historical context and intertextual futurity in *Anna in the Tropics* reflect the transcultural capital that empowers Cuban and Cuban American entrepreneurship while promoting a collective identity that draws from a heritage of art, artisanship, and labor.

Anna in the Tropics dramatizes how Cuban nostalgia plays a crucial role in the entrepreneurial decision-making process, labor relations, capital investment, marketing, and the determination of value. The transcultural capital articulated in Nilo Cruz's play is constituted, in part, from the affective lifeworlds of the Cuban American characters, which reflect the trauma of displacement and the desire to forestall future losses, both emotional and economic.[15] The family portrayed in Nilo Cruz's play relies on cultural traditions and material and bodily practices from Cuba in the North American context, and the depiction of their successes and failures in this ethnic family melodrama epitomizes the transcultural capital that reflects both the idealist and utilitarian discourses of their diasporic imaginaries.

The play centers on the figure of the *lector*, a person employed by the factory to read aloud newspapers, magazines, and novels to the workers while they sort, cut, bunch, and roll the tobacco for the factory's signature cigars. Historically, the tradition of the *lector* developed in Cuba as a means of educating the mostly illiterate workers, and in due time he assumed a key role in promoting and sustaining solidarity, particularly in labor movements and disputes. In Cruz's play, however, the *lector* that comes from Havana to Ybor City also represents a crucial link to the traditions of the homeland, not only on foreign soil where the pressures to assimilate to U.S. culture are pervasive and persistent, but also at a time when industrialization of cigar production is well under way and looming economic crises threaten to decimate the industry altogether. This particular *lector*, Juan Julián, embodies an idealization of the past before the vicissitudes of history bring about the irrevocable losses that set nostalgia in motion.

I have not seen a live production of the play, and it is interesting that the Pulitzer Prize Committee did not see a New York production before awarding it with its highest honor.[16] Yet the stage directions indicate that the staging is minimalist, which focuses the action on the dialogue among the characters. From the first scene in *Anna in the Tropics* to the climax and denouement, the characters' actions and motivations demonstrate how nostalgia, entrepreneurship, and Hispanic/Latinx identity help shape the Cuban American embodied economy. Read more broadly, *Anna in the Tropics* not only dramatizes family conflicts, infidelities, desires, loves, hates, and sexual and homicidal violence, but also stages how the characters' Cuban cultural traditions and gendered habitus are practiced and embodied through an entrepreneurial disposition, as well as how risk and competition in a capitalist system generate social positionings of domination. Cruz begins the play with a clear distinction between compulsive gambling and the kinds of calculated risks that entrepreneurs make when contracting labor and investing in the means of production. The play opens with a fast-paced scene in which Santiago, the owner of the cigar factory, and his half-brother Cheché (aka Chester, "half Cuban, half-American") are placing bets at a cockfight. Simultaneously sharing the stage, Santiago's wife Ofelia and their two daughters, Marela and Conchita, stand by the seaport waiting for the ship from Havana that will bring the factory's new *lector*, Juan Julián. Ofelia admits to her daughters that she sneaked money from her husband's safe to pay for the *lector*'s passage. Ofelia takes on the risk of incurring her husband's wrath in order to continue a Cuban tradition she values as indispensable to running their business and that her daughters idealize as a romantic escape from the drudgery of manual labor. Meanwhile, on the other side of the stage, Santiago is losing large amounts of the family's money gambling at the cockfights. In a show of macho bravura, he refuses to cut his losses and begins to borrow larger and larger sums from Cheché, who has been on a winning streak. Eventually, Santiago becomes so indebted to Cheché he offers him an owning share of the factory, carving the agreement on the sole of Cheché's shoe.

In contrast, the women at the harbor discuss the ideal qualities of the *lector* they have just contracted, and they fret that he may not arrive, prompting Marela, the younger daughter, to admit that she employed a Santería spell to conjure him forth. The women become so overwhelmed with excitement and anticipation that Marela loses bladder control when Juan Julián finally makes his appearance from among the crowd of passengers. This contrasting action between men and women, and the exuberant passions that the characters display in this opening scene, foreshadow the unbridled acquisitiveness, romantic entanglements, and destructive obsessions that build and later climax in the play. The dual action also underscores how speculative risk is not solely a rational calculation but rather a dispositional practice that reflects the embodied habitus of the diasporic characters. The stage is divided to create two gendered spaces in which doxic forms of femininity and masculinity are engaged in, on the one hand, entrepreneurial action and, on the other, games of domination. In both cases, the characters make choices and take action through gendered dispositions, which impacts the family's business for better or worse. Ofelia hires the lector to uphold Cuban traditions associated with art and literature, and Santiago continues to gamble because Cuban machismo demands he never surrender to his male rival, Cheché. The juxtaposed scenes underscore the attempts by the diasporic characters to embody and practice their Cuban habitus in the economic and social fields of the United States.

Although Ofelia makes an executive decision to invest capital in the hiring of a new *lector*, her nostalgia for island traditions appear to run counter to entrepreneurial decision making. Key characteristics of the entrepreneurial outlook are the ability to anticipate and adapt to changes in the economic climate and consumer demand, as well as the willingness to take risks. The nostalgic sensibility, however, lingers on past losses, whether material, personal, or psychological, and attempts to forestall future losses through acts of preservation. In the context of the Cuban American habitus in South Florida, entrepreneurialism and nostalgia have not been incompatible and, to a certain degree, have complemented one another. Mark F. Peterson describes how family mentoring, role models, and personal memories of past experiences play a crucial role in the development of entrepreneurship among Cuban Americans. He writes, "A great deal of both formal and informal teaching, mentoring and advising, occurs through the kind of experience and storytelling that maps onto rich memories."[17] Similarly, Alejandro Portes emphasizes the importance of maintaining social networks within an ethnic enclave: "Premature cultural assimilation, with its concomitant weakening of ethnic ties, may be inimical to economic progress. The alternative suggested by the Cuban experience and other entrepreneurial minorities is instrumental adaptation to the realities of the host economy and labor market, a circumspect approach to the new culture and selective adoption of its traits, and preservation of strong bonds of group solidarity."[18] While these scholars focus on the exile community that emerged in South Florida after the Cuban Revolution, their acknowledgment of the compatibility between entrepreneurship and the nostalgic sensibility sheds light on how the characters in *Anna in the Tropics* attempt to negotiate economic agency with their Cuban cultural heritage in order to make decisions that, although involving risk, have the potential to produce material and affective benefits.

Cruz's play and its portrayal of Cuban American history demonstrate the distinction Svetlana Boym makes between "restorative nostalgia" and "reflective nostalgia." For Boym, restorative nostalgia emphasizes the *nostos* (return home) in nostalgia's etymology; that is, it "attempts a transhistorical reconstruction of the lost home" and "thinks of itself as truth and tradition." Reflective nostalgia, on the other hand, stresses the *algia* (longing) and "delays the homecoming" and "does not shy away from the contradictions of modernity."[19] Similarly, Raúl Rubio distinguishes between literary and performance texts "that utilize the 'discourses of nostalgia' as a narrative means to exemplify the Cuban experience" and "texts that formulate 'discourses on nostalgia' in order to explain the Cuban experience."[20] In *Anna in the Tropics*, the characters at first engage in a wholly restorative nostalgia, in which they attempt to re-create the cultural, material, and bodily practices of their Cuban homeland in the United States. By the end of the play, however, they embrace a reflective nostalgia in which they continue to long for Cuba but also acknowledge and prepare for the historical changes that keep that homeland ever so close but always out of reach. At a metadiscursive level, Cruz's play stages reflective nostalgia for a moment in Cuban American history that precedes the Cuban Revolution and the dominant conservative political imaginary that characterized the early waves of exiles in the United States. The play serves as a longing for a progressive political ideology in which art, artisanship, and labor were not divided into different domains of the culture versus economy, but were complementary and circulated within a broader, more inclusive embodied economy.

Similarly, the very first scene in Eduardo Machado's *The Cook* immediately establishes a dichotomy between control and indulgence—or business versus pleasure—a theme that develops throughout the play as part of the larger critique of class hierarchies, proprietorship, and economic exploitation. Unfortunately, I haven't seen a live production of this play, yet at its 2003 run at the INTAR Theater in New York, cast members circulated among the audience members serving fried plantains, Cuban *croquetas,* and empanadas.[21] The play opens in the kitchen on New Year's Eve 1958 with Adria Santana (the mistress of the house), Gladys (the cook), Carlos (Gladys's husband and chauffeur to the Santana family), and Julio (Gladys's cousin and hired hand). The characters rush about the stage as they prepare hors d'oeuvres and dessert for a party of the Santana's friends—all Batista loyalists. (Through the brief audience participation at the INTAR staging, the audience become the Batista loyalist party guests.) However, sugar takes center stage in this scene through the ice cream and Baked Alaska that Gladys prepares, and later scenes also revolve around different dishes in Cuban cuisine, each one symbolizing various facets of Cuban cultural imaginary. The Baked Alaska, supposedly named to commemorate the U.S. purchase of the Alaska territory,[22] emblematizes Fernando Ortiz's characterization of sugar and the complex processes that facilitate its consumption: "*Por tener todos los azúcares purificados un gusto igual, han de ser consumidos siempre con la adición de otras sustancias que les dan otros sabores*"[23] ("As the taste of all refined sugars is the same, they always have to be taken with something that will give them flavor").[24] Gladys is clearly in charge of the kitchen, and she scolds her husband Carlos as he tries to sneak a taste of the strawberry ice cream that will later become an elaborate Baked Alaska. Although Carlos tries to exert his masculine privilege and demand a taste of the ice cream, Gladys's first duty is to the Santana family and, in particular, Adria, whom she believes is more of a friend. Nevertheless, the staging sets up a clear distinction of class hierarchies, with the wealthy Batista loyalists remaining off-stage and the working-class staff appearing solely in the kitchen. As Adria walks on- and off-stage, we learn how she and her mother gave Gladys an education not only in cooking but in the cultural capital that constitutes the habitus of the white, Cuban elite. Gladys feels indebted to her employers, and Adria praises her as the best cook in Cuba, even better than some of the chefs whose restaurants she frequented in Paris. Despite this ostensible intimacy and mutual admiration, it is clear that Gladys and Adria live in strictly regulated social spaces, and while Gladys may be the best cook in Cuba, she will never be a chef because that profession is reserved solely for white men. The dialogue also reveals the racial discrimination that keeps Gladys in the kitchen while Adria enjoys traveling to U.S. and European capitals where she can move freely through the legitimacy of her whiteness, wealth, and cultural distinction. Consequently, the quarrel Gladys has with Carlos over whether she will allow him a taste of the ice cream emblematizes the means by which bodily and material practices perpetuate relations of power and control and how food serves as a medium through which autonomy and servitude are embodied and normalized in the characters' habitus. The sweet, sugary ice cream belongs to the wealthy, and only through special indulgences will the working-class characters be allowed to have even a small taste.

The Cook portrays three key moments in contemporary Cuban history: the 1959 Revolution; the political purges of the 1960s and 1970s; and the Special Period following the breakup of the Soviet Union. Each of these key moments constitutes a radical shift in society (Revolution), ideology (political purges), and the economy (Special Period). The play portrays these historical shifts through what can be called "Cuban Kitchen Realism"; that is, like the "kitchen sink realism" of British theater in the 1950s and 1960s, Machado's play focuses on the struggles of working-class characters who are also racially and sexually marginalized. The play also maintains the action in the closed space of the kitchen, yet unlike the cramped tenements of British kitchen sink dramas such as *Look Back in Anger* (1956) and *A Taste of Honey* (1958), Gladys's kitchen is part of a sumptuous mansion that belongs to her wealthy, Batista-connected employers, the Santanas. And while Gladys assumes confident authority in the kitchen, her employer Adria Santana makes numerous appearances during the first act to remind Gladys of who is the real owner of the house. The play's characters avoid stock portrayals of heroes and villains; in particular, the protagonist is as prone to exploit others as she is to struggle against the exploitation inflicted on her. Nevertheless, the food and recipes that are part of the action and dialogue serve to evoke a complex affective domain in which desire, power, and need are embodied by the characters as part of their Cuban habitus. As such, the play is a defense of the class politics of the Cuban Revolution as much as it is a critique of the political and social hierarchies that emerge from the Cuban state and the socialist field of power. In the broader context of Machado's work, both in theater and narrative memoir, the play depicts the hysteresis effect of those Cubans who never left and who withstood many of the changes that took place in the Cuban Revolution, yet it also articulates the hysteresis effect of the exile community's nostalgia and desire to return to a Cuba that no longer exists.

Like his play *Havana Is Waiting*, Machado wrote *The Cook* based on his experiences returning to Cuba after years of exile. In an interview with Eduardo R. del Río, Machado recounts the terror he felt when he returned to Cuba in the late 1990s. He feared the Cuba he would find would not be the one from his childhood memories: "I was terrified because not only was I walking back into my childhood but also walking into my fiction."[25] Although his memories of the places and streets where he grew up were accurate enough for him to find his childhood home and school, he also came to grips with the irrevocable changes that had taken place since his family sent him and his younger brother on one of the Pedro Pan flights from Cuba to the United States. Machado's family in the United States considered his return a betrayal, as they still resented the expropriation of their property and businesses that was part of Cuba's socialist Revolution. Nevertheless, this return trip was the first of many for Machado, and in one of his extended stays on the island he developed the material that would later be incorporated into the play, *The Cook*. In his memoir, *Tastes Like Cuba: An Exile's Hunger for Home*, Machado describes the feeling of victory when he wrote this play in Havana, which allowed him to engage with Cuban characters not based on his family, as were those in his most well-known works in the *Floating Islands* cycle: "I had won. I had beat the sons of bitches on both sides of the embargo. I was writing a play and having a drink in my hometown."[26] The feeling of victory was short-lived, however, as Machado begins to perceive on one of his later trips how things in Cuba are "stuck"; "I noticed that there was no movement this time. I knew a lot about it this time, and it was stuck, and I was stuck in my relating to it."[27] Machado's trajectory as an exile returning to his childhood home follows one of the plotlines in his play, *The Cook*, and his experience and theatrical work convey how a reflective nostalgia for the Cuban homeland can mitigate the hysteresis effect and help imagine a future that wrestles with the contradictions of transcultural capital.

CONSUMING PASSIONS

This sense of being "stuck" is closely related to Bourdieu's notion of the hysteresis effect in that Machado, as an Americanized exile, is dispositioned to expect constant change and novelty, which he does not perceive from his habitus. Likewise, in *Anna in the Tropics*, Ofelia's insistence on reproducing the labor conditions of the Cuban homeland reflects the hysteresis of her habitus and dispositional inability to make sense of how a cigar factory could successfully function without the *lector*. Ofelia's decision to hire a new *lector* involves several risks that could potentially hurt the business. First, as the women express in their anxious exchange at the seaport, there is the risk that Juan Julián might not arrive, which would leave Ofelia with a loss of the capital she invested in his passage. Another risk Ofelia took was that she initially contracted Juan Julián without knowing him personally, only having the recommendation of a "gentleman" who described him as the "best lector west of Havana."[28] The women have only a picture by which to recognize him, but this is enough for Marela to fantasize about his level of elegance and good looks. Therefore, Ofelia does not know if the *lector* will meet the principal qualifications of having "good vocal chords, deep lungs and a strong voice" until he actually begins to read at the factory.[29] Furthermore, Ofelia hires Juan Julián at a time when the mechanization of the cigar industry made the role of the *lector* obsolete since his voice could not be heard over the sound of the automated machines. Later in the play, Cheché attempts to introduce a cigar-rolling machine to increase production and compete with other automated factories, but Ofelia and the overwhelming majority of the other family members and factory workers vote to overrule him. Even though investing in technology is no guarantee that the factory will do better to meet changes in consumer demand, the factory owners risk losing their competitiveness by channeling resources to outmoded means of production and redundancy in the labor force. While hiring a *lector* under these circumstances helps to maintain a sense of solidarity among the workers and upholds a cultural tradition from their Cuban homeland, Ofelia's entrepreneurial decision and action involve a consideration of various uncertainties that could prove detrimental to the business' bottom line. Ofelia's main consideration in hiring the *lector* is to reproduce the culture she knew in Cuba, and she acknowledges that this embodied economy forms part of the Cuban American community's attempt "to create a little city that resembles the ones we left back in the island."[30]

Another risk factor in Ofelia's decision to hire Juan Julián is that, historically, the *lector* very often represented the interests of organized labor rather than the profit motives of the cigar factory owners, and in many cases the *lector* was at the center of labor disputes and strikes. The cigar industry had already established a strong foothold in South Florida since the latter half of the nineteenth century, and cigar factory workers had developed well-organized labor unions and fraternal societies in tandem with the industry's growth. Historian Gerald Poyo describes how Cuban and Spanish cigar factory workers formed their own labor groups, inspired by Spanish and Italian anarchism, communism, and socialism. The Cuban *tabaqueros* were often much more politically radical than their Anglo-American counterparts in the Cigar Makers' International Union, and their anarchist tendencies often clashed with the efforts of Cuban nationalists who were promoting separatism from Spain.[31] Nevertheless, Cuban cigar workers developed strong solidarity among themselves and repeatedly opposed attempts by factory owners and management to reduce wages or make changes in working conditions. Labor leaders led many strikes against the factory owners, and in some instances the *lector* played a central role in these labor disputes. The Cuban cigar, its mode of production, and its forms of consumption become emblematic of the class conflicts and alliances that Cruz depicts in *Anna in the Tropics.*

Similarly, the foods that Gladys prepares in *The Cook* mark the political and economic changes that result from the Cuban Revolution. The ice cream that appears in the first act chronicles the passage of time, as Gladys recalls the different flavors she has prepared over the years as part of the New Year's Eve menu. Time and history become a crucial focal point in the scene. Because Mr. Santana is late to arrive at the party, supposedly because he is with his mistress, Adria tries to delay the arrival of the New Year by setting back all the clocks. This attempt to forestall the passage of time also conveys Adria's anxiety at the impending fall of Havana to Fidel Castro's rebels. She receives word from her husband that she must leave Cuba immediately, so while Gladys, Carlos, and Julio continue to serve food to the party guests, Adria prepares her escape, leaving Gladys with five hundred dollars and a command to never let Castro's men into the house. Even as she entrusts her house to Gladys, Adria expresses her skepticism and reminds Gladys that they can never truly be friends on an equal footing:

> ADRIA: All I know is that Batista has told us to leave. Fidel will march into La
>   Habana tomorrow.
> GLADYS: I'm so sorry.
> ADRIA: You don't care about me.
> GLADYS: I do.
> ADRIA: How can you? You work for me.[32]

Both Adria and Gladys deceive one another because the promises they make to forestall time and the radical changes in Cuban society are based on a racial and class hierarchy in which exploitation is disguised as friendship. Although they embrace each other and declare their mutual admiration, Adria suspects Gladys really supports the Revolution and its populist politics. Gladys, in turn, is grateful to Adria for her education in elite cultural capital, yet also resents the authoritarian demands and endless appetites of her employer's wealthy friends. Consequently, Adria's and Gladys's promise to sustain the illusion of friendship is a form of symbolic violence that misrecognizes the relations of power.

In the second act, as the dish Gladys prepares changes from Baked Alaska to Cuban tamales, we see how the hysteresis effect emerges from Gladys's attempt to keep her promise to Adria, even though the Revolution has redefined social progress through historical materialism and has rejected other conceptualizations of history. The transition from the elaborate foreign dessert to the indigenous roots of Cuban food reflects the anti-U.S. discourse of the Revolution, as well as its valorization of *cubanía*. In his culinary memoir, Machado recounts how he encountered a woman who served as the inspiration for his character of Gladys: an Afro-Cuban woman who ran a *paladar* in a home that formerly belonged to a wealthy, white Cuban family.[33] Although she refuses to discuss this personal history, she sends Machado a plate of Cuban tamales at the bed-and-breakfast where he is staying. She sends along a note reminding Machado that the tamales are part of an indigenous legacy that unites Cubans across borders and political divides. This connection through food is different from the ethno-nationalism that privileges white, European, and Anglo-American standards of taste and distinction as the sole determinants of what defines *cubanía*. However, even though the culinary practices that are staged at the beginnings of the first and second acts convey the historical material shift of the Revolution, Gladys continues to hold fast to her promise to Adria and to the belief that she will one day return to reclaim her property. As in his memoir, Machado's play explores how food and culinary practices reflect not only the ethno-national identity that is at the center of nostalgia and the hysteresis effect, but also the hierarchies of taste and distinction that characterize class conflict, racial discrimination, and the colonialism that legitimizes U.S. and Anglo-European cultural values over and above those of local Caribbean communities.

Once again, the ice cream and the Baked Alaska emblematize the transcultural culinary practices that combine the local specialty (Cuban ice cream) and the elaborate U.S. confection (Baked Alaska). However, this form of transculturation perpetuates the hegemonic legitimacy of U.S. upper-class tastes over those of the local Cuban recipes. Gladys and Adria discuss the culinary trends of the United States and Europe, as well as Cuban *cocina criolla* and its own discourses of taste and distinction. They discuss one of the popular Cuban culinary figures of the era, Nitza Villapol, whose cookbook and television show, *Cocina al minuto*, were widely known in Cuba. In his memoir, Machado writes that he came upon an old copy of Villapol's cookbook while browsing the used bookstalls in Havana's Plaza de Armas, and that this book helped him with background research for his play. Ironically, Villapol was a defender of the Revolution who stayed in Cuba until she died in 1998, and her recipes were specifically crafted for the scarce resources available to her Cuban readership. In the play, Villapol's local fame, status as tastemaker, and white, European heritage contrast with Gladys's status as an unacknowledged, Afro-Cuban talent who serves solely at the behest of her wealthy employer. In Adria's compliments and avowals of friendship to Gladys lies a barely concealed assertion of ownership and authoritarianism. Gladys is a fixture of the house that Adria abandons at the end of act 1, and the promise she extracts from Gladys to never let Castro's men take over the property extends her proprietorship onto her cook.

PROGRESS, POWER, AND THE TRADITIONS OF LABOR

Cruz's *Anna in the Tropics* depicts a much more sympathetic relationship between the cigar factory owners, the workers, and the *lector*. It is only Cheché and, to some degree, Conchita's husband Palomo who attempt to introduce machines and thus eliminate the need for a *lector*. Yet these men are motivated by more than just rational decision making and entrepreneurial forecasting; Juan Julián represents a challenge to their sense of masculinity and a threat to the family's stability when he begins having an affair with Conchita. When Juan Julián reports to the factory for his first day at work, he encounters Cheché who immediately attempts to get rid of him. Ofelia and her daughters intervene and reveal why Cheché has such antipathy toward *lectores*:

> MARELA: He thinks that lectors are the ones who cause trouble.
>
> JUAN JULIÁN: Why? Because we read novels to the workers, because we educate them and inform them?
>
> MARELA: No. It's more complicated than that. His wife ran away from home with a lector.
>
> OFELIA: Marela! He doesn't need to know these things!
>
> MARELA: But it's true. She disappeared one day with the lector that was working here. She was a southern belle from Atlanta and he was from Guanabacoa. Her skin was pale like a lily and he was the color of saffron. And of course, now Cheché is against all lectors and the love stories they read.[34]

Cheché's mixed ethnic heritage ("half-Cuban, half-American") and his failed marriage to a light-skinned American woman establish his character as estranged from the traditional Cuban and Latinx community of the cigar factory. As Conchita emphasizes, "He's from another culture."[35] Cheché comes to represent the Anglo-American values of ambition, individualism, and utilitarianism. His complaints against the *lector* reflect not only his personal prejudice but also his belief in the implacable march forward of technology and modernization. Cheché's relentless anticipation of the future takes on the character of an *idée fixe*; at one point, Santiago confronts Cheché's obsession with crossing out the days on the calendar before they have passed. Cheché's attempts to modernize the cigar production process are not wholly unwarranted, since greater efficiency could potentially benefit the factory's profit margin. Yet *Anna in the Tropics* contrasts the modern, North American way with the Cuban traditions of manual labor and the *lector*, which serve the play's nostalgic valorization of the past as well as its articulation of a transcultural Cuban American experience. The play also situates Cheché's ambition within the embodied domain of interracial sexual relations, and the loss of his light-skinned, American wife—a sign of upward mobility and cultural assimilation—to a dark-skinned *cubano* conveys a subversion of the racial and sexual policing of the Jim Crow South.

This valorization of Cuban cultural traditions and the denigration of Cheché's Anglo-American economic ethos resonates with the Calibanesque personification of the United States that Uruguayan essayist José Enrique Rodó articulated in his 1900 essay, *Ariel*. In this turn-of-the-century example of *modernista* Latin Americanism, Rodó casts Shakespeare's Caliban and Ariel as symbolic figures that capture the essence of the U.S. and Latin American characters, respectively. Rodó writes the essay from the perspective of an intellectual delivering a valedictory speech to a group of young Latin American men—the future leaders of the political and cultural elite. For Rodó, Ariel symbolizes the noble spirit of reason, culture, and intelligence that supersedes the base, irrational, and animalistic vestiges of Caliban.[36] The Prospero figure in his essay imparts to his charges an appeal to develop a multifaceted character and to avoid overspecializing their talents and interests to the detriment of individual aptitudes.[37] In contrast, he cautions these future leaders against the dominant inclination of their times that overvalues the pursuit of material utility and quotidian comforts, which hampers the dissemination of those purely ideal preoccupations that are held in high esteem by those who devote to them their most noble and persevering energies.[38] Rodó articulates this pedagogic valorization of idealism for the Latin American cultural and social elite as an oppositional discourse that would neutralize the overwhelming hemispheric influence of Anglo-American utilitarianism and its most menacing representative in the region, the United States. Rodó argues that utilitarianism leads to a populist democracy and entrenchment of Caliban ("*la entronización de Calibán*"), which would gradually extinguish any notion of spiritual superiority other than the most ignoble brutalities of force.[39] Rodó considers the United States the embodiment of Calibanesque utilitarianism, and while he acknowledges the United States' economic and military dominance, as well as its traditions of liberty and piety, he rejects its compulsive drive to aim all its efforts toward practical and pragmatic ends: ". . . *tiene una eficacia admirable siempre que se dirige prácticamente a realizar una finalidad inmediata*"[40] (". . . has an admirable efficiency so far as it is directed to practical ends and their immediate realization").[41] For this reason, Rodó famously says of the United States, ". . . *aunque no les amo, les admiro*"[42] (". . . and I, who do not love them, as you see, admire them still").[43]

In Cuban literature, this opposition to Anglo-American utilitarianism appears in works such as Gertrudis Gómez de Avellaneda's *Sab* (1841) and José Martí's "Nuestra América" (1891); similarly, as the character of Cheché in *Anna in the Tropics* focuses all of his interests on acquiring more authority in running the factory, he disdains traditions like the *lector* as backward and unproductive, and he prefers pulp detective fiction over literary masterpieces, all of which situates him within the pragmatic, industrialized consumer culture of the United States. His mixed ethnic heritage, his paternal illegitimacy, and the violent acts he commits later in the play also cast Cheché as the lascivious "man-fish" Caliban that appeared in the original Shakespearean play. In the family drama that pits Cuban tradition against the forces of U.S. modernization, Cheché clearly plays the role of an unenlightened and unrefined Caliban.[44]

Conversely, Juan Julián embodies all the spiritual and aristocratic aspects of Rodó's Ariel. According to Rodó, the Arielist spirit to which the Latin American leaders of the future should aspire appreciates above all else the universal virtues of beauty and goodness. He writes, *"Yo creo indudablemente que el que ha apren-dido a distinguir de lo delicado lo vulgar, lo feo de lo hermoso, lleva hecha media jornada para distinguir lo malo de lo bueno"*[45] ("I hold it certain that he who has learned to distinguish the delicate from the common, the ugly from the beauti-ful, has gone half the way to knowing the evil from the good").[46] The pursuit and appreciation of beauty in art and in the natural world become moral and ethical imperatives in Rodó's pedagogic prescription, as much for the individual as for societies in general. In the figure of Ariel, Rodó infuses the ennobling character-istics that distinguish the Eurocentric and elitist traditions of Latin America from the mediocrities of U.S. mass culture. For Rodó, Ariel is an epic hero whose influence has lifted primitive man from obscurity to the heights of enlightened civilization.[47]

In Nilo Cruz's *Anna in the Tropics*, Juan Julián describes his role as a *lector* in strikingly similar ways. When Cheché tries to introduce a cigar-rolling machine in the factory, which would cause too much noise and thus make the *lector* redun-dant, Juan Julián offers an impassioned defense of reading to the workers as a form of collective enlightenment:

> My father used to say that the tradition of having readers in the factories goes back to the Taino Indians. He used to say that tobacco leaves whisper the lan-guage of the sky. And that's because through the language of cigar smoke the Indians used to communicate to the gods. Obviously I'm not an Indian, but as a lector I am a distant relative of the Cacique, the Chief Indian, who used to translate the sacred words of the deities. The workers are the *oidores*. The ones who listen quietly, the same way the Taino Indians used to listen. And this is the tradition that you're trying to destroy with your machine.[48]

Juan Julián casts himself as an inspirational leader among the workers, one who transports them from intellectual obscurity to divine knowledge. Much like Rodó's ethereal Ariel, Juan Julián considers himself an intermediary in the community's evolution to a higher plane of civilization. The workers who passively listen to the *lector*'s celestial words are very much like the students in Rodó's essay who serenely take in their master's lecture. As a recent arrival from Cuba, Juan Julián unequiv-ocally represents the nostalgic link to that Latin American idealism that the family struggles to protect from the relentless encroachment of U.S. utilitarianism and modernization. Not only does the play reinscribe the dichotomy of Ariel and Cal-iban as the opposition between Latin America and the United States, in the con-text of the cigar factory the debate pits the demands of the labor force against the interests of ownership and management, a struggle which emblematizes the con-tradictions of transcultural capital in the Cuban American enclave. Furthermore, it perpetuates the Western tradition that privileges the mind and spirit over the body. Yet, as the play progresses, these oppositions become less clear and the embodied economy of the cigar industry redirects the characters' quest for enlight-enment toward romantic entanglements and sexual violence.

In Machado's *The Cook*, Gladys serves the role of the preservationist who polices the material and bodily practices that threaten the restorative nostalgia with which she maintains the space of the kitchen and the house. However, by the start of the second act Gladys has gradually begun to appropriate the private spaces of the house that were once reserved exclusively for Adria's wealthy, white family. In particular, Gladys has taken over Adria's master bedroom and has begun wearing her former employer's clothes. Ostensibly, Gladys begins to embody Adria's elite status by inhabiting the most intimate spaces of her house and wearing her expensive clothes. However, it is the Cuban Revolution's policy of economic expropriation that facilitates Gladys's newfound agency, as well as the political patronage that her husband Carlos enjoys as a member of the Communist Party. The audience also learns that Gladys takes possession of the master bedroom to prevent Carlos from moving in with his young, pregnant mistress. Gladys invokes her promise to Adria as the reason she refuses to share her house with Carlos's lover, which reflects the hysteresis effect that misrecognizes the symbolic violence of the pre-Revolutionary social hierarchies as a bond of friendship. Gladys and Carlos enter into a power struggle in which Gladys assumes the habitus of the former owners of the house to impose an exclusionary boundary, while Carlos reinforces his *machista* habitus through the political and economic intervention of the state.

This state-sponsored machismo serves as the fulcrum upon which Gladys and Carlos attempt to gain leverage in their estranged marriage; it is also the mechanism through which these characters inflict state violence on the body of their gay cousin, Julio. As in act 1, the domestic turmoil in the house reflects the broader historical changes and events in Cuba, the United States, and Europe. In act 1, Julio arrives to help Gladys serve the New Year's Eve party guests. When Adria appears in the kitchen in her mink coat to say her goodbyes and give Gladys final instructions about protecting the house, Julio gawks in fascination at Adria in her finery. He even asks if he can touch her mink coat, thus revealing his own queerness through this staged camp embodiment. By the time he reappears in act 2, as the action has moved forward to 1972, his sexuality and taste for the look and style of mass youth culture of the early seventies place him in danger with the Cuban purges of gays and intellectuals. Gladys and Carlos comment on Julio's bell-bottom pants and queer gender identity. He refuses to change his clothes but asks Gladys to help him evade the neighborhood watch and state agents who have him under constant surveillance. Julio's justified paranoia reflects the persecution, imprisonment, and exile of Cuban intellectuals such as Heberto Padilla, Guillermo Cabrera Infante, and Reinaldo Arenas, all of whom initially supported the Revolution but who later fell into disfavor after Fidel Castro's famous dictum of 1961, "*Con la revolución todo, contra la revolución nada*" ("Within the Revolution, anything goes; against the Revolution, nothing"). The Unidades Militares de Ayuda a la Producción (UMAP) of the late sixties also served to indefinitely detain homosexuals and social and political dissidents, as retold in the documentary film *Improper Conduct* (1984). Julio pleads with Gladys and Carlos to protect him from falling into the hands of the authorities who will arrest and imprison him in the infamous El Morro fortress. While Gladys and Carlos wage their battle over dominance in the house, both relying on the agency with which the Cuban state has empowered them, Julio becomes a pawn in their game of power. Carlos threatens to have Julio arrested if Gladys does not allow him to bring his lover to the house, and Gladys sacrifices Julio in order to keep what she says is her promise to Adria, which reveals her own propensity to inflict violence on others in order to exert power and retain control. While wearing Adria's clothes and sleeping in her bed, Gladys simultaneously embodies the elitism of her former employer and enforces the state violence of the Castro regime. Machado's staging of the hysteresis effect reveals the time lag in the discourses and material practices of the Cuban Revolution, which projected an egalitarian society of "new men" but instead reproduced real and symbolic violence on the Black, queer bodies of its own people.

The history of political purges and persecution of LGBTQ Cubans has been depicted in a number of films, documentaries, and literary works. In Tomás Gutiérrez Alea's and Juan Carlos Tabío's film *Fresa y chocolate* (1993)—based on Senel Paz's short story "El lobo, el bosque y el hombre nuevo" (1990)—the main character Diego recounts his own experience of detention in the UMAP camps. Reinaldo Arenas wrote about these forms of persecution and imprisonment in fictional form in the short novel *Arturo, la estrella más brillante* (1984) and later in his autobiography, *Antes que anochezca* (1992). Lillian Guerra argues that the Castro state policy of enforcing a Revolutionary machismo is not a holdover from previous, patriarchal norms, and that the "gender policing" of the Castro regime, of which the UMAP camps were the most violent form, reflected the economic imperatives of collectivization and the labor demands of the shift toward an agrarian economy.[49] However, the hypermasculinity of the New Socialist Man drew from Romantic antecedents and served as an institutional discourse in the universities, culture, the arts, and sexual relations. The Castro regime encouraged neighbors to denounce neighbors and children to turn in their parents if there were any signs of antisocietal behavior, such as effeminacy, listening to the Beatles or Elvis Presley, or spending too much time with books and culture and not enough performing hard labor in the cane fields for the glory of the Revolution. Although the Cuban woman was portrayed in these campaigns as adopting masculine traits in order to join the labor brigades in the rural sectors, the Cuban state propaganda reinforced traditional femininity through beauty pageants and *talleres* on makeup and hair. However, two important films from 1968—*Memorias del subdesarrollo* by Tomás Gutiérrez Alea and *Lucía* by Humberto Solás—satirize and condemn the hypermasculinity of Cuban machismo and the sexual exploitation of women, and their portrayals use various cinematic storytelling techniques to underscore the persistence of the *machista* habitus at all levels of Cuban society. The persecution of sexual, political, and religious dissidents during the late 1960s reflected the broader shifts in economic policy and the hardline political realignment of the Castro regime, but part of its success at infiltrating institutional and social spaces—from the universities to the nuclear family—occurred because the *machista* habitus of pre-Castro

Cuba was never eliminated by the Revolution, only appropriated as official state discourse under the guise of collectivist values.

Machado's depiction of homophobia and violence against gay men in *The Cook* reprises the portrayals of closeted sexualities and abusive family conflicts that appear in his *Floating Islands* cycle. In 2005, Machado added a sixth play to the ongoing drama of the Marqués family—*Kissing Fidel*—in which a bisexual cousin arrives from Cuba for the funeral of the family's homophobic and tyrannical matriarch. The cousin reveals that the tourist sex trade was his only means of survival in Cuba, but now among the exile community in South Florida, he is expected to clean up his appearance and get into a real business like his exile cousins. While the bisexual cousin's experience in *Kissing Fidel* represents the post-Soviet era and Special Period shift in policy toward homosexuality in Cuba, in *The Cook* Julio experiences the terror in which sexual and political dissidents lived in the 1960s and 1970s. As Gladys prepares tamales in the kitchen, Julio pleads that she close the blinds to prevent the secret police from locating him. He spies them across the street, and although Gladys makes excuses for his behavior and sexual nonconformity, Julio coaxes her into admitting that Raúl Castro and the Cuban state have implemented a punitive policy against sexual dissidents:

JULIO: When did this country become so moralistic?
GLADYS: When Raul Castro went to China . . . and he asked how they handled their homosexual problem. They replied, "We kill them, throw them in the river and then let their bodies float down to town. So they can see what the punishment is for improper conduct." But Cuba, being more humanistic, just puts deviants in camps.[50]

Although Gladys urges him to change his clothes, marry a woman, and "save" himself from persecution, once she argues with Carlos and finds out he wants to bring his pregnant mistress to live in the house, Gladys sacrifices Julio for the sake of maintaining her own pride and authority. She allows Carlos to betray Julio to the secret police, and in doing so reaffirms her authority in the house through her embodiment of Adria's elite, white habitus.

CARLOS: I just told your cousin how you betrayed him.
GLADYS: I'm not betraying myself for any man.
CARLOS: You're black. Do you know that?
GLADYS: Yes. I do.
CARLOS: You're not her.
GLADYS: Yes, I know.
(Gladys serves Carlos a plate of tamales. Carlos eats.)
But in her house, in her clothes, I feel like I am.[51]

By the end of the act, Gladys's tamales have turned out salty and bitter because, in spite of her defense of her autonomy, she becomes complicit with the state violence that will befall her cousin as soon as he leaves the protected space of the house. The embodied practices that are staged in this scene—the food the characters prepare and eat and the clothes they wear—emblematize the violent contradictions of what Carlos calls the "dialectical explosion" of the Cuban Revolution, which, as Gladys and Julio acknowledge earlier in the scene, provides comfort only "For some people. . . . For decent people."[52]

CUBAN CULTURE IN CONTACT AND CONFLICT

As noted previously, Machado's depiction of the hysteresis effect and how the embodied culture of machismo persists in the ostensibly progressive and egalitarian Revolutionary Cuba is consistent with other representations in literature and film produced in Cuba, such as Senel Paz's short story and the films by Gutiérrez Alea and Solás. However, in this case the condemnation of its violent implementation by the state implicates those members of the marginal classes who have acquired agency and power through the Revolution's political and economic reconfiguration of Cuban society. Machado's play also stages this contradiction as a scene in the battle of the sexes, in which Gladys refuses to submit to the demands of her husband as he attempts to wield his masculine privilege. Nevertheless, by the third act the audience sees another set of transitions that point toward reimagined embodiments of agency. The stage directions describe the familiar historical shift, with the action taking place in 1997, and the characters engage in preparing a new culinary dish in the kitchen, this time a Cuban version of *pollo al ajillo*, or garlic chicken. However, the most striking changes that have occurred are that the house has been converted into a *paladar*, one of the family-style restaurants that serve foreign tourists and that permit a form of state-controlled entrepreneurship that is also called self-employment, which is more consistent with Cuba's socialist values that renounce the notion of private property.[53] The audience also immediately meets a new character, Rosa, the daughter Carlos had with his mistress. The inclusion of this character and the transformation of the house into a business suggest that Gladys has reneged on her vow to save Adria's home from any kind of change. Just as the state has had to allow certain forms of market and enterprise in order to emerge from the economic crisis of the post-Soviet Special Period, Gladys, too, relents in her opposition to redefining the nuclear family by including Rosa in the once highly guarded domestic space of the kitchen. Just as the socialist Revolution vowed to never accede to the demands of capitalism, Gladys had vowed never to allow any changes in the home she was keeping for her former employer. By the third act, however, the audience sees in Gladys's business and the transformation of the house how the tourist industry once again becomes one of the main sources of income for both the Cuban state and its people.

In the case of the Cuban American family in *Anna in the Tropics*, the embodied economy they attempt to sustain reflects an anti-U.S. discourse of Latin Americanism, in particular the cultural dichotomy that José Enrique Rodó articulated in his essay, *Ariel*. That is, their support for the tradition of the *lector* echoes Rodó's emphasis on high literary and artistic culture as a pedagogy that promotes Latin

American autochthony. However, as immigrants and participants in the U.S. economy, their Latin American idealism must negotiate with the North American hegemony of modernization, economic liberalism, and utilitarianism. This civilizational opposition plays out as part of the family drama that also revolves around the future of the cigar factory and the kinds of entrepreneurial decisions and labor relations that will impact the business' success or failure in changing times. The family in Nilo Cruz's play attempts to run its business according to the way they imagine themselves as inheritors of a Cuban cultural tradition that they risk losing to the overwhelming influence of U.S. hegemony. Their transcultural position between two embodied economies—between Ariel and Caliban—further complicates their attempts to confront the uncertainties of the future, in terms of both their economic survival and their familial stability.

The materiality of tobacco and the cigar is the foremost constitutive element in the family's embodied economy. Throughout the play, the characters describe the qualities of tobacco and of the perfectly rolled cigar; they rhapsodize over the taste and smell of the cigar smoke; and they defend the manual labor that represents an important cultural legacy. As Fernando Ortiz describes in his *Contrapunteo cubano*, tobacco and smoking are steeped in folklore, legend, and history. His anthropological study details the mystical properties and origins that were associated with tobacco smoking, how the indigenous Arawaks used tobacco in their religious ceremonies, and how the smoke represented a visible form of the spirit and a materialization of tobacco's narcotic and stimulating properties.[54] It is due to these narcotic effects and the social practices surrounding the experience of smoking tobacco that this plant became a major agricultural commodity, traded globally and manufactured both manually and, eventually, industrially. According to Ortiz, Cuban tobacco went on to conquer the world through a process of transculturation, in which cultures come into contact through demographic, political, and material displacements and give rise to new cultural imaginaries that combine elements of their sources.[55]

One of the discursive elements that serves to constitute the transcultural capital of the Cuban American family in *Anna in the Tropics* is Leo Tolstoy's *Anna Karenina*, the first novel that the *lector* Juan Julián reads to the cigar factory workers. With each reading, the characters argue over different interpretations, and they comment on how the novel's plots and characters reflect their personal concerns, family relations, and desires for the future. In addition to the passionate and tragic story of Anna and Vronsky's illicit affair, Tolstoy's novel relates the historical context of nineteenth-century Imperial Russia and the contemporaneous debates on labor after serfdom, land ownership, political economy, and education. Each of the characters in *Anna in the Tropics* sees in Tolstoy's novel that, in love and economic concerns, the genre of melodrama situates characters in moments of crisis that demand making choices and sacrifices. This genre resonates significantly in the Cuban American embodied economy because it reflects the history of exile and migration, in which personal and collective choices have led to both losses and gains, whether affective, cultural, or material.

The affective force of passion and desire constitutes a central theme in the play, and this is nowhere better represented than in Juan Julián's choice of *Anna Karenina* as the first novel he reads at the factory.[56] Not only does Tolstoy's tale of love, marital infidelity, and tragic death take hold of the family and factory workers' imaginations and stir up their passions, the novel also becomes part of the transcultural capital that affects the business decisions that the family makes. While a work of Russian realism, Tolstoy's novel narrates many melodramatic scenes in which characters' passions overtake their capacity to maintain the social veneer of aristocratic propriety; for example, Anna's public emotional breakdown when Vronsky falls from his horse at the steeplechases.[57] As was evident from the initial scene at the shipyard, Marela is the most inclined to gravitate toward the melodramatic elements in the story of Anna Karenina's illicit and unquenchable love for Vronsky. Marela's dialogue with Juan Julián, even before he starts reading from the novel, reveals that she thinks in corporeal metaphors, and therefore visualizes alternate lives for herself and hidden meanings behind the surface of mundane reality:

> JUAN JULIÁN: It's curious, there are no mountains or hills here. Lots of sky I have noticed. . . . And clouds. . . . The largest clouds I've ever seen, as if they had soaked up the whole sea. It's all so flat all around. That's why the sky seems so much bigger here and infinite. Bigger than the sky I know back home. And there's so much light. There doesn't seem to be a place where one can hide.
> MARELA: One can always find shade in the park. There's always a hiding place to be found, and if not, one can always hide behind light.
> JUAN JULIÁN: Really. And how does one hide behind light?
> (*The women laugh nervously.*)
> MARELA: Depends on what you are hiding from.
> JUAN JULIÁN: Perhaps light itself.
> MARELA: Well, there are many kinds of light. The light of fires. The light of stars. The light that reflects off rivers. Light that penetrates through cracks. Then there's the type of light that reflects off the skin. Which one?
> JUAN JULIÁN: Perhaps the type that reflects off the skin.
> MARELA: That's the most difficult one to escape.[58]

This flirtatious exchange captures the dichotomy that the play establishes between spiritual and bodily knowledge, between idealist aspirations and quotidian pragmatism. Juan Julián's observations distinguish the Cuban landscape from that of South Florida, and they reinforce the perception of the United States as an oversized and overwhelming force, one that can absorb all the natural resources around it. The various types of light range from all the ways light manifests itself materially to "light itself," which could include the "light" of reason and awareness. Marela, as a first-generation Cuban American, has found ways to "hide behind light"; that is, she evades the glare of U.S. public life and finds solace and comfort in her Cuban culture. She also hides behind the light that demands rational decision making and inhabits a culturally constituted imaginary of magical thinking and animistic belief. The "light that reflects off skin" is "the most difficult to escape" not only because of the suggested eroticism, in which one's passions are not easily disguised, but also because of the racial connotations implied by skin, making one's racial and ethnic difference "most difficult" to escape in the pre–civil rights era of the United States. Marela so readily embraces the romantic fantasy of *Anna Karenina* and the novel's portrayal of aristocratic Russian life because she has already learned how to live in a world that challenges her sense of reality. Her escape into this shaded comfort zone reflects more than the romantic notions of a young and idealistic girl; this place "behind light" is also the somatic domain in which Marela's Cuban habitus can withstand the onslaught of U.S. rationalism and utilitarianism, as well as the racialization of her Cuban identity.

As Juan Julián reads from the novel, the characters become a "reading community" and begin to share their interpretations of the passages to which they have just listened. Marela is the most susceptible to extrapolating from the novel personal meanings that defy rationality:

CONCHITA: She never remembers anything.
MARELA: I do. I just don't cling to every word the way you do. I don't try to understand everything they say. I let myself be taken. When Juan Julián starts reading, the story enters my body and I become the second skin of the characters.
OFELIA: Don't be silly.
MARELA: We can always dream.
OFELIA: Ah yes. But we have to take a yardstick and measure our dreams.
MARELA: Then I will need a very long yardstick. The kind that could measure the sky.
CONCHITA: How foolish you are, Marela![59]

Ofelia later tells Marela, ". . . people like us. . . . We have to remember to keep our feet on the ground and stay living inside our shoes and not have lofty illusions."[60] Ofelia's remark about "living inside our shoes" recalls the contract for ownership of the factory that Santiago signed on the bottom of Cheché's shoe. The hard practicality of quotidian life and business agreements contrasts sharply with Marela's vivid imagination and her willingness to let herself "be taken" by fiction and fantasy into an alternate reality.

The characters whose dramatic arc most closely parallels the love story in *Ana Karenina* are Conchita and Palomo. Although not as impressionable as Marela, Conchita nonetheless sees in Tolstoy's novel a reflection of her own marital troubles and her dissatisfaction with her husband, Palomo. Conchita uses the reading of *Anna Karenina* to bait Palomo into an admission of infidelity, and she later begins her own affair with Juan Julián in order to manipulate her husband into competing for her affections. Here, too, the characters' passions and memories of the past dramatize the conflict between Anglo-American and Cuban cultures that form part of their transcultural imaginaries. When Conchita and Juan Julián begin the flirtatious dialogue that eventually leads to their affair, Conchita recounts an experience with a young American boy with whom she had a brief relationship. She offered him a braid she had cut from her hair and asked that he bury it under a tree, a custom she had learned from her Cuban culture. The young man rejected the gift and Conchita never saw him again, highlighting how the Cuban *cierta manera*-the material and embodied practices that comprise the habitus of *cubanía*—is not legible in the United States and is even seen as an affront to decency and good taste. Conchita also readily admits to Palomo that she is having an affair with Juan Julián, describing to him details of their encounters in the factory. Although Palomo at first listens voyeuristically, he later tells Conchita:

> PALOMO: *(Grabbing her arm.)* I want you to go back to him and tell him you
>   want to make love like a knife.
> CONCHITA: Why a knife?
> PALOMO: Because everything has to be killed.[61]

Palomo's request parallels the tragic end of Tolstoy's *Anna Karenina*, and it foreshadows the real death that takes place when Cheché murders Juan Julián. With the death of the *lector*, the play anticipates the historical events that soon will put an end to the practice of reading in the cigar factories and, eventually, to the cigar industry in Ybor City. The play closely ties the romantic complications and cultural nostalgia of the Cuban American characters with their embodied economy and historical circumstances.

Similarly, Tolstoy's novel contains more than the tale of Anna and Vronsky's romance; other characters such as Levin, his brother Sergei, and the farmer Sviyazhsky have numerous debates about land ownership, advances in farming technology, agrarian reform, and the status of peasant labor.[62] In *Anna in the Tropics*, Santiago converses with Ofelia and describes his interest in Levin:

> SANTIAGO: That Levin reminds me of when I was young and my father left me
>   to run the factory. It seems as if Levin has dedicated his whole life to his farm.
> OFELIA: Yes, he's a dedicated man.
> SANTIAGO: I used to be like him.
> OFELIA: Yes, you used to be like him.[63]

Santiago laments his unshakeable "agony" and absence from the day-to-day operations of the factory. The novel reminds him of the vigor he once had and the acumen with which he ran his business. Santiago also expresses the feelings of dispossession he has when he loses at gambling: "Every time I lose, I feel that something has been taken from me. Something more than money."[64] Santiago's nostalgia for his youth and the loss of his dignity encapsulate the overall message of the play and the characters' attempts to maintain a way of life and a mode of production that hearken back to a time and place long past. Santiago becomes so inspired by the novel that he resumes his place of leadership in the factory. He takes out a loan to pay his gambling debt to Cheché, thus buying back the ownership of the factory; he rejects the machine Cheché attempts to introduce; and he devises a new, premium cigar called *Anna Karenina*. To a certain extent, Santiago's rejection of technology and modernization reflects the way Levin in Tolstoy's novel also criticizes new agrarian methods and theorizes about the primacy of the Russian laborer in the agricultural industry. Santiago bases his entrepreneurial decision on a longing for the past and an idealized, paternalistic relationship with his labor force.

Even though his decision is based on nostalgia, as an entrepreneur Santiago must determine if future changes in demand will warrant the investment in costly machinery, or if consumers will value traditional manual labor methods enough to sustain a profitable enterprise. Juan Julián convincingly makes this case in his debate with Cheché. Although most of his defense of the tradition of the *lector* is framed in terms that are not at all economic considerations and more mystical in nature, Juan Julián perceives the change in consumer preferences and how it will impact the cigar industry: "This fast mode of living with machines and moving cars affects cigar consumption. And do you want to know why, Señor Chester? Because people prefer a quick smoke, the kind you get from a cigarette. The truth is that machines, cars, are keeping us from taking walks and sitting on park benches, smoking a cigar slowly and calmly. The way they should be smoked. So you see, Chester, you want modernity and modernity is actually destroying our very own industry. The very act of smoking a cigar."[65] Juan Julián's speech acts as a future anterior prognostication of what will have happened after the economic crisis of the stock market crash and the Great Depression. Although both Cheché and Juan Julián attempt to address the changing circumstances that modernization and industrialization have wrought on the cigar industry, it is only Juan Julián who considers a broader range of factors that has impacted changes in consumer demand. Cheché perceives the mechanization of cigar production solely from the managerial perspective, not necessarily from an entrepreneurial one. That is, he focuses on catching up with innovations made at other factories, not necessarily changes in consumer demand. In fact, Santiago chides Cheché for crossing out the days in the calendar before they are over, suggesting he foreshortens his perception of the immediate future in his rush to overcome the cultural stagnation about which he complains. It is up to Santiago to make an entrepreneurial decision by forecasting changes in consumer demand that lie ahead, but even he can in no way anticipate the stock market crash and the ensuing Great Depression that will eventually decimate the cigar manufacturing industry and leave Ybor City as a virtual ghost town for several generations. It is only from the perspective of the contemporary audience that one can see how Santiago's decision will not likely save his business from the general decline that took effect over the whole industry. Nevertheless, Santiago's nostalgia for traditional production methods and his role as the entrepreneur are not necessarily incompatible with discourses and practices that successfully evolve from a transcultural economic imaginary.

Santiago does not know that his business plan will not succeed, nor can any of the characters foresee the transformational events that lie ahead, from the Great Depression to the Cuban Revolution and the subsequent waves of Cuban exiles that will change the cultural and economic landscape of South Florida. At the end of the play, when Cheché rapes Marela and then kills Juan Julián, the play symbolically portrays the community's loss of innocence and the irrevocable loss of a way of life and mode of production. As the representative of the U.S. hegemony of modernization and technological progress, Cheché's violent actions reaffirm the Arielist discourse that depicts the United States as the aggressive usurper of Latin American cultural and economic autochthony. The days of the *lector* are soon to be permanently consigned to the realm of nostalgia, and Juan Julián's death anticipates what will have occurred shortly after the events represented in the play. Historians George E. Pozzetta and Gary R. Mormino describe how the practice of the *lector* was abolished once and for all in Ybor City in 1931 after violent clashes between owners and workers: "On November 27, 1931, the readers' tribunes came down. Some manufacturers dismantled the platforms in the evening; others chose to do so in front of the humiliated workers."[66] Santiago's business plan involves risk, and he cannot fully foresee if his gamble will pay off. He hopes that a cigar marketed with associations of romance and Russian aristocracy will appeal to that shrinking consumer demand that values traditional production methods over machine-manufactured cigars. While his efforts would have most likely failed due to circumstances beyond his control, the yet-to-be Cuban American community of the latter half of the twentieth century will have established itself as a dominant economic force in South Florida, and a large part of their success will have been built on nostalgic transcultural capital.

The climax and denouement of *Anna in the Tropics* depict allegorically the tumultuous political, economic, and social history of the Cuban and Cuban American experience that occurs proleptically from the perspective of the play's dramatic chronotope. As the family celebrates the launch of the new *Anna Karenina* cigar—a scene that the stage directions imbue with pre-Hispanic ritualism—the action and costuming reenact the future anterior history—from the perspective of the twenty-first-century audience—of the antagonistic relationship between a capitalist, free market Anglo-American sphere and the socialist political economy of Cuba. When Santiago, Ofelia, and the others go offstage to fire celebratory gunshots in the air, Cheché violently grabs Marela, who is still wearing the fur coat she borrowed to portray Tolstoy's tragic heroine. The scene goes black before the audience witnesses the implied rape, but this act of sexual violence resonates with the Cold War struggle between the United States and the Soviet bloc, especially if the audience and the reader keep in mind how Cheché serves as an avatar of Rodó's Caliban, which, in turn, symbolizes the industrialized United States and its history of economic exploitation and military interventionism in Latin America. With the idealistic and naïve Marela suffering the indignity and physical violation of Cheché's lust, the play casts Latin America as the helpless victim of U.S. rapaciousness; the fact that Marela is still clutching a copy of Tolstoy's novel and dressed as its Russian heroine underscores as well the eventual collapse of the Soviet Union and its influence in Cuba's economic system. While socialist political and revolutionary movements continue to this day as part of Latin American economic imaginaries and a reinvigorated new left, Nilo Cruz's play depicts the capitalist United States, embodied by the character of Cheché, as the usurping aggressor that overwhelms and disempowers the other nations of the region, in particular the post-Soviet yet still embargoed Revolutionary Cuba. By having the other characters offstage, the play's allegorical portrayal of capitalist exploitation exonerates the family's free market entrepreneurship and status as the ownership class; but as Santiago's illegitimate half-brother, Cheché represents a noxious, destructive force in the Cuban American family and thus an extreme and dangerous element in their pursuit of transcultural capital.

Cheché's violence causes Marela to shrink further into her fantasy world; she appears shortly before the last scene still wearing the heavy fur coat that she used to portray Anna Karenina for the cigar band label. However, Marela's rape is only the prelude to the homicidal violence that Cheché soon inflicts on Juan Julián. Once again, the play weaves together the reading of *Anna Karenina* with the dramatic action as part of the allegorical depiction of conflicting embodied economies. While Juan Julián reads a passage describing Anna's husband's thoughts on dueling his rival, Vronsky, Cheché appears on stage unnoticed and then shoots the *lector* dead. As the mystical intermediary between the workers and literary knowledge, and as the avatar of Rodó's Ariel, Juan Julián's murder resonates with the many incidences of violent U.S. military intervention in Latin America and Cuba; in particular, his death reenacts the assassination of Che Guevara, one of the most idealized global symbols of the Cuban Revolution and socialist political thought. Although the play condemns the history of this political violence through the villainous character of Cheché, with Juan Julián's close affinity to the entrepreneurial Cuban American family at the center of the play, Nilo Cruz rewrites the history of the Cuban exile community and its strong antisocialist politics. *Anna in the Tropics* does not necessarily condemn the Cuban American enclave in South Florida and its success at free market expansion in a global context, yet the play dramatizes this embodied economy from a progressive perspective that canonizes the avatars of Latin American idealism and martyrs the embodiments of socialist, labor-oriented political economies.

Once Cheché murders Juan Julián, the play immediately transitions to the final scene with the other characters back at work, silent, morose, and unable to articulate their grief over the death of their *lector*. Their only solace is to continue to read Tolstoy's novel, and the only character willing to do so is, ironically, Palomo, who suffered a cuckolding because of this very book. Once reliant on the *lector*, the characters take it upon themselves to continue the tradition, and although the audience and readers know that the tradition will not continue for much longer, the end of the play suggests that the survival of the family's cultural sensibility depends on the nostalgic preservation of the past. The ending reaffirms what Conchita had earlier told Juan Julián: "anybody who dedicates his life to reading books believes in rescuing things from oblivion."[67]

In contrast, Machado's *The Cook* imagines a future that is contingent on repurposing the embodied Cuban economy of the past. The third act begins with Gladys, Carlos, and Rosa cooking and debating the economic policies of the Special Period that have made Cubans reliant on tourist dollars and remittances from the exile community. Once again, the culinary practices that are staged in the kitchen reflect the changes in material conditions and Cuban history. Gladys remarks that the garlic chicken she serves has become a big hit with foreign tourists, "an easy way to make dollars."[68] Carlos tries to defend the new economic paradigms as being born out of necessity and as a way to "survive":

ROSA: I want to do more than survive.
CARLOS: Careful, daughter. You're talking like a capitalist.
GLADYS: So? Where would we be without the tourist dollars?
CARLOS: Living on my pension.
GLADYS: You mean starving on your pension?
CARLOS: We're a socialist country. We take care of each other.
GLADYS: With tourists and dollars.[69]

The hysteresis effect in this scene now includes the time-lag between the socialist economy of the first three decades of the Revolution and the post-Soviet economic crisis that led to extreme scarcity and precarity. Carlos embodies this resistance to a historical transition, and while he remains firm in his adoration of Fidel Castro, he has had to put on a white apron and return to the service industry that he denounced as a revolutionary. He asserts that the changes are necessary because of the blockade, and that all Cubans "have to change our way of surviving, but not our ideals."[70] However, as the third act progresses, the action and dialogue suggest that the changes in material practices and economic agency will lead to new ideals as well, in particular, a reconciliation between the collectivist values of the Revolution and the aspirational individualism associated with a market economy.

The climax of the play occurs when, in the midst of these debates, the doorbell rings loudly—a doorbell no one has rung since before the Revolution. The characters wonder who it could be, since it is still early in the day and they aren't expecting any tourists for dinner until much later. The person ringing the doorbell turns out to be Lourdes, Adria's adult daughter, who has traveled to Cuba with her husband. Machado stages this encounter based on his own experience, which he recounts in his culinary memoir. The moment of return is also the central plot in his other play, *Havana Is Waiting*. Other Cuban American authors, such as Ela Troyano (aka Carmelita Tropicana) and Cristina García, have also depicted similar returns to the island, either by the exile generation who left as young children or by the children of exiles who never knew Cuba firsthand. For Machado, the return to Cuba stirs mixed emotions, and in both his memoir and *Havana Is Waiting* he depicts the frustrated attempts of the exile generation to gain access to their former homes, now converted into public institutions. In these, more personal iterations of the exile's return, Machado explores the uneasy reconciliation between those who left and those who stayed behind. In *The Cook*, however, Lourdes's return to her mother's former home sparks a heated exchange over who rightfully belongs in the house. At first, Gladys mistakes her for Adria since the resemblance is so striking. Yet what becomes more evident as the characters argue is that Lourdes embodies many of her mother's cultural and social values, even though she claims to reject what her mother has become: a bitter, angry woman who "lives a wasted life."[71] Lourdes's appearance—a return to a homeland she never knew—stages the hysteresis effect that has perpetuated and nurtured the revenge fantasies of many Cuban exiles who vowed to reclaim what the Revolution appropriated from them. Lourdes serves as a stand-in for her mother, who never forgave those Cubans who stayed behind and supported the Revolution. In particular, Adria came to despise Gladys so much that she erased her from her family history. This encounter is the first time Lourdes ever even heard about Gladys, who up to this point had always lived off her memories of her former life as someone else's cook.

The climax in this third act also stages the confrontation between two very different forms of Cuban nostalgia: from Gladys's perspective, a nostalgia for a friendship with Adria she never really had; from Lourdes's view, a nostalgia for a privileged social position she never had the chance to assume. Lourdes's arrival stages the house, and especially the kitchen, as the site where bourgeois legitimacy and inheritance confront populist will and collective ownership. Yet the characters also reveal the contradictions that lie at the center of these opposing social classes and their correlative habitus. Lourdes conveys the perspective of U.S.-born Cubans who have, as Albert Sergio Laguna argues, inherited the nostalgia of their parents and grandparents, and who reproduce *cubanía* as much through family relations as through the commoditization of memory with the purchase and exchange of foods, antiques, and memorabilia.[72] While Lourdes distinguishes herself from her mother—emphasizing she has married a liberal, white Democrat—she nonetheless engages with Gladys as if she inherited her mother's privileged habitus, which entitles her to claim ownership of the house. With Lourdes's arrival, Gladys reaffirms her debt and loyalty to Adria, but when Lourdes tries to lay claim to the house and reimpose the social order from her mother's era, Gladys finally enunciates and embodies her ownership of the house, a reconfiguration of habitus that had been taking place all along. Gladys acquired knowledge through her employment under Adria, which she misrecognizes as tutelage and friendship. Through hysteresis, she persists in valorizing the social hierarchies that relegated Black women to occupy the spaces of domestic service and servitude. As Bourdieu argues, although radical changes may occur in fields of power, the reconfigurations in habitus and dispositions that ensue observe a different time signature: "Habitus change constantly in response to new experiences. Dispositions are subject to a kind of permanent revision, but one which is never radical, because it works on the basis of the premises established in the previous state. They are characterized by a combination of constancy and variation which varies according to the individual and his degree of flexibility or rigidity."[73] It is only when Lourdes reveals that her mother called Gladys a "nigger" that the former cook relinquishes the last vestiges of her loyalty to Adria and the past life she represents. Gladys takes ownership of her labor and finally rejects the racial and class legitimacy of her former employer. Rosa asks Lourdes to leave, and Gladys says, "A cold reality has just left the room"; to which Carlos replies, "Finally, you understand the revolution."[74] The play portrays how a reconfiguration of habitus occurs over time, and that the conscious acknowledgment of that change facilitates an active engagement with creating a future.

The future the characters imagine is an entrepreneurial one, with Gladys mentoring and teaching the culinary profession to Rosa, whom she adopts as her own daughter. Yet even here, Gladys's dream of Rosa becoming a chef at one of the state-owned hotels and serving the European and North American tourists harkens back to the pre-Revolutionary era. Gladys had always wanted to pursue that profession, but the gendered and raced division of labor under the Batista regime did not allow for it. Even though the state now owns the hotels that once served the foreign elite, these sites of the tourist economy continue to serve a clientele according to European and North American standards of taste and distinction. Rosa can now pursue that dream through the more egalitarian values of the Revolution, a change that reflects a shift toward a feminist and intersectional politics and away from *machista* authoritarianism and white privilege.

For Machado, staging the return of the diasporic Cuban helps to mitigate the hysteresis effect of exilic nostalgia. The return allows for a recontextualization of the past—remembered vaguely from early childhood experiences—with the reality of present-day, Revolutionary Cuba. The use of food and cooking underscores the bodily knowledge that comprises the Cuban habitus of the play's characters. The kitchen becomes the staged space of conflict and emergence from the hysteresis effect, where historical changes reconfigure the habitus of the characters who occupy that space. In the first two acts, the kitchen remains "frozen in time," but the final act shows how the future for Cuba will require reinventing some of the forms of economic agency that the Revolution had ostensibly stamped out.

For Cubans in the United States and Cuba, nostalgia is not only a way to preserve a sense of cultural identity in the face of historical and societal changes, it is also big business and a mode of economic survival. In his analysis of the annual Cuba Nostalgia fair in Miami, Albert Sergio Laguna examines the pedagogical role that a commercialization of memorabilia and souvenirs serves in reproducing an image of Cuba that is frozen in time. He writes, "Nostalgia as a means to assert Cuban identity in the face of a suspicious white majority is no longer necessary in Miami, but Cuba Nostalgia makes it clear that it is still a profitable business strategy. Part of the event's organizing logic is that nostalgia is for sale, and the transaction begins with the price of admission."[75] Yet nostalgia has also served as a major selling point for tourism in Cuba, and when the Obama administration relaxed travel restrictions and reopened the U.S. embassy in 2016, many U.S. tourists flocked to Havana to see it "before it changes." In an op-ed on this short-lived revival of interest in travel to Cuba, Laguna also writes, "What 'changes,' exactly, do people want to avoid seeing when they visit Cuba? The arrival of U.S.-style capitalism? A post-Castro political era? Whatever those changes travelers wish to avoid may be, they stand in stark contrast with the will of the Cuban people, who are very much invested in any change that would bring a brighter future to the island."[76] As *Anna in the Tropics* and *The Cook* show, some forms of Cuban nostalgia are deployed to hold people back and enforce conservative doxic values that resist adapting to change. Yet nostalgia also appears in these plays as a way to endure radical historical changes and envision a future where Cuban cultural identity survives and thrives under new social, political, and economic conditions. This form of reflective nostalgia captures what Fernando Ortiz articulates when he distinguishes between *cubanidad*—a generic condition of the Cuban—and *cubanía*, which he defines as "a cubanidad that is full, felt, conscious, and desired; a responsible cubanidad, a cubanidad with the three virtues said to be theological: faith, hope, and love."[77] These virtues of *cubanía* embrace the complexities and contradictions of Cuban history, and they are part of the reflective nostalgia that reconsiders the past in order to imagine and plan for an uncertain future.

CHAPTER 2

Decolonizing Queer Camp in Novels by Edwin Sánchez and Ángel Lozada

Debt acts as a "capture," "predation," and "extraction" machine on the whole of society, as an instrument for macroeconomic prescription and management, and as a mechanism for income redistribution. It also functions as a mechanism for the production and "government" of collective and individual subjectivities.
—Maurizio Lazzarato, The Making of the Indebted Man

Some day, you're going to see the name of Googie Gomez in lights and you're going to say to yourself [gasps] was that her? And you're gonna answer to yourself, [gasps] that was her! But you know something, mister? I was always her, just that nobody knows it!
—Googie Gómez, The Ritz

In *Anna and the Tropics*, the action opens and closes with scenes of indebtedness. In the first scene, Santiago signs what amounts to a promissory note on the bottom of Cheché's shoe, and by the end of the play he has taken out another loan to pay off his debt to his murderous half-brother. Indebtedness becomes the focal point of the two men's antagonistic relationship and emblematizes Polonius's advice to his son, Laertes, in act 1, scene 3 of Shakespeare's *Hamlet*, "Neither a borrower or lender be / For loan oft loses both itself and friend." Similarly, an expression my father often used to describe a strong relationship of trust and admiration is, "*Él no quiere cuenta conmigo.*" I was always curious to know what that expression meant and speaking to friends and colleagues from Puerto Rico and Latin America, some understand the saying to mean, "He doesn't want anything to do with me." Literally it means, "He doesn't want to have an account or dealings with me," but my father's Puerto Rican version suggests good friendships are built on mutual trust and not indebtedness, similar to Polonius's advice. However, in contemporary neoliberal economies, whether at the personal or national level, worth is assessed by how much debt one can incur, with the assumption that the more credit you are given, the more likely your income and sources of capital will allow you to repay it. Economic anthropologist David Graeber—whose book *Debt: The First 5,000 Years* became a best seller after the 2008 financial meltdown and the rise of the Occupy Wall Street movement—argues that debt is the unspoken, misrecognized logic at the center of socioeconomic relations, from the intimacy of family commitments to the abstract calculations that generate monetary systems and financial institutions.[1] In the United States, consumers measure their level of financial security by means of their credit scores, and innumerable commercials and advertisements equate credit card accounts with personal freedom, success, and stability. Similarly, credit ratings agencies like Standard & Poor's, Moody's, and Fitch Group can impact local and national governments' ability to issue bonds, and a junk status can propel a national economy toward a debt crisis. Puerto Rico's debt crisis has been just one example of how global financial institutions and government policies create perverse incentives that can cripple an economy and politically disenfranchise those who already occupy the most precarious positions in society. Yet, as Graeber shows, the trillion-dollar debts of government are never repaid, just recirculated and resold as speculative investment opportunities.

Indebtedness is also seen as a moral and ethical failing, an inability to live within one's means, and a lapse into debilitating dependency on others. This contradiction lies at the heart of how Puerto Rican writers Edwin Sánchez and Ángel Lozada portray the experience of gay Latino men who emulate the upwardly mobile lifestyle associated with economic success and sexual liberation in New York City. Their novels use various forms of subversive humor, particularly queer camp, in order to expose how the heightened visibility of gays and lesbians establishes a hierarchy of taste—what Bourdieu calls distinction—based on conspicuous consumption, body fascism, and elitist, exclusionary social formations.[2] These gatekeeping criteria ensure that gay Latino men from working-class families must acquire on credit the social and cultural capital associated with the dominant white culture in order to enjoy the personal freedom and autonomy that normalizing discourses promise. The social and cultural capital that the characters in these novels acquire also come at a price; in particular, estrangement from their families and Puerto Rican communities. Because they pursue upward mobility through conspicuous consumption and the commoditization of their raced bodies, they either go into bankruptcy trying to consume an idealized lifestyle or become destitute after losing the only tangible asset they had: their fetishized, youthful Latino bodies. Sánchez and Lozada decolonize queer camp as a way to resituate the diasporic subject from a submissive position of dependency to a position that, while economically precarious, resists the symbolic violence that hegemonic, homonormative values impose on gay Latino men. The logic of debt becomes part of their habitus as upwardly mobile gay men of color, yet just as there are some forms of kinship they can't live without, there are some debts they are obliged to honor in order to survive.

Sánchez and Lozada both write about the experiences of gay Latino men in NYC, and the two novels that form the counterpoint of this chapter portray the contradictions of transcultural capital for those men who aspire to upward mobility but fall on hard times because of these aspirations. Sánchez, a prolific, award-winning playwright, publishes in English and has written numerous works that explore the complexities of dysfunctional family relations, social outcasts trying to find acceptance, and the tortuous emotional conflicts that come from repressed sexual desires. Lozada, a fiction writer who publishes in Spanish, is the author of a number of short stories and two novels that depict many of the same themes found in Sánchez work. The cultural perspectives of the two writers differ in that Sánchez writes primarily about the experience of U.S. Latinxs, while Lozada portrays the lives of Puerto Ricans on the island and their diasporic experience as migrants to the mainland. Sánchez's novel, *Diary of a Puerto Rican Demigod* (2015), is a first-person narration of the life of Javier "Javi" Rivera, a thirtysomething Puerto Rican from the Bronx who at seventeen had a flash-in-the-pan career as a Broadway dancer.[3] Javi abandons his career after his one and only casting when a rich, white admirer—Jason Wilcox—romances and showers him with his wealth and access to the exclusive social circles of NYC's A-Gays. After twenty years of "unwedded bliss," Jason trades Javi in for a younger model, and the novel chronicles Javi's downfall from the heights of social and economic privilege to unskilled unemployment and life in his parents' basement. Lozada's novel, *No quiero quedarme sola y vacía* (2006; *I Don't Want to End Up Alone and Empty*), is a third-person narration of La Loca, a young Puerto Rican from the island who moves to NYC to find work in the financial sector.[4] Unlike Sánchez's use of the more traditional form of the fictional diary, Lozada's novel experiments with multiple narrative voices, often switching from Spanish to English and using a hyperbolic, frenetic prose style. The novel follows the main character from failed relationships to anonymous sexual encounters and narrates his attempts to live an upscale lifestyle by maxing out his credit cards and eventually declaring bankruptcy. The main characters in Sánchez's and Lozada's novels share the habitus of what sociologist Maurizio Lazzarato calls the "Indebted Man," a neoliberal version of *Homo economicus* whose subjectivity is constituted by relations of power that emerge from the creditor-debtor relationship.[5] In the context of the diasporic experience, these relations of power are also operationalized through Puerto Rico's colonial condition and the hegemonic discourses that doxify upper-class white culture as the norm toward which all people of color should aspire. Sánchez's novel explores the contradictions of transcultural capital, which can simultaneously empower economic agency while reproducing asymmetrical relations of power and domination. In particular, Javi's fictional diary shows how debt and indebtedness are central to the economic logic that perpetuates social inequality and even Puerto Rico's colonial condition but can also take the form of the communitarian values of honor and reciprocity. In contrast, Lozada's novel focuses more closely on the deleterious effects of indebtedness, and the narrator offers a metatextual turn that critiques the forms of debt that were incurred as part of the novel's production and publication. Because of a dispute with his publishers, Lozada threatened legal action to have his novel released, and the author uses the narrator's voice to renounce the Puerto Rican literary community that had initially embraced him as a rising, young author.

Contemporary Latinx literature often depicts the contradictions that arise when characters attempt to transform the transcultural capital derived from their diasporic experience and heritage culture into economic capital in U.S. dominant culture. The dominant discourse on immigration and upward mobility emphasizes assimilation into hegemonic, Anglo-American culture and a disavowal of Latinx Caribbean heritage. In this "melting pot" ideology, the Latinx Caribbean cultural heritage is portrayed as a deficit rather than an asset that contributes to economic empowerment. As Chicana education scholar Tara J. Yosso argues, students of color are often perceived as having "cultural deficiencies" while, in fact, they possess various forms of social and cultural capital that comprise what she calls "community cultural wealth"; that is, "an array of knowledge, skills, abilities and contacts possessed and utilized by Communities of Color to survive and resist macro and micro-forms of oppression."[6] However, while an accumulation of transcultural capital ostensibly gives agency to the Latinx subject, it can also reproduce the hegemonic structures of power in a neoliberal economy. In some cases, literary works propose that a decolonial strategy can emerge from radical embodiments of diasporic positionings in different social fields. The analysis of Sánchez's and Lozada's novels that follows will show how that decolonial discourse emerges from the text's formal elements, such as narrative structures, figurative language, and metatextuality. Through an examination of how Sánchez's novel depicts the social relations that constitute diasporic subjects as economic agents, I wish to scrutinize and critique this literary text's potential for articulating a decolonial discourse in the context of neoliberal capitalism in the U.S. Latinx community. Sánchez's novel explores the possibility that the value of Latinx transcultural capital is derived not solely from its opposition to dominant forms of capital, but also from its reinvestment in the collective well-being of the marginal communities from which it emerges. On the other hand, Lozada's novel has a more pessimistic outlook, and its portrayal of bankruptcy and precarity anticipates the economic crises, compounded by Hurricane Maria's devastation, that have recently plagued Puerto Rico.

These two works of fiction explicitly engage with the internal contradictions of transcultural capital through a decolonial critique of the neoliberal state, in which upward mobility and wealth accumulation are institutional mechanisms that perpetuate social and economic inequalities. The Latinx traditions of communitarian values that persist in diasporic ethnic enclaves become the collective means with which to mitigate the symbolic violence inflicted by neoliberal political economies that maintain Latinx Caribbeans in a constant state of displacement, second-class status, and colonialist exploitation. Communitarian values and collective action are not inherently Latinx, but they are part of the array of embodied practices—the diasporic habitus—in which language, race, gender, and sexuality are the means by which the diasporic subject articulates and is articulated by the institutional fields of power that facilitate the disequilibrium in value between different forms of social and cultural capital. In some cases, works of Latinx cultural production reproduce elements of the symbolic violence of trans-cultural capital, which appears as an uncritical embodiment of the logic of social domination, whether in the discourses of upward mobility and wealth accumulation or in the exploitative material and cultural practices that form part of the diasporic experience. Through this critical approach, Sánchez's and Lozada's novels reveal the strategies that gay Latino men have engaged as economic agents to mitigate the contradictory logic of their transcultural capital and, in some cases, imagine ways to position themselves against the institutionalized systems of oppression that perpetuate state violence, economic inequality, and social and cultural disenfranchisement.

Edwin Sánchez, born in Puerto Rico and raised in the Bronx, is the author of over two dozen off-Broadway and short plays, several of which have won regional and national awards.[7] His most well-known works include *Trafficking in Broken Hearts* (1992), *Unmerciful Good Fortune* (1992), *Clean* (1995), *Icarus* (1997), and *La Bella Familia* (2011).[8] Sánchez's plays portray a broad range of life experiences, interpersonal relationships, cultural clashes, and class conflicts. A common char-acter in his dramatic works is the social outsider, who can appear as a street hus-tler (*Trafficking in Broken Hearts*), a disfigured loner (*Icarus*), a gay priest (*Clean*), or a Puerto Rican hit woman (*La Bella Familia*). With his first novel, *Diary of a Puerto Rican Demigod*, the main character goes from a socialite to a reject, and it is through the protagonist's fall from the heights of wealth and social visibility to the depths of poverty and life in his parents' basement that the fictional diary elab-orates a critique of upward mobility and the forms of conspicuous consumption that are associated with taste and distinction.

The novel begins in medias res at the moment when Jason dumps Javi for a younger man. As Javi rereads his old diary entries, the novel portrays the protago-nist's aspirations as a naïve young Latino who is dazzled by Jason's wealth and social connections. He even recounts an episode when he gets to have dinner with Madonna after a charity fundraiser. These flashbacks are interspersed with Javi's current crisis as a middle-aged gay man with no education or professional pros-pects. His fall from grace is somewhat softened by his parents, for whom Jason had previously purchased a three-flat brownstone on the Upper West Side. Unemployed and taking only the designer clothes he has collected throughout the years, Javi moves in with his parents and the extended family comprising his bisexual, down-low cousin Hector, Hector's "baby-mama" Sonia, and their three children. Between his mother who constantly harasses him to get a job and Sonia who calls him "loca" and "pinga jockey," Javi at first finds little comfort with his family. The novel follows his reacclimation to a Puerto Rican working-class community, but now as an openly gay man who has developed the practical habits of the Manhat-tan elite. At the neighborhood gay bar—the Red Castle—Javi also reconnects with his childhood friend, Rob, and he finds a new community of gay Latino men from working-class backgrounds. Although Javi was unceremoniously dumped, he still holds out hope that he can reunite with Jason, and although he has several encounters with his ex throughout the novel, he is devastated when he learns Jason plans to marry his new Latino lover, Eric. Javi's adventures are narrated with humor, yet the novel explores the complex lives of gay Latino men who live on the margins of the dominant, white gay culture and, in some cases, in conditions of extreme precarity. His friend Joel, for example, is a homeless activist who refuses to accept Javi's offers of charity. The central conflict revolves around Javi's return to a Puerto Rican community that shows little interest in the forms of elite cultural and social capital that Javi had when he was living with Jason, yet his family and friends do not necessarily reject wealth and the financial security it provides. Ultimately, Javi has to reconcile the different sets of values that constitute his transcultural capital while reimagining his economic future, with or without Jason.

Ángel Lozada, born and raised in Mayagüez, Puerto Rico, and migrated to the United States as an adult, is the author of two novels, *La patografía* (1998) and *No quiero quedarme sola y vacía*, as well as a number of short stories and a prose poem, *El libro de la letra A* (2013), which reflects his practice of Santería.[9] *La patografía* received much critical attention as a forceful, unflinching look at homophobia in Puerto Rico, and it tells the story of a young boy in Mayagüez who lives in a family dominated by female relatives, some of whom accept and care for the protagonist, whose mother is abusive and father is completely absent.[10] Religion plays a significant role in the protagonist's life, whether in the form of his aunt's Santería or in the evangelicalism to which he turns in order to suppress his homosexual desires. Both of Lozada's novels integrate various experimental narrative techniques, yet his first work is readily identifiable as a coming-of-age fiction while the second book defies any such linear narrative trajectory. *No quiero quedarme sola y vacía* follows the misadventures of La Loca, a young, gay Puerto Rican who has earned his BA, served in the U.S. Navy, and works for Anderson Consulting in NYC. Lawrence La Fountain-Stokes summarizes the many definitions of the term "loca" in the Puerto Rican context, which can mean everything from "'madwoman' in Spanish, but also means 'effeminate man' or 'queer,' similar to English-language usages such as 'pansy,' 'nelly,' 'fairy,' 'Mary,' and 'queen.'"[11] Despite his education and entry into the white-collar workforce, Lozada's protagonist falls on hard times due to his addiction to easy credit. The novel reproduces much of the sloganeering and advertising language associated with the gay consumer market, which is mixed heteroglossically with first- and third-person narrative depictions of La Loca's many sexual exploits and diatribes on Puerto Rican literary and cultural institutions. Although both Sánchez and Lozada include many explicit portrayals of gay sex, Lozada's novel has a darker edge, and La Loca's anonymous hook-ups convey a sense of abjection that is not found in Sánchez's more humorous depictions. Because of La Loca's inability to live within his means, he ends up homeless and panhandling in the streets of New York. Whereas Sánchez ends his novel with Javi surrounded by his community of family and friends, La Loca is left "sola y vacía," alone and empty, with little hope for an economically secure future. The novel not only depicts this life of social isolation but also serves as a metafictional denunciation of Lozada's own banishment from the Puerto Rican literary and intellectual community. *No quiero quedarme sola y vacía* underscores the consequences gay Latino men suffer when they are profligate with their transcultural capital and are unable or unwilling to honor their debts to family and community.

QUEER PUERTO RICAN LITERATURE AND THE POLITICS OF THE LITERARY FIELD

Sánchez's and Lozada's novels share many of the literary themes, bilingual poetics, and uses of humor with other works of fiction that have depicted the diasporic imaginary of queer Latinidad in NYC. As in the works of Manuel Ramos Otero and Reinaldo Arenas, Sánchez and Lozada write about the experience of cultural and social isolation in the city, although Sánchez also portrays in his novel a gay Latino community that is at once marginal to and integrated in the larger Latinx enclave. Sánchez and Lozada address racial and class conflict, same-sex love and loss, nonnormative sexual relations, homophobia, violence, and machismo as recurring themes in ways very similar to the novels and short fiction of Jaime Manrique, Larry la Fountain-Stokes, and Charles Rice-González. While Sánchez's novel is written predominately in English with Spanish phrases and bilingual code-switching mixed sporadically throughout the text, Lozada's bilingual poetics is Spanish dominant and more reminiscent of the highly stylized language games found in novels by Giannina Braschi. Both novels incorporate elements of satire, parody, and camp humor, yet Sánchez's fictional diary also contains melodramatic episodes and plot lines, whereas Lozada's semiautobiographical text experiments with the dark humor of the absurd. What distinguishes Sánchez's and Lozada's novels is their articulation of the diasporic embodied economy that explores the contradictions of transcultural capital, which can simultaneously empower economic agency while reproducing inequitable relations of power and domination, particularly in sexual relations and romantic entanglements. Their works show how debt and indebtedness can take the form of the communitarian and familial value of honor, as well as the economic logic that perpetuates social inequality and Puerto Rico's colonial condition. As I examine how the novels articulate these contradictions and potentialities, I also consider how these literary works circulate within different configurations of the literary field, which imposes their own set of norms and modes of acquiring and accumulating social and economic capital.

In a 2017 interview I conducted with Edwin Sánchez, he related to me why he self-published this novel, in spite of his long career as a playwright and the publication of his plays by theater presses. As Sánchez pitched the novel to different editors, they were more interested in publishing a coming-of-age novel rather than a fictional diary that focused on a middle-aged man. The coming-of-age novel, memoir, and autobiography are some of the most pervasive subgenres in Latinx literature. From the foundational *Down These Mean Streets* by Piri Thomas to the more recent success of Justin Torres's *We the Animals*, the coming-of-age novel has so dominated the literary field for Puerto Rican writers in the United States, it is as if

Puerto Ricans remain a people in perpetual childhood, always becoming but never fully grown.[12] The preferences of literary editors in this case reveal an unwillingness to engage with material in which Latinx men and women are portrayed as adults with complex lives and a wealth of experiences. In order for these subjects to be comprehensible and suitable for a broad reading public, the portrayal of Latinx lives has to align with a discourse of infantilization. The dominant trends in Latinx literature also reveal the importance of the academic readership in the literary market; the coming-of-age novel and memoir appeal to younger readers and are therefore frequently assigned on course syllabi.

Although Sánchez does include passages that reproduce Javi's diary as a young man as well as childhood recollections and reflections from his perspective as an adult, the novel focuses on Javi's adulthood, which explores in detail how the character loses much of his social and economic capital as a consequence of his transition into middle age. This also runs counter to the familiar narrative trajectory of the coming-of-age novel, particularly when the story focuses on the immigrant experience, which follows the protagonist's emergence from poverty and overcoming of personal and professional obstacles. Because Sánchez's novel resists this formulaic depiction of Latinx lives, the author chose to publish and distribute the novel on his own, which has allowed him to make a unique contribution to the Latinx literary field that expands the repertoire of fictional genre and form. The trade-off, of course, is that his novel will not receive the promotional support from an established press, and fewer readers will have the opportunity to engage with this expanded literary repertoire and the complexity of the Latinx lives it portrays.

Lozada directly engages with the politics of the literary field in his novel, and through the use of metafictional discourse the author situates himself in opposition to the Puerto Rican intellectual communities as well as the dominant trends in the U.S. literary market for Latinx fiction. As I will discuss in more detail below, the publication of Lozada's second novel was fraught with accusations of censorship, blacklisting, and threats of litigation. The narrator and protagonist serve as proxies for the author, who denounces the Puerto Rican literary and intellectual establishment that marginalized his work after initially embracing and promoting his first novel, La patografía. While Lozada's second novel directly addresses the politics of publication on the island, it also alludes to the ways the literary establishment in the United States consecrates certain Latinx authors according to marketability and how closely their works hew to the prevailing narratives of the Latinx experience. In a fragmented, stream-of-consciousness passage, La Loca fantasizes about having a successful literary career like that of Esmeralda Santiago, whose three memoirs, *When I Was Puerto Rican* (1993), *Almost a Woman* (1999), and *The Turkish Lover* (2004), have received critical acclaim from U.S. reviewers and remain highly visible on high school and college curricula:

> *Y escribir, no una novela puertorriqueña, sino La Novela Puertorriqueña. Realizar el American Dream y titularla Casi Una Mujer. Escribir un libro para los gringos que tenga un nombre de fruta en el título, muchas escenas tropicales y una maestra*

que me salve y me lleve a Harvard. Escribir mis memorias para latinos semi-
(anal)fabetas con un árbol genealógico en la contraportada. Hacerme millonaria
y que me retraten en un sillón como si fuera Esmeralda Santiago, descalza.[13]

And write, not a Puerto Rican novel, but The Puerto Rican Novel. Achieve the
American Dream and title it *Almost a Woman*. Write a novel for Gringos that
has the name of a fruit in the title, many tropical scenes, and a teacher who
saves me and takes me to Harvard. Write my memoirs for semi-(il)literate Latinos with a genealogical tree on the inside cover. Become a millionaire and have
my picture taken in an armchair as if I were Esmeralda Santiago, barefoot. (my
translation)

Lozada did, in fact, stage a similar photograph for the front cover flap of his first
novel, *La patografía*, although instead of an armchair he is pictured barefoot on a
park bench. Lozada challenges the critical fallacy of confusing the authorial persona with a narrator, a metafictional gesture I will address again in my reading of
Junot Díaz's short stories. The cynical tone of this passage conveys La Loca's disassociation from and disdain for the U.S.-born Latinx community, while also articulating the self-serving dream of achieving success in the literary market that
appeals to that readership. La Loca underscores the banality of Latinx literary
trends and the way they exoticize the authors and their culture with trite, tropical
imagery, the rutinary fixations on family and lineage, and the trope of the white
savior who rescues the Latinx author from obscurity. Even the reference to the book
jacket image of Esmeralda Santiago sitting barefoot in a rocking chair (which
appeared in the 1993 Vintage Books edition of *When I Was Puerto Rican*) serves to
critique the U.S. literary establishment's portrayal of Latinx authors as noble sav-
ages who, although now educated and conversant in English, continue to embody
elements of their primitive origins. This passage exemplifies a mercenary use of
transcultural capital, in which Puerto Rican culture reaffirms the U.S. stereotypes
of exotic, premodern Latins in order to cash in on that heritage and attain high
levels of economic and symbolic capital.

These considerations help outline how the literary field and the market for
Latinx fiction determine what kinds of works are published and which authors are
consecrated by cultural and academic institutions. In his analysis of the kind of
gatekeeping that these cultural institutions perform, Bourdieu argues that "the field
of cultural production is the site of struggles which, through the imposition of the
dominant definition of the writer, aim to delimit the population of those who possess the right to participate in the struggle over the definition of the writer."[14] In
other words, those with the most influence in these fields of cultural production
reproduce the logic of their gatekeeping function by giving access to other participants who share the same interest in perpetuating that logic. Bourdieu calls this
interest the *illusio*, which constitutes the collective belief in the value of playing
the game in a social field and the legitimacy of the rules that establish the field's
boundaries. The *illusio* in the Latinx literary field fetishizes the work of artistic
labor as an authentic expression of a lived experience, as well as an urgent voice

from a marginalized group that deserves to be heard by a broader audience. The value attributed to this *illusio* circulates as "innumerable acts of credit which are exchanged among all the agents engaged in the artistic field."[15] That is, the writers, agents, editors, and reviewers who are invested in playing the rules of the game engage in relationships of indebtedness as they acquire capital and enforce the gatekeeping criteria which perpetuate their positions of legitimacy. Consequently, not only do Sánchez's and Lozada's novels explore how indebtedness comes to constitute the subjectivities of the gay Latino characters, the unconsecrated status of these works also challenges the logic of debt and the hierarchies of taste that define what Latinx identities are considered relatable to a consumer market.

Consumerism, Upward Mobility, and Gay Latino Identity

Through the character of La Loca, Lozada's second novel explores the experience of the queer Puerto Rican diaspora and the kinds of insolvent identities that occur when these subjects buy into the consumer culture that promises economic self-fulfillment and social mobility. Many scholars and critics have undertaken the analysis of homosexuality and its mutually constitutive relation to the structural elements of the economy. John D'Emilio's seminal essay on capitalism and gay identity examined the contradictory way labor mobility under capitalism allowed men and women to move away from their biological families and explore same-sex relations in urban communities, yet at the same time the heterosexual, reproductive family was valorized as the foundational norm of a capitalist, wage-labor society.[16] Ann Pellegrini reassesses D'Emilio's essay and suggests that his very valuable analyses also "articulate gayness with or even as whiteness." She also asks rhetorically, "What if some ways of doing kinship are not dispensable?"[17] Lozada's novel offers a compelling portrayal of these intersectionalities and reveals the economic and colonialist structures that have impacted Puerto Rican families and have simultaneously empowered and violently marginalized the queer Latino subject. If wage labor has performed a key role in constituting gay identity in the United States, as D'Emilio has argued, advertising and consumerism have further entrenched notions of personal liberty and social integration for upwardly mobile queer subjects of color. In her book, *Selling Out: The Gay and Lesbian Movement Goes to Market*, Alexandra Chasin writes: "Just as advertising in the early twentieth century hailed immigrants as members of an ethnic group, offering them a route to Americanization, so did advertising in the late twentieth century have the power to bring a gay community into public being. Simultaneously, it subjected gay men and lesbians to the idea that emancipation could be achieved through the market, particularly in the mode of assimilation, especially through consumption."[18] The main character in Lozada's novel attempts to attain a sense of self-realization and integration into an upwardly mobile gay community through consumerism, but his ability to consume is contingent upon easy credit rather than personal wealth. Eventually his inability to pay for this virtual lifestyle sends La Loca into a cycle of debt and bankruptcy as well as a vortex of self-abjection and isolation, which the novel portrays through an increasingly fragmented and disjointed narrative and which is articulated through La Loca's simultaneous fear and embrace of death.

The narrative voice in *Sola y vacía* recounts numerous binges of consumption, anonymous sex, and fantasies of a virtual self that emerges in the next life:

> *Dios me usará nuevamente. Si descubren la pastilla de la eterna juventud, si logro alterar mi genética, seré totalmente libre. Iré a los baños todas las noches y me hundiré en orgías inimaginables y después me iré a hacer ejercicios y a comer bagels. Si descubren la cura para el SIDA, seré de todos. Seré tuya porque ya no tendré miedo de contagiarme. No me importará ya con quien. Me poseerá la masa urbana y viviré satisfecha y riéndome, mientras el mundo asegura su futuro en NASDAQ.[19]*

> God will use me once again. If they find the pill that grants eternal youth, if I manage to alter my genetics, I will be totally free. I will go to the baths every night and I will plunge myself into unimaginable orgies and then I will go workout and eat bagels. If they find the cure for AIDS, I will belong to everyone. I will be yours because I will no longer fear contagion. It won't matter to me with whom. The urban masses will possess me and I will live satisfied and laughing, while the world secures its future on NASDAQ. (my translation)

The addressee of this passage remains undefined but serves as a disembodied object of desire that is forever out of reach. Very similar to the portrayal in *La patografía* of the persecuted *pato* who metamorphoses into a duck, in this passage La Loca imagines a resurrection from his current state of precarity and emotional isolation. In this case, he desires to be reborn through chemical enhancement and genetic engineering as a queer cyborg that is plugged into a matrix of perpetual sex, consumption, and speculative finance.

The novel prefigures the Puerto Rican debt crisis that would eventually lead to the PROMESA legislation of 2016, the Junta de Supervisión y Administración Financiera, and Governor Ricardo Roselló's declaration of Title III bankruptcy for the island. Although the novel lends itself easily to an allegorical reading, David Graeber and Maurizio Lazzarato argue that debt is the underlying logic behind neoliberal political economies, which not only formulates the public policies of deficit spending but also constitutes the subjectivities of economic agents in contemporary Western societies. Lozada's novel articulates the way diasporic subjects attempt to position themselves in social fields of power by embodying the habitus of indebtedness. Lozada's Loca desires the death of his abject queer body, which will lead to a new "beginning" and "overcoming," yet the novel also shows that the desire for redemption, renewal, and a sense of belonging can cause queer Latino subjects to fall prey to the facile integration into state sanctioned forms of legitimacy. The simultaneous fear and embrace of death reflect a paradoxical rebellion against and desire for belonging, thus interrogating the terms with which we imagine ourselves as a community and with which we gauge our integration into the legitimized spaces of neoliberal democracy. Perhaps present and future queer generations can resist the forces that perpetuate forms of abjection by transforming our existing family ties, creating new support networks and coalitions, or even operating as free agents, and if we want to prevent ourselves from being *solas y vacías*, our embodied economies may be the most crucial part of our communities that we need to radicalize.

Both Javi and La Loca owe the acquisition of their hegemonic cultural capital either to a dominant partner, in Javi's case, or to educational and financial institutions, in the case of La Loca. Javi acknowledges that he "partnered up" and his embodiment of an upper-class habitus is not his "birthright."[20] He reveals in his diary how he dropped out of high school immediately after performing a self-taught forward flip at an audition and landing his first gig in the fictional Broadway show, *FUEGO!* A perpetual victim of gay bashing, Javi wasted no time in dropping out to avoid the daily abuse of the neighborhood bullies who would follow him to school, call him "*maricón*" and "*loca*," swing their hips exaggeratedly, and shout *fua! fua!*[21] He begins an alternate form of education as a dancer and, eventually, as Jason Wilcox's young Latino consort. As a dancer, Javi works and socializes for the first time with other gay men, some of whom display unapologetically the gestures and bodily movements that his high school bullies would imitate to mock him. Javi congratulates himself for earning more money dancing on Broadway than his father ever did after years as a maintenance worker at a suburban hospital. This leads Javi to believe naïvely that he shares equal status with Jason when they first meet. However, when he begins dating Jason seriously and then moves in with him, he receives a crash course on social etiquette and his dominated status. He "was swallowed whole by gay society" where "Jason was one of their Gods and that made [him] a demigod."[22] Lorraine, one of Jason's "besties," instructs Javi on what to expect now that Jason has chosen him as "the one who will complete him as a perfect matched set."[23] While a retinue of personal assistants attend to Lorraine's makeup and wardrobe, she summarizes Javi's personal story as the "Boy from squalor who nabs the Sun King."[24] Javi will be under close scrutiny not only by Jason and his elite social circle, but also the paparazzi and press. Lorraine says: "Mistakes will be tolerated at the beginning and then magnified. I hope you have a good learning curve. Remember everything, especially names, don't gossip or listen to gossip, but if you must gossip and it is traced back to you, deny, deny, deny. Follow Jason's lead when it comes to what parties, bars and charities to favor and dress as if life itself depended on it."[25] It is at one of these parties, when Jason forces Javi to wear silver *lamé* shorts with suspenders while everyone else is formally attired, that a cadre of bitchy queens tells the newcomer, "We're all for sale. Just don't sell yourself cheap is all."[26]

Yet when *FUEGO!* closes and Javi fails to get cast in another show, he abandons his career as a dancer and relies entirely on Jason's wealth and privilege. He even allows Jason to purchase a three-story brownstone for his parents, where he eventually finds refuge after getting dumped. Javi learns and adopts the attitudes, tastes, and mannerisms associated with the A-list society, yet this social and cultural capital has no value for Javi outside of his relationship with Jason. As Bourdieu argues, these forms of capital are worth less when they are acquired over time; the embodied capital of the elite is more valuable because it is perceived as their innate birthright. Bourdieu writes, "This embodied capital, external wealth converted to an integral part of the person, into a habitus, cannot be transmitted instantaneously (unlike money, property rights, or even titles of nobility) by gift or bequest, purchase or exchange."[27] As soon as Javi realizes that Jason has replaced him, he also comes to grips with the loss of his elite status and connection to Jason's circle of friends; he imagines his identity as a "demigod" beginning to fade and eventually feels invisible. Because he owed his acquisition of social and cultural capital entirely to Jason, Javi never fully took ownership of the habitus that facilitated his upward mobility.

The situation for La Loca in Lozada's novel is different because the protagonist does acquire educational capital on his own, although he does so by taking out student loans that he later cannot repay. For La Loca, his educational capital provides the means to join the white-collar workforce, but he aspires to an upwardly mobile lifestyle beyond his economic means and uses credit cards to sustain his obsessive consumerism. During his time in Washington, D.C., La Loca begins a relationship with another young Puerto Rican—a classical pianist who has expensive tastes but whose attempts to ingratiate himself with elite social circles invariably end in disappointment. As a couple, the two men become the gay pets of socialite Pepita Rodeaux and her group of wealthy and well-connected Puerto Rican women who use them for their personal entertainment but treat them condescendingly: "*después que salían de su casa, se burlaban de ellos porque eran patofóbicas bien a fondo*" ("after they would leave their house, they would mock them because they were homophobic to the core" [my translation]).[28]

The affiliation of gay men with wealthy socialite women is a recurring trope in queer camp repertoires, and the role that gay men assume as tastemakers for elite social circles appears in everything from the literary works of Oscar Wilde to television shows like *Queer Eye for the Straight Guy* and *Sex and the City*. In the case of La Loca, he receives a constant barrage of disparaging remarks from his partner and their wealthy friends. They criticize his vocabulary in Spanish and his inability to master the mannerisms and bodily comportment associated with the habitus of the elite:

> *Por andar tanto con aquellas viejas pese a todo aquel chisme, la Acomplejada empezó a imitar a Pepita y a refinarse: mejoró su español, compró libros para aumentar su vocabulario y eliminó de su lengua aquella r de Maricao, esa que se pronuncia en lo más profundo de la garganta, y la remplazó por una más fina, la que se pronuncia con la punta de la lengua. . . . Pero las viejas no perdían la más mínima ocasión para corregirle el español a La Loca: no se dice entrenamiento, se dice adiestramiento. No se dice comando, se dice dominio.*[29]

By running around so much with those old crones in spite of that gossip, Miss Inferiority Complex started to imitate Pepita and act more refined: she improved her Spanish, she bought books to increase her vocabulary, and she purged from her tongue that Maricao r, the one that is pronounced from the furthest depths of the throat, and she replaced it with a much finer one, the one that is pronounced on the tip of the tongue. . . . But those crones never missed the minutest occasion to correct La Loca's Spanish: don't say training, say preparation. Don't say command, say knowledge. (my translation)

The narrator refers to himself here as "la Acomplejada" because the constant derision he suffers from his wealthy friends inculcates in him abjection and a sense of inadequacy. Like Javi, despite his attempts to acquire the cultural capital associated with the elite class, those members who enjoy the privilege of innate ownership of their habitus regulate and deny his access to their social circle. According to Bourdieu, "Language is a bodily technique, and specifically linguistic, especially phonetic, competence is a dimension of bodily hexis in which one's whole relation to the social world, and one's whole socially informed relation to the world, are expressed."[30] As we see with La Loca's attempts to correct the pronunciation of his guttural r—a sign of rural, working-class origins in Puerto Rico—the dictates of distinction reinforce hereditary transmission of social and cultural capital. La Loca, like Javi, is not allowed to assume ownership of the capital that facilitates his upward mobility. Through this dedoxification of distinction, both Sánchez's and Lozada's novels put quotation marks around queer camp and its affiliation with elite cultural production. The novels perform "camp" in a way that resemanticizes the very act of cultural appropriation in order to reveal the hierarchical social contingencies that give value to hegemonic forms of capital.

The novels differ, however, in their exploration of other forms of indebtedness; in particular, the moral and ethical values that emerge from relations of kinship and community. A comparison of these novels shows that the Latinx cultural values of family cohesion—often but not always reflecting paternalistic Latinx traditions—are not a universal experience but remain a doxifying force in the diasporic habitus, albeit from a minoritarian position vis-à-vis the hegemonic Anglo-American model of the heteronormative family. The paternalistic *machista* tradition in Latinx Caribbean culture creates symbolic capital through honor, and debts to honor establish hierarchical relations of power and legitimacy among family and community members. David Graeber, in *Debt: The First 5,000 Years*, argues that honor emerges in societies in which human beings are reduced to commodities, in particular slave societies, because it represents the value of a human being—usually male—that must be protected from extraction by others. Even when men protect the honor of their wives, sisters, or mothers, they are essentially protecting their masculine privilege and dominant status over the women in their families. Graeber writes: "At its simplest, honor is that excess dignity that must be defended with the knife or sword (violent men, as we all know, are almost invariably obsessed with honor). . . . Some of the most genuinely archaic forms of money we know about appear to have been used precisely as measures of honor and degradation: that is, the value of money was, ultimately, the value of power to turn others into money."[31] Bourdieu makes a similar argument in his sociological study of the Kabyle in Algeria. For Bourdieu, in this precapitalist society, honor is "a transfigured expression of the objective relationship between the [economic] agents and their ever-threatened material and symbolic patrimony."[32] However, Graeber elaborates his characterization of honor in support of his thesis that there are two forms of economy: a commercial or market economy and a "human" economy, in which money serves as a measure of social dignity and prestige rather than as a means of engaging in commodity exchange.[33] Bourdieu, on the other hand, consistently critiques the type of economism that separates economic capital and symbolic capital, and he argues that symbolic capital—signs of dignity, prestige, and high status—is derived from economic capital but misrecognized as noneconomic. This puts into question Graeber's proposal that contemporary societies should abandon the market logic that has perverted the social relations of human economies.[34] For Bourdieu, social relations, even in precapitalist societies, are always characterized by the interest—or *illusio*—that drives economic agents to stake a claim on economic and symbolic capital in any social field: "When one knows that symbolic capital is credit, but in the broadest sense, a kind of advance, a credence, that only the group's belief can grant those who give it the best symbolic and material guarantees, it can be seen that the exhibition of symbolic capital (which is always very expensive in material terms) is one of the mechanisms which (no doubt universally) make capital go to capital."[35] In the case of Sánchez's and Lozada's novels, the ability or inability to repay debts to family and community constitute measures of honor or shame, and while that indebtedness may be moral and ethical, it nonetheless adheres to the logic of debt that facilitates access to both economic and symbolic capital.

The Embodied Economy of Gay Latino Sex

As discussed previously, Sánchez's novel explores the way a gay Latino man's youthful body becomes a fetishized commodity, and once Javi reaches middle age, Jason replaces him with a younger Latino named Eric. Javi writes in his diary, "Eric is the one thing I can never be anymore. New."[36] Although Javi has by no means let himself go and still takes care of his physique, the fact that he can "pinch an inch," as Jason points out, means he no longer lives up to the exacting standards of A-Gay body fascism. "No fats no fems" is the ubiquitous phrase that appears on hookup sites and apps, which conveys how forms of masculine domination and misogyny are reproduced in gay sexual practices. I also use the term "body fascism" based on Susan Bordo's feminist analysis of eating disorders and body dysmorphia, which she argues are crystallizations of the Western and Judeo-Christian traditions that privilege the mind and spirit over the body. Bordo cites the pioneering work of psychoanalyst Hilde Bruch, whose female patients of anorexia and bulimia often described the elation of controlling and disciplining their bodies through compulsive dieting and extreme exercise regimens. Many of the respondents characterized the compulsion to control their bodies in masculinist terms, with one woman comparing this mind/body split as living with "a dictator who dominates me."[37] Bordo also finds strong correlations between eating disorders, upward mobility, and highly competitive academic and professional fields.

Gay and straight men—in particular, professional athletes and bodybuilders—also experience these eating disorders and body dysmorphia as a mind/body split. Anglo-American men are socialized to reproduce and enforce hegemonic gender norms, what Charlotte Hooper calls the bourgeois rational masculinity, which aligns with discourses of white nationalism and its values of individual freedom and self-reliance. According to this model, women and colonized people of color are portrayed as slaves to their bodies and passions. Hooper argues, "Bourgeois [white] men, whose behavior was characterized as being governed by pure reason, thus appeared natural colonial rulers and inheritors of the enlightenment."[38] This hegemonic form of masculinity is also pervasive in the advertising industry, which appeals to the upwardly mobile gay male consumer and feeds into what psychologists call the "Adonis complex" with eroticized images of hard bodies that can be controlled and perfected, which in turn promotes the purchase of gym memberships, supplements, and cosmetic surgery, as well as black-market steroid and hormone injections.[39] Body fascism perpetuates an economic feedback loop, in which upwardly mobile gay men aspire to attain the idealized body images that are associated with success, wealth, and power, and who are therefore compelled to expend much of their disposable incomes on controlling and disciplining their bodies to conform to these ideals.

When Javi reconnects with his Latino gay friends, however, he becomes aware of how these standards of male beauty reflect not only the premiums placed on youth and thinness, but also how exclusionary hierarchies that idealize a youthful, muscular body also devalue bodies not conforming to the dominant norms. His childhood friend Rob, the struggling actor, is balding and has a considerable paunch and love handles, and part of the reason he cannot find any work as an actor is due to his looks and ethnicity. Nevertheless, Rob does not devalue his own body; on the contrary, he proudly wears clothing that reveals his full figure, and in the bear and cub scene, he flaunts his physique with confidence. Rob never buys into body fascism and its predominately white, homonormative images of the sexually desirable gay man.

However, Javi's friend Victor—the bartender with the body of a Greek god—undergoes a change in attitude toward his idealized body image. Victor vows never to get fat or show his age, which would relegate him to work as a bouncer rather than at the more lucrative station behind the bar where lustful patrons shower him with tips. Even though all his friends and the bar patrons idolize and lust after his physique, he follows a rigorous diet and exercise routine to achieve ever more exacting standards of perfection. During a two-week hiatus, when everyone thinks he is at an exercise boot camp, Victor actually gains nearly thirty pounds of fat. When he reveals his new body, Javi laments that Victor used to be perfect. "No honey," Victor says, "I was just renting perfection."[40] Victor dissociates from the body image that he held up as the key to his employability and earning potential. As he makes his grand entrance at the bar in a pair of tight spandex shorts, he initially receives jeers and sneers, but as he starts to list all the Puerto Rican foods he can now eat— *pernil, flan, tembleque, amarillos,* and *maduros*—the crowd of Latino men begin to see Victor with new eyes. Victor trades in his obsession with attaining a perfect body to reclaim his Puerto Rican culinary heritage. Finally, Javi's bisexual cousin Hector compliments the "junk in his trunk," which empowers Victor as a fat yet sexually desirable Latino man. As he watches Victor gain confidence and receive more tips than ever before, Javi reflects on how Jason would panic if either of them gained even one pound. Jason's demands for physical perfection epitomize the white, bourgeois rational masculinity that is perpetuated in the idealized body image, which pervades gay-oriented media and consumer culture. Although Javi continues to cultivate his own physique to resume his training as a dancer, he sees in his Puerto Rican friends Rob and Victor ways of embodying Latinidad without conforming to the standards that fetishize and commoditize the gay Latino body, particularly as the colonized sex object of the white male gaze.

Like Javi, La Loca in Lozada's novel fears the effects of aging, since a lithe, muscular body is the standard of male beauty and sexual desirability in gay media and consumer culture. La Loca obsesses over her body—"*por más que rebajaba la loca siempre se encontraba obesa*" ("no matter how much weight she lost La Loca always thought she was obese" [my translation])—and spends much of her income on protein shakes, vitamins, and weight loss supplements. Although she signs up at a gym—"*Quería tener las tetas desarrolladas y la barriga ripiada*" ("she wanted to have her tits well developed and get six-pack abs" [my translation])—she only goes infrequently, and even then it is to cruise other, more muscular men. She idolizes the physiques of the models who appear in the International Male catalogue— "*así mismito quiero tener mi cuerpo*" ("that's exactly how I want my body to look" [my translation]).[41] The stream-of-consciousness narrative exposes the premium on youth and normative, cismale embodiments that constitute La Loca's cultural imaginary and dreams of living in a utopia of surgical and pharmacological enhancements:

> *A los cuarenta comenzaré un régimen riguroso de levantamiento de pesas para ponerme fibrosa y atractiva y levantarme el culo a fuerza de squats, para que las nuevas generaciones me miren y me deseen. Pagaré por implantes de nalgas en California.*
>
> *Pero los avances de la ciencia genética le daban esperanzas: si Dios quiere, no me pondré vieja porque ya pronto descubrirán la pastilla para uno mantenerse permanentemente joven, y enseguida que descubran la cura para el SIDA, me entregaré de lleno a los baños que es lo único que necesito para poder ser productiva. Seré verdaderamente libre cuando descubran la cura para el SIDA y para el herpes.*[42]

At forty I will begin a rigorous weight-lifting regimen to become sinewy and attractive and to lift my ass through sheer force of squats, so that the new generations will look at me and desire me. I will pay for butt implants in California.

But the advancements in genetic science gave her hope: God willing, I won't grow old because soon they will discover the pill that keeps you permanently youthful, and as soon as they discover the cure for AIDS, I will surrender myself completely to the baths, which is the only thing I need to be productive. I will be truly free when they discover the cure for AIDS and for herpes. (my translation)

This passage shows how the standards of beauty and sexual desirability, which become the doxic, homonormative values for gay men, are buttressed by upward mobility and the disposable income that can purchase the gym memberships, butt implants, and pharmaceuticals that will facilitate entry into a utopian space of neoliberal biopower. Keep in mind that Lozada published this book well before the use of PrEP and Truvada as pharmaceutical prophylactics against HIV. Yet this now widely available drug regimen can be costly even with insurance copays, the side effects can be damaging to the liver, and the drug is not suitable for men with high blood pressure. For those who can afford and sustain the daily dose prescription, the sense of freedom to have sex without condoms also puts the gay man in an indebted relation of dependency to the pharmaceutical industry.

La Loca's fantasy is articulated as a form of prayer—"*si Dios quiere*" (God willing)—which further links the embodied economy of homonormativity to a spiritual redemption and salvation. In other words, the idealized, cismale image of the upwardly mobile gay man relies on a discourse of self-fulfillment, individualism, and transcendence through the power of economic agency and technologies of the self, as Michel Foucault theorizes, "which permit individuals to effect by their own means or with the help of others a certain number of operations on their own bodies and souls, thoughts, conduct, and ways of being, so as to transform themselves in order to attain a certain state of happiness, purity, wisdom, perfection, or immortality."[43] Later in the novel, La Loca repeats this fantasy, but also remarks on how this kind of body fascism that pervades the sexual aesthetics of urban gay men also serves as a form of gatekeeping. S/he specifically implicates the gay community in Chelsea, NYC, as a space where the muscle queen can exert power through these embodiments, and the exclusionary practices that they implement establish a class hierarchy in the utopian gayborhood, where men supposedly are free to live openly. The homonormative image reproduces the symbolic violence that misrecognizes the gay man's submission and enslavement to the rigors of a neoliberal technofuture as a form of salvation and personal empowerment.

Lozada and Sánchez have explored gay Latino sexual practices in their previous works, which use graphic language to portray everything from furtive adolescent sex to monogamous sex between long-term partners, down-low sex between straight and bisexual men, group sex, male prostitution, rough trade, incest, and sexual violence. In all these depictions, Lozada and Sánchez situate these practices in the embodied economies where sex for gay Latino men reproduces relations of power around race and class. In Lozada's first novel, *La patografía*, the main character, Luisín, describes his first sexual encounters in Puerto Rico with his friend,

Jesús, "*un mulato—indio—nuyorican*, [que] *tenía un bicho que era casi el doble de grande que el mío*" ("a mulatto—Indian—Nuyorican, who had a dick almost twice as big as mine" [my translation]).[44] When Jesús tries to seduce Luisín's younger brother, their mother threatens to punish them if they see him again. Jesús becomes the dark-skinned predator whose race is associated with hypersexuality, and his status as a Nuyorican places him at the margins of the Puerto Rican national family. Sánchez also explores the racial and class politics of gay Latino sex in his play *Trafficking in Broken Hearts*, in which Papo, a Puerto Rican hustler in NYC, crosses ethnic and class lines in his relations with an upwardly mobile, white attorney and a working-class, white runaway who was a victim of incest and abuse from his brothers. Papo's sexual relations with these white men shift the power differential— who exploits, who is exploited—based on their social class status. In these depictions and others, sex for gay Latino men is transgressive but also aligned with hierarchies of race and class, which perpetuates states of abjection and violence against these diasporic subjects.

Lozada and Sánchez also portray the commodification of sex and how sexual relations can serve as a form of transcultural capital. In his second novel, Lozada uses even more graphic language to depict the sex between La Loca and her pianist boyfriend in D.C. In a passage directed to the ex-boyfriend in the second-person, La Loca recounts:

> *¿Te acuerdas cuando empezamos a meternos dildos? Aquella noche que, después de haber visto la película de Chad Douglas* On Spring Break . . . *y luego te compraste dos plugs, uno para ti y otro para mí, y luego empezaste a ponerte cock rings. . . . ¿Recuerdas cuando me metiste el plug y yo me vine por dentro, mientras veíamos una película de Jeff Stryker, donde él se lo metía a un policía en la cárcel, y nos pegábamos?*[45]

> Do you remember when we started fucking each other with dildos? That night, after watching that Chad Douglas movie *On Spring Break* . . . and then you bought two butt plugs, one for you and one for me, and then you started wearing cock rings. . . . Remember when you inserted the butt plug up my ass and I had an anal orgasm, while we watched a Jeff Stryker movie, where he was fucking a cop in prison, and we would smack each other around? (my translation)

In this passage, the way La Loca and her boyfriend experiment with sexual toys and light BDSM reflects the commodification of sex through pornography and paraphernalia. Their sexual antics reproduce not only the practices they see in pornographic videos, but also the culture of masculine domination in which sexual assault and rape is fetishized and associated with state violence. These sexual practices also encourage the purchase of various toys, costumes, and paraphernalia so that BDSM fantasies generate profits for the adult erotica industry. Similarly, in the case of Sánchez's novel, one of Javi's jobs is as a sales clerk at a sex shop, and one of the carnivalesque sex scenes involves Javi using an electric dildo machine he receives as a Christmas bonus. As discussed earlier, the gay Latino body is a

consumable object in the elite social circles of white men like Javi's ex, Jason. The depictions of gay Latino sexual practices in these literary and theatrical works, which range from the abject to the carnivalesque, underscore how sex in neoliberal societies is defined by consumer culture and market logic, where the racial and class identities of the participants in prescripted sexual encounters serve to reproduce positions of power and, in some cases, the violence of masculine domination and white nationalism.

For example, one chapter in Lozada's novel describes a night of sexual encounters at the gay bathhouse, the West Side Club, and uses the subversive power of the carnivalesque and its foregrounding of the material lower bodily stratum, as Mikhail Bakhtin has elaborated in his analysis of Rabelaisian fiction.[46] Throughout the graphic and scatological descriptions of anal sex and water sports, La Loca's exploits constitute a racial revenge narrative that dethrones white supremacy through the abjection of racialized bodies. La Loca recounts the forms of sexual degradation inflicted on her by a pair of Black men at the bathhouse, getting brutally sodomized and losing bowel control. Yet the protagonist, while covered in urine, spit, and her own excrement, narrates these scenes as a triumph against all the white men who ignore her:

> . . . y salimos del closet y a mí se me cae un mojoncito chiquito bien apestoso en el pasillo por donde caminan todas esas locas de Chelsea descalzas por donde caminan todas esas musculocas que pagan 24 dólares para estar con un attitude cuando yo sin músculos y sin nada me he tirado todos los negros que me ha dado la gana.[47]

> . . . and we left the closet and I dropped a stinky little turd in the hallway where those Chelsea queens walk barefoot where all those muscle Marys walk, who pay 24 dollars to cop an attitude when I, without any muscles or anything, have been fucking all the Black men that I want. (my translation)

La Loca embodies abjection here not only for the erotic degradation she celebrates, but also for her ambivalent racial status: neither white in the Anglo-American sense nor Black or Brown in the Latinx sense. As Julia Kristeva has theorized, the abject is that which occupies the space of a border and, in particular, the transgression of the clean and proper body's external surface by its internal fluids and viscera.[48] However, while La Loca's sexual practices position her as a subversive agent against social dominance of white muscle queens from Chelsea, she performs this abjection of her own body through the commodification of Black men. She fetishizes their gargantuan endowments—"tiene la pinga descomunal, gigantesca, casi de doce"— and their sheer numbers and anonymity serve to dehumanize them in the service of her own abjection. Even though Sánchez includes descriptions of many of the same sexual practices in his novel, neither Javi nor any of the other gay Latino male characters commoditize or dehumanize other men's bodies the way Lozada depicts in La Loca's sexual practices. Whereas Lozada reproduces the logic of domination in his depiction of abject sexual practices, Sánchez's portrayal of BDSM, the use of sexual toys, and fetishes is narrated with a heavy dose of decolonial camp humor.

DECOLONIZING QUEER CAMP

Sánchez's use of camp humor exploits incongruity and uses resemanticization as means to establish a discursive community and a hierarchy of meaning. Susan Sontag famously wrote, "Camp sees everything in quotation marks"; that is, cultural figures or objects are bracketed and repositioned from one semantic context to another.[49] In order to perceive this resemanticization, the audience of a camp performance (or reader of literary camp humor) must have the necessary cultural capital that situates an object in its more familiar context. As Javi comments during a charity rummage sale for his neighborhood LGBTQ Center, "Sometimes I think as gay men we all have the same movie posters, bric brac [sic] and music, so how can we sell to each other?"[50] In the context of Latinx/Puerto Rican queer identities, Lawrence La Fountain-Stokes associates shame with the social hierarchies of taste and distinction that hegemonic forms of gay camp reinforce through mass media and consumerism, as in shows like *Queer Eye for the Straight Guy*.[51]

Through these cultural repertoires, camp serves to regulate and enforce boundaries around class-based social formations much in the way Bourdieu theorizes how distinction and taste represent asymmetrical distributions of social and cultural capital. Bourdieu argues that distinction is the social acknowledgment of a person's or group's cultural pedigree, which refers to the manner in which economic, social, and cultural capital are acquired.[52] Social origins and the conditions in which cultural capital is acquired play a key role in how that capital accrues value in any particular field, and whether that capital has value across different fields. Taste functions as a form of misrecognition that occludes the conditions of acquiring social and cultural capital. A person with good taste is perceived as having a natural capacity for discernment—through habitus—and is able to perform the discursive acts and behaviors that majoritarian culture legitimizes as elite. The more the conditions of acquiring those capabilities can be doxified and obscured, the more legitimacy is attributed to that person's or group's social and cultural capital. For Bourdieu, existing forms of capital and the modes of their acquisition position members of a social formation in a field and assign value to these positionings. In queer camp, the performer and audience share the ability to discern the double meaning of an ironic statement or the cultural repertoires that are cited in the case of parody. Camp also foregrounds the artifice involved in doxifying hegemonic cultural capital, and it combines elements of mimicry and parody—most familiarly through female impersonation or drag—to draw attention to the modalities of capital acquisition.

Queer Latinx embodiments—particularly those emerging from working-class communities and experiences—challenge not only the dominant, white heteronormativity in the United States, as well as the paternalistic traditions of machismo in Latinx and Latin American cultures and societies, but also the white, homonationalist privilege that drives much of the consumer culture in the LGBTQ neoliberal economies and normalizes a particular set of dispositions as part of a gay "lifestyle" that determines what clothes to wear, where to travel, how to cultivate the idealized body types, and so on.[53] Javi's diary, therefore, chronicles a personal and communitarian transposition toward a decolonized embodiment of Latinidad and queerness, in which Javi and his Puerto Rican family and friends resist and undermine the legitimacy of the dominant *doxa* surrounding race, ethnicity, gender, sexuality, and class. The decolonizing camp humor in the novel serves to "dedoxify" the standards of taste and distinction that are associated with white privilege and upward mobility.

Although queer camp dedoxifies legitimized forms of cultural production, it nevertheless reaffirms social hierarchies and their power relations through its repertorial citationality. Queer camp uses irony as a way to engage interlocutors who share a cultural repertoire.[54] In Sánchez's *Diary of a Puerto Rican Demigod* this citationality can refer in some instances to hegemonic, Anglo-American forms of cultural production, while at other times it can refer to Latinx and Puerto Rican popular culture. The two often intersect transculturally, as in the case of Javi's youthful adoration of Rita Hayworth, whom he describes in his diary as "*half Latina, hey, Spain counts.*"[55] Like many of the chapters and sections in the novel, the text reproduces Javi's reading of old diary entries from his early days with Jason, then segues into his adult memories of that era and his more recent circumstances after the breakup. Javi blames the Solid Gold Dancers and Rita Hayworth for his "*demented desire*" to become a dancer, and he describes how he would pretend to be sick and skip school on days he knew a Rita Hayworth movie would be showing on television.[56] The Solid Gold Dancers of the 1980s were explicitly encoded as queer camp with their glittery costumes, heavily moussed hair, and hypersexualized choreography. Hayworth embodies the queer camp appropriation of female Hollywood stars as icons of glamour and femininity. In the queer camp repertoire, the difference between explicitly encoded camp and camp appropriation can be seen in films like *Auntie Mame* (explicitly encoded) and *The Wizard of Oz* (camp appropriation). Film historian Desirée J. García also makes this distinction in the practice of musical film sing-alongs such as *The Rocky Horror Picture Show* (explicitly encoded camp) and *The Sound of Music* (camp appropriation), both of which have become staples in the queer camp repertoire.[57] Javi appropriates the Rita Hayworth image as part of his Latinx camp repertoire, and like many female figures who have become gay icons, Hayworth assumes this status as much for her glamourous portrayal of hypersexual femininity as for her biography and personal struggles.

Hayworth, who took her Irish American mother's maiden name, also made the successful transition from being typecast as a sultry Latin dancer to all-American pinup girl. Film and media scholar Priscilla Peña Ovalle writes, "Rita's evolution from dark-haired señorita to all-American strawberry blonde was a story of upward mobility, an assimilation process that procured more and better roles after her name was changed [from Cansino] to something with 'good old American ring.'"[58] This transformation demonstrates the dominant culture's association of legitimacy and success with whiteness. Javi describes his idolization of Hayworth in his adolescent diary entry, and one of the details of her biography that fascinates him is her shyness around Orson Welles's Hollywood friends (Welles was Hayworth's second husband): "She was so intimidated by his friends that when they were all at a party she wouldn't get up from the sofa cause she thought that everybody would just stare at her. Ms. Rita, of course they gonna stare. You were head exploding beautiful."[59] Javi later experiences the same feelings of intimidation around Jason's wealthy friends, but, like his Hollywood idol, he learns to perform the dominant class habitus associated with whiteness and becomes a celebrated party planner and host to Jason's elite social circle. Nevertheless, Javi's early viewings of Hayworth's films—"under an old ratty bedspread, popping Cheetos and watching them in my underwear"—contrasts sharply with his later experience when Jason buys him all of Hayworth's films to watch in his private home theater, surrounded by a wealth and extravagance that Javi acknowledges is not his birthright.[60] Javi resists consuming Hayworth's image from the position of privilege, which would reproduce the elitism that intimidated Hayworth in her personal life and that Javi experienced in his early days with Jason.

As inspirations to his desire to dance, which represented his ticket out of the Bronx and the constant gay bashing he experienced in high school, Javi acquires cultural capital through Hayworth's glamourous image alongside that of the schlockier Solid Gold dancers. These early influences contribute to the formation of a queer Latinx habitus, whereas the later conditions of his privileged consumption occur in the spaces of dominant culture. As part of a queer camp repertoire, the heterodoxic combination of the Solid Gold dancers and Rita Hayworth also represents for Javi a broad sense of Latinidad much in the way that José Esteban Muñoz defines the "disidentification" of queers of color, whose "different identity components occupy adjacent spaces and are not comfortably situated in any one discourse of minority subjectivity."[61] This disidentification represents a cultural appropriation "from below," and allows for an accumulation of cultural capital that can circulate in both dominant and marginal social spaces. However, the value of that capital in these different spaces is contingent on the conditions of its acquisition, and in Javi's case what once served as a form of aspirational capital while growing up in the Bronx is devalued and diminished in the context of the dominant white culture that Jason's social circle imposes on him.

Sánchez's novel also uses camp to resemanticize and dedoxify the dominant culture that situates Puerto Rican culture in the dominated position. An episode from Javi and Jason's early years relates how Jason tries to win over the acceptance Javi's parents by inviting them to a Puerto Rican dinner at his penthouse apartment. Jason hires a top Puerto Rican chef and the famous musical group El Trío Los Panchos, yet the displacement of Puerto Rican culture to the space of Anglo-American wealth and privilege puts quotation marks around Javi's heritage and enforces an elitist camp colonization. The ingredients, recipes, and techniques of Puerto Rican cuisine—*la cocina criolla*—epitomize the transcultural Caribbean influences of Spanish, African, and indigenous cultures, yet in Jason's re-creation of a "mini Puerto Rico" the food is served on "gorgeous Haitian carved wood plates" that Javi once "thought were place mats until a server plopped some mashed potatoes on them." He makes a mental note of warning his parents, "not wanting them to be embarrassed."[62]

Javi's mother does not allow the situation to marginalize and dominate her, and she resists the elitist appropriation of Puerto Rican culture through her own habitus of *¡jum!*. The habitus of *¡jum!* is constituted by the array of dispositions that engages social relations through skepticism and targets elitism and pretentiousness for unmasking. *¡Jum!*" is also the title of a well-known short story by Puerto Rican playwright and fiction writer Luis Rafael Sánchez (no relation to Edwin Sánchez), in which these dispositions are weaponized by a homophobic mob that persecutes a gay man and drives him to his death for his gender nonconformity. (Ángel Lozada uses magical realism to depict a very similar ending in his first novel, *La patografía*.) In the case of Javi's mother, however, her habitus reclaims the Puerto Rican culture that Jason has repackaged and colonized, ostensibly as a gesture of good will but also as a display of economic and cultural domination. In an example of transcultural linguistic camp, Javi's diary recalls how Mrs. Rivera wastes no time after arriving in Jason's Rolls-Royce to check on things in the kitchen and start seasoning the food more to her liking: "it was looming to be a smackdown in the okei corral." When Javi tries to force his mother to speak English to Jason, she rebels and begins recounting embarrassing anecdotes from Javi's childhood, like how she used to dress Javi in girl's clothes, how he used to be fat and gassy, and the time he did "caca" on himself at the Woolworths.[63] Javi's mother draws from a Puerto Rican cultural repertoire of carnivalesque humor to assert her class distinction as dominant in these circumstances: Jason is trying to win her favor, but she is establishing the terms of how she is going to feel at ease.

Part of her skepticism reflects the cultural values of compulsory heterosexuality, and Javi acknowledges that his parents have not fully embraced their son's gay life: "While this started out as the day to celebrate me it is clear that Jason was trying to win over the inlaws who still looked at him as a temporary lapse in judgment on my part before I settled down and married some nice vecina next door."[64] The habitus of *¡jum!* also dedoxifies the hegemonic position of Jason's cultural repertoire, as well as Javi's pretensions to assume dominance over his parents through Jason's white privilege. The stakes for Jason in this family drama are very low, since his privilege allows him to be indifferent to his own manner, as Bourdieu argues. Jason is among the "recognized holders of the legitimate manner and power to define the value of manners—dress, bearing, pronunciations." Javi is one of the "'parvenus' who presume to join the group of the legitimate."[65] The attempt to climb the social ladder, when race, ethnicity, and class origins mark the boundaries of access, leads to a double-bind in which the upwardly mobile face "a choice between anxious hyper-identification and the negativity which admits its defeat in its very revolt; either the conformity of an 'assumed' behavior whose very correctness or hyper-correctness betrays an imitation, or the ostentatious assertion of difference which is bound to appear as an admission of inability to identify."[66] Javi's parents are not interested in climbing the social ladder, and the mother's campy and "ostentatious assertion of difference" does not "admit defeat" nor concede "an admission of inability to identify"; her habitus of *¡jum!* dedoxifies the manners with which Jason has tried to reproduce Puerto Rican culture, and unmasks Javi's attempts to presume the same privilege that these manners legitimate. Javi's mother undermines the pretentiousness of elitist camp, and after thanking Jason she gives him a "look" that says, "*mono que se viste de seda mono se queda*" ("can't make a silk purse out of a sow's ear").[67] Although Javi interprets that look as a cautionary message to Jason, it also applies to his attempts to assume the habitus of white, upper-class privilege. In this way, Javi's mother decolonizes the queer camp that fetishizes Puerto Rican culture and that positions her Puerto Rican son in a dominated position.

The resemanticization of cultural objects through camp can occur at different positions in a social field, from the elitist ironic discourses of a dominant cultural repertoire to the marginal or subaltern appropriation of heterodoxic sources of cultural capital. Andrew Ross argues that, on the one hand, camp "involves the celebration, on the part of the cognoscenti, of the alienation, distance, and incongruity reflected in the very process by which it locates hitherto unexpected value in a popular or obscure text. Camp would thus be reserved for those with a high degree of cultural capital."[68] On the other hand, camp serves as a means for marginal or "arriviste" groups that "lack inherited cultural capital" to "parody their subordinate or uncertain social status."[69] The narrative voice in Ángel Lozada's novel articulates this type of subaltern camp, although it also portrays how dominant groups use camp from the position of the cognoscenti to exploit gay Latino men. We see this especially in the episodes that take place in Washington, D.C., when La Loca and his social-climbing boyfriend serve as campy yet easily disposable gay pets to a group of wealthy and politically connected Puerto Rican women. Lozada's novel does not explicitly portray the social conditions in which La Loca acquires the elements that comprise his camp repertoire and constitute his early formation of habitus. (Lozada portrays more extensively the conditions of precarity of Puerto Rico's working classes in his first novel, *La patografía*.) In *No quiero quedarme sola y vacía*, the narrator briefly yet sardonically mentions his impoverished childhood in Puerto Rico: "*Celebro que dejé atrás casa de madera y de zinc en el Caribe para venir a encerrarme en depressing apartments que nadie arregla, to repeat the word, arrabales urbanos, mientras la droga se vende en el lobby*" ("I celebrate that I left behind the house made of wood and tin in the Caribbean to come lock myself away in depressing apartments that no one fixes, to repeat the word, urban ghettos, while they sell drugs in the lobby" [my translation]).[70] This commentary uses bilingual poetics satirically to denounce the hypocrisy in ethnic enclaves, where the municipal government condescends to a migrant community through superficial gestures such as renaming neighborhood streets in Spanish, while perpetuating the economic exploitation that follows migrants from their homelands to U.S. urban ghettos.

Like Javi, the protagonist in *No quiero quedarme sola y vacía* combines elements from the dominant culture of high glamour (particularly the figure of Jackie Onassis), mass media and television (*The X-Files, Star Trek: Voyager*), and Latinx pop culture and music; the title of the novel, *No quiero quedarme sola y vacía*, comes from "Contigo o sin ti," a song by Puerto Rican salsa and merengue singer Olga Tañón. However, La Loca does not rely on a rich sugar daddy to acquire sources of cultural and social capital. Although he has educational capital through a university degree, works for Anderson Consulting, and even served briefly in the U.S. Navy before receiving a discharge for his homosexuality, his upward mobility is financed through student loans and credit cards. While he shops at high-end clothing stores and imagines himself as Jackie Onassis being waited on by the sales staff, he occupies a squalid apartment in Washington Heights and often has to borrow money from coworkers just to buy some rice and beans. The figure of Jackie Onassis most likely was part of La Loca's early formation of habitus and, like Rita Hayworth for Javi, represented a desire to achieve success and independence. Yet as a gay Latino in New York this cultural capital is reconstituted as part of the habitus of the Indebted Man, which Maurizio Lazzarato describes as a fiction of freedom in a society that restricts agency through a plethora of false choices. La Loca falls into the credit card trap that portrays debt as a kind of freedom. For Lazzarato: "The debtor is 'free,' but his actions, his behavior, are confined to the limits defined by the debt he has entered into. The same is true as much for the individual as for a population or social group. You are free insofar as you assume the *way of life* (consumption, work, public spending, taxes, etc.) compatible with reimbursement."[71] In the case of Lozada's novel, camp humor lays bare the symbolic violence of the protagonist's subaltern status and colonial condition in a neoliberal economy that doxifies conspicuous consumption as a sign of empowerment and autonomy.

Queers of Color Community in NYC

Another way Sánchez's novel subverts the logic of debt and reclaims his Puerto Rican heritage is through a more expansive and egalitarian definition of kinship and community; in particular, he reestablishes social relations with his childhood friend, Rob, a struggling actor who once shared Javi's dream of success and upward mobility. The two had been very close until Jason Wilcox entered into Javi's life, and once Javi began to be "swallowed whole by gay society," he tried to use his friendship with Rob as a protective screen against the judgmental scrutiny of the elite social classes that now set the standards for his behavior and taste. The friendship collapses when Javi attempts to secure Rob's loyalty through the logic of debt and obligation, offering him expensive gifts that Rob could never reciprocate. As sociologist Marcel Mauss argues in his classic study *The Gift*, gift exchange is central to the logic of credit and honor: "Now a gift necessarily implies the notion of credit. Economic evolution has not gone from barter to sale and from cash to credit. Barter arose from the system of gifts given and received on credit, simplified by drawing together the moments of time which had previously been distinct."[72] Bourdieu extends this argument to consider the role that time plays in how gifts exchanged accrue symbolic value and can signal honor or dishonor in hierarchical social relations: "To betray one's haste to be free of an obligation one has incurred, and thus to reveal too overtly one's desire to pay off services rendered or gifts received, to be quits, is to denounce the initial gift retrospectively as motivated by the intention of obliging one."[73] When Javi reencounters Rob at the neighborhood gay bar, Javi reminds Rob of all the nice gifts he gave him at his annual Christmas parties. Rob replies, "No, the butler handed them out. You were too busy playing Perle Mesta."[74] Rob admits that the gifts were so extravagant, he used them to pay his rent. They had no value for him other than economic, and his inability to reciprocate undermined any bond of friendship they were meant to cultivate. Instead, the manner and circumstances in which they were given established a relation of dominance and asymmetrical obligation, and Rob's refusal to assume the dominated position ends his friendship with Javi until they reunite after the breakup with Jason. Once they are on more equal terms, their friendship can resume through reciprocity rather than unpayable debts. Javi asks Rob:

"So we can be friends again?"

"Buy a girl a drink at least."

I suddenly realize that after my last round and tipping like I was still the me of yore, I don't have enough money for this most basic of social transactions.

"I. . . ."

"I'll cover for you. I didn't fall from Mount Olympus so I still earn my money."[75]

Javi has to relearn the rules of reciprocity in the diasporic community and how to revalue money, debt, and obligation as operative modalities of practical logic in egalitarian social relations. Even though Javi never abandons his feelings for Jason, and their relationship evolves to one of mutual respect and potential reunion, he breaks free from his debt to Jason through a number of decisive actions. Most notably, he donates almost all the designer clothes he kept from his former life to a LGBTQ community center during a fundraising drive. When he was with Jason, they would often write generous checks to various charities and causes and draw attention to themselves as noble benefactors. By giving up the last material vestige of his elite habitus, he forgoes the public acclamations of generosity to the benefit of a community of peers with no expectations of reciprocity, thus redefining honor through sacrifice rather than extraction.

In contrast, La Loca from Lozada's novel does not share the strengthening of familial and communal bonds that characterizes the narrative development of Javi Rivera's story. La Loca's narration scarcely mentions his family relations, and those few instances when the narrative voice describes La Loca's brief telephone conversations with his mother in Puerto Rico are characterized by estrangement, guilt, and abjection. La Loca describes how his mother, even though she lacks the means to pay for medicines, often sends her son some of his favorite Puerto Rican foods and calls long distance just to hear his voice and make sure he is well. Because La Loca spends all his income on gadgets, clothes, and nights out at the gay bars, he cannot afford to send his mother a Mother's Day card. These passages are followed

by more descriptions of La Loca's compulsive consumerism and anonymous sexual encounters, which suggest the cycle of indebtedness and self-degradation occurs
as an attempt to forestall his feelings of social isolation. In one instance, when his
mother calls to tell him that her medical benefits cannot cover her mammograms
or medications, La Loca sends her a check for a hundred dollars that he knows will
bounce. The novel connects La Loca's personal financial profligacy to Puerto Rico's
colonial condition, and after chiding himself for his inability to help his mother,
La Loca lashes out at the homeland he simultaneously loves and hates: "*Y la Pro-
fetisa* lost it: 'I warn you, Bitches of Puerto Bankruptcy, I warn you, like the Bibli-
cal Prophets of the diaspora: One day you will be an Island of Bankrupts!!! One
day you will all loose [*sic*] your houses!!! One day you will all be working under
contratos-basura!!!'"[76] Published in 2006, the novel was truly prophetic in its pre-
diction that Puerto Rico would become an "Island of Bankrupts" with the filing
of Title III by Governor Ricardo Rosselló in 2017. Unable to meet its bond and pension obligations, Puerto Rico took the drastic step to declare bankruptcy and
restructure its debts. At one point, La Loca fantasizes about blowing the island to
smithereens but then laughs to himself because he claims global warming will sink
Puerto Rico and all its homophobic cities: "*Mayagüez, San Juan, Ponce, todos los
focos de patofobia serán inundados*" ("Mayagüez, San Juan, Ponce, all the ground
zeros of homophobia will be inundated" [my translation]).[77] Although that has not
happened yet, Puerto Rico's debt crisis has devastated the island in other ways, most
notably the dramatic increase in migration to the United States; in this instance,
across multiple social classes and most notably to the Orlando-Kissimmee area of
central Florida. Eventually, La Loca has to confront the consequences of his own
actions and after consulting with lawyers and credit agencies, he swallows his pride
along with five Puerto Rican pastries—*polvorones*—and goes to bankruptcy court.
La Loca cannot pay his financial debts nor honor his debt to his family or nation,
which generates in him such feelings of inadequacy and shame that he returns to
the cycle of compulsive behaviors that put him in these circumstances in the first
place. In her analysis of the narratives of narcissism and shame in this novel, María
Celina Bortolotto writes, "The powerful force of narratives or scripts upon subjects stems precisely from this strong hold in the self's affective configuration. It is
probably the case that the love La Loca feels for his island is as strong as the anger
he ignites when he relives the shame and marginalization he experienced there."[78]
Unlike Javi, La Loca does not break free from the corrosive logic of debt, and the
novel and its language become more fragmented and hyperbolic after this inflection point to convey the aggravated social isolation that the subjectivity of the
Indebted Man instills in the protagonist. He places his only hope for redemption in
religion and spirituality, yet even these gestures reproduce the pattern of enthusiastic embrace and obsession, which are then followed by disillusion and disinterest.

Neither does La Loca form any egalitarian friendships or communitarian bonds
as a consequence of his perpetual state of indebtedness. Other than the episode in
Washington, D.C., La Loca does not reveal any evidence of long-term friendships
or networks of support. Throughout the novel, La Loca refers to his antagonistic

estrangement from a Puerto Rican intellectual and literary community, and he uses transparent pseudonyms that barely disguise the real-life targets of his diatribes. These passages function metafictionally to lambaste the circuits of cultural production and literary establishments that the author criticizes in the book's cover flap as well as in online interviews.[79] Although Lozada received wide critical praise for his first novel, the radical narrative style, bilingual poetics, and graphic depictions of gay sex of his second novel were met with skepticism and outright rejection. In a conference paper delivered at Lehman College (April 2, 2011), Puerto Rican writer and critic Carlos Vázquez-Cruz relates the negative reaction by Lozada's own publisher, Isla Negra Editores, and the dispute over the author's attacks on the Puerto Rican literary establishment. The publisher attempted to pull the novel from bookstores, to which Lozada responded with threats of a lawsuit.[80] In the novel, the narrative voice of La Loca, which serves as the author's proxy, makes clear that he has burned all bridges with the intellectual and literary community on the island:

> Oh Bitches of the UPR, haven't you notice [sic], that I can write veintisiete! Haven't you notice [sic], Bitches of the Puerto Rican Academia, what's going on here? Lo que pre/prosigue sólo puede catalogarse como irresponsabilidades descuidos y cosas raras, como horrores ortográficos y gramaticales: oh, Bitches with PhDs y con el pelo mal-pintado con Wella hair products: la novela tiene errores y muchos dos puntos, pero les advierto, que le responderé a todas con un "a-mí-plin."[81]

> Oh Bitches of the UPR, haven't you noticed that I can write twenty-seven! Haven't you noticed, Bitches of the Puerto Rican Academy, what's going on here? What precedes and continues can only be catalogued as irresponsible carelessness and strange things, like orthographic and grammatical horrors: oh Bitches with PhDs and with bad dye jobs with Wella hair products: the novel has errors and many colons, but I warn you, that I will respond to all of you with an "I don't give a damn." (my translation)

The last phrase in this passage, "a-mí-plin," is also one of the many catch phrases attributed to Luis Rafael Sánchez's character of La China Hereje in his canonical novel, La guaracha del Macho Camacho. Rather than serve as an homage to this highly acclaimed writer, La Loca's disdainful remark is a rebuke to his literary predecessors and intellectual mentors. In other passages La Loca reproduces the voices of this intellectual and literary establishment, which castigate him for his poor writing and lack of cultural capital and banish him from any conferences or literary symposia. As with his mother, La Loca does not establish a relation of reciprocity or honor with the Puerto Rican literary community, and his banishment from intellectual circles reinforces his social isolation and fuels his feelings of rage and shame. Bankrupt and friendless, and unable to satiate his compulsive behaviors, La Loca falls into a downward spiral that ends in destitution and homelessness: "Ahora sí que tengo mi credibilidad destruída" ("Now I really have my credibility destroyed" [my translation]).[82] A victim of the logic of debt, La Loca loses his credit worthiness and credibility.

QUEER KINSHIP AND HONOR

Sánchez's novel once again uses decolonial camp to resemanticize the question of honor and indebtedness to family and community. In the dinner episode mentioned earlier, Javi's mother dedoxifies the elitist camp appropriation of Puerto Rican culture, and she uses carnivalesque humor to unmask Javi's attempts to adopt the elite habitus. Once Javi's mother destabilizes Jason's dominant position, his father, Efraín, subverts the *machista* doxa of paternalistic homo/transphobia that very often rejects the son or daughter who comes out as LGBTQ. Javi's father does not share his wife's skeptical disposition and, therefore, does not explicitly embody the habitus of *¡jum!* as she does. He embraces the experience of hearing a live performance of El Trío Los Panchos, one of his favorite groups. However, because of the elitist camp appropriation of this Puerto Rican musical tradition, Efraín cannot understand why the musicians are not joining them for dinner but instead were contracted to play quietly in an adjacent room. Yet rather than portray Javi's father as an embarrassment for not having the cultural capital that is framing this encounter, the novel begins to reveal how Javi has up until that point failed to acknowledge his debt of honor to his parents. After his mother's antics, Javi narrates how his father makes a comment that redirects his son's shame to honor: "By the time we got to dessert I was ready to have myself declared an orphan. Jason was uncomfortable, I was mortified and my Moms blissfully continued her roast of me. Then Pops, who could probably have landed an airplane on the head of a pin, turned to Los Panchos and said, 'Mi hijo bailo [*sic*] on Broadway.' The last word is the only one Jason understood, but it was the money shot. The trio looked at me and nodded with respect and Moms, not missing a beat, added 'I always knew Javi was talented.'"[83] The phrase "money shot" may appear as a simple metaphor for a dramatic climax, or even a veiled reference to the editing of a sexual climax in pornographic film. Yet in this context, and in reference to Javi's brief career as a dancer, it articulates how the one word that Jason understands—Broadway—conveys symbolic capital, particularly in the repertoire of elite queer camp, and is a testament to Javi's Latinx transcultural capital, which facilitated his successful casting in the show *Fuego!* Javi's father reminds everyone that his son accomplished his goal through his own effort and determination, and he takes pride in Javi's achievement, even if short-lived. Efraín's disavowal of the *machista* doxa that enforces heteronormativity through shame also adds impact to the subsequent "look" that Javi's mother gives to Jason, which communicates not only her skeptical disposition but also her own reminder to Javi to honor his debt to his Puerto Rican heritage. The difference between elitist queer camp and the camp performed by queers of color, according to José Esteban Muñoz, "is one in which 'camp' is understood not only as a strategy of representation, but also as a mode of enacting self against the pressures of the dominant culture's identity-denying protocols."[84] The articulation of the diasporic habitus in this episode contributes to the decolonization of queer camp and dedoxifies the paternalistic traditions that otherwise would perpetuate violence against a Latino gay man.[85]

It isn't until later in the novel, after Efraín dies and Javi accompanies his mother to Puerto Rico for the burial, that Javi recollects how he owes his dream of upward mobility not to the dominant culture of media and television, but from his unassuming, working-class father. Javi recollects the long train rides he used to take with his father once every summer to visit the hospital where Efraín worked in maintenance. As they passed stately private homes, Efraín would say, "Someday, mi hijo. Someday," and Javi would imagine himself living in a state of perfection like the characters he would see on TV, who "had no accents when they spoke and their only son was cute and popular and looked a little like me, only better."[86] In other words, whiter. As in his adoration of Hollywood icon Rita Hayworth, Javi dreams of a trajectory toward upward mobility that is facilitated by adopting white, majoritarian culture and embodiments. He fails to appreciate his father's working-class values, which he observes at the hospital where Efraín spent the day mopping floors. After his breakup with Jason, Javi is forced to take on a number of odd jobs—from dog walker, cater waiter, personal assistant, retail clerk at Old Navy, and finally cashier at a high-end sex emporium, "Spanks for the Memory." Reacclimating himself to a working-class habitus, Javi acknowledges the debt he owes to his father's values: "Now I think of Pops and all the years he worked and I am humbled, but in a good way, you know. Hey Pops, I finally get it. Perfection was sitting next to me on the train, not outside the window."[87] Javi always imagined that his father was ashamed of his gay son, the dancer, but once he moves back with his parents and readopts his tastes to the working-class, Puerto Rican habitus, he slowly becomes more aware of how his most enduring dispositions came from his family relations and not from his aspirations to adopt the habitus of the elite.

In a conversation over apple martinis with his mother, shortly after their return from Puerto Rico, Javi admits that he contemplated suicide after his breakup with Jason, and that he regrets never asking his father for forgiveness for not living up to what he thought were the *machista* expectations Efraín had of his son. His mother, without spilling a drop of her apple martini, slaps Javi twice, once for thinking about suicide, and a second time for failing to acknowledge his father's acceptance and support:

"But every time I talked to Pops I could always tell he was disappointed in me."

"No, papito, he was just esad that ju estopped dancing. He thought ju could really dance."

"He didn't think dancing was a little. . . ." And again I do the full Walter Mercado.

And another whack.

"Coño Moms!"

"Jour father loved ju. No forgiveness necessary."[88]

Javi also comes to appreciate his mother's "Sofia Vergara / Googie Gomez" accent, which she preserves as a way of holding on to her past.[89] Mrs. Rivera is a catty, camp diva in her own right, not because she embodies Hollywood glamour or has had a string of toxic relationships with men; on the contrary, she is fierce, loyal, and unapologetic of her Puerto Rican heritage. Through a decolonized queer camp, the novel portrays how Javi reclaims forms of transcultural capital that he once thought had no value. The diasporic habitus he had so carefully tried to unlearn now reveals its potential to facilitate his repositioning away from a dominated status and toward economic and social empowerment. Whereas Javi owed the acquisition of elite social and cultural capital to Jason—a debt that kept him in a dominated position—when he reclaims his Latinx transcultural capital, he shares with his family and community honor without extraction. As his mother says, "No forgiveness necessary."

DIASPORA AND THE PUERTO RICAN NATIONAL FAMILY

When many Puerto Rican LGBTQ individuals leave the island for the urban gayborhoods in the United States, this queer Caribbean diaspora, or *sexilio*, serves as a means of self-preservation and a declaration of autonomy, although it does not obviate the need for other forms of kinship and a sense of belonging. David Eng argues that "the methodology of queer diasporas becomes a theoretical approach for telling a different story about contemporary politics of nation-building and race under globalization, along with its accompanying material and psychic processes of social belonging and exclusion."[90] Such a methodology can help to distinguish among different forms of desire and belonging and take a critical stance against those that perpetuate systems of abjectification and violence. In spite of the promises of upward mobility and cultural legitimacy that global capital offers to queers of the diaspora, in some cases Latino subjects lack the social and cultural capital that facilitates their integration into the consumer culture from which a virtual gay identity and community emerge. The decision to emigrate is fraught with uncertainty, yet it can reflect a desire for new identitarian beginnings and a resurrection of the abjectified queer body.

Both Javi and La Loca confront their relationship to Puerto Rico from the perspective of the diaspora, yet the novels depict radically different outcomes for these characters in their integration into the Puerto Rican national family. When Javi's father dies and he accompanies his mother to bury him in Puerto Rico, he stays with his extended family in Isabela and learns intimate details of his parents' lives and the community from which they migrated to the United States. The contradictions of his diasporic identity emerge as he shares moments of collective mourning, conviviality, and joyful storytelling with his Puerto Rican family. He reconnects with his island heritage and sense of belonging: "I go running later in the day and get a chance to just be Puerto Rican. Not gay, not a failure, not anything but another Puerto Rican on an island full of them."[91] It isn't very long, though, before the machismo of the rural Puerto Rican community and the television and media they consume cause Javi to feel estranged from the heteronormative culture on the island. While he happily plays the role of "the older uncle type," he doesn't perceive any gender or sexual diversity in his family, even among the younger generation of cousins: "What the hell happened to one out of ten?"[92] His family is never directly hostile or homophobic to him, yet when watching a comedy program on television one evening, Javi chafes as his family members laugh at the homophobic jokes that appear on the show: "And I am reminded of why there was always a part of me that forever felt uncomfortable with Puerto Rico. In this macho culture the biggest laughs are reserved for las locas, las mariposas, those mincing, prancing comedians who play maricones and are made the butt of all the jokes. Everyone in the room laughs, everyone but me. I love Puerto Rico, I really do, but I always get the impression that I am only nominally allowed in. That even though I was born in Puerto Rico, I really am only tolerated."[93] Although Javi also experienced violent gay bashing as a young man in the Bronx, even being spit on by one of his tormenters, he also was able to leave his working-class enclave and cultivate an upwardly mobile gay identity through his relationship with Jason. Even this return trip to the island was made possible by Jason, who had already separated from Javi yet lent him his private jet to fly his mother and his father's remains back to Puerto Rico. Javi remarks that in the rural community of Isabela, there is no gay scene, and since he cannot drive, he is further isolated from the kind of gay community to which he belonged in NYC. The irony of Javi's ambivalent sense of Puerto Rican identity is that the homophobia of Puerto Rican machismo—both on the island and in the Bronx—perpetually marginalizes Javi from the national family, yet the embodied economy of upward mobility that facilitated Javi's openly gay life in Manhattan was made possible by his entry into an exclusionary social space of wealth and whiteness that marginalized his Puerto Rican heritage.

Javi experiences an even more violent homophobic encounter with Salvin, a man so effeminate "he looks like a drag queen doing a mall run," but who also killed a man with a machete for calling him gay.[94] Salvin refuses to serve Javi when he goes for some *tocino* (fat back) at the local *colmado* (corner store): "*Yo no le sirvo a los maricones,*" Salvin tells Javi. When Javi calls him a *maricón*, too, Salvin sucker punches him and knocks him out cold. Later while jogging, Javi encounters Salvin again, who this time is wielding a machete and slicing open coconuts. After another exchange in which they call each other *pato*, Salvin hurls the machete and barely misses Javi, who dodges the blade just in time. After disarming Salvin, Javi walks away unscathed but also shaken. As a fictional character, Salvin is the opposite of the character that appears in Luis Rafael Sánchez's short story "*¡Jum!,*" who drowns in a raging river trying to escape a gay-bashing mob. Salvin reproduces homophobic violence while using his queer gender performance as a weapon against the homophobia of his rural community. Even Javi's young, straight cousins fear Salvin, who served ten years in prison for the murder he committed, and who proudly declared he would kill again for the same reason. The machete also serves as a symbol of Puerto Rican rural labor and masculinity, as it was the weapon of choice for men who wanted to settle a question of honor or debt. The machete in this encounter also alludes to the revolutionary movements in Puerto Rico, in particular Los Macheteros, or the Ejército Popular Boricua, a radical *independentista* group that promotes the use of armed force to liberate Puerto Rico from

U.S. colonialism. The contradiction between Salvin's internalized homophobia and queer gender performance erupts in homicidal violence, but it can also be a radical act of defiance and self-defense. As Javi reflects on these encounters, he recalls the gay bashing he experienced in the Bronx and the violent rage he felt could have led him to murder his tormentors: "One hell would have ended and another one would have begun. Salvin can never leave this town, cause here he is feared, anywhere else he would be mocked and he would have to kill all over again just to make it clear that he is not to be messed with. So he stays here, the town's fear a constant reminder to them and him of what he did. And I think that's why he gives me nightmares, cause I know that for a moment of relief, I could have been him."[95] The novel explores the challenges and options that gay Puerto Rican men face when they encounter homophobia and gay bashing. In Javi's case, he chose to pursue a dream of fame and upward mobility as a way to escape the violent culture of machismo in the Bronx. Similarly, as I discuss below, La Loca in Lozada's novel also goes into *sexilio*, an exile to escape the homophobic climate that marginalizes, sanctions, and eradicates through violence anyone who displays nonnormative forms of sexuality. Salvin's compromise anchors him to one place, and while his queer gender performance may serve as a direct provocation to others, the violence with which he maintains that social position also isolates and marginalizes him further. In Javi's case, his move from the Bronx to Manhattan put distance between him and his Puerto Rican community, but also opened up the possibility of integrating into different social spaces.

The ambivalent sense of belonging to the Puerto Rican national family is even more fraught in Lozada's novel. La Loca, whose *sexilio* to NYC reflects his escape from violently homophobic machismo in Puerto Rico, nevertheless holds out hope for the island's political independence: "*A La Loca le fastidiaba el discurso de los independentistas puertorriqueños, porque los encuentra patófobos, pero en lo más profundo de su corazón quiere la independencia para su isla*" ("La Loca was terribly bored with the discourse of Puerto Rican independentists, because she finds them homophobic, but in her heart of hearts she wants independence for her island" [my translation]).[96] Despite this nationalism, La Loca admits that she abhors being Puerto Rican, which she associates with downward mobility and cultures of dependency. La Loca also holds a deep grudge against the Puerto Rican intellectual community. As discussed previously, the novel engages in a metafictional discourse that conveys the falling out that Lozada had with his publisher. Like Cuban exile Reinaldo Arenas, who named and denounced his enemies in his autobiography shortly before committing suicide in New York, Lozada also names several prominent figures in queer Latinx academia and Puerto Rican literary circles. Through a heteroglossic fiction that serves as a revenge narrative, Lozada uses pseudonyms and mimics the voices of the Puerto Rican intellectuals who have shunned him from participating in their social and professional circles. In a passage that shifts between several focalizations, the narrator recounts how La Loca begins posting on blogs and vituperating against Puerto Rican literature: "*no sirve para nada absolutamente nada*" ("it is of absolutely no use" [my translation]).[97] The "Josefita

Vega" named below could be a reference to well-known author Ana Lydia Vega, while the "Instituto" clearly refers to the Instituto de Cultura Puertorriqueña, which publishes its own peer-reviewed journal:

> *Entonces, apedreándole verbalmente, le contesta Josefita Vega: "Resígnate a jamás ser invitada a congresos aburridos de literatura pasteurizada ni a homenajes a Luis Rafael Sánchez ni a Rosario Ferré. Cerradas están, permanentemente para ti, las puertas del Instituto de Cultura."*[98]

> And then, verbally stoning her, Josefita Vega answers: "Resign yourself to never being invited to boring conferences on pasteurized literature nor to tributes to Luis Rafael Sánchez or Rosario Ferré. The doors to the Institute of Culture are permanently closed to you." (my translation)

In a 2012 interview with his former doctoral dissertation advisor, Eduardo Subirats, Lozada declares that among the many facets of his life and experience as a gay Puerto Rican of the diaspora, *rabia*—or rage—has become a part of his literary aesthetic, and the passage above exemplifies how he blurs the line between fiction and reality to rage against what he sees as the hypocrisies of the Puerto Rican literary establishment.[99] The novel serves as a denunciation of the cultural institutions that act as gatekeepers of what constitutes authentic Puerto Rican identity.

In an even more hostile confrontation with Puerto Rican nationalism, the novel also depicts La Loca using a Puerto Rican flag as a cum rag for when he masturbates or after one of his numerous sexual encounters. The Puerto Rican flag has served as a symbol of national unity across the borders between the island and the continental United States, and its visibility in Puerto Rican enclaves in cities like New York, Chicago, Philadelphia, and Orlando marks the presence of the diaspora but also the colonial history and economic conditions that compelled millions of Puerto Ricans to migrate. However, the flag is also part of the commercialization of Puerto Rican identity, and its proliferation in the tourist industry, corporate sponsorships, and mass-produced commercial goods underscores how consumption now facilitates the articulation of identity.[100] The desecration of this ubiquitous symbol of the Puerto Rican national family also recalls the rage and backlash that Madonna caused when she used the flag to wipe her crotch during a 1993 concert in Bayamón. The Puerto Rican House of Representatives passed a resolution to officially condemn her. By invoking this controversial moment in pop culture, and linking it to the explicit and scatological depiction of gay sexual practices, Lozada's literary desecration of the Puerto Rican flag performs a dual satire that, on the one hand, exposes the commercialization of Puerto Rican identity and, on the other hand, condemns the violence and exclusionary practices that compel queer Puerto Ricans to live in *sexilio* and isolation from the Puerto Rican national family. The character of La Loca rages against Puerto Rican cultural institutions and the prominent figures who have blocked her entry into the field of cultural and literary production. Yet the scatological depiction of this estrangement also conveys La Loca's abjection, which further manifests itself in the explicit portrayal of exploitative interracial sexual practices among gay men. Lozada's novel rages against the homophobic violence that has been part of Puerto Rican nationalism, while also satirizing the way La Loca reproduces forms of exploitation and violence on herself and others. Yet La Loca still yearns for sexual fulfilment and an affective, even spiritual connection to Puerto Rico. The novel ends with prosaic definitions of solitude and emptiness, however, reminding the reader of the sexual exile that continues to be a closeted part of the Puerto Rican diaspora.

Like the main characters in Lozada's and Sánchez's novels, which tell two different stories about Puerto Rican gay men, I also have turned to writing (this book, in particular) to explore the intersections of family, debt, and the search for forgiveness, honor, and dignity. In the last weeks before my mother died from ovarian cancer, she had an episode when her blood pressure got so low my family and I didn't think she would make it through the night, and we all started saying our goodbyes around her bedside. At one point, my mother asked me to forgive her, and at the time I couldn't understand why since she had always supported and loved me explicitly. I replied in the same way that Javi's mother in *Diary of a Puerto Rican Demigod* did to her son, "No forgiveness necessary." Much later, I realized my mother was asking for forgiveness because, as a devoutly religious woman, she struggled to reconcile her love for me with my homosexuality. She didn't want to leave this world with that unsettled debt. My mother lived for a few more weeks and passed away at home while I was in Vermont with my partner. Like the protagonist in Lozada's novel, I left home to pursue a career and live openly as a gay man. When I returned for the services held at St. Aloysius Catholic Church in Chicago, I stood in awe at the overflow crowd of friends, family, and community members whose lives had been touched by my mother's humility, wisdom, and care for others. As with Javi in Sánchez's novel, I turned to my family and their values to overcome challenges with bad decisions in my finances and personal life. Neither my own experiences, nor those portrayed in Lozada's and Sánchez's novels, cover the full gamut of how gay Latino men come to terms with family debts and honor. Nevertheless, these stories offer insight into the complex intersections of our embodied economies, in which upward mobility, cultural heritage, and human dignity pursue lines of flight and paths of return, and in which we reconcile the debts that are never supposed to be repaid.

CHAPTER 3

Zero-Sum Games in Fiction by Junot Díaz and Rita Indiana Hernández

There is no stronger evidence that we have been successful in our effort to uncover the unconscious than when the patient reacts to it with the words "I didn't think that," or "I didn't (ever) think that."
—Sigmund Freud, "Negation"

When we try to understand masculine domination we are therefore likely to resort to modes of thought that are the product of domination.
—Pierre Bourdieu, Masculine Domination

In the previous two chapters, the theatrical and literary works in counterpoint interrogate and subvert the hegemonic norms of gender and sexuality and their role in reproducing the logic of domination in the embodied economies of the Latinx Caribbean diaspora. Even the plays by Nilo Cruz and Eduardo Machado, in which the main characters' habitus embody cisgender heterosexuality, as well as the novels by Edwin Sánchez and Ángel Lozada unmask the logic of masculine domination through a queering of the diasporic experience. However, even though Latinx Caribbean migration to the United States and upward mobility are associated with discourses of modernization and development and is often celebrated as creating spaces of translocality and rhizomatic cultures, it also exacerbates economic inequalities and reentrenches the social hierarchies that perpetuate discrimination and violence toward racial, gender, and sexual minorities. The throwback culture of toxic masculinity will often travel and resurface along the geographic and economic trajectories that Latinx Caribbean literature portrays and satirizes. Like the return of the repressed, the material and bodily practices associated with masculine domination appear in monstrous forms in the fiction of Dominican writers Rita Indiana Hernández and Junot Díaz. In Indiana Hernández's novel *Papi* (2005) and throughout Díaz's fiction, especially in his short story collection *This Is How You Lose Her* (2012), toxic masculinity emerges as much from the horrors of Dominican history as it does from the rational logic and calculated play in the zero-sum games of neoliberal market economies and global finance.[1] These games, rather than promote progressive values of egalitarianism and freedom of movement, facilitate the violent domination of women and the gender nonconforming subjects of the Latinx Caribbean. Masculine domination also reinforces racial and ethnic violence, particularly against Haitians and Black Dominicans of Haitian descent. This chapter compares how Indiana Hernández's *Papi* and Díaz's short fiction both use narrative games to engage the reader with a demystification of Dominican masculinity and expose its persistent redeployment along the transnational routes of the diaspora.[2] While these fictions often reproduce the very logic they critique, they also queer its gender politics and decolonize the violent practices of its embodied economy.

Rita Indiana Hernández is among a recent group of Dominican writers born during the Balaguer regime who have developed an urban, multimedia repertoire in literature, music, visual culture, and performance art. In addition to her novels, short stories, and poetry collections, Indiana Hernández is also the lead singer of Rita Indiana and los Misterios, a techno-merengue group whose music has been featured on NPR and has climbed the top of the Latin Pop charts. Lorgia García Peña offers an insightful analysis of Rita Indiana y los Misterios' music video "Da pa lo do," which "theorizes the experience of the Haitian-Dominican border conflicts, engaging the multiplicity of contra*dictions* [sic] and borders of the Dominican experience by deconstructing the traditional gendered and racialized narrative of the nation."[3] Born and raised in the Dominican Republic and currently based in Puerto Rico, Indiana Hernández's literature, music, and performance art is primarily in Spanish yet can be defined as transcultural in a number of ways. She integrates the slang of the urban Dominican experience, makes reference to global pop culture and mass media, and engages with broader Latin American literary and cultural traditions. The language of her novels also incorporates uses of English as well as Dominican forms of Spanglish. Most notably, however, her novels reveal the influence that the Dominican diaspora to the United States has had on the culture, politics, and economy of the island nation. As Maja Horn argues, Indiana Hernández's work explores the transformational impact that economic, social and cultural remittances have had in the Dominican Republic.[4] Juan Flores defines cultural remittances as "the ensemble of ideas, values, and expressive forms introduced into societies of origin by remigrants and their families as they return 'home,' sometimes for the first time, for temporary visits or permanent re-settlement, and as transmitted through the increasingly pervasive means of telecommunications."[5] That is, in addition to the money and consumer goods that Dominicans send or bring back with them from the United States, they also return with social and cultural values that challenge and often conflict with dominant norms on the island.

Pulitzer Prize–winning novelist and short story author Junot Díaz has consistently written fiction in which the narrative voice is characterized by a dual register that, on the one hand, reproduces a heteronormative masculine identity associated with Dominican machismo while, on the other hand, undermines the essentialist and exploitative values to which this form of masculinity subscribes.

Jennifer Harford Vargas analyzes the way Díaz uses narrative techniques and formal structures to simultaneously denounce political dictatorship while appropriating dictatorial powers in the act of writing in his novel, *The Brief Wondrous Life
of Oscar Wao*.[6] Yunior, the recurring narrator in Junot Díaz's fiction and quite plau-
sibly the author's alter-ego, considers himself a postmodern *plátano*—that is, a
diasporic Dominican subject who straddles multiple linguistic, cultural, and economic imaginaries—and he uses humor and sarcasm to articulate a self-aware
pose while he reproduces the womanizing behaviors and macho braggadocio he
learned from his father and other family members and friends. Linda Hutcheon
describes the politics of postmodernism as a complicitous critique in which art
and literature perform through satiric parody the ideological discourses they seek
to unmask and dedoxify.[7] One of the most prominent *machista* values that Díaz's
complicitous critique performs and unmasks is the competitiveness between
men, particularly the obsessive gaming involved in the seduction and sexual
conquest of women. These games between men operate under the logic of rational
individualism and an adherence to a zero-sum mentality. There can be only one
winner, and the loser suffers a diminished sense of masculine privilege and, in
some cases, loses his life. Díaz's fiction reveals the symbolic violence that perpetuates political and intersubjective forms of masculine domination as well as undergirds the economic logic of coloniality and neoliberalism. Even as the narrator
portrays the deadly consequences of these games of masculine domination, he is
also engaged in a playful and not entirely innocent game with the reader, who is
seduced into taking pleasure in the textual performance of violence, conquest, and
colonization. Nevertheless, the dual register of the narrative voice—which employs
irony and sarcasm, narrates in asynchronous sequencing, and speaks in the second person—simultaneously unmasks the exploitative logic of these homosocial
games while ostensibly celebrating their eroticism and seductive character. This
tension takes on a profound critical edge when considering the controversies surrounding sexual harassment accusations against Junot Díaz and his confessional
revelations of having been a victim of sexual violence as a youth.

For Indiana Hernández and Díaz, the combination of gaming and rational individualism occurs at the intersection of *Homo ludens* and *Homo economicus*—the
"Domo economicus"—where Dominican machos who play for keeps operational-
ize the neoliberal logic of self-economization as part of their diasporic experience
and their accumulation of transcultural capital. The novel *Papi*, for example, follows the surreal fantasies of a Dominican girl of about eight years old who waits
for her father's return from the United States. The image of the absent father takes
on a dreamlike quality of hypermasculine excess and is imbued in all the wealth and
material goods his family and friends eagerly await upon his return to the DR. As
such, his upward mobility and economic success are defined in terms of how much
U.S. capital he has accumulated and is able to redistribute to his community and,
indeed, his island nation. Junot Díaz describes these forms of social and cultural
remittances in the novel *The Brief Wondrous Life of Oscar Wao* as a "Diaspora

engine" that has been slapped into reverse: "airports choke with the overdressed; necks and luggage carousels groan under the accumulated weight of that year's cadenas and paquetes, and pilots fear for their planes—overburdened beyond belief—and for themselves; restaurants, bars, clubs, theaters, malecones, beaches, resorts, hotels, moteles, extra rooms, barrios, colonias, campos, ingenios swarm with quisqueyanos from the world over. Like someone had sounded a general reverse evacuation order."[8] Both Díaz and Indiana Hernández associate the ostentatious displays of wealth that U.S. Dominicans bring back to the island as markers of status that create a false image of prosperity and of achieving the American Dream.

In the case of Indiana Hernández's *Papi*, the hyperbolic language and surrealist images serve to demystify the symbolic violence that these forms of social and cultural remittances inflict on the Dominican imaginary. Through the psychoanalytic topography of the unconscious, as well as Bourdieu's notions of habitus and symbolic violence, we can see how the narrative games in Indiana Hernández's *Papi* use figurative language and narrative techniques to demystify the forms of masculine domination that are articulated and practiced in the embodied economy of the Dominican diaspora.[9] One of the games that masculine domination plays is through rational logic, and its discursive, material, and bodily practices reproduce forms of symbolic and state violence that it then negates as external to itself.

The first-person narrative voice in the novel belongs to an eight-year-old girl who visualizes the impending return of her estranged father. Papi lives in the United States and has attained a great measure of economic success as a car dealer. These fantasies are narrated in the figurative language of dreams—through metonymic association and metaphoric displacement—and the hyperkinetic poetics with which these images are depicted takes on a stream-of-consciousness quality of random thoughts and desires. From the very outset, the larger-than-life figure of the girl's father (neither of the two are ever named) appears as an uncanny, monstrous return of the repressed. He is everywhere and nowhere at once, always on the verge of violently emerging from the hidden depths of the little girl's psyche:

> *Papi es como Jason, el de* Viernes trece. *O como Freddy Krueger. Más como Jason que como Freddy Krueger. Cuando uno menos lo espera aparece. Yo a veces hasta oigo la musiquita de terror y me pongo muy contenta porque sé que puede ser él que viene por ahí. . . . Papi está a la vuelta de cualquier esquina. Pero uno no puede sentarse a esperarlo porque esa muerte es más larga y dolorosa.*[10]

> Papi is like Jason, the guy from *Friday the 13th*. Or like Freddy Krueger. But more like Jason than Freddy Krueger. He shows up when you least expect him. Sometimes when I hear that scary music, I get really happy cuz I know he might be coming this way. . . . Papi's there, around any corner. But you can't sit down and wait for him cuz that's a longer and more painful death.[11]

The protagonist's desire to reunite with her father is expressed as an estrangement of the familiar and a mixture of terror and pleasure, that is, as "the uncanny," which is the key psychological reaction that the horror movie genres she cites are supposed to trigger. Just as she eagerly anticipates her father's violent return, like Jason with a baseball bat or hatchet ready to strike, she also has to repress that desire by occupying herself with mundane activities, like watching cartoons all day or taking a walk. By starting her novel with the allusions to Hollywood slasher films of the 1980s, Indiana Hernández establishes from the outset a link between the father's absence, his return, and an act of violence. What the protagonist imagines as a joyful return is a misrecognition of the violence that the father committed when he abandoned his family in the first place.

Psychoanalytic interpretations of Hollywood horror films provide a compelling account of how staged acts of violence perpetuate dominant social norms. In the case of the slasher films from the Eighties that Indiana Hernández cites, this subgenre conveys a conservative discourse of masculine domination through the figure of the monster. Film scholar Robin Wood argues that the monster appears as the embodied dramatization of the "dual concept of the repressed/the Other."[12] That is, the audience derives pleasure from the horror film because the monster embodies many of the taboos that society represses and simultaneously projects onto figures that threaten patriarchal social norms, such as foreigners, women, racial minorities, and queers. According to Wood, "One might say that the true subject of the horror genre is the struggle for recognition of all that our civilization represses or oppresses, its reemergence dramatized, as in our nightmares, as an object of horror, a matter of terror, and the happy ending (when it exists) typically signifying the restoration of repression."[13] Carol J. Clover analyzes more specifically the forms of sexual repression that encode gender identification in modern horror films. Although many examples in the slasher genre position a virginal female character as the "Final Girl" who survives the monster's onslaught, the films nevertheless appeal to the male audience who simultaneously identifies with the male slasher and the female survivor. The male killers are feminized or castrated, usually through some traumatic childhood episode that results in a sexual dysfunction and obsession. The female survivors are rendered masculine or phallic, particularly in the final sequences when she wields a weapon to fight back against the monster. "It is not that these films show us gender and sex in free variation; it is that they fix on the irregular combinations, of which the combination masculine female repeatedly prevails over the combination feminine male."[14] In Indiana Hernández's novel, Papi is the monster that embodies repressed desires and Otherness yet whose return also facilitates the restoration of repression. And as the novel progresses, the readers see the way hypermasculinity is at the core of the Dominican embodied economy and is performed through public displays of conspicuous consumption. Yet the female protagonist begins to appropriate and reproduce the phallic power that is reserved for men like her father. As in the case of Junot Díaz's complicitous critique of Dominican masculinity, Indiana Hernández uses the narrative allusions to mass media to show how the social norms of masculine domination are what really constitutes monstrousness, both horrific and seductive at the same time.

One way to understand these contradictions is through Bourdieu's own appropriation of psychoanalytic terms; in particular the notion of (de)negation, or *Verneinung*, and misrecognition, or *méconaissance*. Although Bourdieu explicitly distanced his sociological approach from psychoanalysis, scholars have shown that many of the terms he uses in his work are directly connected to those developed by Freud and Lacan. This disavowal is perhaps Bourdieu's own form of (de)negation, an articulation and recognition of structures and objects of knowledge that he nonetheless discredits or denies. As George Steinmetz argues, "His treatment of Freudian psychoanalysis more often takes the form of admitting Freudian terminology and even some psychoanalytic arguments into his texts while surrounding these passages with rhetorical devices that seem to condemn psychoanalysis."[15] Bourdieu's own use of the concept of (de)negation does not refer to the relationship between analyst and analysand, as quoted above in the epigraph by Freud. With his focus on the structures of the habitus, Bourdieu referred to (de)negation as a disavowal of history in the way social groups embody their values and norms. As Steinmetz describes, this usage is not contradictory to its Freudian definition, in particular in the analysis of gender identity formation: "Psychoanalytic theory has long been concerned with the same problem that Bourdieu sets out to explain here, namely, the ways in which masculine domination is *historically* reproduced as a *dehistoricized* form."[16] In Indiana Hernández's novel about Papi's monstrous masculinity, the embodied economy of sexual promiscuity and displays of conspicuous consumption disavows the colonial and racial histories that have contributed to the formation of this habitus and essentializes the material and bodily practices through which it reproduces itself as authentic Dominicanness.

The first chapter of Indiana Hernández's novel establishes the link between the embodied economy of the masculine domination and the (de)negation of the colonial and slave histories that are part of the diasporic experience. The novel uses carnivalesque imagery that invokes the material bodily lower stratum and a Rabelaisian excess of consumption to portray the acquisition of symbolic capital with which the diasporic father figure returns to the Dominican Republic. In figurative language reminiscent of Virgilio Piñera's short fiction, the narrative voice portrays the entire Dominican nation celebrating the economic remittances to which Papi's friends and family now feel entitled.[17] These remittances become part of the national economy, and as Papi's return is broadcast live on national television, he becomes a public figure in which the nation places its dreams and desires. The dollars he showers on his compatriots taste like sugar—"*una ducha de billetes verdes que saben a azúcar de pastelería*"—a metaphor that implies the Caribbean history of sugar plantocracies and the slavery that facilitated this economic model.[18] The entire carnivalesque scene of Papi's return, narrated from the perspective of his young daughter's imagination, situates the father figure at the center of national identity and as the driving force of the island's economy. However, as the protagonist visualizes her father as the center of attention, the final image in this chapter reveals how her desires to share in the wealth and privilege emerge from narcissism and a desire to draw attention to herself. The diaspora becomes the image in which the Dominican nation visualizes and affirms itself:

> *Me asomo al balcón para ver si ya llega y lo que llegan son las vanettes de los canales de televisión a esperarlo, una hilera de presentadores en la acera, micrófonos en mano señalando hacia aquí. Yo saludo con la mano desde el balcón de Cilí [her grandmother] y cuando entro, para ver si en las noticias dicen por dónde anda papi, me veo en la pantalla en el balcón de Cilí diciendo adiós con una mano.*[19]

> I go out to the balcony to see if he's here yet, but all I see are the TV station's vans waiting for him, a line of newscasters on the sidewalk, mics in hand, pointing up here. I wave at them from Cilí's balcony, and when I go back inside to see if the news can tell us where Papi is, I see myself on the screen, waving from Cilí's balcony.[20]

This passage conveys the complex intersections of specularity, desire, and the socially relational subject. In Lacan's terms, the young girl encounters the socially constructed image of herself through a reenactment of the mirror stage, yet in this case the surface in which the subject sees herself is the national media. This leads to the misrecognition (*méconaissance*) of the protagonist's body, which she perceives through the technologies that channel her desire for her father.[21]

The disavowal leads to a misrecognition of the self and the structures of power that material and bodily practices reproduce. For Lacan, the *méconaissance* occurs when the emerging subject perceives his or her body as fully integrated and autonomous, when this image is always already overdetermined by its family and social formations. Similarly, Bourdieu argues that misrecognition occurs when the economic and social histories of habitus are naturalized and perpetuated as doxic values. In Indiana Hernández's novel, the narrative devices and figurative language lay bare both of these forms of misrecognition. The description of the young girl who sees herself through the mediated eyes of the nation—that is, as a televised image waving to herself—embodies the collective desire to take part in the return of her father, which constitutes her subjectivity. This desire is channeled through the remittances the father distributes among the members of the Dominican nation, which enter into the embodied economy of consumer goods and sexual practices. The girl sees herself as the central figure in the spectacle of her father's return, yet her desires are conflated with those of the national family that desires the economic largess the diasporic Dominican brings back from the United States. In his theory of the mirror stage, Lacan writes, "It is this moment that decisively tips the whole of human knowledge into mediatization through the desire of the other, constitutes its objects in an abstract equivalence by the co-operation of others, and turns the I into that apparatus for which every instinctual thrust constitutes a danger."[22] The "danger" of this collective desire to this mediated image of the self is the threat to its cohesion and uniqueness. As the novel progresses, the girl competes with the numerous claims that family and community members make on her father's time and wealth. By staging this form of misrecognition, in which the girl perceives herself as the object of the desire of others, Indiana Hernández's novel reveals the narcissism that drives the embodied economy of masculine domination. The girl's selfhood and the Dominican nation constitute themselves through desire for the father figure and as the deserving recipients of diasporic wealth redistribution. Indiana Hernández integrates the figurative language of dreams and the cultural scripts from mass media and pop culture in a narrative game with the reader that reveals, reproduces, and resists the material and bodily practices of masculine domination.

The Rules of the Game

Whereas masculine domination appears in Indiana Hernández's novel as the monstrous and indestructible serial killer, in Díaz's fiction the toxic legacy of the father figure reemerges in Yunior's and his brother's embodiment of *donjuanismo* and the serial seduction of women. The diasporic Dominican habitus that Yunior and other male characters embody in Díaz's fiction in many ways enforces the logic of domination through the adherence of the dominated, which Pierre Bourdieu defines as a type of symbolic violence. It is crucial not to misrecognize discourse as empowering simply because it adopts an oppositional stance. Bourdieu writes, "When the dominated apply to what dominates them schemes that are the product of domination, or, to put it another way, when their thoughts and perceptions are structured in accordance with the very structures of the relation of domination that is imposed on them, their acts of cognition are, inevitably, acts of recognition, submission."[23] In Díaz's fiction, a self-aware narrator reflects on and exposes the narrative structures that articulate and reinforce the symbolic violence of masculine domination. He lays bare the rules of the game of the Dominican diasporic habitus in order to subvert the symbolic violence that narrative fiction can recirculate into discourses of identity and cultural authenticity. Yet this voice does so through a performative embodiment of these doxa and therefore adheres to the logic of masculine domination in order to play a narrative game with the reader. The reader must break the rules of this narrative game in order to resist adhering to the habitus of the dominated and thus break the cycle of symbolic violence.

In Dominican society, the forms of male homosocial play that enforce heteronormative masculinity often resort to abuse and violence, which reflect the larger political and historical context of dictatorship, U.S. invasion and occupation, and neoliberal globalization. E. Antonio de Moya argues that in the Dominican Republic, "masculinity is thus a totalitarian notion that produces intricate strategies (power games) for men to oppress other men and to prevent oppression by them."[24] The rules of the game in the embodied economy of Dominican machismo create a field of binary oppositions that delineate the spaces in which material and bodily practices legitimate masculine privilege. De Moya provides a list of these rules based on his participant observation and interviews with Dominican men and women. Among the rules that young boys must follow in the game of masculine domination, de Moya includes:

• He must stand up, walk and sit down in a straight fashion.

   . . .

• He should not gesticulate much or show "feminine gestures," such as soft hand movements.

   . . .

• He cannot wear his mother or sisters' clothes, shoes, make-up or jewels.

   . . .

• He should put on shirts from behind, without raising his arms.

   . . .

• And by age twelve or thirteen, at puberty, he should show a vivid and visible erotic interest in all females that come close to him (mostly girls his age and their mothers) when he is with his peers.[25]

The men who play by these rules must continually display their capacity to emulate the impossible standards of authentic masculinity, which, as Bourdieu argues, "leads to sometimes frantic investment in all the masculine games of violence, such as sports in modern societies, and most especially those which most tend to produce the visible signs of masculinity, and to manifest and also test what are called manly virtues, such as combat sports."[26] In the Dominican Republic, baseball crystallizes not only the "manly virtues" that can be proven through sports, but also the most sought-after avenue through which men can achieve upward mobility. Ironically, the highest achievement in this masculine pursuit is making it to the professional leagues in the United States, which reinforces the role that the diaspora plays in sustaining embodied economy of masculine domination in the Dominican Republic. The rules of the game that Dominican men play to reaffirm the legitimacy of their machismo also serve their positioning in the fields of economic and political power.

We see this in *Oscar Wao*, for example, when Oscar becomes involved in a violent test of endurance and superiority with a Dominican police captain during a visit to the island. Because Oscar falls in love with the *capitán*'s girlfriend, Ybón, he becomes the target of the *capitán*'s jealous rage and violent reprisals. The *capitán* had been one of Balaguer's soldiers during the U.S. invasion and suppression of the political left on the island, and his use of terror and murder was little more than a game for him to achieve status in the military. The *capitán* is also sarcastic and playful in his encounters with Oscar, even though his demeanor hides a murderous intent. The first time he detains his rival, Oscar offers a weak defense and attempts to hold up his U.S. citizenship as a protective talisman; but the *capitán* dismissively declares his own status as a naturalized U.S. citizen, neutralizing any privilege Oscar thought he had. When he has his men brutally beat Oscar, they sadistically tease their victim and feign nonchalance and politeness before thrashing him mercilessly: "It was like one of those nightmare eight-a.m. MLA panels: *endless*."[27] The playful metaphor—articulated by Díaz's recurring character and narrator Yunior—describes this act of extreme violence through a metafictional form of humor that engages with a select group of scholarly readers. This critical

self-reflexivity articulates the postmodern critique of the violent passages in the text. Even as this episode reproduces many of the cultural stereotypes associated with Dominican machismo, and it is a fictionalized throwback to the Spanish colonial legacy that privileged notions of male honor and positioned women as the disputed property between male contestants, the ludic performance of heteronormative masculinity takes place at multiple diegetic levels, ultimately engaging the critical yet complicitous reader.

In the most basic applications of game theory in the social sciences, one of the first principles in the calculation of payoffs is to never play a dominated strategy and to always choose the strategy with the least bad outcome.[28] Oscar survives his first round with the *capitán* and his men, and he returns to New Jersey to recuperate and put this episode behind him. However, he continues to pine for Ybón, and when he returns to the Dominican Republic to pursue her, he and the *capitán* enter into a deadly game with Ybón as the prize. Although he was a master at the fantasy games like Dungeons and Dragons that he played with his friends back in New Jersey, Oscar knows he cannot win this high-stakes game but risks his life anyway because he sees Ybón as the only woman with whom he has developed a mutually intimate relationship. The zero-sum logic of the homosocial game that Oscar plays with the *capitán* forces the contestants into violent competition as a legitimating performance of Dominican masculinity. This logic is similar to that which gave license to Dominican autocrats like Joaquín Balaguer, who centralized power and wealth and persecuted any and all political rivals; Balaguer once said that "Dominican history had taught him that anyone who had ruled the country, sooner or later would rule it again."[29] This history of dictatorship and colonialism is part of the cursed lineage that Díaz defines as the *fukú americanus*. Within these structures of power and zero-sum logic, the outcome of Oscar's game with the *capitán*, which happens to take place during Balaguer's sixth term as president, is a foregone conclusion; however, what is at stake for Oscar is not power or wealth but rather a choice between his life and his manhood. Even though Oscar eventually loses this game, by entering into it he assumes the heteronormative masculine identity that had eluded him his entire life. In her analysis of the novel's ending, Maja Horn writes, "Though it explicitly critiques this masculinity, implicitly it cannot entirely renounce its desirability and evaluates the male characters' success or failure through some of its standards."[30] Nevertheless, Yunior's telling of Oscar's story—with all its metanarrative techniques and forms—shows how the intersectionality of masculinity and national/ethnic/racial identities confers on Dominican male subjects social legitimacy, privilege, and power. Although for most of his life Oscar has no "game" as a Dominican macho, he gambles his life for the chance to finally lose his virginity with Ybón, and the novel's afterward reveals that he, in fact, was able to consummate his relationship with her. Although his game with the *capitán* is a suicide mission, he pays the ultimate price in order to achieve some semblance of heteronormative legitimacy. Oscar plays the game of masculine domination from the positionality of the dominated.

A similar set of games appears in Indiana Hernández's novel, *Papi*, in which Dominican machismo is not portrayed as a premodern or primitive form of masculine domination but is consistent with the neoliberal values of rational action that define what Wendy Brown calls the *Homo economicus*. Derived from the classical liberal economic theory of Adam Smith and reappraised through Michel Foucault's notion of biopolitics, Brown traces the evolution of "economic man" to the contemporary neoliberal age, in which people are imagined as forms of human capital and entrepreneurs of the self. Like the zero-sum game of masculine domination, *Homo economicus* has eliminated all other forms of human sociability, in particular *homo politicus*, that is, the relational self that Brown situates at the center of democratic forms of statehood and that is "realized beyond the struggle for existence and wealth accumulation." Brown writes, "Neoliberalism retracts this 'beyond' and eschews this 'higher nature': the normative reign of *homo oeconomicus* in every sphere means that there are no motivations, drives, or aspirations apart from economic ones, that there is nothing to being human apart from 'mere life.'"[31] In Indiana Hernández's novel, when Papi returns to the cheering crowds of Dominican family and friends who await the largess of his material and cultural remittances, his daughter imagines him running triumphantly through the streets like a champion athlete, "*sonriendo y juntando sus dos manos por encima de su cabeza como los ganadores*"[32] ("smiling and holding his hands together above his head like a winner").[33] This image synthesizes the competitive, winner-takes-all logic of Dominican machismo and the doxic values of individualism and self-reliance that constitute the neoliberal *Homo economicus*. Brown also argues that this figure, or "creature," although often generalized as universal, adheres to the hierarchies of an embodied economy in which gendered forms of labor are valued or devalued. For Brown, "when *homo oeconomicus* becomes the governing truth, when it organizes law, conduct, policy, and everyday arrangements, the burdens and the invisibility of those excluded persons and practices are intensified."[34] Once again, in the passage that reproduces the mirror stage, when the young girl sees herself through the technology of mass media that has focused on her father, the spectacle reveals the misrecognition that directs the dominated subject to see herself through the perspective of domination and to embrace its logic as natural and universal. In this way, the *Homo economicus* gives rise to the *Domo economicus*, a masculine ideal toward which the Dominican nation strives, even as it relies on the transnational economy of the diaspora to sustain the fiction of its cultural autonomy.

The daughter in Indiana Hernández's novel allies herself with the violence that this dominant form of masculinity perpetrates on women, ostensibly as the father's sidekick in a sci-fi action film. The novel's portrayal of the father-daughter relation parodies a science fiction or comic book scenario, in which Papi and the young protagonist ascend toward outer space in a sports car/space ship. They are followed by a caravan of carnival floats teeming with a bacchanalian multitude of Papi's ex-lovers, "*dando golpes de barriga y de pechuga tan intensos que a veces se les brota una tripa o un ojo, furiosas, demoníacas, preciosas, horribles fulanas de tal*"[35] ("beating themselves on the stomach and chest so intensely that sometimes an intestine peeks out, or an eye. They're furious, demonic, beautiful, horrible nobodies").[36] The language here utilizes images of the material bodily lower stratum, and the women who demand Papi's attention become a demonic mass of monstrous femininity that threatens to consume Papi and his daughter. Papi hands his daughter a pistol, and she begins to exchange gunfire with their pursuers. Their car transforms into a spaceship and takes flight, but their escape is impeded by the women who now sprout wings and turn into bat-like creatures, clinging to the vehicle with their claws and teeth. The daughter is finally able to dislodge them from their ship by sticking a blue lollypop in the eye of the lead harpy, "*la infierna que grita muy fuerte cayendo y arrastrando a todas las demás, una por una, hacia el fondo del mar, levantando una corona de espuma, muy blanca y muy linda, por lo menos desde aquí arriba*"[37] ("she screams loudly and falls, dragging all the others, one by one, to the bottom of the sea, raising a crown of froth, very white and very beautiful, at least from way up here").[38] The phantasmagoric image of the women who compete to possess and consume Papi reveals how the daughter draws from mass media and popular culture to imagine the threat that a voracious femininity represents to the Dominican macho, whose masculine privilege allows him to use as many women as he can and then dispose of them indiscriminately. As a sidekick, the daughter becomes complicit in the dehumanization of other women, and those who try to lay a claim to her father deserve the violence that is inflicted on them. The weapon that finally overpowers the horde of women—the blue lollypop— emblematizes the child's appropriation of a phallic object to enforce the logic of masculine domination. As cartoonish as this narrative sequence may seem, it conveys a psychosexual form of symbolic violence in which the daughter allies herself with and becomes the agent of the commodification of women. Bourdieu argues that "girls internalize, in the form of schemes of perception and appreciation not readily available to consciousness, the principles of the dominant vision which lead them to find the social order, such as it is, normal or even natural."[39] Consequently, women assume traditional domestic roles or pursue forms of labor and/or professions associated with "women's work," such as in education or the health care industry. By allying herself with her father, the protagonist rejects these female-gendered roles. The passage cited above shows how that vision is reinforced through sci-fi, comic books, and global mass media, and the young girl internalizes and reproduces the dominant gender norms that perpetuate the logic of masculine domination.

Through the naïve perspective of the young female protagonist, the novel shows how authoritarianism reconstitutes itself in the neoliberal policies and political discourses of progress and modernity of the postdictatorship governments of the Dominican Republic. Maja Horn argues that Indiana Hernández's fiction reflects a skeptical critique of neoliberalism's promise to democratize and modernize the Dominican nation. The political propaganda of Leonel Fernández, the first president after the decades-long regime of Balaguer, promised that the Dominican Republic was "moving forward," yet despite the opening up of the country to foreign investment, free trade zones, and tourism, the same forms of clientelism and authoritarianism continued to live on and perpetuate structural inequality. Horn writes, "The radical opening of the country to outside forces and the dramatic transformations this has resulted in have thus ultimately helped to further compound existing political patterns rather than proffering a decisive challenge to them."[40] Although the Dominican Republic has opened its economy to global interests, and the Dominican diaspora has brought about an influx of social and cultural remittances that offer alternative gender and sexual identities, masculine domination revives and reappears—like Jason or Freddy Krueger from the slasher films—even in those queer appropriations of the embodied economy of Dominican machismo.

The games of masculine domination that constitute Dominican masculinity encourage men to derive pleasure from the abuse and oppression of others. There is also the pleasure derived from taking something of value away, of dispossessing someone (of their virginity, chastity, or property). Masculine pleasure is also an expression of triumph over breaking down defenses and taking away a prize. In addition to the ludic element in Dominican masculinity, Díaz's fiction explores how play intersects with the self-economizing sensibility of the *Domo economicus*. Díaz's short stories narrate this gendered symbolic violence as part of the diasporic experience, which redefines a man's role in the institution of the family but also facilitates the performance of gendered behaviors associated with male privilege. The *machista* tradition is passed down from one generation to the next, and Yunior can trace his ambivalent stance toward heteronormative masculinity to his abusive father, Ramón. Yunior is as much an apprentice as he is a victim of his father's abusive behavior, and details in the short story collection *Drown* point toward Ramón's past experience in the Dominican military during the U.S. invasion as indicative of his affinity for violence and domination over others. (Yunior reveals in *Oscar Wao* that his father, like the *capitán*, supported the U.S. invasion in 1965.) The military, as part of the repressive state apparatus, enforces and is sustained by these *machista* codes of conduct. Additionally, the conditions of labor after Ramón's military service, which saw increased rates of Dominican migration to the United States, make possible reaffirmations of and challenges to the dominant masculine ideal and the role of men in the Dominican family. Díaz portrays Ramón and the social values he embodies as embedded in the political context of armed conflict, colonialism, and state violence, as well as the neoliberal restructuring of the global economy and its impact on the gendered division of labor.

Another way that Díaz engages in a literary game with readers is through nonlinear narrative sequencing—telling tales out of chronological order. The narrative sequencing of Ramón's migration experience in *Drown* is reminiscent of the extended analepsis in Julia Álvarez's *How the García Girls Lost Their Accent*. However, whereas Álvarez's novel traces backward the biographies of the García sisters, Díaz's short story collection presents a nonlinear ordering of set pieces that ends with what is ostensibly Ramón's first experiences in the United States, before he commits to bringing over his family from the Dominican Republic. His itinerant bachelorhood leads to bigamy when Ramón marries Nilda, a single mother he meets in the laundry mat. Nilda owns her own restaurant and takes up piecemeal clothes mending on the side; she is self-supporting and resourceful, and she is the primary income earner in her relationship with Ramón. They even concoct a game in which Ramón has to find the cash she hides on her body before embarking on the dangerous bus commute home from the restaurant. By marrying Nilda, Ramón eventually obtains legal status, and he has to weigh whether he will abandon his family in the Dominican Republic or reunite with them and reassume his role as *padre de familia*. He chooses the latter, in large part because Nilda, with whom he has a third son, begins to make demands of Ramón and forces him to choose between his two families. He also physically and emotionally abuses her when she asks too many questions about his family back on the island.

Eventually, and at the urging of his Puerto Rican friend Jo Jo, Ramón chooses to reunite with his Dominican family and bring them to live in the United States, though he exerts a tyrannical dominance over Yunior, his brother Rafa, and Virta, their mother—Yunior calls him "My Father the Torturer." In his article on this short story, John Riofrio argues, "To not send for his family is to admit that he has come to the US and failed to regain the role of provider Dominican poverty had stripped him of."[41] Even after he reunites with his family, Ramón continues to have extramarital relations with "the Puerto Rican woman," one of his many *sucias*, as Yunior learns when his father obligates him to tag along on one of his sexual encounters. Eventually, Ramón and Virta separate, as is indicated in the titular story "Drown," and Ramón takes up with yet another woman in Miami even as he tries to reconcile with Yunior's mother through secret, long-distance phone calls. In all his family relations, Ramón exerts the privilege of having choices that are reserved for men. He can choose to leave his family and migrate to the United States, just as he can choose to enter into sexual and marital relations with other women while still maintaining his rights as *padre de familia* with his family back on the island.

The ability to make these choices for himself and others, with the fate of his wives and children contingent on what he perceives as the most advantageous options for himself, reflect the individualistic ethos of the self-economizing man, or *Homo economicus*, as Wendy Brown argues. Unlike Oscar in Díaz's novel, the character of Ramón in *Drown* has "game" and violently asserts his mastery of the social and cultural norms that define Dominican masculinity. Ramón's male prerogatives reflect a broader cultural norm that legitimates a Dominican macho's "right to have up to three or four women (to satisfy his 'natural' sexual appetite)."[42] Díaz shows how this male supremacy epitomized the Trujillo regime in *Oscar Wao*, and its noxious ethos of female subjugation filters down into the personal relationships of nearly all the male characters in his fiction. Ramón's *negocios* are as much about social and economic mobility as they are about negotiating the welfare of others in his pursuit of male heterosexual privilege and his performance of Dominican *machismo*.

Yunior also learns the logic of masculine domination through his older brother, Rafa. Díaz's depiction of the sibling rivalry between Yunior and Rafa demonstrates the links between heteronormative masculinity, games of domination, and economic self-interest. Rafa, whose name evokes that of the dictator Rafael Leónidas Trujillo, uses ridicule, fear, and violence to manipulate and subjugate his younger brother. The psychological games of domination that Rafa plays with Yunior are consistent with the survival tactics he uses to mitigate his economic precarity. For Rafa, his masculine privilege can be maintained only by consistently playing the dominant strategy in search of a payoff, whether in terms of his social and familial status or as an economic actor. In his games of domination with his brother, Rafa reproduces the discourses of military discipline, self-economizing, and misogyny as part of a broader symbolic violence that normalizes the fragmentation of families and corrosive sibling relations that emerge from the transnational Dominican diaspora.

Queer Redeployments of Masculine Domination

The opening chapter and later passages in Indiana Hernández's *Papi* deconstruct the misrecognition of the Dominican macho as a self-contained, impenetrable subjectivity that characters like Ramón and Rafa aspire to embody. In addition to the carnivalesque depiction of the economy of desire that constitutes the subjectivities of the protagonist and her father, Indiana Hernández's novel describes how Papi is a member of a fraternity of *socios* (business associates) who engage in games of one-upmanship through their wheeling and dealing, as well as through their sexual traffic in women. In one passage, the protagonist describes how she often accompanies her father on his business meetings at high-end restaurants, where he and his *socios* consume extravagant amounts of the most expensive foods like lobster, whose shells they crack without the use of any utensils. As they speak, they spit bits of food in every direction, which often land on the protagonist's glasses and face. As hypermasculine men, their feats of strength and excess accompany boasts of sexual conquests and cuckoldry, which pits the *socios* against each other in a perpetual game of *quién es más macho*. They also sexualize any passing female, including young girls who are close in age to the protagonist:

> *Se aflojan la correa y el botón del pantalón cuando han terminado de comer y cuando pasa una muchachita que todavía no usa brasier dicen "qué pezoncitos" y papi dice "la niña la pinta y la santa maría" para que se acuerden que estoy ahí, para que se acuerden que yo también tengo pezoncitos. Y entonces tosen en la servilleta y cambian de tema y ahora hablan de sus compadres, y de las hijas de las mujeres de sus compadres y de lo mucho que se parecen estas hijas a ellos y de nuevo un garbanzo salivoso cae sobre mis lentes.*[43]

They loosen the belts on their pants when they're through eating. When a young girl who doesn't wear a bra yet walks by, they say, Oh what little nips, and Papi says, The Niña, Pinta, and Santa María, so they'll remember I'm present, so they'll remember I also have nips. That's when they cough into their napkins and change the subject and then talk about their pals' wives, about their pals' wives' daughters, about how much those daughters look like them, and that's about when a spit-covered chickpea lands on my glasses.[44]

As in the passage depicting Papi's return, Indiana Hernández portrays the homosociality that empowers masculine domination as a grotesque display of the material bodily lower stratum. Here the high-end food, expanding male stomachs, explosive laughter, and feats of strength and violence emblematize the way excessive consumption is embodied in Dominican machismo. Women serve as objects of sexual consumption, and the cuckolding of one another solidifies the stature and power that Papi's homosocial community of *socios* strives to attain. Papi's masculinity can be constituted and affirmed only through these homosocial relations, which undermines the notion that the Dominican macho is a fully autonomous, self-contained subject. Furthermore, as the young daughter is pelted with the masticated bits of food that land on her glasses, we see that this hypermasculinity empowers itself through violence against others, in particular women. The young girl's gender identity is constituted by the exhibition of male desire, and the flecks of food that land on her glasses distort her vision and perception, which alludes to the misrecognition of her self-image as an autonomous individual and inheritor of Papi's masculine privilege.

The father's allusion to Columbus's three ships—"*la niña la pinta y la santa maría*"—provides another example of (de)negation as well. The father directs these famous names at his *socios* in order to misdirect his daughter's attention away from the masculine desire for sexual conquest that constitutes her gender identity. An unspoken irony here is that the Dominican Republic is one of the reputed sites of Columbus's remains, and there is even an ostentatious monument and museum that makes this contested claim. As I will soon discuss, the figure of the dead patriarch and his remains appears later in the novel when Papi becomes a zombie. Indiana Hernández layers these allusions in the narrative description of the young girl's queer initiation into the homosocial games that her father and his *socios* play in order to attain positions of power and wealth accumulation, always at the expense of others. These kinds of bawdy, hyperbolic displays of masculine privilege are usually reserved for an exclusively male group, and young boys will often have a seat at the table in order to learn the codes, mannerisms, and modes of speech that are part of the habitus of the Dominican macho. The novel queers this depiction of male bonding through the perspective of the daughter, whose sexual and gender identity positions her both inside and outside the homosocial space. By drawing attention to his daughter's presence (through misdirection), the father establishes the boundaries that situate her in the dominated position as a potential object of male sexual conquest, which is one of the measures of authentic Dominican masculinity. The naming of Columbus's ships not only serves as a corrective *indirecta* to police his *socios'* behavior but also invokes the history of conquest in the Americas, the Dominican Republic's nationalist claims to the colonizing figure of Columbus, and the intersection of civilizational conquest and the sexual exploitation of women. By trying to protect the daughter from his *socios'* desires for sexual conquest, the father reveals how the daughter is a queer witness to her own domination.

The novel further queers the performance of masculine domination as it depicts the young girl reproducing the material and bodily practices she learns from her father and his group of *socios*. The protagonist describes how she becomes sexually attracted to women, in particular María Cristina, her father's Cuban girlfriend, whom she meets when traveling to the United States. She spies on her father and his girlfriend lying naked in their hotel bedroom and fantasizes about María Cristina waking up and kissing her on the mouth: "*Y yo nunca había deseado algo tanto en mi vida*"[45] ("I've never wanted anything so much in my life").[46] The young girl also starts to develop crushes on her female friends and engages in erotic games with them. She narrates that, because of her straight hair, she is constantly plagued with lice and, therefore, has to have her head shorn, which makes her look like a boy:

> *Y fue por eso que cuando jugábamos al papá y a la mamá mis amiguitas querían que yo fuera el papá.*
> *Y fue por eso que me le subí a Natasha debajo de su cama.*
> *(Y a Mónica y a Sunyi y a Renata y a Jessy y a Franchy y a Zunilda y a Ivecita.)*
> *Y fue por eso que doña Victoria, la abuelita de Natasha, le dio un correazo.*
> *(Y a Paola y a Lily y a Sandrita y a Gabi y a Julia y a Karina.)*
> *Y fue por eso que mami empezó a ponerme vestidos solamente.*[47]

And that's why when we play that we're mom and dad, my friends want me to play dad.
And that's why I climbed on top of Natasha under her bed.
(Same with Mónica and Suny and Renata and Jessy and Franchy and Zunilda and Ivecita.)
And that's why Doña Victoria, Natasha's grandmother, whipped her with a belt.
(And Paola and Lily and Sandrita and Gabi and Julia and Karina.)
That's why Mami started dressing me only in dresses.[48]

Not only does the protagonist adopt a masculine appearance with her short hair, she assumes the male role in her erotic games with her female friends. The uninterrupted list of names that chronicles her erotic exploits reproduces the serial seductions of women that her father and his *socios* use as a measure of their virility and domination over other men. The daughter's queer practice, however, is policed and sanctioned by the adult women in her and her friends' families. Her mother enforces a feminine gender identity by obligating her to wear dresses exclusively. Nevertheless, the protagonist continues to emulate the freedom and power that are associated with her father's machismo, and she persists in reproducing the embodiments of toxic masculinity.

Although the novel queers the culture of masculine domination with the female focalization of its narrative voice, the subversion of gender norms through material and bodily practices does not necessarily challenge or undermine the forms of violence and domination that this embodied economy reproduces. Bourdieu argues that women will reproduce symbolic violence against themselves through misrecognition; that is, adopting as natural the gender norms that maintain her in a dominated position. The dominated subject adheres to the "cognitive instruments" she shares with the male figure that dominates her, and "the schemes she applies in order to perceive and appreciate herself" emerge from the embodied logic of patriarchal sexual hierarchies. Bourdieu emphasizes the role that the unconscious plays in the reproduction of symbolic violence, and that the dominated subject engages in a cognitive practice "that is profoundly obscure to itself."[49] The daughter in this scenario adopts the bodily practices of her Dominican macho father, mounting her female friends successively as a show of domination and reproducing the logic of gender hierarchies and power that situates her in a dominated position, *"para que se acuerden que yo también tengo pezoncitos."*

Misrecognition, in this sense, distinguishes Bourdieu's analysis from that of Judith Butler, who has consistently underscored the iterability and performative aspects of gender. For Butler, gender norms are not biologically determined, but circulate as repertoires of bodily practices that are performed continually so that their legitimacy is enshrined in social relations. The material practices that assist in the legitimation of these gender norms—clothing, adornments, bodily modification, food, gender-segregated spaces—form part of the embodied economy that dictate positions of power and access through cycles of conspicuous consumption. Butler argues that it is in the instability of these discourses and practices that gender norms can be subverted, and that in case of drag performance, for example, the contingency of gender is foregrounded and deconstructed.[50] However, the iterability and performative construction of gender occurs repeatedly in Indiana Hernández's novel through the young protagonist's desire to wear her father's expensive clothes, adopt his masculine bodily practices, and reproduce his domination over women. These appropriations may be queer, on the surface, yet their performance does little to subvert the social hierarchies that are enforced by masculine domination. On the contrary, the daughter becomes the father's sidekick and helps him stave off the hordes of women who compete to lay claim to his wealth and sexual favors. In *Pascalian Meditations*, Bourdieu argues that "it is naïve, even dangerous to suppose and suggest that one only has to 'deconstruct' these social artefacts in a purely performative celebration of 'resistance' in order to destroy them."[51] The debate between Butler and Bourdieu centers on what kind of agency, if any, can emerge from the disruption or queering of gender norms, with Butler arguing for the subversive potential of queer performativity and Bourdieu arguing that such appropriations do not necessarily escape the logic of masculine domination if they are performed by those who occupy a dominated position.[52] As in the case of Indiana Hernández's female character and protagonist, the queering of masculine domination reproduces the symbolic violence that entrenches the power dynamics of these material and bodily practices.

Nevertheless, Butler's notion of the performativity of gender helps shed light on the way Indiana Hernández's novel uses ludic and oneiric imagery to depict the embodied economy of Dominican machismo. In particular, the protagonist catalogues the vast collection of clothing that her father possesses, which underscores the way gender norms are reproduced through the material and bodily practices associated with conspicuous consumption. The narrative voice addresses an unnamed interlocutor in the second person—*tú*—and boasts of how many closets full of clothing her father owns, more than anyone else's father. The narrative voice emphasizes the competitive nature of Dominican machismo as she teases her interlocutor that his father does not know what it is like to enjoy so much wealth. The accumulation of clothing, jewelry, expensive cars, and other consumer goods reaches such hyperbolic levels that her father loses track of all his belongings: "*Papi tiene tanta ropa y tiene tantos clósets para guardarla que a veces cuando quiere ponerse una camisa tiene que comprarla de nuevo porque se olvida en cual clóset es que está*"[53] ("My Papi has so many clothes and so many closets to keep them in that sometimes, when he wants to wear a particular shirt, he has to buy it new cuz he forgets which closet he put it in").[54] In order to sustain the masculine ideal, her father has to display a nonchalant attitude toward waste and excess. The performativity of the masculine ideal is achieved not only through the type of clothing her father wears but also through the quantity and disposability of material goods that wealth and privilege provide.

The novel juxtaposes fragmented, oneiric imagery in a queer appropriation of the material and bodily practices that constitute Dominican machismo and dominant gender norms. Although this queer appropriation underscores the instability of gender norms, it also reproduces the zero-sum logic of masculine domination and its empowerment of social hierarchies. In one passage, the protagonist describes how she raids her father's many closets and wears his oversized clothes. In particular, she enjoys wearing the monogrammed jackets her father receives at VIP parties and events.[55] While her father watches a broadcast of the film *Rocky III* on television, his daughter tries on his numerous padded jackets, which are too heavy for the Caribbean climate in the Dominican Republic. The father complains that watching her try on his jackets makes him feel hot—"*a él le da calor verme con ellos puestos y yo no entiendo*"[56] ("he starts sweating just looking at me wearing them, but I don't understand").[57] Although it is not uncommon to say that a person feels hot seeing someone else overdressed in warm weather, and in Spanish there is a clear difference between saying "*le da calor*" and "*se pone caliente*," this passage offers a narrative portrayal of the Oedipal family romance in which the parent-child relation is marked by pent-up erotic desire or what Freud calls "cathexis." The daughter puts on more and more of her father's clothes because these objects are metonymic extensions of the father's bodily presence, as well as symbols of his social and economic capital. She attempts to stave off his imminent departure by wearing his clothes, yet this causes discomfort to the father as he watches his daughter appropriate the consumer goods that are part of the erotic repertoire of his masculine status.

However, the oneiric imagery of the scene also conveys a queer appropriation of the material and bodily practices associated with Dominican machismo. The more of his jackets that she tries on, the more her father literally sweats and melts away. The last sign of Papi is a TV remote control that floats in a puddle where his body used to be. She starts taking off the jackets *"porque no quiero quedarme sin papá"*[58] ("cause I don't want to be without my dad"),[59] but all that is left of her father is a wet stain on the sofa, *"y sobre la cara de Rocky ruedan los créditos mientras él llama: ¡¡¡¡¡Adrian!!!!! con la boca torcida"*[60] ("and the credits are rolling over Rocky's face as he screams, his mouth twisted: Adrian!!!!!").[61] This passage presents a dreamlike image in which the metonymic contiguity between gender identity and clothing also serves as metaphorical similarity between masculinity and power.[62] The ostensibly random juxtaposition of objects—the men's jackets, the Rocky film, the remote control—all form an oneiric metonymy in which the objects are extensions of the male body. By playing dress-up in her father's clothes, the daughter attempts to embody his masculine privilege. As the daughter appropriates the accessories that are associated with that masculinity, the father diminishes and disappears. The final image of Rocky's twisted mouth further reinforces the randomness and dreamlike quality of this passage, as the scene the narrator describes is actually from the original *Rocky* film, when the title character loses to Apollo Creed and reunites with his love interest, Adrian. This allusion underscores the competitive gamesmanship that constitutes the logic of masculine domination. The scene to which this passage alludes shows Rocky in the boxing ring, where there can be only one champion. By integrating the fragmented images and objects that are associated with the male body, wealth, and privilege, the novel portrays the relation between gender identity and its material and bodily performativity, as Judith Butler has incisively argued. However, the act of appropriation does not subvert Dominican machismo, and the queering of gender reproduces the zero-sum logic of masculine domination. In the end, the daughter desires to revive her father and therefore casts off the clothes that serve as extensions of his male body and symbolize his wealth and privilege. The protagonist is not the only woman to appropriate the material and bodily practices that reproduce masculine domination; her cousin, Milly, along with her twin brother Puchy, begin to dress and behave according to the logic of Dominican machismo, and eventually they both become Papi's *socios* in training. In her analysis of Indiana Hernández's novel, Maja Horn writes, "The position of hegemonic masculinity is here not necessarily tied to a biological essence in the novel; however, neither does the narrative suggest that these transgressive-seeming female appropriations in any way modify the hegemonic masculine script or temper its virulent effects."[63]

A queer appropriation of the material and bodily practices that constitute Dominican machismo cannot, on its own, deconstruct masculine domination and its positioning in the fields of power. Indiana Hernández also shows how the myth of the self-contained male body depends on the homosocial networks that are created and sustained by zero-sum games of domination. This occurs in the novel's portrayal of the *socios* who make up Papi's exclusive social circle. As already discussed, the *socios* form homosocial bonds around their business dealings (legal or otherwise), the traffic in women, cuckolding, and the material and bodily practices of conspicuous consumption. As Bourdieu has argued in *Distinction*, conspicuous consumption is not solely a practice associated with the upwardly mobile, and members of diverse social formations signal their sense of belonging and affiliation to their group through consumptive practices.[64] The *socios* to which Papi belongs signal their legitimacy as members of their group through the public display of hypermasculinity, and this nexus of material and bodily practices constitutes the embodied economy of Dominican machismo. These social networks sustain the fiction of the autonomous and self-contained Dominican macho, a figure similar to the Mexican macho Octavio Paz described in his famous *El laberinto de la soledad*. Indiana Hernández's novel opens up the Dominican macho to critical scrutiny and, through the perspective of the young girl, penetrates the homosocial spaces where upwardly mobile Dominican men play the zero-sum games of masculine domination.

Just as these social networks provide access to economic fields where upwardly mobile men can accumulate wealth and privilege, they create risks through the instability of the games of domination. Today's winner can be tomorrow's loser, and an ally and friend can easily become a rival and enemy. Once again, the narrative portrayal of Papi's *socios* explores this aspect of the embodied economy of Dominican machismo. Inevitably, the *socios* turn against and betray Papi, and the protagonist recounts the day she and her family receive the news that Papi has been murdered by his former associates. In the zero-sum logic of the games of masculine domination, Papi is eliminated from the field of power. He becomes an obstacle to the upward mobility of those who compete against him. Although the novel uses oneiric imagery to depict this murder and the daughter's perception of it, the violence of this embodied economy reflects the Dominican Republic's history of dictatorship and political oppression. During the Trujillo and Balaguer regimes, the authoritarian state maintained its power through the arbitrary implementation of violence against its own people. At any point, neighbors, friends, or family members could benefit by betraying one another for being a political subversive or even for being insufficiently enthusiastic in the obligatory displays of loyalty to the state.

The Political Economy of the Dominican Hustle

The justification of the androcentric social order combines and condenses two operations: it legitimates a relationship of domination by embedding it in a biological nature that is itself a naturalized social construction; and it ritualizes the institutional division of the sexes, as in the rites of separation of the boy from his mother.[65] Díaz's short story "Ysrael," which appears as the first story in *Drown*, can be read as a rite of separation for Yunior. Rafa separates his younger brother from his mother and leads him in a game of initiation into the logic of masculine domination. Rafa sets up this ritual as a game whose rules he improvises from his habitus as a Dominican male—from his "feel for the game," not necessarily a rational calculation—and he derives the pleasure of dispossessing his victim of dignity with the brutal unmasking of the titular character, the No-Face boy. Díaz therefore establishes early on in his fictional works that the Dominican male ethic can be summed up in one concept: having game. In Junot Díaz's story, the brother plays homosocial games of male domination with Yunior and exerts power through a strategy of creating uncertainty—of faking his brother out. The connection to time also embeds these practices in history, and in the case of Díaz's story, Rafa and Yunior reproduce in their male domination games the totalitarian practices and discourses of the Dominican state; the dispositions and patterns of behavior that comprise their habitus are put into practice in the larger sociopolitical field of dictatorship as a form of governmentality.

In Eric Berne's transactional theory of psychological games, sibling rivalry and rebelliousness against parental figures are not necessarily based on rational choice, but rather on patterns of goal-oriented emotional manipulation. What they do have in common with rational choice game theory is that these psychological games, especially between and among families and close relations, is that the players engage with each other expecting a payoff from the game. These payoffs are forms of what Berne calls "stroking"; that is, an expression for the need of affective and sexual gratification.[66] In some cases the desired gratification comes from the reinforcement of relations of power and social hierarchy, with players occupying dominant or submissive positions. Some of the games that Rafa plays with Yunior, while abusive and bullying, also teach the younger brother to be wary of others' intentions and falling into logical traps. For instance, Rafa shows Yunior a knife and tells him if he can stay quiet, he can keep it. As soon as Yunior asks, incredulously, "Yeah?," Rafa snatches the knife back and says, "See. You already lost it."[67] Rafa makes Yunior think that he brought the misfortune on himself, that his own actions caused him to lose the game.

Rafa embodies what Wendy Brown describes as the self-economizing man of neoliberalism: "*homo œconomics.*" He entrepreneurializes himself and he survives by using others' motives and desires to his advantage. Brown develops her notion of the *Homo economicus* through a critical reading of Michel Foucault's 1978–1979 lectures at the Collège de France, who proposed that neoliberal man is "for himself his own capital, his own producer, the source of his earnings."[68] Brown also writes that "whether he is selling, making, or consuming, he is investing in himself and producing his own satisfaction. Competition, not exchange, structures the relation among capitals, and capital appreciation through investment structures the relation of any capital to itself."[69] In the short story "Ysrael," Rafa displays this talent for "scheming," and he invokes the machismo of their absent father to shame Yunior for hesitating and feeling shame during one of his conniving hustles. Rafa teaches Yunior how to economize and take advantage of any situation, particularly if it involves stealing, cheating, or tricking others in order to come out on top. For Rafa, not only is there nothing wrong with theft and abuse as long as he doesn't get caught, but not to do so is a sign of weakness and effeminacy, that is, acting like a "pussy." Whether he is plotting a violent assault—as when he and Yunior jump Ysrael—or when he abuses women and exploits them sexually, Rafa exerts his dominance by preying on other people's emotional dependency. Yunior both admires and despises his older brother, as Deborah R. Vargas argues in her essay on what she calls *"lo sucio"* (the dirty), which "operates as a structural metonym for nonnormative constructions of intimacy, sexual desire, sociality, and kinship."[70] Vargas writes: "Rafa represents a love for Yunior that he despises. Rafa is the embodiment of *lo sucio* that Yunior does not want to become but cannot ever quite overcome. In actuality, most of Yunior's sexually intimate relationships appear and disappear through the ebbs and flows of his violent yet adoring relationship with Rafa."[71] Ultimately, Rafa takes no responsibility for the way he uses others, since in his mind they were not smart enough to beat him at his games, and they were stupid enough to play his games in the first place. For Rafa the people he hurts deserved what he does to them because they were foolish to trust him. He is a self-contained and impenetrable macho, much in the vein of Octavio Paz's famous description of the Mexican *chingón*. Rafa's refusal to acknowledge the externalities of his actions and choices allows him to play the dominant strategy regardless of how his games affect other people. In this way, he personifies the self-generating capital of the *Homo economicus* as well as the socially engaged actor of the homo ludens; that is, he asserts his self-interest as a Dominican macho through the manipulative games he forces others to play.

E. Antonio de Moya describes hegemonic forms of masculinity in the Dominican Republic as "a totalitarian and contradictory political discourse."[72] From the private space of the household to the public spaces of business and politics, numerous terms such as *hombre serio, hombre de pelo en pecho*, and *padre de familia* to *burgués, cacique, ejecutivo*, and *empresario* connect a man's virility to his privileged position at all levels of society.[73] This association between wealth, power, and hypermasculinity not only reflects the economic imaginary of the Dominican dictatorial regimes in the twentieth century, but is also part of a long-standing, colonialist tradition in the Spanish-speaking world. While the hypermasculine men in Dominican fiction can appear simply as boorish throwbacks to an unenlightened age, their *machista* self-interest and self-economizing pathologies, which do indeed emerge from the long history of colonial rapaciousness and centralization of political power in the Dominican Republic, also epitomize the neoliberal *Homo economicus* that has facilitated the reproduction of Dominican machismo in the diverse spaces of the diaspora. The same logic of rational choice and self-economization that propels the globalization of the Caribbean and its ensuing outflows of Dominicans to the United States also begets the toxic masculinities that prevail in Dominican society and among the transcultural subjects of the diaspora.

Dedoxifying the Diaspora through Narrative Schemes

Habitus is simultaneously the principle that generates classes of practices and the schemes of perception by which we judge those classifications. In other words, we discern the classifications through the cognitive instruments that emerge from the principle that generates those classifications.[74] In the case of Díaz's self-reflexive narrator, Yunior's habitus is constituted by the experience of migration and translocality, and he internalizes this experience into a disposition that, on the one hand, positions him as a player in games of masculine domination and, on the other hand, as a decolonial critic who perceives through self-reflexivity the negative externalities generated by his economic actions, that is, his *machista* games. In spite of the critical self-reflexivity that Yunior has acquired from the dual positionality of a diasporic subject—his transcultural capital—he remains a victim of the colonialist symbolic violence when he adheres to the logic of masculine domination through the practice of Dominican *machista* games.

The transcultural capital of the diasporic subject is accumulated and expended through the dual positionality as insider and outsider to two (or more) fields. This allows the diasporic subject to move between fields without fully adhering to the habitus of the dominated—a form of disidentification. The parallel field provides a space to which the diasporic subject can migrate out of hierarchical social relations and thus escape from a cycle of symbolic violence, yet this does not necessarily mean the subject takes up the dominant position in another field, although this is certainly possible. These lateral, nonhierarchical moves, which are not necessarily performed consciously or rationally, are similar to what I called *jaibería* in relation to the discursive strategies of self-reflexive humor in Puerto Rican literature and its "eccentric" reformulation of national identity.[75] In a broader sense, the transcultural capital of the diasporic subject can be simultaneously empowering and disempowering, since every accumulation that it enables in one field is perceived as withdrawal from another. For the diasporic subject, loss is misrecognized as a gain according to the logic of the hegemonic field, whereas a gain in that field is misrecognized as a loss according to the logic of the minoritarian field. The aim of decolonial discourse, then, is to articulate a break from the zero-sum equilibrium of transcultural capital and the habitus of the dominated that constitutes the diasporic subject's schemes of perception. The diasporic subject cannot achieve this break by deconstructing the logic of one field through the equally dominated habitus from another set of conditions of existence, that is, the lived experience in either a hegemonic or minoritarian field.

In the collection *Drown*, while Yunior narrates his apprenticeship on heteronormative Dominican masculinity and its tradition of cruelty, the chronological sequencing of his personal narrative—the "story" as opposed to the "discourse"—establishes from the outset a postmodern critique of this gender logic.[76] The reader encounters early on Yunior's nonconformist perspective, and while his sardonic and self-aware narrative voice has already prepared the reader to reject his father's *machista* values, the story of his father's migration told in "Negocios"—the final story in the collection—is simultaneously critical of and empathetic to Ramon's experiences. In the titular story "Drown," which precedes "Negocios" in the collection but follows chronologically the narration of Ramón's experiences, Yunior categorically rejects any dealings with his estranged father, as it becomes apparent that his parents have separated and Ramón makes repeated attempts to reconcile with Yunior's mother.

The story's main plot also portrays Yunior's friendship with Beto, which ends after some ambivalent homosexual experimentation and because Beto leaves for college in New York City—a choice Yunior views as a racial and class betrayal. In the story "Negocios" that appears later in the collection, Yunior's narrative voice describes a "postmemory" of his father's experience, and he empathizes with the self-economizing logic of the Ramón's *machista* prerogative, privilege, and ability to "hustle."[77] As a new immigrant, Ramón initially bases all his actions on whether they will benefit him without much regard for his family in the Dominican Republic. Although he sends them money on occasion, bringing them to the United States doesn't figure into his plans until many years after his arrival. Because the reader comes to Ramón's story after already having encountered Yunior as a small boy in the Dominican Republic waiting for and idealizing his father's return, having read about Yunior's subsequent estrangement from his father, and Yunior's homosexual experimentation with Beto, these earlier rejections and queerings of Dominican machismo provide a critical lens through which we perceive Yunior's empathetic narration of his father's immigration experience and all the human frailties it reveals behind the *machista* mask.[78]

Similarly, Indiana Hernández's novel, *Papi*, and its use of narrative collage, in which multiple references to pop culture clash against erotic and violent imagery against women, reproduces the figurative structures of dream language, such as the Freudian concepts of displacement (metonymy) and condensation (metaphor). For example, the protagonist imagines herself committing violent acts against the hordes of Papi's lovers, and her imagination compares the women to purebred dogs. The hyperbolic portrayal of Papi's promiscuity incorporates the language of the corporatist bureaucracy, and his multiple relations with women are compared to the clientelism of the Dominican authoritarian state. The traffic in women becomes a commercial market, a labor movement, and a competitive field in which the female body serves to position the competitors and clients advantageously to access the structures of state power. The women both support and undermine one another, and the graphic depiction of women's pregnancy and abortions conveys how they perpetrate violence against themselves in the patriarchal order of the authoritarian state.

The novel depicts the young daughter as an imaginative yet naïve devotee of her father's social position, wealth, and sexual potency. However, as in the scene at the restaurant when she witnesses the displays of hypermasculinity among Papi's *socios*, the protagonist only partly understands the contradictions of her complicity in reproducing the material and cultural practices of Dominican machismo. The protagonist recounts how, while traveling with Papi to Orlando, they drive endlessly on the interstate highways and sleep at the rest areas. In one instance, the daughter gets out of the parked car and stands at the edge of the highway, feeling the vibrations of the cars as they speed past:

> *Una vez me dieron ganas de cruzarla y estuve allí con un pie en la acera y otro en la carretera para sentir cómo vibraban los camiones y carros que pasaban muy rápido por delante de mis ojos, hasta que mi propio pie con su sandalia sobre el*

asfalto me pareció el pie de otra niña, como un pie en una foto y me dio miedo y
volví al carro a hacerme la dormida.[79]

One time I wanted to cross and stood there with one foot on the sidewalk and
one foot on the highway so I could feel the vibrations of the trucks and cars
passing so quickly before my eyes, until my own sandaled foot on the asphalt
started to look like some other girl's foot, like a foot in a photo, and I got scared
and went back to the car and pretended to sleep.[80]

Whereas the novel opens with a scene in which the protagonist experiences misrecognition when she sees herself on television, in this scene she experiences a
moment of bodily disassociation, as if her body belonged to another person whose
foot she sees in a photograph. These narrative depictions of split subjectivity underscore how the female protagonist creates a masculine persona that reproduces the
machismo she fetishizes through her father. Yet as a young girl, she sees herself and
her body from that masculine perspective, which induces fear and self-abjection. As
the passage above implies, she quickly returns to the safety of the fantastical world
in which she is Papi's sidekick on a road trip adventure. All the while, Papi engages
in criminal activity at their various stops, and at one point he murders a man in
front of his daughter, tells her he is simply suffering from an illness, and stages the
dead man's body at the wheel of his car to look like a suicide. While in Orlando, the
father leaves his daughter alone in the hotel room and forbids her to step outside.
She fears he will never return and spends her day watching television with the volume on high in order to drown out the sound of other children playing by the hotel
pool. Eventually, Papi does return, but the next morning there is a boot on the wheel
of his car, once again signaling his underground criminal activity, which his
daughter does not, or refuses to, fully comprehend. The daughter takes all this in
from the naïve perspective that shields her from the violent reality of the machismo
she idolizes. She is more concerned with visiting Disney World and Epcot Center,
and her biggest disappointment is that her father takes her to the Seaquarium
instead.

The transition from Orlando to the DR is sudden and suggests the translocality of the Dominican diaspora, for which the United States and the island dissolve
into each other as a borderless, neoliberal zone of migration, trade, and tourism.
The underground economy of Papi's criminal activities takes advantage of these
transnational routes of commerce, which the novel portrays through the image of
Papi's Mercedes-Benz speeding across an endless network of highways on both
sides of the border. Once back in the Dominican Republic, the hyperbolic portrayal
of Papi's promiscuity incorporates the language of the corporatist bureaucracy, and
his multiple relations with women are comparable to the clientelism of the Dominican authoritarian state:

Las novias de papi van más rápido que nadie y se han puesto ellas mismas una
oficina para organizarse, para ir concertando citas con papi, y ahora ellas tienen
su propia secretaria para que se comunique con la secretaria de papi (que entre

secretarias se entienden mejor) y son todas tan bellas y tantas (las secretarias tanto como las novias) que a veces tienen que alquilar un hotel para conocerse todas y se intercambian tarjetas de presentación que además del nombre, profesión y teléfono de la novia tienen el turno que les toca en la lista de citas de papi.[81]

Papi's girlfriends are faster than everybody and they've set up an office to organize themselves so they can coordinate their dates with Papi. They now have their own secretary who communicates with Papi's secretary (cuz secretaries understand each other best) and they're all beautiful and there are so many of them (both secretaries and girlfriends) that they sometimes have to rent out a hotel to get to know each other and trade business cards, which, besides the girlfriend's name, profession, and telephone number, also shows her turn on the long list of dates with Papi.[82]

The protagonist takes on an administrative role to process the claims of all the women who have given birth to one of the multitudes of Papi's children. The scenario parodies the paternalist role that the Dominican authoritarian state plays in the distribution of favors and entitlements to single mothers. The other women in the protagonist's immediate family—*la familia real*—also serve as administrative functionaries in the traffic in women, and while they feign sympathy, they also dehumanize Papi's lovers, whispering to each other, "*¡Cuantoooo cueroooo!*" ("What a bunch of sluts!"). The novel's carnivalesque narrative, which contains elements of magical realism, exaggerates the number of Papi's lovers to the point that the line they form reaches out into the street and to the malecón, and some of the offspring grow up waiting in line, underscoring the lifelong debt that the impoverished Dominican owes to the state for her survival. Through this dreamlike imagery, the novel transposes the logic of the administrative state to the sexual economy of male promiscuity and the *machista* values of virility and sexual potency. The governmentalities that administer the distribution of favors and entitlements is coextensive with the logic of masculine domination and the traffic in women. With the multiple references to Papi's upward mobility, material wealth, and conspicuous consumption, the novel portrays Papi as the embodiment of the authoritarian state that assumes the paternalist role in relation to its citizens/children and that attains wealth and power through unrestrained capitalist markets, where women exist and compete against each other as disposable commodity fetishes.

The novel uses absurdist imagery and hyperbolic description to portray the unchecked infrastructure growth that emerges from the neoliberalization of the Dominican economy. As new high-rise buildings and commercial centers multiply across the island, the narrator also chronicles the human cost of this economic boom. Workers fall into vats of wet cement, they are decapitated by falling debris, and Haitian workers fall from these construction sites and impale themselves on exposed rebar. These deaths are dismissed by the architects and the general public, who accuse the Haitian workers of throwing themselves off the buildings on purpose in order to survive the fall and claim disability benefits. The novel connects the island's economic growth to the dehumanization of its expendable population, just as Papi's *novias* become interchangeable and disposable bodies. Despite these destructive and deadly effects, the inaugurations of new construction projects are publicly celebrated with out-of-date images of Papi that festoon promotional materials and mass media. All aspects of governmentality are enmeshed with the neoliberal growth of the economy, from entitlements to the lottery, which raffles off appointments with Papi, to cash, jet skis, and electric knives, all to distract and placate the public. The unchecked growth and overpopulation of urban centers causes pollution and devastating environmental impacts on the island (this is a theme Indiana Hernández takes up again in her later novel, *La mucama de Oriunclé*).

In spite of the industrialization of the island economy, a wave of unemployed neighbors and distant relatives gather around the protagonist's home in hopes of obtaining some kind of handout from Papi's "official" family. They all claim some affiliation or parentage, yet they appear as an undifferentiated mass of human impoverishment. As Steven Gregory argues in *The Devil Behind the Mirror: Globalization and Politics in the Dominican Republic*, the neoliberal restructuring of the Dominican economy, which occurred under the presidencies of Joaquín Balaguer and especially Leonel Fernández, shifted away from agriculture toward manufacturing and the tourist industries. Yet these formal sectors of the economy exacerbated social divisions of labor and entrenched the inequities to access that reflect discrimination based on race, gender, and citizenship. The barriers to access spurred the creation of informal sectors, which could take the form of unlicensed food service to sex tourism and the drug trade. State and local authorities stringently police the informal sectors of the economy, which serve to criminalize the survival strategies that the poor, Black, and undocumented immigrants deploy in order to make a living on the margins of the formal economy.[83] Indiana Hernández's novel uses the hyperbolic imagery of magical realism and absurdist humor to show the deleterious effects of the neoliberal economy, which creates growth and wealth for the politically connected but also spreads poverty and idleness to the disenfranchised population on the island.

Transcultural Capital and the Simulacra of Authenticity

In *Masculine Domination*, Pierre Bourdieu argues that the androcentric vision of the world is founded on the social construction of male and female bodies, which "imposes itself as neutral and has no need to spell itself out in discourses aimed at legitimating it."[84] The "virilization" of boys and men is part of a symbolic order in which "all the differentiated and differentiating practices of ordinary existence (manly sports and games, hunting, etc.), encourages the break with the maternal world."[85] This process compels boys and men to occupy the public spaces of the marketplace and politics, while confining women to the domestic sphere. Bourdieu writes: "The explanation of the primacy granted to masculinity in cultural taxonomies lies in the logic of the economy of symbolic exchanges, and more precisely in the social construction of the relations of kinship and marriage alliance which assigns to women their social status as objects of exchange defined in accordance with male interests to help reproduce the symbolic capital of men."[86] Men accrue this symbolic capital through games and rituals that confer honor on those who can exert domination over other rivals. In the case of the male characters in Junot Díaz's fiction, the men play these games with each other as a way to mitigate their economically marginal status and the race and class discrimination they experience as Dominican migrants in the United States. As Bourdieu argues, "When the dominated apply to what dominates them the schemes that are the product of domination, or, to put it another way, when their thoughts and perceptions are structured in accordance with the very structures of the relation of domination that is imposed on them, and their acts of *cognition* are, inevitably, acts of *recognition*, submission."[87] When Yunior reproduces the symbolic violence of masculine domination that he learns from his father and brother, his self-reflexive, "narcissistic" narrative reveals his subaltern status as a racialized subject of the diaspora. The games he plays with the reader do not exculpate him from his violent and exploitative behaviors; instead, they allow the reader to see how Yunior has submitted to this symbolic economy in which power over others reaffirms an ostensibly authentic Dominican masculinity.

The paternal figure in Díaz's *TIHYLH* reflects the complicit critique of masculine domination that has appeared throughout the author's fiction, from *Drown* to *The Brief and Wondrous Life of Oscar Wao*. Like Papi in Indiana Hernández's novel, we see Díaz's recurring narrator, Yunior, waiting for his father's return from the United States in *Drown*, and like the female protagonist who idolizes her father and attempts to reproduce the material and bodily practices associated with his Dominican machismo, Yunior also fetishizes the figure of his absent father, but also fears and loathes his cruel authoritarianism and the abuse he metes out to his family. This includes the father's promiscuity and multiple extramarital affairs. Nevertheless, Yunior and his brother, Rafa, reproduce these behaviors in their own relations with women and each other.

Throughout the stories in *TIHYLH*, the narrative voice associated with Yunior's character engages directly with the reader and, in some cases, adopts the second-person voice in order to comment on and criticize his own toxic masculinity. These instances function as metafictional narrative devices that draw the reader's attention to their own expectations and consumption of the text. How much do the readers buy into Yunior's rationalizations for his toxic masculinity, while also assuming the critical distance that denounces these forms of sexual violence and domination? One of the ongoing conflicts in Díaz's fiction is Yunior's attempts to straddle these contradictory positions, and although the reader is encouraged to engage vicariously with this ethical ambivalence, she might not be so easily seduced into playing the narrator's literary game.

Another dual register that emerges from Yunior's heteroglossic narrative voice reflects, on the one hand, the experience and perspective of the upwardly mobile generation of Dominicans who have acquired levels of higher education and pursue careers in education, the arts, and white-collar professions. On the other hand, the games the narrator plays with the reader situate the consumption of the text in a field of knowledge and cultural production familiar to urban professionals and, in particular, non-Dominican readers whose interest in ethnic literature is consistent with a politics of self-aware whiteness. This is particularly notable in the scant use of Spanish in the text, even in dialogue that diegetically takes place among Spanish-speaking characters in the Dominican Republic.

The first story in this collection begins this metafictional game with the reader by setting up an ironic pose toward the narrator's toxic masculinity. By asking the reader to mitigate her judgment of Yunior's behavior, the story establishes him as a sympathetic but unreliable narrator. The reader is now engaged to condemn Yunior's rampant narcissism, while still empathizing with his self-awareness. The non-Latinx readers, particularly those in the professional fields of education and the creative arts, are often called upon to testify about their progressive bona fides in regard to race, gender, and sexual politics. The proliferation of whiteness studies and university and corporate workshops on white privilege and antiracism offers progressive readers a collective and public forum in which they can demonstrate their self-aware whiteness. The narrator in Díaz's fiction appropriates this reflexive pose in order to testify about his sexual indiscretions and masculine privilege. Nevertheless, as a Dominican male from the diasporic, working-class community in the Northeast, these progressive *testimonios* are partially shielded from the reader's critiques.

These games also allow Yunior to position himself as an autoethnographer with insider knowledge. He serves as a complicit interlocutor who can speak to different linguistic, ethnic, and class communities. He participates in the material and cultural practices that confer legitimacy in these various social formations, even though the dispositions that characterize one group are not accepted by members of another. In this way, Yunior embodies the diasporic habitus of being an insider/outsider in different and often conflicting ethnic, class, or gendered social formations. The metafictional games Yunior plays as a narrator allow him to reposition himself in order to elicit empathy while engaging in material and bodily practices that his readers find alternately strange and abhorrent. Yunior's games imagine a reader who will indulge his bad behavior as long as he demonstrates the self-awareness that has served as a mitigating positionality for the privileged classes. The reaction from Latina feminists has been quite different to the effusive accolades Díaz's fictions have received from the mainstream press and U.S. literary establishment, and their condemnation of the complicitous critique of Dominican machismo has extended to the author's own professional and personal relations with women of color.[88]

In 2018, just prior to public accusations of sexual harassment made against him by Latina writers, Junot Díaz published a lengthy confessional in the *New Yorker* in which he recounted his own experience as a victim of sexual violence.[89] The accusations against Díaz were serious enough for him to step down as a board member of the Pulitzer Prize Committee. A debate emerged over whether Díaz's stature in Latinx literature should be questioned or if criticism against him reaffirmed racist stereotypes of hypersexual Latino men who perpetrate violence against women.[90] Yomaira Figueroa-Vázquez writes, "I believe that Díaz's work does the important labor of bearing witness to how misogyny, gender violence, and patriarchy are formed and perpetuated. His actions, however, further reveal deeply entrenched forms of domination."[91] The controversy also reveals another aspect of Díaz's fiction and its prominence in U.S. ethnic literature and American studies curricula: how the Latinx experience is commoditized for a literary market and consumed by readers who include upwardly mobile racial, ethnic, and sexual minorities, as well as self-aware white elites. In the previous chapter, I explored this aspect of literary production in relation to the obstacles both Edwin Sánchez and Ángel Lozada faced when attempting to publish novels that did not fit the institutional paradigms of U.S. and Puerto Rican literary establishments. Ralph Rodríguez also underscores the way the publishing industry creates expectations for what constitutes Latinx literature through policing ethnic identities: "Moreover, this policing can lead to a cult of ethnicity that has deleterious effects on literature, for wittingly or not, it places a burden of representation on the writer. Publishing houses come to expect Latinx writers (all ethnic writers for that matter) to write on a certain set of themes, and if they do not, an agent or editor will often tell them that it is not ethnic enough, stifling their imaginations by forcing them into knowable boxes."[92] Consequently, when we consider how Díaz constructs a complicitous critique of masculine domination in his fiction, we must also situate these forms of cultural production in a field that is highly guarded and to which access is determined by the attainment of educational credentials and hegemonic forms of cultural capital. The dual positionality made operational by Díaz's narcissistic narratives straddles these reading communities by acknowledging "selling out" to white, hegemonic forms of material and bodily practices, while also reproducing the language, attitudes, and behaviors associated with "authentic" Dominican, working-class culture and social values.

This dual positionality also recalls the well-known parable by Jorge Luis Borges, "Borges y yo" ("Borges and I"). Reflecting on his authorial persona, Borges writes: "It is no effort for me to confess that he has achieved some valid pages, but those pages cannot save me, perhaps because what is good belongs to no one, not even to him, but rather to the language and to tradition. Besides, I am destined to perish, definitively, and only some instant of myself can survive in him. Little by little, I am giving over everything to him, though I am quite aware of his perverse custom of falsifying and magnifying things."[93] Through the character and narrative voice of Yunior, Díaz engages with the contradictory expectations of his diverse readership, which includes upwardly mobile people of color who expect a certain measure of cultural authenticity in Latinx literature, as well as self-aware whites who consume literature and culture that affirms their progressive values and attitudes toward communities of color and sexual minorities. Does Yunior serve as Díaz's alter ego, "falsifying and magnifying things?" As in Ángel Lozada's novel, there is an unstable distinction between Díaz the author and his recurring character. Ralph Rodríguez argues that these kinds of indeterminacies are not necessarily meant to be resolved, but instead force readers "to question why we lean so heavily on an author's identity in valuing a work of literature."[94] In the final story of *TIHYLH*, the character of Yunior relates how he is a tenured professor of creative writing at MIT, a position Junot Díaz holds at the time of this writing. Once again, the authorial persona, who up until the accusations of sexual harassment was a highly visible public intellectual, reveals himself while hiding behind the fictional narrator in his stories. This dual positionality is facilitated by transcultural capital, which the Latinx literary field generates for authors who are legible as sufficiently "ethnic" yet whose metafictional narratives expose and critique the very conditions which provide their access to a cultural marketplace. These games with the reader simultaneously establish an ironic complicity while also allowing for a metafictional back door through which the authorial persona can slip when questions of authenticity come knocking.

These literary games are especially relevant when engaging with depictions of sexual violence that invite a voyeuristic thrill, even when these fictions condemn and critique the violent acts and the sexist motivations behind them. However, Yunior tells his story from the perspective of an abusive sexual predator who turns a blind eye to the motivations behind his violent acts. He often resorts to characterizing his chronic philandering as a Dominican thing, behaviors and attitudes that are normalized and legitimated as culturally authentic in his ethnic and class heritage communities. Nevertheless, the narrative games Yunior plays with his readers reveal the childhood traumas that he suffered at the hands of his father and brother, the two male figures in his life who unapologetically embodied the values perpetuated by the legacies of masculine domination and Dominican machismo. In this way, Yunior's complicitous critique mirrors the preemptive testimony that Díaz published when he faced accusations of sexual harassment. The literary text serves to condemn masculine domination even as the purveyors of these literary voices (Yunior/Díaz) benefit from the cultural legitimacy that Dominican machismo confers on them in the eyes of their diverse readers.

The first and last stories in the collection frame the narrator's perspective and retelling of his personal experiences. Nearly all of the other stories remain in this first-person narrative voice. The short story, "Alma," is told from Yunior's perspective but in the second person. However, "Otravida Otravez" is the first-person account of Yasmin, one of Ramón's other women with whom he shares a life in the United States. The first and last stories are the most reflexive fictions, whose location in the overall organization of the collection not only draws attention to the vicious cycle of Yunior's infidelities and troubles with women, but also underscores Yunior's social and class positioning as a diasporic Dominican writer and tenured academic. With the first story, Yunior's reflexive, first-person narration focuses on his relationship with Magda, his Cuban American fiancée at the time, and their trip to the DR. Although they had planned this trip for some time, just prior to their vacation Magda learns of Yunior's affair with a coworker. They decide to go on vacation to the DR anyway, even though they both acknowledge that their relationship is unlikely to recover from his betrayal. As narrator and protagonist, Yunior addresses the reader in a fraternal tone and offers advice on how to manage having multiple sexual partners while maintaining an innocent pose. He characterizes the homosocial communities that are involved in his troubled relationship with Magda as "his boys" and "her girls." These gendered social formations perpetuate the *machista* values that encourage men to have multiple sexual partners. "His boys" and "her girls" wage a battle of the sexes in which men and women either stand in solidarity with their ethnic brothers and sisters or undermine each other by stealing one another's sexual and romantic partners.

Throughout the story, Yunior considers his dual status as an island-born Dominican who makes an effort to reconnect with his family and early childhood conditions of rural poverty and deprivation, as well as a returning migrant who has achieved considerable success through higher education and as an academic professional. He resents Magda because she thwarts his efforts to reassume his status as an authentic Dominican. Yunior had plans to stay with his grandfather and explore some areas of the island's interior. Magda, on the other hand, has an emotional meltdown and insists on leaving early for their reservations at one of the largest and most developed tourist resorts on the island, Casa de Campo. Although Yunior concedes to placate Magda, the change in plans provokes him to assume the ironic pose of a postmodern *plátano* who can stay at luxury resorts his family never could have afforded when he was a child. His attempts to engage with the resort staff, as if he were on equal terms, fail because the local Dominicans recognize the all-too-familiar awkwardness of the diasporic Dominican who returns as a tourist but clumsily tries to assert his cultural and class solidarity. Yunior's attempts to recuperate his connection to the DR are further undermined by a literal return to the native soil that occurs when he meets two other Dominican men, a character he calls the Vice President and his bodyguard, Bárbaro. The homosocial bond they form not only reaffirms the values of Dominican machismo but also underscores the link between state power, economic mobility, and masculine domination.

The narrative voice also uses the subjunctive and conditional to draw attention to the story's narrative devices: "If this were another kind of story, I'd tell you about the sea."[95] This metadiscursive modality allows Yunior to describe the impoverished conditions on the island from both the insider perspective—his family home and the street where he grew up—and the outsider perspective as a diasporic Dominican who is no longer bound by the economic conditions that were part of his childhood experience. Yunior is hyperconscious of his dual status and that of his reader. At the resort, he chafes at the thought that he is among the wealthy and elite, and that he should identify more closely with the staff who change the sheets: "Let's just say my abuelo has never been, and neither has yours. This is where the Garcías and the Colóns come to relax after a long month of oppressing the masses, where the tutumpotes can trade tips with their colleagues from abroad. Chill here too long and you'll be sure to have your ghetto pass revoked, no questions asked."[96] Yunior also characterizes his discomfort through the racial difference between

Magda, the European male tourists who flirt with her, and himself. He always associates himself and his boys with Black men, or "niggers" as he constantly repeats. Magda is an "octoroon," or light-skinned Cuban American. Yunior's self-aware narrative and his ambivalent racial and class positioning brings to mind Frantz Fanon's analysis of the "black skin, white mask" syndrome that he diagnosed as the Caribbean colonial condition. Fanon argues that Blacks (he uses the word *nègres* in the original French) will uncritically adopt and reproduce the language as well as the material and bodily practices of the dominant white culture, particularly in the colonial context of the Caribbean, but also in the diaspora and the spaces of the metropolis where they acquire economic, cultural, and social capital. This is the "white mask" Blacks and colonized people of color wear when they uncritically buy into the dominant cultural values that facilitate upward mobility and distance themselves from their heritage cultures, their Créole languages, their racial identities, or their working-class origins—all of which they now perceive as unevolved, retrograde, and ultimately abject.[97]

Yunior is not deluded into thinking he can achieve whiteness by adopting the material and bodily practices that comprise the European and Anglo-American habitus of the wealthy and elite. However, the reflexive metafictional discourse of his stories draws attention to the conditions of cultural production that give legitimacy to the author's work. Yunior's fictions are surrounded and acclaimed by the publications and cultural institutions that cater to readers who share these hegemonic forms of educational and cultural capital. In contrast to Fanon's figure of the assimilated Black man, Yunior identifies as Black Dominican, particularly according to racial categories in the United States. As Ginetta Candelario argues, Dominican racial politics are structured on othering Haitians as the abject *negros*, whereas Dominicans of Afro-Caribbean descent perform different shades of whiteness, which are nevertheless marked by how much "black behind the ear" a person is perceived to retain.[98] As a writer and tenured professor at MIT, which the reader learns in the final story, Yunior has the cultural and educational capital that gives him access to critical forms of racial discourse. The reader does not encounter Yunior in a university setting, although he alludes to conversations and interactions that take place "at work" (this is where he meets the woman, Cassandra, with whom he cheats on Magda). However, Yunior's dual narrative voice often betrays his struggles with the imposter syndrome, not only as an academic from working-class, Dominican origins, but also as a working-class Dominican who has acquired elite forms of capital that are legitimated and regulated by the dominant white culture.

Even though Yunior addresses a Dominican male reader who shares his diasporic experience, the published book—authored by Junot Díaz—in which this voice articulates his dual status is framed by blurbs from the most prestigious U.S. literary and cultural journals, magazines, and newspapers. Neither Yunior nor Díaz attempts to masquerade as white, yet the narrative games they play place a Black mask on the non-Dominican readers who confer critical legitimacy on these literary works. This allows the educated and cultural elite to position themselves among the insider community of Black and mixed-race Dominicans and Latinxs of the Caribbean. Nevertheless, Yunior's discomfort at the expensive resort underscores the ethical and existential contradictions of a native son who is slumming it as an upwardly mobile expat. These contradictions extend to the non-Dominican reader who vicariously empathizes with the toxic masculinity that is supposedly a sign of Dominican cultural authenticity.

An Undead Economy (The Return of Masculine Domination)

Rita Indiana Hernández's *Papi* also explores the contradictions that emerge when countercultural expressions of rebellious youth culture serve to reproduce the commodified forms of masculine domination. The story follows the young protagonist from her early childhood fantasies as she enters into early adolescence. Now a rebellious teenager who skateboards and wears T-shirts emblazoned with satanic images from heavy metal bands, she becomes the target of neighbors and family members for her gender nonconformity. She and her friends are brutalized by a national campaign of compulsory heteronormativity, and she recounts how the heavy metal subculture is scapegoated as a public menace. Those who display any of the paraphernalia associated with this group have their hair shorn and their clothes and music collections confiscated. The novel depicts this form of censorship and scapegoating as a reaction to the influence of global pop culture, which is contrasted with the authentic and autochthonous Caribbean culture, music, and forms of religious syncretism. As a musician and performer, Rita Indiana Hernández has been a part of the alternative and hardcore music scene in the Dominican Republic, and other bands such as Abaddon RD and Archaios have combined some Caribbean influences in their heavy metal sound. Nevertheless, these musical forms are often dismissed as foreign imports that do not reflect Dominican national culture. Although the novel explores how the heavy metal subculture challenges this censorship, it also shows how the music and its associated merchandise are lucrative commercial enterprises, even when the purchase and exchange of music and clothing go underground.

The protagonist's sexual maturation also underscores the contradictions in her desire to appropriate dominant forms of masculinity while deviating from the heteronormative logic of gender conformity. Back in the Dominican Republic, the narrator recounts her experiences at a summer camp and how she and the other adolescents begin to reach puberty. Once again, the protagonist reveals her lesbian desire, this time for one of the female swim instructors, while the other adolescents begin experimenting sexually with each other. The novel conveys the sexual maturation through images of disgust and abjection, in particular descriptions of rotting food, disease, and bodily fluids. One of her more sexually mature female friends, Julianna, tells her an urban legend about a man with AIDS who cuts himself and contaminates vats of Coca-Cola with his infected blood. The novel integrates these abject images with descriptions of sexual experimentation as a way to demystify the coming-of-age narrative, which often depicts adolescent sexual awakening as an ecstatic revelation of desire and identity fulfillment. Instead, the abject images in *Papi* confuse erotic attachments and bodily boundaries, and sexual desire is stripped of its romantic idealism as well as its heteronormative determinism.

The deconstruction of adolescent sexuality culminates in Papi's actual death. While at the summer camp, the protagonist's mother suddenly appears to announce that Papi has been killed by a hit-and-run driver, and the protagonist imagines her father's body being pulverized by the runaway vehicle. The images of abject adolescent bodies suddenly transition to images of the crushed and mangled body of the patriarchal figure. Papi is completely dehumanized and the protagonist visualizes him as a crash test dummy flung across the highway. As in the previous passage that depicted Papi's body melting, in this episode the father's body is liquified and destroyed at a moment when the protagonist begins to experiment with nonconforming gender identity and queer sexuality. The reader later learns that the father was murdered—shot in the head—and that the protagonist's fantasy of the hit-and-run accident reflected her experiences and memories of riding with her father in his car, moments when she felt closest to him and imagined herself as the heroic sidekick in a surreal road trip narrative.

The father's death interrupts the protagonist's maturation and induces a return to childhood dependency, which is once again mitigated through consumption and consumer goods:

> *Cuando vuelvo a abrir los ojos tengo la boca llena de Count Chocula y leche y babeo, estoy desnuda en una silla del comedor y por el balcón sigue entrando un solecito, mami me estriega un brazo con una esponja y me avisa: "llamaron esta mañana, mataron a tu papá."*[99]

> When I open my eyes again, my mouth is full of Count Chocula and milk and I'm drooling. I'm naked and sitting at the dining room table while sun continues to filter in through the balcony. Mami scrubs my arm with a sponge and reminds me: They called this morning; they killed your father.[100]

The breakfast cereal she consumes emblematizes infantile tastes and dispositions, and the description of its textures, sweetness, and how it colors the milk conveys a borderless, presubjective state. In order to emerge from this regressive state, the family initiates a series of rituals and gendered bodily practices that reinforce compulsory heteronormativity. The protagonist is taken to a beauty salon to prepare her for the wake and funeral services, which contrasts sharply with the rebellious subculture of heavy metal and demarcates a highly segregated gendered space where her previous androgyny is transformed by means of standard forms of feminine dress and makeup. Throughout the novel and particularly in these chapters, the major milestones in the protagonist's childhood and early adolescence are mediated through consumerism, brand-name merchandise, and mass media. Just as Papi's hypermasculine body is constituted by the clothes, colognes, shoes, jewelry, and other accessories that convey his social mobility and male privilege, the

young protagonist also constructs her identity and her awareness of social relations through the proliferation of consumer goods and the rhetorical structures
of marketing and advertisement. This coming-of-age story narrates more than the
young protagonist's journey toward maturation; it also reveals how both heteronormative and queer identities rely on consumerism and all its paraphernalia as
signposts for mapping out memory and history.

The novel ends with two starkly contrasting sequences. The first continues to
recount the events that follow Papi's death, and the narrative parodies the magical realism of Gabriel García Márquez's *Los funerales de la Mamá Grande*. At one
point, when Papi's coffin, a funerary cortège, and various accoutrements are air-
dropped onto a crowd of mourners that has gathered at Papi's rural, childhood
home, a note that lists the container's contents includes a eulogy written by García
Márquez. The novel uses the carnivalesque imagery of the lower bodily stratum to
depict not only Papi's rotting corpse, but also the grotesque mass of mourners.
Papi's death also occasions an opportunity for mass media and the tourist industry to converge on the crowd, which underscores how the patriarchal figure
remains at the center of economic activity and consumerism, even in death.

The protagonist, however, refuses to believe that the corpse is actually her father;
instead, she believes it is a robot or replica made in Miami that has been perfected
by mortuary science. She is even unconvinced by the dental work she sees when
she opens the corpse's mouth. She removes one of the dead man's teeth and flees
with it into the forest as her family and the crowd of mourners descend on her for
desecrating her father's corpse. She swallows the tooth, which invokes the legend
of the Buddha's tooth, a sacred relic that a female disciple saved from the Buddha's
funeral pyre. The legend claims that whoever possesses the tooth has a divine right
to rule.[101] However, swallowing Papi's tooth, as Judith Butler argues through the
Freudian principle of erotogenic transferability of body parts, also symbolizes the
lesbian phallus.[102] In this way, the protagonist incorporates into her own body
the phallic power she has emulated in her father:

> *Papi estaba en mí y yo en papi. Yo hasta me chupaba la salsa picante de las cutícu-
> las impecables de papi. Yo era igualita a papi. Yo era papi. Yo soy Papi.*[103]

> Papi was in me, and I was in Papi. I even licked the salsa picante from Papi's
> impeccable cuticles. I was exactly the same as Papi. I was Papi. I am Papi.[104]

Juan Duchesne-Winter argues that the use of the lower-case "p" for *papi* in the original Spanish-language novel is a way to emasculate the father figure and delegiti-
mize his deification.[105] This passage, which ends with the word "*Papi*" capitalized,
shows that the protagonist, after ingesting the phallic tooth, assumes the role
of messianic leader to the Dominican nation. Along with her cousins, Puchy and
Millie, she becomes a fugitive and leads a cult that has formed around the con-
spiracy theory that her father is not really dead. The novel relates these adventures
with allusions to evangelical movements that have become pervasive in Latin
America and the Caribbean, as well as the cult followings that continue to lionize

despotic figures like Trujillo. The collective desire to place Papi at the apex of the Dominican nation helps to reanimate his corpse. He reappears as a mute zombie and gestures toward his open mouth, demanding that his daughter return the tooth she swallowed and has already defecated. She, in turn, becomes a kind of priestess who distributes favors and indulgences to Papi's many followers. The mass movement degenerates into a series of hysterical sightings of Papi, a spectacle of unhinged devotees, and finally a military crackdown and genocide of Papi's followers. In a few short pages, the novel synthesizes so much of the Dominican Republic's history of totalitarian dictatorships, the delusional psychology of religious mass movements, and the Latin American literary traditions that have engaged with elements of the fantastic to depict these recurring, violent repressions. The compulsion to consume, even in the symbolic swallowing of Papi's tooth, pervades the history, political institutions, and forms of embodiment that enshrine and reproduce masculine domination at all levels of society. As Bourdieu argues, "When we try to understand masculine domination we are therefore likely to resort to modes of thought that are the product of domination."

In contrast, the final chapter takes a sudden turn to the anticlimactic and focuses on the protagonist and her mother, who up until this point had only been a minor character, completely overshadowed by the father's hypermasculinity. The narrative shifts from the graphic and surreal violence of the previous chapters and recounts how the protagonist's mother is hospitalized after having several benign tumors removed. Duchesne-Winter argues that this final chapter shows how the protagonist goes from being "*la hija de papi*" to "*la hija de mami*":

> *La hija de mami es la hija adorable de mami, pero ella no necesariamente está en mami ni mami está en ella, sino que ella lee y escribe junto a mami el enigma abierto, interrumpible, los signos opacos, de un cuerpo de hija de mami.*[106]

> Mami's daughter is Mami's adorable daughter, but she is not necessarily in Mami nor is Mami in her, rather she reads and writes alongside Mami the open enigma, interruptible, the opaque signs, of a body of Mami's daughter. (my translation)

The protagonist visits her mother while she recovers from surgery, and although the focus is no longer on the material and cultural practices that perpetuate masculine domination, a number of references to brand-name goods and television programs demonstrates how the pervasive consumer culture continues to define key moments in the protagonist's life. Even as the focus shifts to an intimate relationship of caregiving between women, the protagonist still fears that zombie Papi will reappear at any moment, in particular when she goes to get her mother snacks from the vending machines, a location where many of the hysterical sightings of Papi's reanimated corpse occurred among his cult followers. Even in death, the specter of Papi's hypermasculinity is most active around automated forms of consumerism. The protagonist also recounts how her aunt takes her to a concert while Mami is still convalescing, and she watches as Dominican president Joaquín

Balaguer enters the cathedral where the concert is being held. Blind and infirm, Balaguer is helped to his seat by his sister as the protagonist fantasizes about laying her hands on him to heal his blindness. Balaguer was a ruthless *caudillo* who imprisoned, tortured, and disappeared thousands of his political opponents, just as had been portrayed in the previous chapter. Although she is "*la hija de mami*" in this chapter, the protagonist continues to gravitate toward the patriarchal figure at the apex of a society built on masculine domination. Nevertheless, Mami has the last word in this novel, and she simply states that she will need her daughter's help from now on to go to the bathroom. The descending action of this final chapter and its quiet denouement bring the family of women into a closer, more interdependent relationship. However, just as at the beginning when Papi's visits were characterized as a monstrous return of the repressed, the young girl is still haunted by the desire to embrace masculine domination and all its violent forms—a compulsion inculcated in her by the inescapable consumerism that structures her queer Dominican habitus.

PLAYING OFF THE FIELD

In Díaz's *TIHYLH*, while the metafictional games serve to decolonize Dominican masculinity and its resurgence along the transnational routes of the diaspora, they nonetheless carry the baggage of the violent material and bodily practices they purport to contest. We see this in the way the opening story articulates a dual register that reflects the contradictions in Yunior's diasporic identity. The story promotes conspiratorial familiarity with which Yunior addresses the reader, as if we were among "his boys," but also as if we were outsiders who need to be initiated into secret knowledge about the DR from an insider's perspective. On the one hand, the story relates the mundane series of events that lead to Yunior's breakup with Magda. At this register, the reader is in on the secrets of philandering Dominican machos. Yunior claims he cannot speak for all Dominican men, even though Magda's friends and family attribute his chronic infidelities to his Dominican machismo. On the other hand, the story assumes the reader knows little about the DR, and Yunior serves as an autoethnographer whose experiences convey a diasporic Dominican sensibility as he describes the landscape, the people, and the history of his homeland. It is through the dual register of the narrative voice that Yunior's otherwise uncompelling story of yet another failed relationship in a string of failures articulates how fraught Yunior's return to the DR really is, and how the story's metafictional discourse deconstructs the figurative language that links diasporic identity to a compulsory return to the native land.

The scene in which Yunior accompanies the VP and his bodyguard on a nighttime trip to the rural outskirts of the resort village brings these dual registers together to depict how Yunior simultaneously occupies contradictory positionings in his relationship to the DR, and that a literal return to the native soil does not allow for a full recuperation of what Yunior has lost due to his diasporic experience. First, we see Yunior's stubborn dependency on measuring his self-worth on his ability to seduce women. Even though he is breaking up with Magda, he trains his Don Juan gaze on other women at the resort to find a quick replacement for the woman he is about to permanently lose. This sense of urgency to hook up with anyone even slightly attractive shows how his masculinity is contingent on the ability to play the game of seducing and sexually conquering women. Second, Yunior's conversations with the VP and his bodyguard reposition him as a player representing a homosocial community. The three commiserate over the inscrutability of women and the continual need to conquer and deceive them in order to remain in good standing among other Dominican machos. After copious amount of cognac, the VP tells Yunior he wants to show him "the birthplace of the nation."[107]

His ride out to the rural Dominican countryside with the VP and his bodyguard synthesizes these multiple contradictions by invoking a widely used literary trope: the return to the native soil. This return to the earth and the homeland also reaffirms the homosociality that often compels Yunior to adopt the *machista* material and bodily practices of his Dominican peers. Finally, the scene invokes this literary tradition and reaffirms the habitus of masculine domination through a reflexive narrative that invites the reader to engage the scene with skepticism and irony. Yunior also conveys a sense of danger, since as Díaz portrayed in *The Brief Wondrous Life of Oscar Wao*, these remote, rural outskirts past the cane fields are where Trujillo's and Balaguer's men would often take their victims to beat, torture, and kill. At one point, the VP's bodyguard, Bárbaro, who had gotten sentimental and showed vulnerability on the car ride over, produces a machine gun as they make their way to a deep fissure—the supposed Cave of the Jagua, the birthplace of the Taínos. The two men hoist Yunior by the ankles and lower him down into the hole. However, as he peers into the abyss with a powerful flashlight, rather than gain some insight into his Dominican origins, he can only think of Magda and how they first met: "And that's when I know it's over. As soon as you start thinking about the beginning, it's the end."[108]

On the one hand, Yunior's peering into the abyss is emblematic of the *real maravilloso* that Alejo Carpentier described in his introduction to *The Kingdom of This World*. The *real maravilloso* is the amazement or *asombro* that overwhelms the subjects of history who perceive themselves through the Latin American landscape, its monuments, and its built spaces. The "real" in Latin America is "marvelous" because it synthesizes the myriad contradictions of its history of conquest, colonization, genocide, revolution, and dictatorship, as well as the many instances of U.S. military, political, and economic intervention. For Carpentier, there is a collective faith that allows the Latin American subjects of history to perceive the marvelous in the real. He writes: "*¿Pero qué es la historia de América toda sino una crónica de lo real maravilloso?*"[109] ("But what is the history of all of America if not a chronicle of the real marvelous?"; my translation). The way the scene in Junot Díaz's short story invokes the *real maravilloso* also distinguishes itself from the way he integrates elements of magical realism in *The Brief Wondrous Life of Oscar Wao*. In both cases, the narrative depiction of a return to the wild interior of the DR conveys the island's violent history—the *fukú* that has cursed Dominicans for centuries. Yet in *Oscar Wao*, the amazement that overwhelms the characters is with the supernatural, which again is traced back to the Black Caribbean heritage, religious beliefs, and folklore that pervades the Dominican diasporic imaginary. In this short story, however, one way to read Yunior's amazement is at the level of bare life in its most naked form. The scene lacks the fantastical animism with which Díaz portrayed sexual and political violence in *Oscar Wao*. Yunior's descent into the abyss is not only a literal return to the native soil and the birthplace of the nation, it is also a gaze into his own Caribbean Blackness and its origins in the violent history of the DR. In his short story, "Monstro," Díaz takes up this theme through a sci-fi allegory, in which the Blackness—or *negrura*—of Haitian zombies becomes the return of the repressed history of racism and genocide that has been normalized in Dominican society.[110] Frantz Fanon describes a similar gesture made by the "educated Negro" who strives to return to his people: "And it is with rage in his mouth and abandon in his heart that he buries himself in the vast black abyss."[111] Yet, on the other hand, Yunior's narrative voice never ceases to convey the ironic perspective of the outsider who does not fully embody Latin Americanness nor shares the collective faith in its traditions, and the acquisition of U.S. educational and cultural capital through the experience of the diaspora puts the *asombro* of the *real maravilloso* in quotation marks for Yunior and the other postmodern *plátanos* reading about his exploits.

Despite the telluric trope and gaze into the abyss that otherwise would provide Yunior a transformative experience, his self-awareness and ironic pose serve to undermine the redemptive return to the native soil. The scene also invokes the literary and artistic traditions that portray the landscape as the female body. The Cave of the Jagua to which the VP and Bárbaro take Yunior, and which is supposedly the birthplace of the Taíno people, is clearly a metaphor for the vagina and the womb. In fact, as Yunior is lowered into the pit and he fails to have a transformative experience, he begins to cry not because he is overwhelmed with the power of the *real maravilloso*, but because he knows he will no longer have access to Magda as a sex object. When his companions lift him out of the hole and see him crying, the VP says, "God, you don't have to be a pussy about it."[112] This admonishment synthesizes the narrative and affective contradictions that constitute Yunior's masculine identity as well as his voice as a narrator. It conveys the *machista* values of stoicism and impermeability that are part of Yunior's habitus as a heterosexual Dominican male. Its dramatic irony also unmasks Yunior's self-loathing as a failed macho who, although he reproduces the abusive and exploitative sexual practices that are expected of Dominican machos, the cultural and educational capital he has acquired as a diasporic Dominican have "feminized" his perspective, and it is from this critical position that he sees himself through the eyes of the women he has betrayed.

This form of self-reflection appears again in the story "Alma," when Yunior recounts another of his failed relationships through the second-person narrative voice. This story also performs metadiscursively by providing the collection with its title. When his girlfriend, Alma, reads his journal and discovers all the other women with whom he has had sexual relations, Yunior tries to assume his Dominican macho privilege: "You glance at the offending passages. Then you look at her and smile a smile your dissembling face will remember until the day you die. Baby, you say, baby, this is part of my novel. This is how you lose her."[113] Yunior confronts his *donjuanismo* from Alma's perspective, which he internalizes and claims he will remember until the day he dies. Yunior's failure to live up to the *machista* values he reproduces reflects his dual status as a Dominican who narrates his experiences from both inside and outside his heritage culture.

Yunior's skepticism about the redemptive power of his return to the native soil also establishes the empathy he hopes to inculcate in his educated readers, who would recognize the clichés in this scene and would expect the transformative experience to fail. As Christopher González argues in his reading of this story, Yunior's failed relationships with women can be regarded as failures only from the position of his romantic optimism and his assertions that he is not like those other Dominican men.[114] The games he plays with his readers simultaneously deconstruct his embodiment of Dominican machismo as well as the postmodern ironic gaze with which he distances himself from the unshakeable compulsions that define his Dominican masculinity. The abyss into which he gazes does not provide Yunior nor his readers with a moment of redemption, yet it becomes the ground zero of the narrative collapse into which toxic masculinity and ironic detachment undermine one another. For the readers, the risk of playing this game is that we empathize with an abusive character who uses women to sustain the fiction of his Dominican cultural authenticity, regardless of our level of "wokeness" that allows us to see through the literary clichés. We empathize with a toxic *machista* who really isn't all that bad and not like those other Dominican men, whom we perceive without the ironic quotation marks that seduce us into complicity with Yunior's acts of sexual violence. The symbolic violence this narrative game perpetrates on the reader is convincing us that Yunior's vulnerability—his crying like a "pussy"—lies somewhere outside his toxic masculinity, when it really is one of *donjuanismo*'s most successful facilitating strategies.

Another way the narrative voice in Díaz's fiction articulates a complicitous critique of Dominican machismo is through the use of the second-person narrator, which in most cases represents Yunior's self-reflexive consciousness and thoughts. In stories like "How to Date a Black Girl, Brown Girl, White Girl, or Halfie" from *Drown*, or "The Cheater's Guide to Love" in *TIHYLH*, the second-person narrator is also the protagonist of the stories, in each case Yunior at different moments of his life. These stories also portray Yunior's many sexual exploits and infidelities to women, as does the novel, *Oscar Wao*, in which Yunior develops a tumultuous sexual relationship with Oscar's sister, Lola. In the cases of "How to Date a Black Girl" and "The Cheater's Guide to Love," the second-person narrator depicts Yunior's womanizing career in the form of instructions to other wannabe *tígueres*, and the use of the second-person creates a narrative instability and is as much an address to the coconspiring reader as it is an ironical pose that allows Yunior to observe himself as he reproduces the *machista* behaviors he deplores in his father and brother. In "How to Date a Black Girl," although the self-help parody ostensibly addresses other young men who want to learn how to "date" girls from different racial backgrounds, the "you" in the story describes Yunior's attempts to score with girls and his own insecurities about his race and social class.

As a self-help manual for racialized seductions, the story employs the second-person narrative voice in what Matt DelConte calls a "completely-coincident narration," when "the narrator, protagonist, and naratee are all the same and exist on the same diegetic plane."[115] Marisel Moreno analyzes the parodic reproduction of self-help discourse in Díaz's story and argues that the underlining irony shows the tenuous grasp the narrator has on his authority as an expert on multiracial dating; after all, Yunior very rarely "scores" and the second-person narrative suggests some of his conquests could be more fantasy than reality.[116] Furthermore, self-help discourse reflects the dominant cultural paradigm in the United States that promotes individualistic conceptualizations of subjectivity, in which the subject is an autonomous, rational actor whose life choices and behaviors can have a transformational impact on the individual's social status and sense of self-worth. Heidi Marie Rimke argues, "Self-help literature, which exalts the individual over the social (and negates the inherent sociality of being) is elaborately consistent with the political rationalities promoted in advanced liberal democracies. Self-help literature aids in the production, organization, dissemination and implementation of particular liberal modes of truth about the social world."[117] Díaz's story demonstrates how the transcultural habitus, through which Dominican men of the diaspora embody the doxa that govern their masculine identities, lies at the intersection of the traditional Dominican values that promote male sexual promiscuity and the neoliberal U.S. values that promote the ethos of self-economizing, in which every individual is a potential entrepreneur of the self.

Once again, the narrator plays a game with the complicitous reader in which the objective is to deconstruct the cultural codes that legitimate heteronormative masculinity and the rationalistic thinking that establishes these norms as achievable and conquerable goals toward self-improvement and authenticity. Despite the preordained hardships and histories of failure that Yunior identifies as the *fukú americanus*, the *Domo economicus*—the self-economizing Dominican macho—is tirelessly engaged with the payoffs from playing against the odds and accumulating social and economic capital. As a "postmodern *plátano*," Yunior is skeptical of the promises that the *Domo economicus* holds out as a transformational ethos, since its ideological affiliation with rationalistic individualism serves to isolate subjects into constant competition. Nevertheless, Yunior is embedded in the transcultural habitus where these discourses and behavioral norms set the stage for Dominican men to perform as social agents and economic actors. Therefore, his narrative games help to dedoxify his own reproduction of the erotic games and self-economizing logic that can serve as forms of symbolic violence.

Reprising the self-help discourse he used in "How to Date a Black Girl," Yunior employs the second-person narrative voice once again in "The Cheater's Guide to Love" in order to convey metafictionally the embodied economies that allow cultural and social critique to circulate as wealth-producing texts. No one benefits more from a self-help book than its author, who seeks to capitalize on a store of knowledge gained through education and experience. In "The Cheater's Guide to Love," Yunior recounts his numerous sexual exploits and infidelities to his girl-friend, as well as all the rationalizations and self-recriminations he shares with his friend and coconspirator, Elvis. By the end of the story, Yunior's girlfriend has left him and, as a final gesture to expose his checkered sexual history, she sends him a folder with all the emails and photos from "his cheating days."[118] As they read the incriminating emails, Elvis tells Yunior, "You should really write the cheater's guide to love."[119] The reader becomes aware that the so-called self-help "guide" is Yunior's attempt at redemption as well as remuneration, because even though his writing "feels like hope," as a self-help manual the text serves to individualize his experi-ence and allows him to claim ownership and profit from it.

In *Distinction*, Bourdieu states, "Intellectuals could be said to believe in the representation—literature, theatre, painting—more than in the things represented, whereas people chiefly expect representations and the conventions which govern them to allow them to believe 'naively' in the things represented."[120] This calls to mind the ending of "The Cheater's Guide to Love" and the two readers of the text: Yunior's friend Elvis—a well-experienced cheater and "postmodern *plátano*" himself—and the implied reader—who occupies a space of literary appreciation and discernment. This narrative doubling creates a critical reflexivity that objec-tifies the rules of the game the narrator plays with the implied reader. The com-plicitous critique of Dominican machismo is articulated, as Bourdieu argues, "at the level of the field of positions [from which it is] possible to grasp both the generic interests associated with the fact of taking part in the game and the specific inter-ests attached to the different positions, and, through this, the form and content of the self-positionings through which these interests are expressed."[121] Not only is the reader obliged to examine the position from which he or she reads "The Cheat-er's Guide to Love" (both as fiction and as self-help manual), but the metafictional narrative doubles back onto the narrator's voice and undermines his authorial per-sona; it was his girlfriend, after all, who compiled the disparate texts and bound them for Yunior to read.

Later, as an adult and "postmodern *plátano*," Yunior narrates his own machismo and womanizing through the schemes of perception of the dominated, having been dominated by his father, his brother, and by his experience as an economically disadvantaged person of color. A dispositional analysis—one that reads Yunior's narrative as a complicitous critique—moves beyond the forced choice between mechanical coercion and voluntary consent. This reading shows how Yunior exposes the rules of the game as he plays it, a game whose symbolic violence is exerted in the context of colonialism, racism, misogyny, and homophobia. These are the "structuring structures" that constitute the diasporic Dominican habitus in contemporary conditions of neoliberalism and transnational globalism. The metafictional elements in Díaz's fiction epitomize what Linda Hutcheon calls the "narcissistic narrative," which "demands that [the reader] participate, that he engage himself intellectually, imaginatively, and affectively in its co-creation."[122] The playful narrative, with its self-aware poses and hybrid linguistic registers, is the *Domo economicus*'s testimonial of how he has paid the price for negotiating a contested masculine identity under conditions of racism, economic inequality, and colonialism while, nevertheless, enjoying the benefits of social and cultural capital that come with the violent masculine domination he critiques himself for reproducing. As Indiana Hernández's novel and Díaz's short story collection suggest, the logic of masculine domination threatens to emerge from ostensibly safe spaces of communitarian discourse and practice, perhaps most uncannily from queer embodiments of traditional gender norms or the pages of semiautobiographical Latinx fiction. The embodied economy of the diaspora offers queer and decolonial discourses to dedoxify the hegemonic cultural norms of masculine domination. However, the very literary implementations of these disruptive strategies can also embed the diasporic subject in a field of cultural production where the rules of the game redeploy the structures of power that these works of fiction seek to unmask and contest.

CHAPTER 4

The Gentrification of Our Dreams in Lin-Manuel Miranda's Musical Theater

Part of the inertia of the structures of social space results from the fact that they are inscribed in physical space and cannot be modified except by a work of trans-plantation, a moving of things and an uprooting or deporting of people, which itself presupposes extremely difficult and costly social transformations.
—Pierre Bourdieu, "Site Effects"

They are all counting on me to succeed.
I am the one who made it out!
The one who always made the grade.
But maybe I should have just stayed home . . .

—Nina Rosario, In the Heights

In one of the most poignant scenes of *In the Heights*, the neighborhood matriarch Abuela Claudia raises her winning lottery ticket to the heavens and asks the spirit of her long-deceased mother, "And ay mamá / What do you do when your / dreams come true? / I've spent my life / inheriting / dreams from you."[1] Abuela Claudia's signature song, "Paciencia y fe," epitomizes her credo that better days will come with patience and faith, and like the other characters in the show, Abuela Claudia is unprepared when circumstances contrive to situate her before that longed-for inflection point. Abuela Claudia has only ever lived in the urban spaces of poverty, hard work, and low wages, first as young girl in the impoverished neighborhood of La Víbora in Havana, then as an immigrant in the working-class Washington Heights of NYC. Abuela Claudia has grown accustomed to deferring her dreams of a better life, so when the moment for decisive action arrives, she does not have the ready knowledge of what to do with her ninety-six-thousand-dollar winnings. Abuela Claudia is disposed to confront and accept the vicissitudes of deprivation and precarity, not the empowerment of wealth and economic security. She inherits and has internalized her mother's dreams, with which she has always mitigated her dislocation and precarious economic conditions. These dreams survive as part of her diasporic habitus—that is, the embodied array of social dispositions that is shaped as much by tradition and conventional wisdom as it is by the physical and social spaces in which she has lived all her life.[2] Abuela Claudia is disposed to live off a dream deferred, and when it finally materializes, she faces a critical moment of doubt in everything she has held dear.

Similarly, in Miranda's *Hamilton*, it is the character of Eliza Hamilton whose song at the finale delivers a powerful invocation of the theme of yearning and doubt. As the betrayed wife and widow, Eliza sings about preserving Alexander's legacy after his death, but wonders, "Will they tell my story?"[3] The question suggests to the audience that Eliza is the hidden voice behind Alexander Hamilton's story, as Ron Chernow's biography—Miranda's source text—suggests with the epilogue dedicated to Hamilton's widow and her efforts to preserve her husband's place in U.S. history.[4] Yet as the character in Miranda's musical retelling of that story, and through the show's race-conscious casting, Eliza's question also conveys the voice of the minoritized subjects that the musical *Hamilton* ostensibly mutes. The audience must consider whose legacy the musical portrays, and the indeterminacy of this finale foregrounds the repositionings of symbolic power that can occur when artists of color appropriate the narratives of U.S. white nationalism. As a form of symbolic capital, Miranda's *Hamilton* reconceptualizes the history of the white Founding Fathers as an immigrant story, which articulates the diasporic imaginary of an economically empowered Latinx community. Miranda's musicals mix genres, from Broadway ballads to hip-hop to salsa and bolero, which also reflects the transcultural history and experience of the Caribbean and its multiple diasporas. However, Miranda's musicals also reengage with hegemonic forms of capital that reproduce symbolic violence in the field of cultural production, in particular the space of Latinx theater and performance. The same transcultural capital that empowers Latinx economic agents and creates wealth also recirculates in a field of power where positions of inequality constantly reconstitute themselves and where the Brown and Black bodies of the Latinx Caribbean are displaced and dispossessed of their own cultural traditions.

While the previous chapters have placed literary and theatrical works from two different authors into counterpoint, this chapter focuses on two works from the same author, Lin-Manuel Miranda. Both *In the Heights* and *Hamilton: An American Musical* exhibit the mixing of musical genres, theater traditions, and performance repertoires that are characteristic of transculturation in art and literature. Fernando Ortiz coined the term *transculturación* to counter the prevalent notion at the time of acculturation, which describes a one-way shift from a dominated culture to the dominant one. Ortiz argues that in Cuba, and more generally in the Americas as a whole, the history of conquest, geographic displacements, and demographic shifts shows how transformation occurs in multiple directions, even as power structures establish themselves along lines of technological and economic dominance. In Miranda's musicals, transculturation gives rise to new forms of artistry and performance and occurs as a deliberate stylization, while it also reflects the history of the Latinx Caribbean diaspora and cultures in contact.

TRANSCULTURAL APPROPRIATIONS

Considering Miranda's musicals in counterpoint reveals the difference between transculturation as a practice of survival for minoritized subjects and as a cultural appropriation of discourses of power in social relations. On the one hand, the integration of Latin salsa, bolero, rap, hip-hop, and Broadway show tunes of *In the Heights* reflects the transcultural appropriation and mixing of styles and genres that characterize the Latinx diasporic experience and the hybrid forms that emerge from the show's portrayal of the enclave community. On the other hand, *Hamilton's* combination of rap, hip-hop, and Disney-style ballads to retell the story of the titular Founding Father and the U.S. Revolutionary War represents a type of cultural appropriation that Richard A. Rogers defines as "cultural dominance": "the use of elements of a dominant culture by members of a subordinated culture in a context in which the dominant culture has been imposed onto the subordinated culture, including appropriations that enact resistance."[5] Rogers identifies four types of cultural appropriation; in addition to cultural dominance and transculturation, cultural exchange represents an ideal of "reciprocal exchange" between two or more cultural groups, and cultural exploitation constitutes the appropriation of elements belonging to a dominated culture by a dominant one "without substantive reciprocity, permission, and/or compensation."[6] While *In the Heights* appropriates the national symbolism of July 4 and U.S. Independence Day celebrations to tell the story of immigrants and the Latinx diasporic community in New York, the dramatic conflicts and character arcs keep close to the lived experiences of the Washington Heights residents. *Hamilton* reimagines the foundational narratives of Anglo-American nationalism through the staged embodiments and musical traditions of people of color, whose histories and lived experiences are largely absent from the dominant version of the story the musical tells. Lyra D. Monteiro argues, "The idea that this musical 'looks like America looks now' in contrast to 'then,' however, is misleading and actively erases the presence and role of black and brown people in Revolutionary America, as well as before and since."[7] Now a major motion picture in which Miranda plays the role of the *piragüero*, *In the Heights* portrays the struggles of a dispossessed and underresourced community trying to accumulate greater cultural and economic capital. With *Hamilton*, Miranda demonstrates how members from that very same community who possess high levels of capital can appropriate elements of the dominant culture to redefine the foundational narratives of U.S. national imaginary. As Rogers states, instances when a dominated culture appropriates elements of the dominant culture can be forms of resistance that highlight "the agency and inventiveness of subordinated peoples."[8]

As an example of transculturation, in which cultural production and expression derive from multiple sources and destabilize essentialist notions of bounded cultures, *In the Heights* recounts from various cultural perspectives and experiences the events on a sweltering July 3–4 in Washington Heights. Transculturation also describes the social relations and historical conditions that bring cultures into contact and, as Rogers argues, accounts for the inequities in power between dominant and dominated cultures.[9] With *In the Heights*, the appropriation of Independence Day constitutes a deliberate act of artistic license that gestures toward the social relations and historical conditions that have brought about the transcultural imaginary of the diasporic community. Through the diasporic experience, the Independence Day celebrations can convey multiple meanings, not only the dominant discourse of U.S. patriotism and national unity, but also the history of independence movements and struggles against colonialism in the Caribbean. Likewise, in *Hamilton*, the race-conscious casting and musical hybridity perform a cultural appropriation of the dominant culture, while gesturing toward the transculturation that the official versions of U.S. American foundational narratives ignore or attempt to erase.

In Latin American studies, the notion of transculturation has developed from Cuban anthropologist Fernando Ortiz's early iteration to later theories and practices of literary discourse by Peruvian Antonio Cornejo Polar, as well as Uruguayan Ángel Rama.[10] Silvia Spitta has also shown the continuities and disjunctures between transculturation and theories and practices of the borderlands and mestizaje that have emerged in U.S. Latinx art and literature.[11] In her analysis of European travel writing in Latin America, Mary Louise Pratt argues: "Ethnographers have used this term [transculturation] to describe how subordinated or marginal groups select and invent from materials transmitted to them by a dominant or metropolitan culture. While subjugated peoples cannot readily control what the dominant culture visits upon them, they do determine to varying extents what they absorb into their own, how they use it, and what they make it mean. Transculturation is a phenomenon of the contact zone."[12] The various uses of transculturation have generated debates over the term's endemic elitism and what John Beverley has called "a fantasy of class, gender, and racial reconciliation."[13] As in the case of the cultural remittances that appear in the narrative fiction of Rita Indiana Hernández and Junot Díaz, the transculturation that takes place through outflows of consumer goods and U.S. material practices in the Dominican Republic can reproduce and entrench the logic of domination. However, a theory of transculturation is relevant to the analysis of contemporary Latinx Caribbean literature and the diasporic experience in as much as it remains attentive to the inequalities of power that occur at the point of transcultural contact. For Rogers, transculturation "refers not only to a more complex blending of cultures than the previous categories but also to a set of conditions under which such acts occur: globalization, neocolonialism, and the increasing dominance of transnational capitalism vis-à-vis nation states."[14] The theory of habitus is consistent with this definition of transculturation since it conceptualizes both conscious, deliberate acts of cultural appropriation as well as the unconscious embodiments of social values in competitive fields of power.

This definition also helps to shed light on how Miranda's musicals mobilize transcultural capital in order to convey the diasporic community's aspiration for economic independence and upward mobility. The plot of *In the Heights* centers on the economic challenges and changes that impact the three businesses in the neighborhood: Usnavi's bodega, Kevin's car service, and Daniela's hair salon. Usnavi at first wants to sell the bodega and move to the Dominican Republic, but later decides to keep the business open and stay in New York. Kevin and his wife, Camila, sell their business in order to pay the college tuition for their daughter, Nina. Daniela can no longer afford the rising rents and relocates her salon from the Heights to the Bronx, or as her employee Vanessa says, "Gettin' out the barrio, and headin' to the hood."[15] In the 2016 Chicago production I attended, the sets for the bodega and the car service were constructed back-to-back on a rotating platform, with the salon stage left.[16] Apartments and a fire escape occupied an upper level over the businesses and street. The set emphasizes the proximity of lived space to the commercial space of resident-owned small businesses. The rotating set also reminds the audience of the volatility of the real estate market and the risk involved in capital investment: as one business survives another is sacrificed.

Numerous scholars and researchers have documented the gentrification in the Latinx neighborhoods of NYC that have dispossessed and displaced many low-income residents.[17] A Housing Policy Brief published by the CUNY Dominican Studies Institute documents how "the price of all housing in Washington Heights/ Inwood has appreciated six-fold between 2000 and 2015, placing the neighborhood second among all New York City neighborhoods."[18] The study includes a table that shows the increases in out-of-pocket rent (after subsidies are subtracted), rental contracts, and median income. The report clarifies that the increase in median income does not reflect an equitable distribution across racial/ethnic lines, and that it is due mostly to the influx of upper-middle-class, white professionals. According to the authors of the study, this disparity "exacerbates economic inequality while laying the grounds for the eventual exodus of low-income residents whose incomes remain stagnant in a neighborhood where the cost of living continues to rise."[19] Nevertheless, with *In the Heights* the business decision to stay or sell is also made based on Latinx cultural values, whether that be as a commitment to preserving an ethnic community's cultural heritage or to the priorities of the Latinx nuclear family. The objective material conditions that impact the economic status of the musical's characters are mitigated by the transcultural imaginary of their Caribbean diasporic experience and their dreams that become a legacy.

The characters of *In the Heights* have many dreams, most of which involve accumulating some species of capital in order to leave or transform their urban enclave. Usnavi, the neighborhood bodega owner, longs to sell his store and retire on a secluded beach in the Dominican Republic near the town where his parents were born. Even though Usnavi was born in the United States after his parents migrated, once they pass away he inherits their store and their dreams of returning to an island he only knows through the stories they told: "and [they] left me with these memories like dyin' embers / from a dream i can't remember."[20]

Like Abuela Claudia, Usnavi inherits his dreams from his parents' trauma of dislocation and economic precarity, which become part of Usnavi's own diasporic
habitus. When he discovers that the winning lottery ticket was sold to someone at
his bodega, but still does not know Abuela Claudia is the winner, Usnavi and the
other characters sing about what they would do with the ninety-six thousand dollars. Usnavi declares he would give some to his friends, sell the store, and use the
rest to "fly me down to Puerta [*sic*] Plata, I'll make the best of it."[21] Usnavi conveys
the general consensus among the barrio residents that the best way to enjoy the
sudden wealth of the lottery winnings is to leave Washington Heights. The
"crazy hypotheticals" in which the characters engage underscore the disjuncture
between the physical space of the Latinx urban enclave and the social space of
privilege and upward mobility. A sudden and unexpected acquisition of economic
capital sets in motion the disposition of their inherited diasporic habitus and
their desire to leave behind the Latinx urban enclave where they have only ever
experienced deprivation and disappointment.

Only his cousin Sonny imagines using the ninety-six thousand to revitalize the
neighborhood for the sake of the Latinx residents. He would use the money to forestall the rapid process of gentrification taking place:

> I'll cash my ticket and picket, invest in protest!
> never lose my focus till the city takes notice
> and you know this man! I'll never sleep
> because the ghetto has a million promises for me to keep![22]

Sonny commits to ameliorating the residents' precarious economic conditions by
investing in their "edumacation," a purposeful neologism that accents the hegemonic forms of cultural capital with streetwise Latinx transcultural capital. The
accumulation of these forms of capital helps create what Tara J. Yosso calls "community cultural wealth," a term she develops in order to center her education
research lens "on the experiences of People of Color in critical historical context"
and thereby revealing "accumulated assets and resources in the histories and lives
of Communities of Color."[23] Whereas the majority of the characters dream about
taking flight from their Latinx urban enclave, Sonny commits to making his neighborhood a place where his community will want to stay and thrive. His promise
to resist the forces of gentrification, to "invest in protest," seeks to accumulate and
grow the community cultural wealth that emerges from Latinx traditions of ethnic and class solidarity.

Eventually, Abuela Claudia shares her winnings with her adopted sons, Usnavi
and Sonny, who then spread the wealth to some of the other characters for whom
this cash infusion will help them realize their own dreams. Once Sonny learns that
Abuela Claudia has left him a third of the lottery winnings, he follows through on
his promise and enlists the character Graffiti Pete to paint a mural on the bodega
gate in honor of Abuela Claudia and her signature phrase, *Paciencia y fe*. The homage compels Usnavi to change his plans to sell the bodega, which now stands as
a bulwark against the encroaching gentrification of the neighborhood. Abuela

Claudia's signature musical number is crucial not only because it moves the plot forward to the bittersweet resolutions for nearly all the main characters, but also because it articulates the show's central theme of how individual desires can only be fulfilled through collective action and Latinx communitarian values of family and shared labor. Although many of the characters visualize their personal success in terms of American individualism, and they have been compelled to adopt the hegemonic value of pulling one's own weight in life, the fortuitous economic capital they receive only has value if the entire community can benefit from it. As Jorge Duany argues, "Diasporas often sustain social, economic, cultural, political, and emotional bonds to their countries of origin. The enduring links to a real putative homeland through collective memories, myths, and rituals constitute one of the basic criteria for most definitions of diaspora."[24] The characters' dreams of a better life straddle the centripetal and centrifugal forces of the diasporic imagination. They profit from transforming their transcultural capital—the Latinx Caribbean cultural values that have survived their diasporic displacement—into economic capital, which empowers them to claim ownership of their physical and social spaces.

Abuela Claudia's scene also captures the multidirectionality of the characters' social relations and the overlapping of physical and social spaces: the invocation upward allows wealth to spread laterally, which strengthens the social bonds among characters and helps revitalize the physical space of the neighborhood. Many of the other characters imagine their trajectories through physical and social spaces vertically and horizontally, where upward mobility means moving out of the barrio. Meanwhile their Latinx communitarian values bring them back down and toward the center, back to the urban terrain of their Washington Heights neighborhood where they share a common cause. For example, two of the young female characters, Nina and Vanessa, share a dream of one day leaving their Washington Heights neighborhood in NYC through economic upward mobility. However, Nina and Vanessa have very different means by which they plan to achieve this dream, and the songs they sing, which combine traditional Broadway instrumentation with Latin genres such as bolero, salsa, and bachata as well as the urban rhythms of hip-hop and rap, reflect on the amount of social, cultural, and economic capital they already possess and what they will need in order to find the better place in life they seek.

Nina is the neighborhood good girl, a scholarship student at Stanford University and daughter of hardworking, Puerto Rican parents who have sacrificed so much to give their daughter a chance of fulfilling their dreams of upward mobility. Vanessa, on the other hand, works for low wages at the neighborhood hair salon and takes care of her abusive, alcoholic mother. Even their relationships with men are diametrically opposed, with Nina shyly falling in love with her father's non-Latino protégé Benny, while Vanessa is popular with all the men and has the reputation of a Latina spitfire. These female characters reprise and reimagine the roles of María and Anita from *West Side Story*, with Nina's relationship to Benny invoking the forbidden love between María and Tony, and Vanessa's goal to leave the

Heights reminding the audience of Anita's famous desire to "live in America." The gendered dispositions of these characters also play a role in what each young woman allows herself to dream. For Nina, the support she receives from her parents and the straight-and-narrow path she has chosen provide her with early aspirations to aim high: "I used to think we lived at the top of the world, / when the world was just a subway map / and the one slash nine climbed a dotted line to my place."[25] Nina's dreams take shape as a vertical trajectory, and in another song she also sings about how she used to climb "to the highest / place, on every fire escape, restless to climb / just me and the GWB, asking, 'gee, Nina, what'll you be?'"[26] In spite of her attempt to "make it out" of her neighborhood, when Nina abandons her studies at Stanford due to poor grades and the subsequent loss of her scholarship, she wonders "maybe I should have just / stayed home. . . ."[27]

Vanessa also sings of the elevated trains that pass by her apartment, with hopes of climbing aboard one headed downtown and never returning:

> The elevated train by my window doesn't faze me anymore.
> The rattling screams won't disrupt my dreams.
> It's a lullaby, in its way.
> The elevated train drives everyone insane, but I don't mind, oh no.
> When I bring back boys, they can't tolerate the noise
> and that's okay, 'cuz I never let them stay.
> And one day, I'm hopping on that elevated train and I'm riding away!
> It won't be long now![28]

Vanessa plans to escape the barrio life by relocating to a more upscale neighborhood downtown, and even though she imagines that the elevated train will help elevate her economic status, unlike Nina she is more concerned about where rather than who she will be. Nina hopes to achieve her goals through higher education, a form of cultural capital that will transform her into a different version of herself. Meanwhile, Vanessa saves and hustles to have enough money for a security deposit on her new apartment, a form of economic capital that will allow her to change her surroundings but not necessarily her identity. Their social and economic statuses are contingent on the physical and social spaces Nina and Vanessa traverse and occupy. In either case, however, the characters can only realize their dreams by leaving their neighborhood, yet when Nina returns defeated, she recovers her self-confidence through the support of her community, while Vanessa declares that if she were to "make it out," she would never turn back. The similarities and differences in these two Latina characters show how their existing forms of capital and their gendered dispositions shape the trajectories they choose for attaining upward mobility, as well as their senses of belonging to a community and a place they feel compelled to leave behind.

The contrast between Nina and Vanessa underscores the importance of the educational or academic field in the accumulation of social and cultural capital. In general, a social field is analogous to a field of play, in which agents position themselves competitively according to how much capital they already possess and how well disposed they are to accumulate more.[29] Furthermore, economic agents develop strategies and plot trajectories of motion in a field according to the amount and kinds of capital to which they have access. The value of these forms of capital, however, is unstable and contingent on the type of field in which an economic agent strives to occupy an advantageous position. When Nina goes to Stanford, even though she was the neighborhood good girl and excelled academically in NYC, she lacks the social, cultural, and economic capital to succeed in this much more competitive field. The strategies that Nina developed at home positioned her advantageously to make it out of her neighborhood; once transplanted to the wealthier and whiter academic field of Stanford, her strategies place her at a disadvantage.

Nevertheless, everyone in her community perceived her as having a privileged position in comparison to her peers in Washington Heights; she, in turn, believes she is indebted to but also constrained by the community's support and expectations. In a scene when Nina's father Kevin announces he has decided to sell his car service business to pay for her tuition, Nina protests and refuses to accept the money:

> NINA: Wait. Dad, I'll find a job. I can take night classes!
> KEVIN: What so you end up just another girl stuck in el barrio?
> VANESSA: Why you gotta look at me when you say that?[30]

Meanwhile, Vanessa desires to make it out of her neighborhood as well, even though she lacks the species of capital that supposedly were Nina's ticket out. Her strategy is to accumulate the economic capital that will help fulfill her dreams, and eventually Usnavi uses some of the ninety-six-thousand-dollar lottery winnings to secure a deposit on the downtown apartment Vanessa had been so anxious to rent. Even though Nina and Vanessa share a dream of leaving Washington Heights for a better life, they have different strategies based on the species of capital they already possess and the relation of these capitals to the very different social fields in which the characters compete.

The "rules of the game" in any particular field are also contingent on the historical and political context in which economic agents compete for the accumulation of capital. We see this when we compare Nina to the main character of Lin-Manuel Miranda's second Broadway hit, *Hamilton: An American Musical*. In this musical, Miranda foregrounds Alexander Hamilton's Caribbean origins and features songs such as "My Shot!," in which the titular character proclaims his determination to rise to the top of colonial American society: "Hey yo, I'm just like my country / Young, scrappy, and hungry / And I'm not throwing away my shot!."[31] Like Nina, Miranda's version of Alexander Hamilton lacks the economic, cultural, and social capital that give the elite like Aaron Burr and Thomas Jefferson— Hamilton's rivals—access to the best educational, professional, and political opportunities available. In the opening scene, the character of Aaron Burr sings:

> How does a bastard, orphan, son of a whore and a
> Scotsman, dropped in the middle of a forgotten

Spot in the Caribbean by providence, impoverished, in squalor,
Grow up to be a hero and a scholar?[32]

Even though he is an illegitimate child and a poor immigrant, Hamilton gains his first entry into public discourse and the backing of well-connected businessmen when he writes a moving letter seeking aid after a hurricane devastates his native island of Saint Croix. For both Hamilton and Nina, Miranda's characters draw from their immigrant origins in the Caribbean—their transcultural capital—to accumulate other species of capital that will fulfill their dreams of upward mobility and access to the "field of power."[33] These dramatic arcs depict the process by which immigrant economic agents transform their transcultural capital into the hegemonic species of capital—educational and economic—that facilitate occupying dominant positions in U.S. social fields. However, *Hamilton* is less about cultural uplift for communities of color as it is about reimagining the problematic U.S. history of white settler colonialism from the perspective of contemporary ethnic and racial politics.

Hamilton notably casts the Founding Fathers and American revolutionaries with actors of color, and infuses the Broadway musical with urban hip-hop, rap, and R&B. Ostensibly, this race-conscious casting and transcultural musical aesthetic reimagine the U.S. national narrative through the perspective of the minoritized subjects who have been excluded from this foundational story. The musical performs a political discourse of inclusion and immigrant empowerment that is consistent with the progressive social and cultural values characteristic of the Obama era (more on the musical's intervention on the Obama-Trump transition below). At the February 9, 2017, production I attended in Chicago, the lines delivered by the characters of Lafayette and Hamilton drew some of the loudest applause: "LAFAYETTE: Immigrants: / HAMILTON, LAFAYETTE: We get the job done."[34] However, *Hamilton*'s dramatic plot of the scrappy individualist who pulls himself up from his bootstraps contrasts sharply with the "community cultural wealth" that gives agency to the characters from *In the Heights*. In this way, Miranda's second musical misrecognizes how the capacity to accumulate capital is contingent on the amounts and species of capital that economic agents already possess and the value of these capitals in the sociohistorical fields in which they compete. As Lázaro Lima argues in his interrogation of the bootstrap narrative that characterizes U.S. Supreme Court justice Sonia Sotomayor's biography, "The historical amnesias that bind us to the narratives of bootstraps ultimately forestall the possibility for a national accounting that would make these stories of success and advancement ethically just and democratically meaningful."[35] When contrasted to the casting of people of color in the roles of the Founding Fathers, the dramatic arc in *Hamilton* commits an act of symbolic violence against those like Nina who position themselves in a white, hegemonic social field where the racial disadvantages against them are systemically reproduced and assumed to be logical and natural. As I discussed in the previous chapter, the notion of misrecognition describes how the dominated classes perceive their social position from the logic of domination, which perpetuates violence against their own agency and forecloses their capacity to speak in their own voices. Lyra D. Monteiro makes a similar argument in her analysis of *Hamilton* when she writes, "Despite the proliferation of black and brown bodies onstage, not a single enslaved or free person of color exists as a character in this play."[36] Monteiro also notes that the most explicit condemnation of slavery in *Hamilton* comes during the rap battle between Hamilton and Jefferson over whether the newly independent nation should establish a central bank. It is not without irony that Miranda portrays Hamilton's role here heroically; as founder of the financial system that allowed the federal government to issue bonds and incur debt, Hamilton should stand as the avatar of everything that went wrong with Puerto Rico's debt crisis.[37] Miranda's version of Hamilton conveys a mixed message in its conflation of all immigrants who "get the job done," regardless of the advantages and disadvantages with which they engage in competitive social fields. By appropriating the figure of Hamilton through a racialized embodiment, the Puerto Rican artist also occludes the history of his own people's colonial condition and diaspora.

BETWEEN LINEAGE AND LEGACY

An analysis of economic, cultural, social, and symbolic species of capital cannot elucidate how power structures are formed and reproduced in a social field unless one considers an agent's habitus; that is, the ways agents embody and perform the social and cultural values that they derive from their social relations. Furthermore, the capital that agents possess may have varying degrees of value in relation to the configuration of power and domination in a particular social field. In the educational field, transcultural capital will generate value through the social capital that obtains from the dominant positions of masculine and white privilege that facilitated Alexander Hamilton's access to educational, economic, and political capital. In contrast, Nina's Latinx transcultural capital, which can be understood in terms of Yosso's notion of "community cultural wealth," generates less value in the educational field because of the dominated position she occupies as a working-class woman of color. Although Miranda portrays these characters as autonomous subjects who consciously pursue goals in the educational field, the objective historical circumstances that contribute to the constitution of their habitus empower or disempower their agency and their capacity to transform transcultural capital into economic capital. Consequently, while *In the Heights* proposes collective agency through the transformation of transcultural capital into economic capital, *Hamilton* stages a subversive form of race-conscious casting that puts Black and Brown faces on the foundational narratives of white nationalism. *Hamilton*'s race-conscious casting simultaneously stakes a claim on cultural proprietorship—Blacks and Latinxs sing and perform hip-hop and rap—while appropriating the white nationalist narrative of the Founding Fathers to articulate the cultural and economic imaginaries of contemporary people of color and immigrant communities.

As with Abuela Claudia and Usnavi, the theme of legacy and inheritance is also key to understanding the different habitus that Nina and the character of Hamilton embody. Nina's relationship with her parents, in particular her father Kevin, dramatizes what Bourdieu calls the "contradictions of inheritance."[38] The paternal figure stands as the embodiment of the immigrant's dreams of upward mobility. These dreams form a "project" or "conatus," that is, "a striving, inclination, natural tendency, impulse or effort" that is passed down from one generation to the next through, on the one hand, a deliberate moral education. On the other hand, the father's "whole way of being," that is, the array of dispositions that comprise his habitus, is also passed down unconsciously as the natural state of affairs, the unquestioned conventional wisdom that become doxic values. Nevertheless, sons and daughters can consciously accept or reject these inherited values and the projects that perpetuate them as a family legacy. Kevin from *In the Heights* sings about his own rebelliousness against his Puerto Rican father, who expected his son to carry on the family legacy through agricultural labor. In his song "Inútil" ("Useless"), Kevin recounts how he shared his own aspirations of upward mobility with his father:

But I told him, "Papi, I'm sorry, I'm going farther.
I'm getting on a plane.
And I am gonna change the world someday."
And he slapped my face.
He stood there, staring at me, useless.
Today my daughter's home and I am useless.[39]

The spatialized language of Kevin's song ("going farther," "getting on a plane") demonstrates how he had already inculcated in Nina his own dreams of upward mobility and the embodiment of a diasporic habitus through the outward traversal of geographic and social spaces. Kevin's song describes how the dispositions and cultural values of one generation are passed down to the next, but the second generation does not always meet with paternal expectations. Nina has certainly reembodied the inheritance of aspiring toward upward mobility from her father, even though Kevin rejected the values his father expected him to accept.

The risks Kevin took by leaving Puerto Rico and opening his own business compel him to be insistent and domineering with Nina when she drops out of college and jeopardizes the dreams they both share. During one of their arguments, Nina's mother, Camila, points out that Kevin is reproducing the patriarchal tyranny he challenged as a young man. Kevin invokes the doxa of masculine domination in order to impose his will. Although he does not turn to violence as his father had done with him, Kevin nevertheless tries to force Nina to comply with the dreams he embodies and has taught her to adopt as her own. However, Camila and Nina challenge this patriarchal order by threatening to leave. Finally, because Nina shares her father's dream of "going farther," she eventually accepts her paternal inheritance and decides to return to Stanford once her father sells his business to raise the needed tuition money.[40] The family is united around the potential that Nina's accumulation of educational capital will ameliorate the sacrifice of their economic capital. Once again, the Latinx transcultural capital of family unity and communitarian support serves to position Nina in a social field where she can compete to accumulate a hegemonic species of capital.

With the portrayal of Hamilton in Miranda's musical, however, the interpretation of the Founding Father's illegitimate lineage, based on Ron Chernow's biography, articulates one of the persistent myths of American individualism and melting-pot ideology: that immigrants reinvent themselves upon arrival and succeed by fending for themselves in a contest of survival of the fittest. Although the historical figure of Alexander Hamilton lived in the era of Enlightenment values, emerging bourgeois capitalism, and classical liberalism, the character of Hamilton that appears in Miranda's musical epitomizes the neoliberal, rational male subject known as *Homo economicus,* a supposedly self-possessed economic agent who is constantly engaged in the "spirit of calculation."[41] As discussed previously, Wendy Brown describes the evolution of this figure in Western society and how its current dominance in economic thought has degenerated the egalitarian values that have served as the cornerstone of democracy: "Thirty years ago, at the dawn of the neoliberal era, *homo oeconomicus* was still oriented by interest and profit seeking, but now entrepreneurialized itself at every turn and was formulated as human capital."[42] As *Hamilton* conflates the dreams of white, Anglo-Saxon immigrants of the eighteenth century with those of today's immigrants of color, the musical attributes both to the neoliberal "spirit of calculation" without accounting for the conditions of history and habitus, which make the transformation of cultural capital into economic capital contingent on racial, gender, and sexual hierarchies.

These hierarchies include forms of linguistic capital, as well, and the way a person speaks and gestures can facilitate or hinder the upwardly mobile dreams of the rational actor who, according to the logic of American individualism, is fully capable of transforming the self in order to "play the game" in competitive social fields. It's just a matter of having enough "grit" or "spunk." Both Nina and Benny— the non-Latino dispatcher who works for Kevin—confront their lack of linguistic capital and the obstacles this presents when they try to achieve their goals. Benny does not speak enough Spanish to impress Kevin, whose Puerto Rican and Dominican drivers need dispatch directions in both varieties of Caribbean Spanish. And while Nina describes how she learned Spanish as part of her education and tries to teach Benny, at Stanford the elite students "spoke a different kind of English," in which "weekend" is a verb and "cabin" serves as a "blasé word for mansion."[43] Nina's Latinx Caribbean "certain way" has no purchase in a context where a national language of the elite displays marks of distinction and privilege not solely based on a speaker's linguistic repertoire and accent, but also on the authority and social legitimacy already invested in the speaker's habitus.

With the character of Hamilton, even though he lacks the lineage and economic and social capital that his elitist rivals Burr and Jefferson enjoyed, as a prolific writer who also spoke French, Hamilton's linguistic capital attains more value when it is leveraged by his racial and gender privilege. In Chernow's biography that served as Miranda's source material, the young Hamilton was not without his own social network of relatives and patrons, and as a student at King's College—now Columbia University—Hamilton's first successes as a politician came from his skills as a writer, orator, and debater. Chernow characterizes the New York City of that era as a multiethnic crossroads of cultures, languages, and commerce. Yet in the smaller circle of educated white men, a skillful polemicist like Hamilton with recognized linguistic capital is much more likely to gain an advantageous positioning in the political field than a late twentieth-century, working-class Latina who competes for educational opportunity in an era of standardized testing, credentialism, and quantitative admissions criteria. Although Nina strives to meet these institutionalized standards, her transcultural capital has little value in the academic field, and she lacks the gender and race privileges that Alexander Hamilton enjoyed in his era, which are still the standard by which all other forms of capital are measured. The symbolic power of that privilege determines the value of an economic agent's linguistic capital, and the race-conscious casting of the show *Hamilton*, with its rewriting of the American immigrant story, transposes onto an eighteenth-century slave society the social and cultural values of contemporary multiculturalism and, therefore, occludes the disparities in symbolic power that one immigrant group may have over another.

In the Heights performs a similar transposition of multicultural values, however in this musical the panethnic Latinx identity contributes to the creation of community cultural wealth rather than individualistic entrepreneurialism of the self as in *Hamilton*. *In the Heights* portrays characters from Cuba, Puerto Rico, and the Dominican Republic, but what unites them is their shared habitus in NYC and their pursuit of a Latinized American Dream. There is even a nod toward mixed heritage Latinx identity in the character of Carla, who declares, "I'm Chile-Domini-Curican, but I always say I'm from Queens."[44] However, there is very little explicit acknowledgment in the show of the colonial conditions that have brought these various Latin American and Latinx Caribbean groups together. The closest reference to this history is in the name of the protagonist, Usnavi, a Hispanicized pronunciation of U.S. Navy, the words his parents saw on a ship when they arrived from the Dominican Republic. Usnavi's name implicitly recalls U.S. Marines invading and occupying the Dominican Republic in 1916–24 and the subsequent intervention in the Dominican Civil War in 1965. There is no mention of U.S. colonial history in Puerto Rico or intervention in Cuba. *In the Heights* more explicitly portrays the NYC community's shared disenfranchisement and the collective effort to preserve a Latinx cultural heritage as well as achieve divergent objectives of upward mobility. In the ensemble number "Blackout" the characters react to electrical power failure on the night of July 3, the eve of Independence Day celebrations, and as panic and pandemonium take over, they sing the refrain, "We are powerless."[45] Various groups of characters simultaneously scramble to find one another, find safe exit from the neighborhood nightclub, and protect Usnavi's bodega from looters. The scene ends act 1 with all the characters looking up at the fireworks that

"Light up the night sky / en Washington Heights."[46] The scene is reminiscent of José Luis González's short story, "La noche que volvimos a ser gente," in which the Puerto Rican residents of El Barrio recuperate a sense of community after a black-out leads them to gather on their apartment building rooftops and see the moon and stars as they once did when they were in Puerto Rico.[47] This story was also the inspiration for the critically acclaimed musical, *El Apagón / The Blackout*, produced and performed by Pregones Theater / Puerto Rican Traveling Theater since the 1990s. The characters of *In the Heights*, though, look up at the Independence Day fireworks as "powerless" residents of a Latinx urban enclave, and they direct their collective will toward the promise of their American Dream, which ironically has levied a heavy price for their compatriots back in the Caribbean.

In the Heights redirects the sense of belonging from a Caribbean homeland to the NYC neighborhood and promotes a panethnic, transnational Latinx imaginary, particularly in the song "Carnaval del Barrio," another ensemble number sung after the July 3 blackout. In the production I attended in Chicago, the cast performs a flag of nations parade, even waving the Mexican national flag although there were no Mexican characters in the show. In this way, the musical establishes a cross-cultural sense of Latinidad, as Juan Flores argues is one of the different stages of Nuyorican literature: "By its Nuyorican stage, Puerto Rican literature in the United States comes to share the features of 'minority' or noncanonical litera-tures of the United States. Like them, it is a literature of recovery and collective affirmation, and it is a literature of 'mingling and sharing,' of interaction and exchange with neighboring, complementary cultures."[48] William Orchard finds that *In the Heights*, as an example of a successful Latinx-themed musical on Broad-way, presents a somewhat sanitized portrayal of urban life, but "it does possess a politics, however muted, that is directed at the effects of economic violence and rapid gentrification on a community whose resources are rapidly fading."[49] In this vein, the "Carnaval del Barrio" number also serves as a call to action to the characters, to do more than just complain about their situation and join together to revitalize the neighborhood. As Cristina Beltrán argues, a panethnic Latino identity emerges from mass movements, political action, and collective agency, not through preexisting, universally shared experiences, cultural values, or politi-cal ideologies.[50] Although *In the Heights* occludes the specific histories of the Latinx Caribbean nations and how distinct colonial conditions form part of an array of dispositions and embodied values, the musical performs a panethnic Latinx imag-inary as an expression of collective agency and as a claim to ownership of the urban enclave from which it emerges.

Transcultural Capital and Communitarian Returns

On November 18, 2016, *Hamilton* cast member Brandon Victor Dixon, just finishing a performance as Vice President Aaron Burr, addressed then VP-elect Mike Pence, who had just attended the show. Dixon reassured the audience, "There's nothing to boo here; we're all here sharing a story of love." Although Dixon articulated the alarm and anxiety felt by "the diverse America" since the election of Donald Trump to the presidency, his call out to Pence displayed "the audacity of hope" that had been one of President Barack Obama's guiding principles. Like the other actors of color in *Hamilton* who have portrayed the story of the white Founding Fathers, Dixon embodied the appropriation and redefinition of American values that he exhorted Pence to uphold and protect. *Hamilton* composer and star Lin-Manuel Miranda later defended the bold political agency Dixon performed that evening (he helped write the words Dixon delivered).[51] Like the protagonist of Alexander Hamilton he played in the original Broadway production, Miranda has used his words and lyrics to convey a vision of America's past, present, and future, but from the diasporic imaginary that reflects his Puerto Rican heritage and Latinx urban experience. The confrontation with VP-elect Pence marked a dramatic realignment of the musical's political engagement from when Miranda first debuted the opening number for President Obama's White House Poetry Jam on May 12, 2009. Miranda's success on Broadway and high visibility in the U.S. entertainment industry exemplify the possibility of empowering minoritized subjects as political and economic agents through their own cultures and communitarian values.

Ironically, it would be almost one year later that Lin-Manuel Miranda faced his own group of protestors at the University of Puerto Rico. On November 8, 2017, Miranda visited the campus in Río Piedras to announce he would reprise his role as Hamilton for a charity performance to assist the reconstruction efforts after Hurricane María. Five students took to the stage with signs that read "Free Puerto Rico" and "Lin-Manuel, ¡nuestras vidas no son tu teatro!"[52] The students were protesting Miranda's early support for the Ley PROMESA, which was signed by President Obama and imposed an unelected board to oversee Puerto Rico's debt crisis. Although the protestors were in the minority in their criticism of Miranda, the Ley PROMESA that he supported has been widely condemned by Puerto Ricans on the island and in the diaspora. Miranda's gesture to use the cultural, social, and economic capital he has accumulated as a Broadway star was not universally embraced, and the protest underscored the tensions and contradictions that characterize Puerto Ricans' status as colonized subjects who, nevertheless, can access pathways to upward mobility as U.S. citizens.[53] In spite of the protests and controversies surrounding this performance, *Hamilton* debuted on January 10, 2019, at the Centro de Bellas Artes to much acclaim, and Miranda received a standing ovation for his performance and for waving the Puerto Rican flag at the end of the show.[54]

The portrayal of collective and individual economic agency in Miranda's musical theater closely reflects his own trajectory as an artist and activist. An advantageous positioning for a writer, filmmaker, visual or musical artist opens an opportunity in the field of cultural production to accumulate social and economic capital. Even artists considered underground or radically experimental can assume this cultural and political legitimacy if, like more conventional or commercial artists, they already possess the species of capital that have value in the hegemonic field of power.[55] As a contemporary, second-generation Puerto Rican from New York, Miranda has achieved high levels of cultural and political legitimacy, as well as a great deal of economic success, through the transcultural capital of his two Broadway musical hit shows. Miranda has attained an advantageous positioning in the U.S. hegemonic field of power and has recirculated his cultural and political capital to intervene in public policy debates and electoral politics. Miranda accumulated social and cultural capital through the promotion and marketing of both his shows, particularly on social networks such as YouTube and Twitter.[56]

He also inherited these species of capital through his politically connected and well-educated family. His father, Luis A. Miranda Jr., is one of the founding partners of MirRam Group, LLC, a political consulting and lobbying firm that has strong connections to the Democratic Party in New York. Miranda's mother, Dr. Luz Towns-Miranda, is a clinical psychologist with an advanced degree from NYU. In various interviews, Miranda credits his parents' Broadway cast album collection and his older sister's hip-hop and rap collection as the inspirations for his musical tastes and eventual pursuit of the creative arts. Miranda has also compared his father's experience as a first-generation migrant to the biography of Alexander Hamilton.[57] No doubt that his family's professional success and high political profile gave Miranda access to the kinds of social and cultural capital his characters from In the Heights do not share. Yet as a student at Wesleyan University, he developed many of the concepts and some of the songs that would later appear in this show.[58] Although Miranda's musicals tell the stories of immigrants who fight against the odds with little to no forms of capital in competitive social and economic fields, his own trajectory as an artist and activist underscores how advantageous positionings in these fields are facilitated by existing forms of capital that a Latinx economic agent already possesses and their value in the hegemonic field of power.

Because Miranda has found success in the Broadway musical industry, the celebrity status that accompanies that success reinforces the logic of American individualism. Miranda's lyrics in Hamilton—"I'm not throwing away my shot!"—are as much a musical rendition of this logic as they are a self-reflexive metadiscourse that places Miranda at the center of the Great American Success Story. A recipient of the prestigious MacArthur Fellows Program award in 2015 and with numerous Drama Desk, Tony, and Emmy Awards for In the Heights and Hamilton, which also received the 2016 Pulitzer Prize in drama, Miranda has claimed an unprecedented level of hegemonic legitimacy and economic capital in the U.S. field of cultural production. Subsequently, Miranda has joined Disney for a number of collaborations, including writing the music for the animated feature Moana and costarring in the film Mary Poppins Returns. Nevertheless, Miranda also takes a cue from the character Usnavi from In the Heights, who reinvests his capital into the community from which he draws his values and inspiration. Miranda has promoted legislation, social justice causes, and political campaigns, most notably in the 2016 presidential campaign as a Hillary Clinton supporter and fund raiser.[59] As a public intellectual, Miranda has written op-eds, performed, and created mass media visibility for a number of causes and campaigns. Miranda published an op-ed in the *New York Times* (June 7, 2016) on the practice of automated "ticket bots" that purchase mass quantities of Broadway show tickets, thus raising resale prices and making shows inaccessible to broader audiences. He also teamed up with Jennifer López to perform a benefit song in honor the victims of the Orlando Pulse night-club shooting, which took the lives of dozens of young Latinxs in the gay community.[60] After Hurricane María devastated Puerto Rico, Miranda teamed up once again with López as well as Rita Moreno, John Leguizamo, Luis Fonsi, Gloria Estéfan, and other Latinx pop stars to release a charity song and video, "Almost Like a Prayer." As mentioned previously, Miranda committed to reprising his role as Alexander Hamilton for a 2019 production at the University of Puerto Rico's Teatro UPR. Tickets for the show, which can cost hundreds of dollars or more on Broadway and in other U.S. cities, were supposed to sell for ten dollars and be released through a lottery. Miranda is quoted as saying, "When I last visited the island, a few weeks before Hurricane Maria, I had made a commitment to not only bring the show to Puerto Rico, but also return again to the title role. In the aftermath of Maria we decided to expedite the announcement of the project to send a bold message that Puerto Rico will recover and be back in business, stronger than ever."[61] Miranda has consistently used his star power and high level of media visibility to invest in causes that support Puerto Rico and the Latinx community more broadly.

Not all of Miranda's interventions in public discourse have been fortuitous or without controversy. In addition to a *Times* op-ed (March 28, 2016), Miranda also appeared on John Oliver's *Last Week Tonight* on HBO (April 24, 2016) to perform a rap in favor of congressional action on Puerto Rico's debt crisis. The PROMESA legislation that was later approved and signed by President Obama helped forestall a looming default on the island's bond debt repayments, but it established an unelected review board to govern the island's fiscal future. In this instance, Miranda's intervention received criticism for defending the neoliberal policies that have perpetuated Puerto Rico's colonial status and its economic dependency on the United States.[62] When President Obama commuted the sentence of former FALN member Oscar López Rivera, Miranda took to Twitter to declare he was "sobbing with gratitude" and would reprise his role as Hamilton especially for the Puerto Rican *independentista* who had been convicted of sedition.[63] How much a militant separatist would enjoy a musical that lauds the U.S. Founding Fathers remains an open question. Nevertheless, Miranda's visibility in the entertainment industry and his connections to mainstream political figures have given him a prominent platform from which to engage in political and cultural debates. As such, his musicals combine an artistic vision with progressive political advocacy, yet they also convey the contradictions of transcultural capital and its potential for reproducing hegemonic discourses of power.

Miranda's *Hamilton* has not only become a Broadway and mass media phenomenon but also grown into its own cultural industry and generated everything from a PBS episode of *Great Performances: Hamilton's America* to *Hamilton: The*

Exhibition, a "360-degree immersive exhibition inspired by the revolutionary musical."[64] A recent collection of scholarly essays examines *Hamilton*'s impact in numerous cultural and political debates.[65] As Brian Eugenio Herrera writes in his contribution to this collection, *Hamilton* has a vast array of supplemental tie-ins and a global presence online through its own YouTube channel.[66] Other essays examine the musical in light of pedagogies of American history, Alexander Hamilton's role in establishing U.S. financial institutions, the representation of masculinity, marriage and gender, and the history of slavery during the revolutionary era.[67] In her essay, Patricia Herrera asks, "Does the hip-hop soundscape of *Hamilton* effectively drown the violence and trauma—and sounds—of slavery that people who looked like the actors in the play might have actually experienced at the time of the nation's birth?"[68] Despite these criticisms, Miranda remains committed to promoting the arts in Puerto Rico, and when he reprised his role as Hamilton for the limited run at the Teatro UPR in 2019, a portion of ticket sales proceeds went to the Flamboyán Arts Fund, "an initiative dedicated to preserving, amplifying, and sustaining the arts in Puerto Rico by supporting all facets of the arts community including music, theater, visual arts, dance, literature, and youth arts education."[69] Because of *Hamilton*'s outsize impact both on- and off-Broadway, and Miranda's emergence as a spokesperson for Puerto Rico and the diasporic community in the United States, the show and its author have received a great amount of praise as well as critical scrutiny.

One of the definitive signs that Miranda and his show *Hamilton* have become a massive cultural phenomenon is that the artist and his musical are the targets of the spoof, *Spamilton: An American Parody*. Written and directed by Gerard Alessandrini, creator of the *Forbidden Broadway* series, not only does *Spamilton* rework Miranda's original songs and lyrics for laughs, but its parodic versions of "His Shot" and "Straight Is Back" (originally "My Shot" and "You'll Be Back") serve as pointed critiques of Broadway and the politics of the entertainment industry. In "His Shot," Lin-Manuel Miranda becomes a character who lauds his own career and loves "being a hot big shot." The character sings about the mixed reviews for *In the Heights* and his subsequent success with *Hamilton*, which has him "on a roll." Miranda describes the enormous financial stakes involved in producing a Broadway hit, yet the size and spectacle of a production are no guarantee of a show's quality. He takes on the mission to save Broadway as long as he remains the center of attention and the number one star in every production:

> Essentially, new shows stink relentlessly
> They fill them with hot air and have a spending spree
> Everything is overblown condescendingly
> But there will be a revolution in this century Enter me!
> (He says with reverberie-rie-rie-rie-rie)
> And don't be shocked when theater history mentions me
> I will root out the rife mediocrity
> And eventually, all shows will be starring me!

This parody of the anthemic "My Shot" transforms the aspirational lyrics of the original and their articulation of the American Dream into a critique of Miranda's supposed savior complex, as well as Broadway's perverse economic incentives to create shows for the masses that convey little artistic merit.

This theme reappears in "Straight Is Back," a song that parodies the music and lyrics sung by the character of King George in the original show. In *Hamilton*, the character of King George is cast with a white actor, and his music, unlike the rap and hip-hop of the majority of the show, is more reminiscent of a Beatles pop song. The original character of King George is portrayed as a fey sociopath who sings gayly about retaliating against the upstart colonials: "I'll send a fully armed battalion / To remind you of my love!" This casting and characterization establish a heteronormative sexual politics around ethnic and racial identities. The Black and Brown actors who rap to hip-hop rhythms embody legitimate forms of masculinity, while the white villain is portrayed as an effeminate figure of comic relief. The parody in *Spamilton* underscores the racial and sexual politics of the original casting and characterization. The title refers to how Miranda's musicals have made Broadway a safe space for heterosexual audiences:

> Why so sad?
> Remember how musical theatre was cloyingly gay?
> 'Till the public got mad
> Now *Hamilton*'s new rearrangement has changed the fad
>
> Straight is back
> Soon you'll see
> Campy musicals went out with Glee
> Straight is back
> Time will tell
> Kinky Boots is going straight to hell

In addition to these spoofs, *Spamilton* also takes aim at the outrageous ticket prices for the original Broadway show. A series of beggar women enter the stage and implore the Miranda character for tickets, only to reveal themselves as different Broadway divas such as Bernadette Peters and Liza Minelli. In the Chicago production I attended, one particular surprise appearance also lampooned *Hamilton*'s race-conscious casting, and the parodic stunt resulted in two minutes of uninterrupted laughter from the audience. A great admirer of *Hamilton*, Gerard Alessandrini writes in the digital booklet that accompanies the *Spamilton* cast album, "Anything that takes itself so divinely seriously is ripe for parody and all sorts of mischievous inspiration."[70] Lin-Manuel Miranda was spotted at a performance of *Spamilton* and was overheard saying, "'Yeah, he made fun of my singing. That's all fair game,' Real Miranda told me after the show. 'If I can be okay with the praise, I better be okay with people making fun of my singing. If you can't take a joke, don't do this.'"[71] The spoof does more than just let the air out of a public figure who has been inflated by fame and success; it also lays bare the politics of cultural production and the ways in which a "revolutionary" show such as *Hamilton* can reproduce the hierarchical structures and exclusionary social formations that the original race-conscious casting was meant to subvert.

Miranda's musicals can be read as bookends for the Obama era and the hope for an egalitarian society where empowered minorities restage the nation's story. *In the Heights* articulates the promise of collective action, a discourse consistent with the values and political strategies of Obama's early community organizing. *Hamilton*, in spite of its ebullient reinterpretation of U.S. foundational fictions, portrays its protagonist as a tragic hero, which if read allegorically brings Obama's promise of hope and change to a crossroads and anticipates an uncertain transition. With the results of the 2016 presidential elections, Miranda's musical could not be more prophetic, and when Van Jones characterized the Donald Trump victory over Hillary Clinton, he accurately described it as a "whitelash"; that is, as a white nationalist renunciation of Obama's progressive agenda and panethnic, multiracial, and gender and sexually inclusive constituencies.[72] Like the classical Greek tragedy, *Hamilton* serves as a morality tale and a didactic warning against the corrupting effects of hubris. Although Barack Obama does not share the character traits that led to Alexander Hamilton's downfall, Miranda's musical foreshadows how President Obama's political legacy has been contested and, in some cases, overturned by the white nationalist Trump agenda, in particular the executive orders that expedite family separation and the deportation of undocumented immigrants.

As mentioned earlier, Miranda addressed the anger, anguish, and anxiety of the progressive coalition when, by proxy, the actor playing Vice President Aaron Burr—Branden Victor Dixon—addressed VP-elect Mike Pence at the final curtain call of a November 18, 2016, performance of *Hamilton*. Miranda used considerable social, political, and media capital to denounce the Trump agenda. This radical critique of white nationalism tore down the theatrical fourth wall in order to condemn the policies of the incoming president who had promised to construct a physical wall along the U.S.-Mexico border. Nevertheless, Pence later said he enjoyed the show because, despite the activist coda that called him out directly, in the Alexander Hamilton story he had just seen, a predominately Black and Brown cast perform on stage the story of white immigration and national identity. In this way, and because the denunciation came from a Black actor who had just played the villain VP in the show, the coda served to deny Pence the opportunity to claim this narrative as his own. *In the Heights* and *Hamilton* tell the story of U.S. national identity from the subaltern perspective, and the two musicals convey the social and cultural values that constitute the habitus of immigrants and communities of color.[73] That these works grapple with their own structural contradictions helps elucidate the nonbinary diasporic imaginary and the contingent value of transcultural capital in fields of power.

Miranda's musical theater also demonstrates how an accumulation of economic and social capital may facilitate advantageous positionings for Latinx artists in the hegemonic field of cultural production. Yet that success does not necessarily change the rules of the game in that field. When Alberto Sandoval-Sánchez assessed the state of Latinx theater in the 1980s and 1990s, he described it as "an octopus with many legs" because of its artistic, linguistic, and cultural heterogeneity, its racial, ethnic, and gender diversity, as well as its decentralized forms of production, from grassroots, community-based theater to major Broadway musicals. Nevertheless, it is this same complexity that has kept Latinx theater at the margins of U.S. and Latin American canons, either for being too "Latin" or for not belonging to any Latin American national tradition.[74] Sandoval-Sánchez marks the 1990s as a transitional moment when Latinx theater practitioners moved from the grassroots to Anglo-American regional theaters: "Latino theater has thus moved from being a collective endeavor to the exaltation of the individual, the playwright, a transformation that registers increasing commodification and commercialization."[75] With Miranda's musical theater, the crossover onto the mainstream stage does not necessarily reflect an erasure of Latinx subjects or even of the diasporic imaginary that emerges from their enclave communities. However, the success of *In the Heights* does suggest that its reimagining of the American Dream relies on middle-class conventionalism that is more palatable to a non-Latinx audience. Similarly, *Hamilton* affirms the role of immigrants in the founding of the nation, yet it does so by telling the story of a white, Anglo-Saxon immigrant, even if he is played by a Latino actor. Other than his staged embodiment, the Latino actor who plays the character of Hamilton performs little to no identifiably Latinx culture, thus leaving open the question of whether this musical can be described as Latinx theater at all. Miranda's musicals have definitely broadened the kind of material that garners success on Broadway, and his political activism off stage demonstrates how a highly visible artist can put his accumulated social and economic capital to use for progressive causes. Despite these achievements, *In the Heights* and *Hamilton* convey hegemonic values and conventional wisdom about upward mobility and paternalistic legacies that undermine the transformative potential of transcultural capital in the field of cultural production.

Miranda's star continues to shine brightly, and he remains thoroughly engaged in theater, film, television, and the arts. His personal website, linmanuel.com, features past, present, and ongoing projects that span a broad swath of pop culture and media landscapes. In addition to the film version of *In the Heights*, released in June 2021, the website offers a production diary, written in collaboration with Quiara Alegría Hudes and Jeremy McCarter, which aims to "give readers an intimate look at the decades-long creative life" of this musical.[76] Hudes, the librettist for the original Broadway musical, is also the screenwriter for the film version and is a Pulitzer Prize–winning playwright for her stage play, *Water by the Spoonful*. Likewise, Jeremy McCarter is the coauthor of the show *Hamilton* as well as the glossy, behind-the-scenes account of the show's conception and development, *Hamilton: The Revolution*. Miranda's website shows that he is in constant collaboration with many artists and writers, both in the United States and in Puerto Rico. With projects ranging from *Fosse/Verdon*—a biographical miniseries Miranda executive produced and in which he plays the actor Roy Scheider—to a gallery café in Vega

Alta, PR—La Placita de Güisin—dedicated in honor of his grandfather, Miranda has translated his success into multiple platforms that extend the scope of his cultural production beyond the more traditionally Latinx themes and stories that appear in *In the Heights*.

Nevertheless, Puerto Rico and the Latinx community remain at the core of his artistic enterprise. In one of the promotional YouTube videos for *In the Heights*, Miranda comments satirically on the challenge a Latino artist and producer faces when trying to convince a mainstream Broadway audience that shows about Latinxs are safe and well within their expectations and sensibilities:

> Is it alright for me to rep my people with pride?
> For kids to see Latinos in a positive light?
> For tourists to ride up to Washington Heights without lockin' their
>   car doors tight?
> Maybe rolling down the windows buyin' piraguas from the man
>   on the side of Riverside Drive?
> Or seeing life through his eyes?
> He's just like you and I, he's just trying to get by.[77]

Miranda and his collaborators broke ground where previous Latino-themed Broadway shows were unable to tread, and through a multiplatform marketing scheme not only made a show about working-class Latinxs palatable to the predominately white, upper-middle-class Broadway audience, but also helped diversify the Broadway audience by making musical theater more accessible to the very same communities represented in the show.[78] Many of Miranda's non-Latinx projects convey a communitarian sensibility that is more muted in *Hamilton*, which focuses more on the individual tragedy (or is it the tragic individualism?) of the eponymous character. Although this blockbuster hit retells the Anglo-American immigrant story through the music and poetics of Black and Latinx cultures, the stories that emerge from those cultures and experiences take a less than supporting role in the central story of the white Founding Fathers. Given the diversity of Miranda's work in multiple media and genres, his next Broadway hit may or may not focus on a working-class Latinx community. That doesn't necessarily mean the artist has moved on and sold out, yet it does show how transcultural capital can create a pathway into hegemonic forms of cultural production but does not always transform the political economy of a global entertainment industry, nor does it necessarily decolonize the dominant narratives of the American Dream even when repackaged through the music and embodied performances of minoritized subjects.

CODA ON COLORISM

The film version of *In the Heights* was released in theaters and on HBO Max on June 11, 2021, just as this book was in its final stages of production. The film received enthusiastic reviews, yet many critics denounced the lack of Black Latinx actors cast in any of the starring roles—except for Leslie Grace who plays Nina. The controversy gained national attention when Felice León of *The Root* challenged director John M. Chu for the "erasure" of dark-skinned actors in a film about Washington Heights, also known as Little Dominican Republic, where Black Latinx people and culture are highly visible.[79] Lin-Manuel Miranda issued an apology on Twitter, saying, "I'm seeing the discussion around Afro-Latino representation in our film this weekend and it is clear that many in our dark-skinned Afro-Latino community don't feel sufficiently represented within it, particularly among leading roles. I can hear the hurt and frustration over colorism, of feeling still unseen in the feedback." The criticism generated numerous articles and interviews in the press; in a discussion among Latina writers and editors at the *New York Times*, art critic fellow Isabelia Herrera states: "Yes, we understand that this is a musical, a story with surreal and fantastical elements. Even if we accept the view that a fantasy does not have to be representative, that argument assumes that Black Latinos do not belong in these imagined worlds anyway."[80] Although many of these same critics acknowledge the work that Miranda has done to make Black and Latinx actors more visible on Broadway and in Hollywood, the debate of colorism reflects how minoritized cultures are made more palatable for mass audiences. *In the Heights* originally reimagined the way Broadway portrays Latinx communities, and purposefully steered away from the negative stereotypes of poverty and criminality that characterize shows like *West Side Story* and the unsuccessful *The Capeman*. Yet this "gentrification" of Latinx communities not only erases dark-skinned Latinas and Latinos but also adds a glossy veneer of respectability to urban enclaves that continue to struggle with systemic racism, police violence, and economic precarity. Can a musical or a film about Latinx characters be uplifting while not turning a blind eye to the realities that confront our communities? Miranda ends his Twitter apology by promising to "do better" in his future projects. Nevertheless, the logic of capital that runs the entertainment industry is as much to blame for the erasure of those Black Latinx faces that supposedly don't "sell" to large audiences. If the "medium is the message," as Marshall McLuhan argued, the economic field in which cultural production takes place also determines whose material and bodily practices have value and legitimacy. Under these conditions, it is unlikely that any Broadway or Hollywood productions will ever "get it right" when it comes to decolonizing their own industries.

Race, Sex, and Enterprising Spirits in Works by Dolores Prida and Mayra Santos Febres

Before the "body" there is the "flesh," that zero degree of social conceptualization that does not escape concealment under the brush of discourse, or the reflexes of iconography.

—Hortense Spillers, "Mama's Baby, Papa's Maybe:
An American Grammar Book"

Black Lives Matter. Black Latina Lives Matter. Despite the self-evidence of these statements, Black, Indigenous, People of Color (BIPOC) must continually prove their worth when they enter hegemonic fields of power and pursue an upwardly mobile trajectory. The epigraph by Hortense Spillers emphasizes how slavery stripped Black women and men of their humanity and reduced them to commoditized bodies, whose only value was in their capacity to endure physical labor and reproduce themselves through childbirth. Spillers continues: "Even though the European hegemonies stole bodies—some of them female—out of West African communities in concert with the African 'middleman,' we regard this human and social irreparability as high crimes against the *flesh*, as the person of African females and African males registered the wounding. If we think of the 'flesh' as a primary narrative, then we mean its seared, divided, ripped-apartness, riveted to the ship's hole, fallen, or 'escaped' overboard."[1] Spillers's definition of the "flesh" and its "ripped-apartness" brings to mind Gloria Anzaldúa's metaphor of the U.S.-Mexico border as "*una herida abierta* where the Third World grates against the first and bleeds. And before a scab forms it hemorrhages again, the lifeblood of two worlds merging to form a third country—a border culture."[2] The "flesh" and the "wound" foreground the violence that plantation economies and settler colonialism have inflicted on Black, Indigenous, and Mestiza women. Rita de Maesneer and Fernanda Bustamante make a similar argument in their analysis of recent Dominican fiction, Caribbean literature and art, and more broadly the "post-metaphysical paradigm" of contemporary Western thought:

El cuerpo es abordado como representación y se localizan en él signos y experien-cias que le son inherentes. Es el caso para la violencia que se exterioriza a partir de la herida-huella que se puede convertir en cicatriz. Este gesto disruptivo de poner en evidencia el cuerpo, y con ello, su vulnerabilidad, es propio de las nar-rativas y el arte del Caribe, el cual ha venido asociándose con el cuerpo al menos desde el mismo "Descubrimiento."[3]

The body is addressed as representation, and inherent signs and experiences are localized *within it*. This is the case with violence that manifests itself as the wound-trace that can become a scar. This disruptive gesture of revealing the body and, with it, its vulnerability, is characteristic of the narrative and art of the Caribbean, which has been linking itself to the body since the "Discovery." (my translation)

This violence is reinflicted symbolically when women of color are coerced into adopting the hegemonic forms of whiteness that are associated with success in edu-cation, professionalization, and economic upward mobility. The gentrification of the flesh attempts to disguise and veil the wounds that Black Latinas carry as a legacy of slavery and colonialism. This chapter looks specifically at Dolores Pri-da's play *Botánica* (1991) and Mayra Santos Febres's novel *Fe en disfraz* (2009), in which violence against the female protagonists occurs in tandem with the gentri-fication of the flesh; that is, a reorientation of a Afro-Latina *cierta manera* toward an embodiment of coloniality and domination. The main characters in these works—Milagros in *Botánica* and Fe in *Fe en disfraz*—choose radically different means to negotiate their transcultural capital while attempting to break the cycles of enslavement and exploitation that have commoditized their bodies. Despite these different embodied strategies of resistance, as their names suggest, both Milagros and Fe make interventions in the material world through traditions of Black Latina spirituality and the supernatural.

As a dramatic work that has been staged off-Broadway and has become a staple in high school and college productions, Prida's *Botánica* offers a clear example of contemporary Latina theater in which gendered, transcultural subjects capitalize on the transgressiveness of destabilized identities, even as they resist economic exploitation and racial violence. While they may be as much victims of neoliberal economic inequalities as they are oppressed minorities in the context of systemic racism in the United States, their entrepreneurial spirit turns to the Latina spirit world to draw from their diasporic imaginaries and find a sense of rootedness in their urban ethnic enclave. Their transgressive gender and ethnic identities gen-erate financial and cultural capital through a contestation of the status quo, recon-figuring the Latina embodied economy through transculturation. As Alberto Sandoval-Sánchez writes in *José Can You See: Latinos On and Off Broadway*, the play's main character is "a survivor, always taking into consideration that her iden-tity is determined by antagonisms, binary oppositions, oscillations, vacillations, discontinuities, plurality, ambivalence, and constant negotiations as she formulates a new, hybrid, second-generation U.S. Latina identity."[4] Beyond the play's comedic portrayal of intergenerational conflict and the vicissitudes of gender and racial identity formation in the Puerto Rican diaspora community of El Barrio, *Botánica* offers an economic lesson on how oppressed minorities resist cultural and financial dispossession under conditions of urban gentrification as well as the ideological imperatives that privilege whiteness as the end goal for individual upward mobility.

As the college-educated granddaughter of Doña Geno, the Puerto Rican matriarch, Santería practitioner, and owner of the titular *botánica*, or herb shop, Millie struggles to assimilate to the cultural and economic values that were inculcated in her at the prestigious New Hampshire college she attended, where she also experienced violent acts of racial bigotry at the hands of her white, upper-class sorority sisters. As Doña Geno calls it, *"ese college de blanquitos"* (that college of whities) has transformed Millie, distancing her from her Afro-Indigenous roots, which the play represents through the image of a huge ceiba tree painted on the walls of the herb shop.[5] Millie's absent father is also Cuban, which adds to the multiethnic, transcultural heritage that becomes an object of shame and self-loathing while Millie studies business administration. The play's main conflict is between Millie's aspirations to move away from El Barrio and begin working for a corporate bank in downtown Manhattan, and Doña Geno's desire that Millie use her newly acquired educational capital to take over the family business. Ultimately, Millie finds herself negotiating cultural values and economic value, striking a deal with her Afro–Puerto Rican traditions in order to simultaneously pursue her corporate career path while tapping into an entrepreneurial potential for local wealth creation and proprietorship in an urban ethnic enclave.

In Santos Febres's *Fe en disfraz*, the high value placed on innovation and authenticity in the academic professions performs a similar set of contradictions when an Afro-Venezuelan woman stakes her claim in a space of privilege dominated by white men. Here, the lure of whiteness takes on a literal embodiment in the sexual relationship between Fe Verdejo, a highly accomplished Latin American historian who directs a prestigious seminar at the University of Chicago, and Martín Tirado, a white, Puerto Rican digital archivist who works for Fe. The novel recounts Martín's first-person reminiscences—in his words *"apuntes"* or notes—of how his collaboration with Fe on the history of manumitted female slaves in Latin America turns into a bondage–discipline/domination–submission/sadism–masochism (BDSM) ritual that appropriates the material artefacts of the history they are researching. The transgressive nature of their erotic encounters does not necessarily stem from their intercollegial affair. The graphic descriptions of their sex acts, narrated from Martín's perspective, are imbued with a Sadean eroticism that ritualizes the history of master-slave, white-Black, and male-female exertions of power, domination, and dependency. As in *Botánica*, the appearance of Latina empowerment and economic mobility thinly veils the systems of exploitation and cultural appropriation that constitute the history of Black women in the Caribbean, Latin America, and the United States. *Fe en disfraz* reaches far back into Latin American colonial history and the unrecounted experiences of manumitted Black women, while situating the narrative chronotope within the virtual reality of contemporary neocolonialism, globalization, and post-American hegemony.

As in the case of Nina from *In the Heights*, the acquisition of educational capital does not necessarily facilitate an upwardly mobile trajectory that acknowledges and embraces Latinx transcultural capital. The values of American individualism and white nationalism conflict with the community cultural wealth that is rooted in the Latinx urban enclave where Nina first aspired to make it out of Washington Heights and achieve her family's dreams of success in higher education. As a woman of color from a working-class background, her levels of achievement do not prepare her for the other forms of gatekeeping she encounters as a scholarship student at Stanford. Ultimately, she returns to her community and the values of collective struggle she learned from Abuela Claudia and her mother, Camila, the two women who represented a counterpoint to the male-dominated spaces of the family home and business.

Similarly, the main characters in Prida's *Botánica* and Santos Febres's *Fe en disfraz* turn to education as a means of achieving upward mobility. The protagonists in these works also face the racially and sexually exploitative legacies of white settler colonialism and slavery that characterizes Caribbean, Latin American, and U.S. histories. However, as they empower themselves through educational capital, they also risk commoditizing their cultural heritage and reproducing the forms of material and symbolic violence that have been inflicted not only on them but also on their Afro-Latina ancestors and families. Prida's play and Santos Febres's novel both explore how that repressed history—the history of the flesh—insists on being acknowledged and made visible through traditions of faith and spirituality. More so than any of the other works I discuss in previous chapters, *Botánica* and *Fe en disfraz* propose that Black Latina spirituality has the potential to mitigate and resist the culturally deracinating imperatives that secular education imposes on Caribbean women of color.

THEATER, FICTION, AND LATINA EMPOWERMENT

As one of the key figures in the development of Latinx theater, along with her extensive career in journalism, Dolores Prida (1943–2012) consistently addressed the conflicts that emerge for upwardly mobile Latina women who struggle to negotiate a balance between their cultural heritages, racial identities, and gender and sexual autonomy, all while attempting to acquire high levels of educational capital and professional success in the United States. Born in Caibarién, Cuba, Prida came with her family to the United States in 1961 and soon established herself in New York City. Alberto Sandoval-Sánchez writes, "Dolores Prida's theatrical works offer a model of/for the construction of bilingual and bicultural identities. Prida successfully represents in her work how, through continuous negotiations and accommodations, her protagonists can function in both Latino and Anglo-American cultures."[6] In addition to plays such as *Beautiful Señoritas* (1977), *The Beggar's Soap Opera* (1979), *Coser y Cantar* (1981), and *Casa Propia* (1999), Prida also contributed to a number of journalistic publications, such as *El Diario / La Prensa*, *The Daily News*, and *Latina Magazine*, where she wrote the popular advice column, "Dolores Dice" ("Dolores Says"). In the replies to her Latina readers, Prida offers advice that mirrors many of the transcultural negotiations her characters act out on the theatrical stage. For example, when *Sexy in Chicago* asks about a "non-Latina coworker" who always greets her in Spanish, Prida advises her not to assume the coworker is being condescending, and that she might just want to practice her Spanish.

> On the other hand, if you can see she's being patronizing or snide, unleash some humor on her. Next time she asks you, "¿Cómo estás?" give her the old Ricky Ricardo fast-and-furious riff:
>
> "Estoybiengraciasaydiosmioestamujermiraqueselodigoyselodigoysiempremepreguntalamismabobería"—or something like that.[7]

Prida also suggests that *Sexy in Chicago* should explore her "feelings of discomfort about being addressed in Spanish."[8] This piece of advice is consistent with the dramatic and comedic staging in her plays where Latina protagonists not only have to face up to multiple forms of discrimination, but also have to come to terms with their own estrangement from their Latinx heritage cultures.

Mayra Santos Febres (1966) is among a group of Puerto Rican writers loosely known as *la generación del 80*, and she shares with authors such as Rafael Acevedo, Ángel Lozada, and Urayoán Noel a postmodern sensibility that continues and accelerates some of the decentering, postnationalist literary projects that have characterized Puerto Rican literature since the Seventies.[9] Santos Febres's works additionally have found international distribution and critical acclaim, thus placing her among other Afro-Caribbean women writers like Nancy Morejón, Maryse Condé, Michelle Cliff, Edwidge Danticat, and Jamaica Kincaid. Santos Febres has published poetry, essays, short stories, and novels; she has also written for television and film and created a literary blog. Santos Febres's literary production reaches across the Caribbean to address the history and experiences of migration and diaspora, not only from the islands to the U.S. mainland, but from one Caribbean island to another as well as to South America and Europe. The main characters in her novels range from a young, *mulata* drag performer and bolero singer (*Sirena Selena vestida de pena*, 2000) to a white, middle-class, male journalist (*Cualquier miércoles soy tuya*, 2002), a Black Puerto Rican madam based on a historical figure from the early twentieth century (*Nuestra Señora de la Noche*, 2006), and a Black Puerto Rican maid who has a brief and intense love affair with Argentine tango singer Carlos Gardel (*La amante de Gardel*, 2015). She has also published a fictionalized biography of Puerto Rican poet Julia de Burgos (*Yo misma fui mi ruta: La maravillosa vida de Julia de Burgos*, 2014). This multiplicity of genres, themes, geographical settings, and characters reflect Santos Febres's constant search for new ways to diversify and expand her work, always with an eye for promoting a transcultural, multiracial representation of the Caribbean and the many diasporic, gendered subjects who inhabit its neocolonial spaces. In an interview with Melanie Pérez-Ortiz, Santos Febres states:

> Yo quiero explorar la convergencia de raza y clase y explorar, contestarme algu-
> nas preguntas que tengo sobre ese sundae de racismos que tenemos, que son el rac-
> ismo hispanófilo y el racismo gringo, mezclaos. Y me llama la atención la
> pigmentocracia y el asunto del género. El proyecto a largo plazo es escribir mucho
> [lo dice con énfasis]. Yo quiero ser una de esas escritoras que tienen 17 novelas en
> los costaos, que tienen 25 libros de cuentos y de ensayos y de todo. Yo quiero ser
> una de esas.[10]

> I want to explore the convergence of race and class and explore, find answers to
> some questions I have about that sundae of racisms that we have, which are the
> Hispanophile racism and the Gringo racism, mixed together. And something
> that calls my attention is the pigmentocracy and the issue of gender. The long-
> term project is to write a lot [she says with emphasis]. I want to be one of those
> women writers who has 17 novels under her belt, who has 25 books of short sto-
> ries and of essays and of everything. I want to be one of those women writers.
> (my translation)

In her efforts to undertake such a prolific and variegated literary enterprise, Santos Febres has also accumulated a significant amount of critical capital, shedding light on those unseen margins where Black, mixed-race, poor, and disenfranchised Caribbean subjects struggle to conquer their own terrain and achieve a measure of recognition, self-determination, and economic security. The characters in her novels face trade-offs that arise when their entrepreneurial spirits lead them to commoditize their raced bodies, profit from their transgressive sexualities, or utilize others to achieve their self-promoting ends. The decisions these characters make at critical moments, when they must negotiate self-interest against communitarian ethics, reflect the opportunities and disenfranchisements that a history of exploitation and experiences of discrimination have imposed on subaltern Latinx Caribbean subjects for centuries.

A number of literary works portray the roles that education, religion, and the diaspora play in the upward mobility of Latinx characters who live in working-class, urban communities in the United States. Ernesto Quiñonez's novel *Chango's Fire* (2004) depicts a male protagonist—Julio Santana—who lives in the rapidly gentrifying Puerto Rican neighborhood of Spanish Harlem; Julio turns to Santería as a means of forging his own cultural identity in the midst of an influx of white artists and urban professionals and as a way to escape the underground economy of insurance scams that has helped finance his property ownership.[11] Angie Cruz's novels *Soledad* (2001) and *Let It Rain Coffee* (2005) tell stories of Dominican women who also strive to attain the American Dream but who must contend with the ghosts of their dysfunctional families and their violent pasts.[12] Loida Maritza Pérez also portrays these generational tensions in her novel *Geographies of Home* (1999), in which the main female protagonist has to abandon her university education to return home and confront the toxic legacies of paternalism and domestic abuse that characterize her strict Christian upbringing, while also reclaiming an Afro-Dominican spirituality that intervenes in the misogynistic violence that plagues her family.[13] Julia Álvarez and Cristina García are well known for their fictions that depict the clash of Latinx family values with the dominant, white cultural norms that young immigrant and exile women negotiate in order to establish autonomous identities as educated and upwardly mobile subjects.[14] García's novels, especially *Dreaming in Cuban* (1992) and *The Agüero Sisters* (1997), integrate elements of magical realism and depict the rituals of the Santería tradition in order to critique the discourses of cultural assimilation and liberal feminism that relegate Latinx culture to an underdeveloped stage of personal and social evolution.[15] All of these works would lend themselves well to a comparison to either *Botánica* or *Fe en disfraz*, but what makes a counterpoint between these two particular works compelling is the radically different ways in which the female protagonists turn to faith, spirituality, and ritual in order to make visible the wound-trace that the history of colonialism and slavery has inflicted on their "flesh." This embodied resistance serves to realign their positionings in the fields of power to which their educational and economic capital give them access. Their different approaches both show, nonetheless, that despite the upward mobility and institutional legitimacy their educational achievements facilitate, as Afro-Latinas the legacies of colonialism, slavery, and sexual exploitation are staged and inscribed on their bodies and must be made visible and legible rather than obscured and erased by the acquisition of educational capital.

The most obvious difference between the two works is in the genres of theater and fiction. With Prida's play, the dialogue, set design, and the kinetic components of stage acting serve to articulate the debates over upward mobility and cultural deracination. Each character represents a different side of this debate, and their dialogues and monologues stage the arguments over the value of Latinx culture versus the hegemonic, Anglo-American individualism that Millie adopts as part of her elite education. Although I have yet to attend a live performance of this play, the set design, as described in the stage directions, allows the audience to see the Afro-Caribbean visual and material cultures that are associated with Santería practices and the alternative medicinal remedies that are the *botánica*'s stock and trade.[16] Set design, which is variable from one live production to another, can also stage the fantastical and magical realist aspects of the play's plotline. Depending on the production budget, the theater space, and the use of lighting, sound, and special effects, the set design engages audiovisually with the audience so as to create an experiential engagement with its central themes and debates. The actors' bodies, gestures, and movements on the stage—what Augusto Boal has called the ritual and kinetic images in theater—underscore the way cultural heritage and economic imaginaries are embodied and embedded in time and space.[17] Finally, the play's active engagement with the audience reaffirms the collective and communitarian values that contrast with the individualist and exclusionary modes of cultural production and consumption that characterize elite forms of artistic expression. Commissioned and first produced by New York's Repertorio Español in 1991, the play's bilingual script privileges the Spanish-speaking generations of Latinx migrants in New York City, while remaining attentive to the hybridized and transcultural forms of expression that reflect the second and third generations of diverse, diasporic communities that reside in these ethnic enclaves. This makes the play accessible to an audience that normally does not attend live theatrical performances, particularly English-only productions at high-priced Broadway and even off-Broadway venues.

In contrast, Santos Febres's novel uses the dialogic discourse of narrative fiction to give voice to the forgotten and silenced Black women of Latin America's colonial slave era. The novel brings together the fictional story of an interracial love affair between the two Latin American historians with an apocryphal archive of slave testimonials that appear in unpublished colonial era court documents. The intercalation of these texts serves to portray the archival labor that is a core methodology of the historian's profession, and while these apocryphal texts are loosely based on established historical research, the multivoiced narrative of *Fe en disfraz* calls on the reader to suspend disbelief in order to fill in the blanks left behind by the dominant forms of historiography that privilege the white male perspective.[18] With its choice to narrate the love story through the first-person voice of Martín— the white male lover—the novel deploys an ironic destabilization of truth claims and historical accuracy, which are contingent on the structures of institutional and economic power rather than on the easily appropriated narratives of experience or conventional notions of chronological order.

Whereas the set design in Prida's play gives the audience visual and material access to the embodied spaces where Afro-Caribbean culture is practiced and reinvented, Santos Febres's novel relies on the disruptive effects of analepsis and prolepsis—flashbacks and flashforwards—to demonstrate how the material culture of the past can be repurposed and fetishized by the institutional discourses of the present. Finally, while *Botánica*'s theatrical staging of special effects and ritual and kinetic movement allow for a comic disidentification with Afro-Caribbean spiritual traditions, *Fe en disfraz* conveys through figurative language and allegory the syncretic convergence of multiple traditions that deconstruct not only racial hierarchies of discursive power and legitimacy, but also the Judeo-Christian theological and philosophical traditions that oppose and isolate body, mind, and spirit from one another, which have served to privilege and give prominence to white men in official Latin American history, while relegating Black women to the ephemeral domain of popular or even "primitive" cultures.

Despite the differences in these works by Prida and Santos Febres, they both explore how the Afro-Latina body becomes the site where the legacies of colonialism, slavery, and the sexual exploitation of women are restaged, reinscribed, and resisted. The protagonists in these works offer up their own bodies for ritualized reenactments of these violent legacies. On the one hand, the hazing rituals described in *Botánica* facilitate Millie's assimilation into the hegemonic culture of white, university sororities and her acquisition of dominant forms of social and cultural capital. On the other hand, Fe in Santos Febres's novel engages in BDSM rituals with her white, male colleague in order to embody and deconstruct the history of slavery and sexual exploitation that is the main line of inquiry in her academic scholarship and her professional career in the United States. As a play, *Botánica* provides the staging of these contradictions and their possible mitigation, particularly through the dialogue and debate between the characters, but also through the use of special effects and a fantastical deus ex machina that bring together Afro-Latina spirituality and the technology of commerce and finance. With *Fe en disfraz*, the novel provides the narrative structures that position the main story of Fe and Martín's affair alongside the intercalated texts that archive the violent erotic histories they reenact in their BDSM encounters.

These works invoke the legacy of colonialism, slavery, and sexual exploitation to challenge and overcome the perpetuation of violence with which contemporary Black Latina women must contend as they pursue educational capital and economic empowerment, as well as their reintegration into a matrilineal community of Latin American women of color. However, what these works also show is that the bondage into which these characters enter of their own free will is also an enduring social structure—a habitus—that keeps Black Latinas in constant struggle against their own best interests. The different approaches to these contradictions also show how Prida's play promotes a transculturation of capital in order to achieve the reconciliation between past, present, and future female empowerment. Santos Febres's novel, however, turns to a Jungian notion of mythic structures that underlie multiple cultures and racial formations in order to dissipate the violence against Black women so that it becomes a shared history for which we must all take responsibility. Nevertheless, while *Botánica* conveys more explicitly Afro-Latina economic empowerment directly from the female protagonists' perspective, *Fe en disfraz* uses the male voice and gaze to document the female protagonist's attempt to liberate herself from the violent history that binds her. The novel shows that there is no resolution to this violence, which perpetually haunts Black Latinas even when they enter the fields of power that they ostensibly conquer and dominate.

EDUCATIONAL CAPITAL AND THE LURE OF WHITENESS

Millie and Fe accumulate high levels of educational capital in the United States and, in Fe's case, in Latin America and Europe as well. As women of color, their achievements place them among a select group in the academic field, and the elite institutions where they attain their credentials further enhance the value of their educational capital. In Millie's case, she overcomes the odds against her not only as a woman of color, but also as the daughter of a single mother and as a first-generation college student. Millie's family—a matriarchy headed by the grandmother, Doña Geno—is neither destitute nor wealthy. As owner of the building where she runs her *botánica*, Doña Geno does have more economic capital than many of her working-class clientele and is definitely in a far better economic position than the homeless character, Pepe el Indio, who serves as the play's wise fool, very much in the Shakespearean tradition. Nevertheless, Doña Geno's business is at risk, partly because of the gentrification that is rapidly dispossessing and displacing the Latinx community in Spanish Harlem/El Barrio. A real estate investment company has been pressuring Doña Geno to sell her property at an extortionary low price, and Millie is all too ready to make the sale in order to send her grandmother packing to Puerto Rico. The *botánica* is also at risk because Doña Geno tries to manage her business the way she advises and prescribes *recetas y remedios*—recipes and remedies—to her clients: from memory and through intuition, informality, and good doses of hopes and prayers. When Millie returns from college, she finds her grandmother has not adopted the more regimented and orderly form of business accounting Millie had prepared for her. Millie tries to use her educational capital to modernize her grandmother's business, but Doña Gena resists adopting the hegemonic forms of business administration and returns to her informal practice of reciting from memory her remedies and ritual prescriptions. She also allows her customers to run a tab and take home on credit the various herbs, aerosol sprays, and Santería paraphernalia that they need to carry out Doña Geno's prescribed rituals. Doña Geno is more concerned with remaining faithful to her spiritual traditions and making sure her legacy lives on through Millie. The name of her shop—*Botánica La Ceiba*—refers to the strong, deep-rooted Caribbean tree that is also pictured prominently in the play's set design. This metaphorical image embraces the seeming contradiction between the diasporic displacement of the Afro-Caribbean spiritual practices and beliefs and the rootedness that Doña Geno declares as her right to remain in her home in NYC. However, her rootedness reflects the long-standing Latinization of New York as well as her economic status as a property and business owner. While Millie's educational capital eventually helps fulfill Doña Geno's dream and maintains her place in her Latinx community, it isn't until Millie realizes that the dominant discourse of cultural assimilation that promotes a disavowal of her Puerto Rican heritage does not necessarily make for good business and is not economically sustainable in the contemporary landscape of urban gentrification.

As a first-generation college student, Millie acquires her elite education and academic credentials through an affirmative action scholarship. She readily acknowledges that her access to these forms of cultural and symbolic capital was made possible through her hard work, but also because she was the *"spic del turno"*—the token spic—whose scholarship reflected the diversity policies of the university she attended (presumably Dartmouth College in New Hampshire). Although Doña Geno has economic capital through property ownership, the family is far from enjoying the kinds of wealth and privilege that characterize the upper- and upper-middle-class student body that attends Ivy League institutions and whose parents will pay "full freight," particularly if they are legacy admissions.

In contrast, Fe Verdejo in Santos Febres's novel comes from a well-educated family who consistently sent their daughters to exclusive Catholic institutions for their education. The novel suggests that the women in Fe's family history would also consistently fall astray from their plans to pursue a religious calling and join the convent, yet they remained prosperous and independent women in a matriarchal lineage. Fe acquires her academic credentials from prestigious Latin American, European, and U.S. institutions, and she rises to a prominent position in her field as a seminar director at the University of Chicago, considered one of the Ivy Plus institutions. Unlike *Botánica*, however, the novel does not portray Fe returning to her family home to mitigate a financial crisis. Because the novel is narrated by her white, male lover, Martín, readers learn very little about Fe's relationship to her immediate family. Instead, the narrator situates her heritage more broadly in the context of Black Latinas and the history of slavery and sexual exploitation in colonial era Latin America. There is never a suggestion that Fe obtained access to higher education through affirmative action programs of the type available to Millie and other U.S. students from underrepresented groups. Yet her racial heritage and gender identity mark her as a singular success story in a profession dominated by men. Martín writes:

> *No son muchas las estrellas académicas con su preparación y que, como Fe, sean, a su vez, mujeres negras. Historiadores como Figurado Ortiz o como Márquez hay cientos de miles. Somos hombres de extensa preparación libresca, tan blancos como los pergaminos con los que nos rodeamos para sobrevivir nuestra inadecuada pertenencia al mundo de los vivos.*[19]

> There are not many academic stars with her preparation and who, like Fe, are, in turn, Black women. There are hundreds of thousands of historians like Figurado Ortiz or like Márquez. We are men with extensive scholarly preparation, as white as the parchments with which we surround ourselves in order to survive our inadequate belonging to the world of the living. (my translation)

In this passage, the bodies of the white male historians become indistinguishable from the material objects of their labor, which biologically essentializes Fe's outsider status but also, as the novel progresses, invokes the erotic fetishization of the material culture and archives that Fe and Martín integrate in their BDSM rituals.

Like Millie, Fe sees how her profession rewards the kind of labor that reaffirms the legitimacy of its elite institutions. She is well aware of how research projects get funded and uses her knowledge of the system to appeal to *nouveaux riches* Latinx alumni whose wealth will sponsor scholarship on the history of their community. Unlike Millie, Fe does not consider herself a member of a U.S. Latinx community, so her initial attempts to rescue the research seminar from budget cuts is more of a calculated move to flatter the cultural pride and assimilationist sensibilities of her upwardly mobile Latinx donors. At first, Fe proposes a sort of prehistory of Latinidad in Chicago that would establish a false lineage between early Spanish settlers and the Brown, Latinx alumni from working-class Mexican and Puerto Rican backgrounds to whom she appeals:

> *Pensaba en algo así como organizar un recuento de la inmigración a la ciudad. Su montaje ilustraría quiénes fueron los primeros en llegar a estas inhóspitas tierras antes de la copiosa migración de braceros puertorriqueños y mexicanos. Fe*

andaba buscando una prueba que diera con asentamientos peninsulares: comerciantes españoles, marinos portugueses, gente que corroborara la herencia europea de la comunidad latina de Chicago. Eso les interesaría a los ex alumnos (latinos y nouveaux riches) que, de vez en cuando, rondaban el seminario. Quizás, así atraería a posibles mecenas.[20]

She thought of something along the lines of organizing a retelling of immigration to the city. She would set it up to illustrate who were the first to arrive to these inhospitable lands before the copious migration of Puerto Rican and Mexican manual laborers. Fe searched for proof of Peninsular settlements: Spanish merchants, Portuguese sailors, people who would corroborate the European heritage of the Latino community in Chicago. That would interest the alumni (Latinos and *nouveaux riches*) who, every now and then, made the rounds at the seminar. Perhaps that way she could attract potential donors. (my translation)

Ultimately, a fortuitous discovery of unpublished slave narratives allows Fe to successfully pitch a completely different proposal while recuperating the lost history that more closely reflects her own racial and gender heritage. In this way, both Millie and Fe use their educational capital and academic credentials to "return home" and reengage with a Latinx and Latin American heritage that their elite education has devalued and disappeared. Nevertheless, the levels of distinction they obtain through their educational capital situate them as dominated subjects who must constantly prove their legitimacy by adopting the cultural and linguistic registers that are associated with the dominant power structures. Their affirmation of Black Latina heritage is in constant peril of erasure as the lure of whiteness persistently establishes the norms toward which they aspire.

The lure of whiteness appears in different guises in these works, but in both *Botánica* and *Fe en disfraz* the Black Latina characters embody and reenact the symbolic and sexual violence that is part of their cultural and historical legacies. Millie recounts how she is shamed into abandoning her Hispanic name—Milagros—and the Afro-Caribbean spiritual practices that differentiate her from the other entitled, white students at the elite college "*de blanquitos,*" as Doña Geno calls it. She insists on being called Millie, even when she returns home after graduation. At school, she hides all the Santería charms and candles that her grandmother would send as protection and encouragement. The other students ridicule her name—"Miracles, what kind of name is that?"—and declare her a witch for all the Santería paraphernalia she hides under her dorm room bed.[21] When Doña Geno and Anamú (her single, fortysomething mother) prepare a celebratory batch of Puerto Rican *pasteles* to take to the graduation ceremony, Millie lies to them and gives them the wrong date so that she is not embarrassed by their boisterous arrival and their cultural and racial difference. Her tastes in food also change, and she adopts the more health-conscious diet of upper-middle-class Anglo-American culture, disdaining the *comida criolla* that she used to relish with her family. As Bourdieu argues in *Distinction*, "Taste, a class culture turned into nature, that is, *embodied*, helps to shape the class body. It is an incorporated principle of classifi-

cation which governs all forms of incorporation, choosing and modifying everything that the body ingests and digests and assimilates, physiologically and
psychologically."[22] Millie rejects her family's culinary traditions because the starchy,
meat-filled *pasteles* are associated with the rural, peasant culture of the Puerto
Rican *jíbaro*, a throwback to some of the earliest waves of migration from the island
to the mainland and their unassuming, premodern tastes. Her assimilation into
the dominant Anglo-American culture associated with her educational capital
compels her to adopt the health-conscious, pork-free diets that reflect upper-
middle-class preferences for slimness and self-control. Puerto Rican culture is too
much—too loud, too colorful, too fat, and too Black—for the regimented and culturally austere spaces of the New England campus of her college.

For Fe in Santos Febres's novel, the lure of whiteness not only characterizes her
love affair and BDSM rituals with Martín but also is consistent with the neoliberal logic that defines success in her profession and innovation in her academic
field. As Latin American historians based in a prestigious and wealthy U.S. institution, Fe and Martín produce knowledge according to the academic standards
and criteria that give them access to well-funded and competitive grants. Fe's
exhibition, *Esclavas manumisas de Latinoamérica* (Freed Slave Women Of Latin
America), opens many professional opportunities for her, yet it also raises some of
the concerns and critiques that Bourdieu and Wacquant make about what they call
the "ethnocentric intrusions" of U.S. hegemony in social science scholarship and
academic publishing.[23] In this polemical essay, the authors argue against and condemn the ahistorical export of U.S. racial and social categories onto so-called
"minority" or "underclass" populations in other parts of the world. They write,
"Indeed, cultural imperialism (American or otherwise) never imposes itself better than when it is served by progressive intellectuals (or by 'intellectuals of colour'
in the case of racial inequality) who would appear to be above suspicion of promoting the hegemonic interests of a country against which they wield the weap-
ons of social criticism."[24] Bourdieu and Wacquant refer specifically to a book by
Michael Hanchard on Black political and cultural movements in Brazil.[25] Their critique was hotly debated and contested by other Latin Americanists and U.S.
scholars of color who undertake research projects in postcolonial studies.[26] George
Yúdice summarizes the importance of both sides of this debate: "Bourdieu and
Wacquant are correct in pointing out that U.S. scholars are permeated by views
that emanate from the specific force field of U.S. social relation, yet this does not
mean that these views cannot be rearticulated in consonance with social justice."[27]
In the case of Santos Febres's fictional exploration of this debate, the characters in
her novel appropriate and extract from Latin America the archives, oral histories,
and material culture that would otherwise be the patrimony of a nation and its
people. There is a long history of cultural theft from Latin America, Africa, and
Asia that has accompanied U.S. and European colonialism.[28] Xica da Silva's dress,
which is one of the artifacts in Fe Verdejo's exhibition, symbolizes the lure of
whiteness as both a fetish object for the upwardly mobile Black women who have
worn it, as well as an object of Brazilian material culture that becomes a historical

artifact and circulates in U.S. cultural and academic institutions. Acting as an agent of those institutions, when Fe takes the dress out of Brazil and uses it in her BDSM rituals, she is simultaneously depriving Brazil of its material cultural heritage while appropriating it to situate herself as an embodiment of that history.

Botánica and *Fe en disfraz* interrogate the terms under which Black Latinas gain access to educational capital as well as the rigid criteria of scholarly "rigor" and "impact" that attributes value to their labor. Their experiences reflect the manifesto published by the Black Latinas Know Collective, a group of scholars, activists, and knowledge producers who collaborate to challenge these standards, especially in the academic institutions that purport such scholarly rigor is colorblind. They write:

> WE KNOW . . . that all scholarship comes from particular personal experiences. Our scholarship is informed by our intimate experiences with Black Latina womanhood. From early experiences of having our Latinidad and Blackness questioned, to dealing with white Latinx standards of beauty that exclude us, to being invisibilized, to being designated as incapable of occupying our places as professors, intellectuals, and knowledge producers, our insights are important and unreplicable.[29]

Millie and Fe struggle to resist the lure of whiteness, even as the professions and spaces of privilege they seek to enter establish Eurocentric norms as the standard to which they must aspire.

LEGACIES OF RACIAL VIOLENCE IN *BOTÁNICA*

Botánica stages the transcultural heritage of the Afro-Indigenous Caribbean through ritualized violence and the invocation of the histories of conquest, colonialism, and genocide. Millie recounts the sorority hazing ritual she endured, which reenacted the history of lynching and the extermination of indigenous peoples in the Americas. At the climax of the play, Millie has a heated confrontation with her grandmother when she refuses to settle down and live out Doña Geno's dream of taking her place as proprietor of the herb shop. She finally reveals to her grandmother the abuse she suffered as a first-generation, nonwhite student at the elite college where she acquired her educational capital. The other students made fun of her name and the many *remedios y resguardos*—remedies and protection spells— she received from home. Finally, at her induction into an exclusive sorority, her so-called sisters decide to play a cruel joke on her:

> *Me llevaron al bosque, de noche . . . me vistieron con una toga, me hicieron caminar descalza sobre los pine cones, me amarraron a uno de los pinos . . . a mis pies pusieron un montón de tissue paper—rojo. Parecía una hoguera. Encendieron velas. Me vaciaron encima una botella de ron. Una de ellas golpeaba un pequeño tamborcito de juguete, las demás bailaron a mi alrededor, como una danza india y . . . yo sé que fue un accidente, pero . . . a una de ellas se le cayó la vela . . . y*

aquella hoguera de papel se convirtió en una hoguera de verdad. En la confusión, en lo que me desamarraban, mis pies, empapados de ron. . . . My feet got burned, abuela! (Geno la abraza.) But I didn't quit, I didn't quit. Porque eso es lo que quieren, que nos demos por vencidos. Pero gané. Y me gradué. Summa Cum Laude.

GENO: *(Meciéndola en sus brazos. Sin reproche.) Pero, m'ijita, de que sirve ganar si dejas de ser quien eres. . . .*

MILLIE: *¿Y quiénes somos, abuela? ¿Quiénes somos?*[30]

They took me to the forest, at night . . . they dressed me in a toga, they made me walk barefoot on the pinecones, they tied me to one of the pine trees . . . they put a pile of red tissue paper at my feet. It looked like a bonfire. They lit candles. They poured a bottle of rum over me. One of them beat a tiny toy drum, and the others danced around me, like an Indian dance and . . . I know it was an accident, but . . . one of them dropped her candle . . . and that paper bonfire became a real bonfire. In the confusion, while they untied me, my feet, soaked in rum. . . . My feet got burned, abuela! (*Geno* hugs her.) But I didn't quit, I didn't quit. Because that is what they want, that we surrender and give up. But I won. And I graduated. Summa Cum Laude.

GENO: (Rocking her back and forth in her arms. Without reproach.) But, m'ijita, what good is it if you stop being who you are. . . .

MILLIE: And who are we, abuela? Who are we? (my translation)

As noted earlier, the *"college de blanquitos"* in *"Nu Jamprish,"* as Doña Geno refers to it, is a thinly veiled reference to Dartmouth College, an Ivy League institution whose retired, racist mascot was an Indian and where, in reaction to the radical Orozco mural—*The Epic of American Civilization*—Dartmouth alum Walter Beach Humphrey painted the controversial Hovey Murals, which depicted drunken and half-naked Indians cavorting in the forest with Eleazar Wheelock, the college's founder. Millie's burning at the stake also brings to mind the traditional homecoming bonfire, around which all first-year students run multiple laps according to their graduation year. Although the practice is currently prohibited, in the past students tried to touch the fire for good luck as they ran around it. Millie's experience might seem melodramatic, yet it is based on a legacy of racism and genocide that lies at the center of elitist educational institutions.[31] The racist violence her white sorority "sisters" inflict on her mixed-race, Brown body serves as an initiation into the elitist spaces of an Ivy League institution.

Nevertheless, the hazing ritual reaffirms and restages the legacy of conquest and genocide that marks Millie as a subordinate member of her class, even though she graduates summa cum laude. Her acceptance into the exclusive realm of the power elite is contingent on her continued and perpetual status as a dominated subject, and with her burnt feet, her body is forever branded as property of the dominant institutions that facilitate her upward mobility. By having Millie recount the episode in this monologue, Prida's play avoids visually restaging the violence as a prurient and sensationalist theatrical device. Millie's monologue also gives her the voice to "own up" to her willingness to submit her body to racist exploitation for

the sake of acquiring elitist forms of social and cultural capital. Did Millie's hazing ritual follow an Anglo-American and white nationalist narrative in which she
is the body marked for extinction, or is the ritual violence already part of an Afro-
Caribbean sacrifice, in which Millie's body restages the violent history of colonialism, slavery, and genocide as a kind of *limpieza o expiación*—cleansing or
expiation?

In order to fit in with the dominant culture at her college, not only must she
work twice as hard to prove she earned her place at a prestigious institution, she
also modifies her name, appearance, and the material and bodily practices that
mark her as a working-class Latina. For Millie, whiteness represents the legitimate
habitus that facilitates her educational and professional success, and the transcultural capital of her fluency in Spanish is merely a means of securing a position in
international finance. The play depicts various instances when Millie's adoption
of white cultural norms clash with the communitarian ethos her grandmother has
cultivated as a spiritual leader. Nevertheless, the play does not depict Millie's bicul-
turalism as a fatal or tragic flaw; rather, through the influence of family and
friends, as well as the divine intervention of the saints and orishas, Millie is able
to negotiate between her Black Latina roots and the hegemonic educational capital she associates with whiteness. The play depicts her initial clumsy efforts to
impose on the botanica's clientele dominant forms of knowledge through self-help
advice and Freudian psychoanalysis. These foreign concepts are unwelcomed in
the Afro-Caribbean space of the *botánica*, and her refusal to value her grandmother's beliefs and practices bring cultural conflicts to a climax when Doña
Geno is overcome with anxiety and falls ill.

Millie eventually learns one of Bourdieu central arguments: that logic and reason alone are not enough for her to understand her place in the world and her
impact on it. When she returns from college and tries to implement the quantitative rigors of business administration, she fails to acknowledge the repression of
her embodied Latinidad, even though she uses her education and knowledge of
Freud to diagnose the repressed erotic attachments of her grandmother's clientele.
For Bourdieu, this form of denegation—bracketing off of the structures of power
at the moment of their implementation—is endemic to the symbolic violence that
hegemonic educational capital reproduces in the material and bodily practices of
upward mobility.[32] Millie misrecognizes her educational capital as a rebellious liberation from the Afro-Caribbean heritage she perceives as a constraint on her
upward mobility, yet in her zeal to prove she has "won" her place at a prestigious
academic institution, she reprises the role of a colonized subject and victim of geno-
cidal violence. It isn't until she pays homage to the spirit world that she is able to
negotiate her elite education and the embodied knowledge of her Black Latina
heritage.

Millie has to make a pact with the saints, represented by Santa Bárbara's disembodied voice, and she seals her promise to help run the botanica with her gold
graduation ring, which symbolizes her achievements in the pursuit of legitimacy
in the dominant culture of white, Anglo-America. It is at this point that she under-

stands Pepe el Indio's repeated exhortation: *no dejar que te maten los búfalos*—don't let them kill your buffaloes. Millie, like the indigenous peoples who were dispossessed of their culture and heritage once they lost their land and their main economic resource, is in danger of selling out her family's heritage and livelihood for the sake of acquiring what the dominant white culture values and legitimates. Yet Millie does not—or cannot—simply reject and disavow the educational capital she worked so hard to acquire. Instead, she adapts her hard-won business acumen to uphold the communitarian ethos embodied by her grandmother and her Afro-Caribbean spiritual traditions.

The way the plot and resolution of *Botánica* depict the Puerto Rican diaspora and transculturation is dramatically different from the canonical Puerto Rican play, *La carreta*, by René Marqués. First published in 1953 during the early years of the Puerto Rican commonwealth government of Luis Muñoz Marín and the industrialization of the island's economy, *La carreta* chronicles the waves of migration that displaced many Puerto Ricans from the rural countryside to the urban slums of San Juan and, eventually, to the ghettos of New York and other mainland cities. The play's central male character, Luis, is obsessed with the technological advances that drive the industrialization of Puerto Rico, and his curiosity to discover how the factory machines work lead to his tragic death when he is crushed by the gears and motors that symbolize the dehumanizing labor conditions many Puerto Rican migrants have faced. Upon his death, his family decides to return to Puerto Rico, not only to bury their eldest son, but also to reclaim their rural heritage and land. His sister, Juanita, says to her mother, Doña Gabriela, "*¡Uhté y yo, mamá, firmeh como ausuboh sobre la tierra nuehtra, y Luis descansando en ella!*"[33] ("You and I, mama, as firm as the bulletwood tree on our land, with Luis resting beneath her!" [my translation]). *La carreta* does not imagine a reconciliation between Puerto Rican heritage and the economic forces of modernization and technological progress. Like the ceiba tree that appears in *Botánica*, the ausubo tree that Juanita mentions represents the rootedness of Puerto Rican heritage in the soil of the homeland. However, for Doña Geno in *Botánica*, she plants her ceiba in New York's El Barrio, and the rootedness of her cultural identity is contingent on the home she establishes in the metropolis rather than on the island.

Nuyorican poet and playwright Tato Laviera had already challenged the pessimistic outlook of Marqués's play with his own collection of poems titled *La Carreta Made a U-Turn*, which celebrates Puerto Rican diasporic identity in its New York urban context. The tragic ending of *La carreta* also differs from the comedic reconciliation that occurs at the end of *Botánica*, and although there is no pair of lovers who unite in marriage as in a Shakespearean comedy, the union between Anglo-American educational capital and Afro-Caribbean communitarian spirituality offers a felicitous marriage of conflicting social and cultural values. This marriage—made official when Millie sacrifices her gold graduation ring to the saints—does not occur without striking a bargain between the beliefs and rituals of Doña Geno's Santería tradition and the digital technology that Millie introduces in order to bring the family business into the modern age. Unlike the deadly machines in *La carreta* that destroy Luis's body and his dreams of assimilation, the computer Millie brings home from her job at Chase Manhattan Bank serves to archive and preserve Doña Geno's vast store of cultural knowledge. Although the computer at first causes a blackout at the shop and appears to fail Millie's objectives, after performing a Santería blessing the device functions perfectly and allows Millie and Doña Geno to reconcile their own professional and spiritual aspirations. The stage directions further emphasize the comedic marriage between these contrasting values by indicating that the scene ends with the song "El yerbero moderno" by Celia Cruz and the projected image of Santa Bárbara winking from a computer screen. The play's conclusion stages what Millie's friend, Rubén, had already argued previously, that his sense of belonging and rootedness was the transcultural combination of both U.S. and Puerto Rican identities: "*¿Qué quiere decir 'ser de aquí'? . . . es mango y strawberries . . . alcapurrias y pretzels . . . Yemayá y los Yankees . . . Yo no veo la diferencia.* What's the big deal?"[34] ("What does it mean to say, 'to be from here'? . . . it's mango and strawberries . . . alcapurrias and pretzels . . . Yemayá and the Yankees . . . I don't see the difference. What's the big deal?" [my translation]). The big deal is the bargain Millie and Doña Geno are able to negotiate in order to pursue upward mobility by appropriating hegemonic educational capital while preserving the Afro-Caribbean communitarian values that are also the main source of the family's economic future.

Nevertheless, this transcultural future is contingent on the boom-and-bust cycle of neoliberal finance and, in particular, the volatility of the real estate market. Another of Prida's plays, *Casa Propia* (1999), restages many of the themes and social conflicts that appear in *Botánica*, such as the mutual support shared by a community of Latina women and the aspirational goals of upward mobility. It is the conditions under which the play was written and produced that exemplify how the contradiction of transcultural capital can reproduce the structures of inequality and exclusion that characterize the neoliberal economy. Prida debuted *Casa Propia* as the winning entry in the "American Dream" Playwriting Contest organized by El Repertorio Español and sponsored by the Fannie Mae corporation.[35] The Fannie Mae corporation is the government-sponsored enterprise created during the FDR administration that guarantees home mortgage loans and backs their securitization.[36] The play depicts Olga, a Cuban American woman and head of household, who pursues economic stability and a sense of personal autonomy through home ownership. In one scene, Olga and her adult daughter, Marilis, pore over the Fannie Mae application forms that will facilitate the purchase of a single-family home in East Harlem. Although the play reaffirms the communitarian values and economic mobility of the earlier *Botánica*, its sponsorship by Fannie Mae reflected the expansion of the subprime mortgage market that eventually contributed to the financial meltdown and bank bailouts of 2007–2008. Situated in this broader context, both *Botánica* and *Casa Propia* convey the transitory nature of economic mobility for the working-class communities of color, whose acquisition of hegemonic forms of capital is contingent on the neoliberal market forces that can destabilize global finance as well as dispossess the at-risk communities the federal government is ostensibly trying to support.

In the realm of real estate and the housing industry, the state speaks through the narratives that valorize ownership of property.[37] While the house is imbued with mythopoetic values that affirm family lineage and celebrate its unity and continuity, the ability to purchase a home depends on the structure of capital and the dispositions of the economic field that is "inhabited by the state."[38] These considerations provide a means of understanding how certain kinds of knowledge and experience can or cannot engage as cultural capital with the economic field in which the activity of home ownership is embedded. Those who possess the cultural capital associated with upward mobility, education, and professionalization can engage in the quantitative discourses that govern real estate transactions; as such, these exchanges position the potential home owner as an autonomous individual with buying power, even though the "spirit of calculation" situates her as a subject of the state.[39]

In the case of marginal subjects who live in communities of color, potential homeowners can stake a claim in this field through alternative forms of cultural capital. Latinxs often engage these economic institutions through communitarian values, ethnic identity, and cultural nationalism. Sociologist Melvin Delgado argues that in the case of Latinx small business success, "cultural capital, unlike social capital, which stresses connectedness and relationships irrespective of ethnic and racial backgrounds of residents, specifically taps values, traditions, and beliefs."[40] Economist Bárbara J. Robles further distinguishes Latinx cultural capital from other types of knowledge and practices: "*Cultural capital* takes on a distinct meaning when applied to communities of color. In this context, cultural capital is defined as the ability to navigate two cultural systems: one's own community and the mainstream institutional, social, and market systems. . . . For communities of color, cultural capital is the ability to switch behavioral attributes that gain acceptance and be leveraged in differing cultural constructs. For example, the ability to language switch and to engage in translating activities when managing consumer activities is a form of cultural capital."[41] Ostensibly, Latinxs can engage in economic activity by leveraging their ethnic identities and cultural practices, which "gain acceptance" across different "cultural constructs." Yet not all of a community's knowledge, traditions, or values are accepted as a form of cultural capital, and the relationship between the community and mainstream economic institutions is defined by a "profound dissymmetry" of power.[42] Arlene Dávila documents this dissymmetry and the limits of Latinx cultural capital in her analysis of tourist empowerment zones in East Harlem, or El Barrio: "East Harlem does not lack cultural resources, nor places, nor memories, nor a willingness to market its culture; rather, it lacks the resources to promote its values, which are at odds with dominant aesthetic hierarchies that devalue ethnicity in favor of universally sanctioned culture."[43] As Latinxs negotiate their cultural capital with the spirit of the state that haunts the economic field, the expenditure of these resources can devalue and displace the local knowledge and collective memories these marginal subjects already possess. Moreover, the economic field of home ownership inevitably sets in motion a physical displacement of poor communities of color through gentrification and urban renewal. If Latinxs monetize and quantifiably appraise their culture, does this negotiation with the state lead to a gentrification of their collective spirit? Because the science of economics is "haunted by state thinking," in what ways does cultural capital reproduce the rationalizing imperatives of the "spirit of calculation" when discursively engaged in the economic field of the ownership of space?

Furthermore, it is often the members of the Latinx community who become the gentrifiers in their own neighborhoods, and although their property ownership can help maintain the cultural character of an ethnic enclave, their economic activity is no less prone to displace other Latinx residents who do not have the financial means to remain in a neighborhood where rents and property values rise at ever increasing rates to meet the demand for upscale housing. *Botánica* and *Casa Propia* portray through comedic structure the felicitous reconciliation between Anglo-American values of individualism and economic self-reliance with Latinx forms of communitarian support and spiritual traditions, yet these happy marriages also restage the structural inequalities that are endemic to the fields of elite education and private property.

When Millie confronts her grandmother and reproduces these structures of inequality by valuing her elite education over her family's economic prospects and property ownership, Doña Geno suffers a mild heart attack and has to leave her business in her granddaughter's care. Desperate that she has put Doña Geno's life at risk, Millie turns to her grandmother's Santería deities in an attempt to bring her back to health. Hesitant at first, she addresses a statue of Santa Bárbara in English with her request, but in a moment of theatrical magical realism, the voice of the Cuban spirit replies in a voice-over, "*No falla. Nada más que se acuerdan de mí cuando truena. Y mira, chiquitica, yo no spika inglis*"[44] ("It never fails. They only remember me when trouble strikes. And look, girlie, I don't spika inglis" [my translation]). Millie is then obliged to make her case to San Lázaro, who is bilingual, and while she follows all the rituals and makes the mandatory sacrifices of gold and bread—her class ring and a half-eaten croissant—she drives a hard bargain with the Santería spirit so that she can continue on her chosen career path while helping to modernize her grandmother's *botánica*. The herb shop becomes a boutique, and Millie combines her grandmother's *remedios* with self-help advice that the regular female clientele use to gain confidence and independence. She also introduces technology through a computer, which will serve as a digital archive for her grandmother's cultural memory. When the family is finally reunited on stage and has successfully integrated Millie's management skills with their Afro-Caribbean traditions, Millie receives a phone call from the real estate developer who presses her to sell the building. She replies, "my buffaloes are not for sale," invoking Pepe el Indio's constant reminder to never sell out to the white power structure.[45] In an interview, Dolores Prida remarks that she derived this theme from Joseph Campbell's *The Power of Myth*: "When white men killed the buffalo, they cut the roots of Indian culture. Millie suffers a similar loss. She goes through convulsions in college when she tries to reject her past. Later she must find the balance between the bank and *la botánica*."[46] Not only was the extermination of the buffalo a cultural loss for the Native American population, it constituted an obliteration of their economy through the loss of their principal source of food and trade. Millie refuses to sell her buffaloes because she finally acknowledges that her Puerto Rican culture is also an ethnic economic resource that will provide income for her family and retain property and wealth within her East Harlem community. By the end of the play, Millie has reassessed the personal and professional trajectories that would have upheld and conformed to a hegemonic social and economic status quo. With a little help from the spirit world, she draws from the experience of transculturation to reorient her embodied economy toward local strategies of survival, betterment, and social transformation.

WRITING HISTORY ON THE BLACK FEMALE BODY IN *FE EN DISFRAZ*

Although Prida's play stages a reconciliation between Millie's Afro-Caribbean heritage and the elite forms of capital she acquired through the shaming rituals of racist violence, it leaves unresolved the libidinal investment, or cathexis, in ritualized violence and the sexual economies of domination. In contrast, the way Santos Febres's novel engages in the narratives of ritual violence shows how the libidinal investment in sexual domination not only generates a series of contradictions in its relation to power and capital accumulation but also circulates in a consumer market for the paraphernalia, clothing, gear, and pornography that serves as fetish material culture for the BDSM community. In her ethnography of the BDSM community in San Francisco, Margot Weiss explores the contradictions between what practitioners consider transgressive sex and the way these practices reaffirm and reproduce the logic of the market in neoliberal capitalist economies, particularly in the proliferation of toys and gear. She writes: "Toys are an integral part of contemporary SM. In concert with the development of a more formalized, professional, and rule-oriented scene, there has been a tremendous expansion in the market for SM paraphernalia and the techniques that these new toys engender. And in the same ways that this new scene produces SM practitioners and communities in accordance with classed and racialized understandings of risk, safety, and subjectivity, buying and using SM toys produces certain kinds of subjects in accordance with larger social, political, and economic relations."[47] As historians, however, it is not enough for Fe and Martín to include mass-produced sex toys or off-the-rack costumes into their ritualized sexual encounters; they appropriate the historical artifacts that were once in direct contact with the very bodies their BDSM rituals reinvoke. This narrative gesture toward historical authenticity serves as a counterpoint to the commercialized forms of ritualized violence described by Weiss. Nevertheless, the objects are imbued with the embodied economies of the colonial slave era that are then reinscribed on Fe's and Martín's bodies.

In particular, Fe appropriates an elaborate gown that once supposedly belonged to Xica da Silva, the Brazilian manumitted slave who became a wealthy courtesan and society matron. Fe wears this garment every Halloween night when she and Martín meet to reenact the history of white-Black sexual relations in Latin America. A tight-fitting, metallic harness is sewn into this gown, and its corroded, rusted wires protrude through the fabric and lacerate Fe's skin and flesh, leaving keloidal scars that permanently inscribe not only her sex games with Martín, but also the history of slavery and subjugation that was perpetrated on the bodies of the Black female ancestors the gown comes to symbolize. While Martín reproduces the role of white master in this ritualization of slavery's sexual history, it is really Fe who assumes the dominant position in their relationship, both professionally and erotically. In her analysis of the novel, Patricia Valladares-Ruiz writes:

> Hay que tomar en cuenta que solo Fe es la encargada de dosificar e, incluso, agudizar su propio dolor. En este juego sexual, Martín no interpreta el papel de un amo dominante, sino que funciona como un elemento más de un ritual orquestado por Fe.[48]

> It should be noted that only Fe is in charge of rationing and, in addition, aggravating her own pain. In this sexual game, Martín does not play the role of a dominant master, but rather he functions as one more element in the ritual orchestrated by Fe. (my translation)

Nevertheless, as the dominant narrative voice in the novel, Martín also exercises his own desire to control the outcome of their sex games and how the reader engages with their story. The multiple inversions and masquerades that occur in this Sadean performance of the carnivalesque dramatize the transcultural economic imaginaries that emerge when contemporary values of academic professionalism and knowledge production in the United States—as well as the technologies of informatics and virtualization—confront, appropriate, and exploit for profit the history of enslavement, dispossession, and subjugation that characterizes the experience of Black women in Latin America and the Caribbean.

In Carlos Diegues's film *Xica* (1976), economic power, sexual bondage, and the master-slave narrative are all inscribed on and performed by the Black, female body of the titular protagonist. Her secret sexual skills overwhelm her masters to such a frenzied state, they at first protest vociferously through external diegetic sound, "*Isso não, Xica*" (Not that, Xica), but then are heard screaming at the top of their lungs once Xica performs her signature sexual maneuver. The film never reveals what this maneuver is, but the male's resistance and release suggest some form of anal penetration, which is consistent with Xica's nickname—*Xica que manda*, or Xica who commands. While she conquers her masters and seduces her way to freedom, she also acquires wealth and power by reproducing the structural and bodily violence of the Brazilian slave system. Most notably, the film associates Xica's empowerment with wardrobe and nudity, and as she attains more autonomy and power, her costumes become more elaborate and extravagant. As soon as she starts to dress in more expensive clothes, she starts violently beating other slaves and arbitrarily issuing despotic commands. In one scene, when she finally convinces her master to free her, she parades her letter of liberty—*carta de alforria*—through the streets wearing a powdered wig and expensive gown. Even though she and her retinue of slaves dance jubilantly toward the town square, the priest slams the doors of the church in Xica's face, since the church only allows eighth-generation whites to enter. Xica misrecognizes her freedom as social power, and soon she becomes more extravagant, cruel, and violent. Her power is short-lived, and when her lover, the *contratador* for the royal diamond mines, runs afoul of the king and is called back to Portugal, Xica goes from "*a Xica que manda*" to "*Xica rabuda*"—or big butt Xica. This cinematic portrayal of Xica da Silva displays many of the same contradictions in *Fe en disfraz*; both works show that when an empowered woman reproduces the real and symbolic violence of an embodied economy, their autonomy and agency remain contingent on the white power structures. Hortense Spillers makes a similar argument in her well-known essay "Mama's Baby, Papa's Maybe: An American Grammar Book":

> The captive body, then, brings into focus a gathering of social realities as well as a metaphor for value so thoroughly interwoven in their literal and figurative emphases that distinctions between them are virtually useless. Even though the captive flesh/body has been "liberated," and no one need pretend that even the quotation marks do not matter, dominant symbolic activity, the ruling episteme that releases the dynamics of naming and valuation, remains grounded in the originating metaphors of captivity and mutilation so that it is as if neither time nor history, nor historiography and its topics, shows movement, as the human subject is "murdered" over and over again by the passions of a bloodless and anonymous archaism, showing itself in endless disguise.[49]

Whatever trappings of power and legitimacy they wear, Xica da Silva's and Fe Verdejo's bodies are perpetually scarred by race and gender domination. The thin veneer of respectability that economic and educational capital confer on them is contingent on their willingness to veil the wound-trace that the histories of colonialism and slavery have carved into their flesh. In both cases, they reenact and relive the violence and trauma of those histories precisely at the moment they assume the habitus of whiteness that is their ticket to economic mobility.

Fe Verdejo's story conveys this gentrification of the flesh through a series of narrative devices that mediate her voice through the intervention of the dominant narrator: her white, male lover, Martín. The reader first learns of Fe's successful academic career through Martín's recounting of their BDSM session. Fe tells him how she marshalled resources to save her Latin American studies seminar from the university's funding reallocations. The layering of these homodiegetic narrative voices has a Scheherazade effect, in particular when Fe divulges her story to Martín as they lie together in a moment of postcoital bliss. This framing device not only connects Fe's professional biography to libidinal desire, but also reveals the way Fe's historiographical practice is contingent on an erotic embodiment of a repressed and unwritten history of Black female empowerment in the Americas. Fe's story of how she rescued her academic career relies on a series of racial masquerades that affiliate wealth and upward mobility with aspirational whiteness. She imagines that she will gain financial support from these upwardly mobile Latinx donors if she obscures their working-class Puerto Rican and Mexican origins in Chicago and, instead, traces the origins of the city's Latinx community to a more palatably white, European ancestry that predates the waves of migration that brought the majority of Latinx residents to their ethnic urban enclaves. It is unclear whether this proposal to "dress up" mestizo and mulatto Latinxs with white, European ancestry is a purposeful misreading of racial identity politics on the part of Fe Verdejo—a well-educated Afro-Venezuelan with little connection to these communities—or on the part of the author, Santos Febres—a well-educated and successful Afro–Puerto Rican from the island. Nevertheless, this ahistorical genealogy runs counter to the dominant narrative in U.S. discourses on upward mobility and the redemptive storylines that depict successful Latinxs emerging from poverty and deprivation to overcome economic barriers set in place by structural racism; in other words, the stories associated with characters like Millie and Nina from *In the Heights*.

Ultimately, Fe is saved from making such a miscalculated pitch by the fortuitous discovery of an uncatalogued collection of colonial-era court documents that chronicle the lives of manumitted Black women in Latin America. It is at this point in the novel that the mediated narrative—Martín's voice telling Fe's story—reveals the complex interconnections between the history of slavery and exploitation of Black women, and the economic and professional empowerment that a Black female scholar derives from the publication and dissemination of that untold history. In other words, the frame narrative of Fe's and Martín's postcoital conversations shows how the lovers write and embody that history, or rather, how that history has always been inscribed on their bodies:

> *Aquel fue el primer día de su rito. Aquel fue el primer día de esta historia que terminará inscrita aquí, en el pergamino de esta pantalla electrónica, de esta mi pálida piel.*[50]

> That was the first day of her rite. That was the first day of this story that will end up inscribed here, on the parchment of this electronic screen, of my pale skin. (my translation)

Between Martín's episodic *apuntes* of his erotic affair with Fe, the novel intercalates apocryphal legal documents from the Latin American colonial slave era that describe court cases involving the abuse and exploitation of Black women—both slave and free. At one point, Fe also sends Martín a separate electronic file that contains the personal story of her childhood in Venezuela, her studies at a Catholic convent, and how she found and rescued from obscurity the antique dress that becomes the fetish object in her and Martín's BDSM rituals. Martín becomes so obsessed with Fe that he eventually breaks off his engagement with his Puerto Rican fiancée, a doctoral candidate who ends up having her own affair with her dissertation director. The narrative juxtaposition of these historical extracts alongside the characters' first-person accounts highlights for the reader the kind of scholarly labor through which Fe and Martín produce and disseminate knowledge, even as they are seduced by the material and intellectual histories they are committed to preserving and analyzing. What also becomes clear as the novel progresses is how scholarship, while imbued with the intellectual ethos of recovering the forgotten histories of Afro-Latina subaltern subjects, functions largely as an economic activity that involves finance, entrepreneurship, labor, marketing, and technology. Fe and Martín share a professional commitment to the recuperation of marginal voices from the slave era, yet their endeavor is simultaneously a labor of love, an erotic performance, and a scholarly enterprise that reflects the embodied economies that have played a significant role in constituting their racial, gender, and sexual identities as Latinx Caribbean subjects.

When she comes across the untitled collection of female slave narratives, Fe redirects her efforts and submits a proposal for researching the history and material culture of the slavery era in Minas Gerais, Brazil, a project that she expands into a multimedia public exhibition. The serendipitous find of these female slave narratives solidifies Fe Verdejo's successful academic career and places her in a unique position among the white, male majority of scholars in her discipline. Nonetheless, Fe maintains her dominant position as seminar director while she assumes a gender and sexual ambiguity in her BDSM encounters with Martín, one of the junior members of her team. The colonial slave history that she preserves and disseminates through her profession is also a racial inheritance that she embodies and which she performs ritualistically through sexual transgression. As a subaltern subject who appropriates and exploits the economic conditions of her First World professional institutions, her reenactments of that violent history through BDSM and sexual role-play act as a psychological and spiritual purge. The synthesis of active and passive, master and slave in Fe Verdejo's character allows the novel to trace the history of Black women's exploitation in Latin America while projecting female empowerment within the context of neocolonialism in the contemporary era.

The depiction of these BDSM rituals, in which Fe and Martín serve as avatars of the history of colonial slavery in Latin America, exhibits many of the elements in the Sadean fantasy that imagine a libidinal economy, particularly the commoditization of the body and the exercise of power through sexual exploitation.[51] The pornographic quality of the sex scenes, narrated from the white male perspective, simultaneously reenacts and critiques how BDSM eroticism commoditizes the Black female body, extending her subservient position from the slave era to contemporary consumer culture. While Santos Febres's novel positions the reader as a consumer of interracial pornography, which aligns the reader's perspective with that of the white male, the intercalation of apocryphal slave narratives lays bare the commoditizing effect that the pornographic image has on the Black female body. The accounts depicted in these slave narratives are no less titillating, and their inclusion in the novel exposes the reader's comfortable anonymity from which she or he participates in the voyeuristic exploitation and subjugation of the subaltern subject. A radical feminist critique of BDSM practices sees no discontinuity between the "real" world and the "scene" world of the BDSM; both worlds are overlapping spaces where sexuality and power reproduce discourses of domination and inequality. Margot Weiss argues that:

> SM is produced through social power, that sexuality (scenes, erotics, desire, and fantasy) is always social, and that "none of us is exempt" from this condition. In this, SM sexuality is like all sexuality: it is not possible to sever sexuality from power; sexuality is a social relation within an already existing social world. At the same time, the spectacularity of SM's play with social power makes its politics more visibly problematic; such a crowded social field demands ethnographic consideration. The radical feminist argument can begin to reveal how the construction of the scene as a safe or bracketed space is itself a way of pushing aside the social relations of power that form SM desires, and that SM communities and scenes produce.[52]

The BDSM rituals in which Fe and Martín reenact the "violence and violation" perpetrated against Black women conjure up the history of colonial slavery in Latin America, and their narrative articulation reveals the discursive mechanisms that enable the continued commoditization of subaltern subjects even as they assume the material and bodily practices of the upwardly mobile and the habitus of the empowered.

Nevertheless, the historico-sexual drama that plays out in *Fe en disfraz* raises the question of how much of an Afro-Latina's empowerment in a capitalist society is contingent on her willingness to submit to the economic and sexual exploitation enforced on her by white male privilege. Feminist critics have scrutinized this Sadean impulse, in which the female subject strives for liberation through submission, and for every dimension of sexual and existential liberty the female subject gains, she risks participating in her own subjugation, rape, torture, and death.[53] Hortense Spillers argues that in the case of the African slaves, their bodies were captured and severed from their "motive will." This captive body

> focuses a private and particular space, at which point of convergence biological, sexual, social, cultural, linguistic, ritualistic, and psychological fortunes join. This profound intimacy of interlocking detail is disrupted, however, by externally imposed meanings and uses: 1) the captive body becomes the source of an irresistible, destructive sensuality; 2) at the same time-in stunning contradiction-the captive body reduces to a thing, becoming being for the captor; 3) in this absence from a subject position, the captured sexualities provide a physical and biological expression of "otherness"; 4) as a category of "otherness," the captive body translates into a potential for pornotroping and embodies sheer physical powerlessness that slides into a more general "powerlessness," resonating through various centers of human and social meaning.[54]

This scene of "pornotroping" occurs as Fe Verdejo allows herself to explore the sexual dimensions of captivity while becoming Martín Tirado's commoditized object. Alexander G. Weheliye argues, "Pornotroping, then, names the becoming-flesh of the (black) body and forms a primary component in the processes by which human beings are converted into bare life."[55] Martín, in turn, uses his written documentation of these erotic encounters as a way to acknowledge his desire to assert a dominant masculinity and assume the white privilege that his professional and intellectual commitments decry as a historical crime. Fe literally offers the tools of her own subjugation to Martín, first through the gown and its tortuous harness, then through the gift of an antique Spanish razor that Martín uses to shave his own body in preparation for their rituals, and eventually uses on Fe's body, at her request, to inflict further lacerations with even more direct force. Neither are their sexual encounters limited to the Halloween / All Saint's Eve rituals, as they occur while the seminar team travels to academic conferences in the Americas and Europe, and, in one instance, in the back seat of Fe's car in the upscale Edgewater neighborhood of Chicago's Northside. It is immediately before this exhibitionist episode that Fe lauds her own success while telling Martín that her most recent lecture exceeded all expectations in its presentation of the other face of slavery—"*la otra cara de la esclavitud*"—the one visible in the slave narratives she discovered: "*la que muestran los relatos de sus esclavas que, sin dejar de ser víctimas azotadas por los amos, se convierten en algo más*"[56] (the one shown to us by the stories of her slaves that, while still being victims whipped by their masters, become something more" [my translation]). As an Afro-Latina at the height of her career and in control of her economic and sexual autonomy, Fe nevertheless submits to Martín's domination in order to achieve an existential transcendence she interprets in the very historical documents with which she attains a highly valued measure of bourgeois dignity.

As a Latin Americanist in the U.S. academy, Fe distinguishes herself by meeting the demands for innovation and individual achievement that dominate her profession. In her historical research, she explores areas of scholarship that have received scant attention by a conservative, white male establishment. Her academic institution provides her with a great amount of self-determination, which she uses to pursue subjects that draw critical praise and lucrative funding, and in turn enhance her prestige and respectability. When she discovers the unpublished collection of slave narratives, she mobilizes her resources quickly to capitalize on their rarity. Fe's success in Anglo-American academia reveals the irony of an institution that prizes innovation and entrepreneurial spirit yet rewards those individual efforts that promote the politics of collective identities and communitarian values. On the one hand, Fe stands apart as a unique figure in her profession and discipline, but on the other hand the archival and material history that constitute her scholarly research link her to a subaltern lineage, which she embodies every time she and Martín reenact sexually the violent legacy of slavery and exploitation. In the Anglo-American embodied economy of her professional life, Fe appropriates the values of self-reliance and innovation to achieve individual success, but she uses the archives and objects to which her profession gives her access in order to relinquish mastery over herself, handing power over to her professional underling and thus reliving the indignities and repression that characterized the embodied economy of the Latin American colonial era. As Fe exerts her hard-won dominance in her field, she pays for her success through the Sadean rituals that connect her to the collective experience of Black women who have suffered sexual violence and economic exploitation in the Americas since the slave era and still today.

Similar to Millie from *Botánica*, Fe Verdejo acquires her educational capital through the efforts of her grandmother. However, Fe discovers that her grandmother is well-connected and has amassed a considerable fortune, the origins of which remain unknown. As the only Black student at an exclusive Catholic school for girls, Fe follows in her mother's footsteps who also attended a religious school but was expelled at age fourteen when she became pregnant with Fe. In order to appease her grandmother, Fe avoids contact with young men by secluding herself in her school's library, where she reads the biographies of female Catholic saints whose lives of devotion and abnegation fascinate her. However, the religious figures she admires, like Santa Teresa de Jesús and Sor Juana Inés de la Cruz, are white women whose biographies describe their cloistered lives of sexless self-sacrifice. The written biographies of white Catholic saints contrast sharply with the lives and unwritten histories of the Black and mulatta nuns of the Brazilian convent where Fe conducts her research and where she obtains the infamous gown worn by Xica da Silva, the eighteenth-century slave turned courtesan. These nuns, like Fe's mother, were victims of sexual violence and, therefore, joined their religious order not so much from devotion as from shame and social opprobrium. The dying nun who tells Fe where to find Xica da Silva's ornate gown warns her not to wear it, as it is inhabited by the history of Black women who fell victim to the lure of whiteness that it represents. By tracing the history of the dress to Xica da Silva, the novel imbues this material object with the desire of a Black woman to assume a position of power and prestige in a racist and misogynistic society. Fe is unable to resist the lure this dress symbolizes, and when she puts it on and its wire harness inflicts its painful lacerations on her body, she assumes her place in the legacy of sexual violence that maintains empowered Black women in positions of submission and servitude. As Spillers argues, "the human subject is 'murdered' over and over again by the passions of a bloodless and anonymous archaism, showing itself in endless disguise."

Once again, the novel frames this part of the narrative through Martín's profession as an archivist. As Patricia Valladares-Ruiz notes in her analysis of these narrative devices, this chapter appears in the same format as the series of colonial era documents that Martín intercalates throughout the text.[57] Fe sends a digital attachment to Martín in which she recounts her childhood in Maracaibo, Venezuela. This is the first and only time that the reader encounters Fe's first-person autobiography, yet it appears as one among several archival documents that chronicle the history of Black women and their sexual exploitation. Through this framing device, the novel situates Fe as the inheritor of a centuries-old legacy in which Black women's empowerment and self-determination are facilitated by white men and an assertion of their sexual privilege. In Fe's case, she manages to avoid this fate until her fifteenth birthday when, after celebrating her *quinceañera* with great fanfare and opulence, she is raped by her white escort. This narrative once again underscores the connection between history, historiography, and the violence inflicted on Black women's bodies. Rather than deny this legacy, Fe becomes its willing inheritor, and she recounts in her own voice that she took great pleasure in the sexual violence that marked her initiation into Black womanhood. The dress, then, becomes the material object that allows Fe to ritualize this violence and that connects her bodily and spiritually to the historical archive that is at the core of her professional success and economic empowerment. At the same time, Fe's use of the dress in her BDSM rituals desacralizes it as a rare and valuable object of colonial-era material culture that her profession as a historian is charged with protecting and preserving.

Santos Febres's novel raises the thorny issue of how Black women achieve self-determination in a capitalistic society where they traditionally occupy the most marginal realms of subalternity and where emergence from these domains of oppression is often contingent on exertions of power over others and/or allowing others to exert power over oneself. In a similar vein, Mae G. Henderson compares Sherley Anne William's novel *Dessa Rose* to Pauline Réage's *The Story of O* in order to examine how the Sadean narrative positions women in a role where they are complicitous with their own subjugation, while positioning the reader in a submissive role in relation to the explicit violence depicted in the text. Henderson concludes: "But as reader-critics, we must ask ourselves how this process of sexual/textual mastery positions us; what happens when we yield to the mastery of the text? [. . .] In other words, how can we avoid being constructed as victims 'by texts that master us' as readers who derive our pleasure from a 'position of subjection'? How can we avoid victimization when we experience our subjugation as 'a pleasurable repetition of [our] own history of loss and recovery'?"[58] These questions are germane to considering the way Santos Febres's novel represents the instability of the relations of power between Blacks and whites, women and men, the Third World and the First World. In what ways do Fe Verdejo's professional interests commoditize and exploit the experiences of those slave women—"*her*" slave women, as Martín emphasizes continually throughout the text—whose stories appear in archival and material history? Does Fe Verdejo achieve a liberatory experience through rituals of self-debasement, or is she complicitous in the perpetuation of an embodied economy in which she commoditizes her own body for the satisfaction of another's appetite for power? Are readers similarly "liberated" from their passivity by participating in a narrative commoditization of subaltern subjects? Jennifer Nash poses a similar series of questions in her analysis of Black female pleasure in pornographic films. She interrogates the feminist critique that considers pornographic images of Black women as incontrovertibly exploitative. Through the concept of "racial iconography," Nash argues that certain pornographic films show "black female protagonists rendering explicit racial mythologies, at times toying with them, at times finding pleasure in them, and at times problematizing them. In so doing, they center racial fictions' inextricable connection to sexual fictions, and emphasize that race is necessarily a pornographic fantasy."[59]

Chrissy B. Arce also undertakes a thorough exploration of these questions in her analysis of *Fe en disfraz*. Arce also acknowledges the complicitous role that Fe Verdejo plays in her own sexual exploitation, but because of her subaltern status as a Black Latina she is invariably positioned as a commoditized object available for the erotic consumption of white men, whether or not she assumes this position of subjugation as a means of bettering her social and economic status. Arce argues that the revelation of the past along with the sexual arousal of the characters' bodies merges and gets confused with the experience of reading the novel, which sheds light on the muted history of the female slave while at the same time enflaming the bodies of the present.[60] The postmodern self-reflexivity of this novel serves to implicate the exchange between authorship and readership in the history of racial and sexual exploitation in the Americas. Ultimately, knowledge alone cannot absolve the sins of the past; the novel suggests that a continual rearticulation and parodic subversion of the violence of history serve to reopen old wounds and bring to the surface the hidden lives of the subaltern subjects whose legacy survives in our contemporary embodied economies. As Martín acknowledges in his anticipation of seeing Fe reprise her role in their Sadean sex game, "*Se convertirá en cortesana haitiana de los tiempos de Henri Christophe, en la mismísima Xica Da Silva, en todas esas mujeres negras, transplantadas por un extraño curso del azar (y de la Historia) a ese traje, a esa otra piel*"[61] ("She will become a Haitian courtesan in the times of Henri Christophe, the very same Xica da Silva, all those Black women, transplanted by a strange twist of fate (and of History) into that dress, into that other skin" [my translation]). Fe Verdejo's racial and sexual identities emerge as a performative legacy that is enabled by the subversive appropriation of the historical archive and material culture of the past.

By the end of the novel, Fe and Martín fully surrender to their Sadean pantomime, and in his final electronic diary entry he suggests that their upcoming reenactment of the Latin American slave narrative will constitute a point of no return. The ominous tone he adopts prepares the reader for a scene of extreme violence and perhaps murder. Martín narrates the final erotic encounter in the future tense as a fantasy of what will occur when he and Fe meet again on All Hallows' Eve, and he imagines that Fe will want to escape her body. He foresees himself brandishing the Spanish razor against her skin, but instead of dealing a deathblow, Martín cuts through the straps and wires of the fetishized gown in order to liberate Fe from the material representation of slavery's history: "*Salir de este cuerpo*" ("Leave this body").[62] The last line of the novel—"*Abandonarse es, a veces, la única manera de comenzar*" ("Abandoning oneself is, sometimes, the only way to begin")—declares that only by abandoning themselves to the violent intimacies of their embodied economies can they avoid being constructed as victims by the texts that master them. By narrating the fantasy in the future tense, the text also implicates the reader's imagination in this transgressive performance, shifting the focus from prurient interest to ethical complicity. Do Fe and Martín free themselves from history's shackles, or is a Black woman's freedom contingent on what she can get a white man to do for her? Does the reader gain knowledge and insight about the exploitation of Afro-Caribbean women, or is readership complicitous in the commoditization of Black women's bodies? Considering the final encounter is told as Martín's fantasy, in which he plays the role of white, male liberator, can readers imagine a different ending? Perhaps Fe takes the razor from Martín and cuts the harness off herself, or perhaps she forces Martín to wear the harness in a BDSM role reversal. As the novel uses Martín to speculate on this culminating moment, it fails to give readers a more radical or queer subversion of the master-slave narrative and instead reinscribes white mastery over Fe's Black body.

The history of racial and sexual exploitation in the Caribbean is more than a tale to be told; it is a lived experience that contemporary subaltern subjects embody whenever they participate in the embodied economies of labor and wealth creation. The Afro-Latina characters in Prida's *Botánica* and Santos Febres's *Fe en disfraz* empower themselves through a transcultural embodied economy in which they mitigate their subalternity by negotiating the virtues and vices of capitalism in neoliberal conditions of coloniality. However, they must also contend with the history of their own subalternity, which lays ethical and communitarian claims on their dreams of success and struggles to attain self-determination. Millie Castillo and Fe Verdejo come from radically different upbringings, and their paths in life could not be more dissimilar, yet they share a trans-Caribbean history of social, political, and economic marginalization, and they also rise above their circumstances through talent, hard work, and an entrepreneurial spirit that never misses an opportunity to get ahead. They also offer up their own flesh—Millie's burned feet and Fe's lacerated torso—in pursuit of social and economic capital, thus reenacting the historical violence of slavery and genocide as a means of attaining upward mobility. They take calculated risks with their racial, gender, and sexual identities, fully aware that racial and sexual violence are ever close at hand.

Conclusion

But I've come to see the American Dream for what it really is: a lie my parents had little choice but to buy into and sell to me, a lie that conflated working hard with passing for, becoming, and being white. I believed the lie for long enough to acquire the tools needed to dismantle it.

—Jennine Capó Crucet, My Time among the Whites:
Notes from an Unfinished Education

When Millie recounts the college hazing ritual that burned her feet, the play's audience situates this allegorical reenactment within the history of violence and genocide perpetrated against Blacks and indigenous people at the hands of white settler colonialists. However, in October 2019 a real burning took place when students at Georgia Southern University torched copies of Jennine Capó Crucet's novel *Make Your Home among Strangers* (2015). Capó Crucet had just spoken to the first-year class of students, who had read her novel as part of their first-year experience program. Students in the audience challenged Capó Crucet's definition of white privilege, which led to high tensions and raised voices in the auditorium. The Cuban American author had to be moved from her lodgings in town after a group of protesters started converging on her hotel. Videos of the book burning were shared on social media, and although the university administration stated that book burning does not align with the institution's values, it was still "within the students' First Amendment rights."[1] Capó Crucet's novel and her follow-up collection of essays—cited in the epigraph above—dedoxify the conventional wisdom about the American Dream; that is, it is a dream you achieve by looking and acting white. Dismantling this conventional wisdom threatens not only those who are thoroughly invested in discourses of white nationalism, it also interrogates the value of higher education and its role in perpetuating the symbolic and real violence that is committed against students, faculty, and administrators of color whose embodied practices do not align with the dominant white norms of appearance and behavior.

The many examples of Latinx Caribbean literature and theater I have examined in this book offer diverse interpretations of what the American Dream looks like from the perspective of diasporic communities. In many instances, as in the chapter on Edwin Sánchez's and Ángel Lozada's novels, these fictions and dramas reflect my own experiences of coming to terms with my parents' expectations, the "unwritten" rules of the game in education and professional academia, and when and in what contexts does my Latinx heritage facilitate or hinder my ability to play by those rules. Similarly, Capó Crucet writes in *My Time among the Whites:*

> I go places and read from my books, and sometimes my parents are in the crowd and they look a little baffled. They seem surprised that the audience isn't solely comprised of people who know me personally—*who are all these people and why are they here?* While they understand that by many measures, I'm successful in ways they've learned to recognize, they don't totally understand how I did this while asserting—rather than muting—my ethnic heritage in my work. They don't understand why I would do this work when they'd given me what they thought was a key to escape it, a way of avoiding the work entirely.[2]

Capó Crucet's emphasis on "work" underscores the amount of labor that goes into a successful academic career, even one built on the often denigrated "me studies" that focus on issues of culture and identity. Part of that labor, as the previous chapters have attempted to show, comes not only from acquiring the hegemonic forms of capital that facilitate upward mobility, but also from the daunting task of negotiating a Latinx Caribbean heritage in those fields of power where whiteness is the model by which one achieves success. Those who perform this kind of labor put themselves at risk of always occupying a dominated position in these fields or, as in the case of Capó Crucet, of becoming the target of a violent backlash when they interrogate and attempt to dismantle those norms.

The various stories and dramas analyzed in the previous chapters all depict the challenges that Latinx Caribbeans of the diaspora face when pursuing upward mobility. They also explore the contradictions that arise when those upwardly mobile characters negotiate their transcultural capital to acquire hegemonic forms of capital, which often leads to reproducing the real and symbolic violence that is endemic to the fields of power that legitimize and regulate the social and cultural values associated with wealth and elite class status. However, some of the works also imagine the possibility of working class, Latinx economic agents whose upward mobility contributes to community cultural wealth. In the embodied economies of the Latinx Caribbean diaspora, transcultural capital can simultaneously create spaces of shared prosperity and provide strategies for decolonizing the material and bodily practices with which we reimagine and reshape our economic agency.

The competing economic value systems that drive the melodramatic plot of *Anna in the Tropics* underscore the role that collective memory and nostalgia play in mitigating the real and symbolic violence of industrialization, particularly for those entrepreneurs whose businesses would be hard pressed to survive without adapting to technological progress. However, as portrayed in *The Cook*, nostalgia can also become a straitjacket that binds the characters to an irrecoverable past and an embodied economy that is no longer operative and has no future. In *Diary of a Puerto Rican Demigod* and *No quiero quedarme sola y vacía*, the acquisition of cultural and social capital is no guarantee of economic autonomy, yet the radically

different family and community relations shared by the protagonists play a significant role in how they regain a sense of selfhood and purposefulness under
conditions of precarity. Heteronormative gendered communities, as in those
depicted in the fictions of Junot Díaz and Rita Indiana Hernández, serve to reproduce the political, economic, and social structures of domination, particularly in
the albeit self-conscious narrative celebration of toxic masculinities. We see this
diversity and divergence in the multiple dreams of the characters from *In the
Heights*, which reflect different points of origin and arrival, and whose emergence
from community cultural wealth differs greatly from the neoliberal invocation of
U.S. founding principles that appears in *Hamilton*. Yet nonnormative embodiments
alone will not transform those fields of power, and as in the case of the protagonist in *Fe en disfraz*, racial and sexual exploitation can be misrecognized as individual empowerment. Upward mobility and the acquisition of educational capital
always come at a cost, and as Millie learned in *Botánica*, community cultural wealth
is strengthened when she sacrifices the symbols of her success in order to recuperate what the history of conquest and colonization has stolen from her people.

The previous chapters explored how transcultural capital for the diasporic subject is accumulated and expended through the dual positionality as insider and
outsider to two (or more) fields. This allows the diasporic subject to move between
fields without fully adhering to the habitus of the dominated. The parallel field provides a space to which the diasporic subject can migrate out of hierarchical social
relations and thus escape from a cycle of symbolic violence, yet this does not necessarily mean the subject takes up the dominant position in another field, although
this is certainly possible. These lateral, nonhierarchical moves, which are not necessarily performed consciously or rationally, are similar to what I called *jaibería*
in relation to the discursive strategies of self-reflexive humor in Puerto Rican literature and its "eccentric" reformulation of national identity.[3] In a broader sense,
the transcultural capital of the diasporic subject can be simultaneously empowering and disempowering, since every accumulation that it enables in one field is perceived as withdrawal from another. Bourdieu writes, "The dialectic of conditions
[of existence] and habitus is the basis of an alchemy which transforms the distribution of capital, the balance-sheet of a power relation, into a system of perceived
differences, distinctive properties, that is, a distribution of symbolic capital, legitimate capital, whose objective truth is misrecognized."[4] For the diasporic subject,
loss of Latinx cultural heritage is misrecognized as a gain according to the logic of
the hegemonic field, whereas a gain in that field is misrecognized as a loss according to the values of the minoritarian community. The aim of decolonial discourse,
then, is to articulate a break from the zero-sum equilibrium of transcultural capital and the habitus of the dominated that constitutes the diasporic subject's schemes
of perception.

While transculturation has been theorized as an evolutionary process of societal change, the literary texts and plays I analyze in this book demonstrate how
transculturation is a form of habitus; it creates its own conditions for existence and
implementation and provides diasporic subjects with a logic of practice, a set of

dispositions, an economic unconscious, a dialectic between the rational and the reasonable, and embodied knowledge, all within an array of fields of structured and structuring action. Through this analysis we can discern the social conditions in which transculturation is generated and in which it is experienced, which allows us to understand the relation between social institutions and the subject in the context of cultures in contact and conflict. An analysis of the transcultural habitus foregrounds writing as a creative art in the literary field, and through genres such as comedy, melodrama, and narrative fiction, these performances and texts articulate the economic imaginaries of diasporic subjects and their communities. This body of theater and fiction delineates the structuring structures of the fields of education, finance, family, religion, government, and civil institutions, while also accounting for the revolutionary imaginary that resists and decolonizes the doxa that situate the diasporic subject in conditions of social and economic marginalization and subaltern status.

At the beginning of this book, I undertook the analysis of Latinx Caribbean fiction and theater within the reflexive framework Bourdieu proposes for sociological study. For comparative literary studies, this involves close readings of form and performance, a consideration of the social relations through which individuals and collectives develop and implement their schemes of perception, and an examination of the historical contexts in which material and bodily practices facilitate the *cierta manera* that is often taken for granted as an essentialized Caribbeanness.[5] I also propose that critical reflexivity demands from literary scholars an explicit awareness of how they position their academic labor in relation to the forms of cultural production they undertake to analyze. In other words, what do I get out of it, and what does my labor offer others who have read this far? As in the case of Fe Verdejo in Mayra Santos Febres's novel, the academic profession is complicit in the logic of profit making for scholars and their institutions. And as Jennine Capó Crucet's experience shows, critical reflection of this logic is often met with rejection and sometimes violence.

This book has allowed me to reflect on the role that transcultural capital has had in my own experience and professional trajectory. I have developed my scholarship and teaching because I endeavor to learn as much as I can about Puerto Rican history and culture, a body of knowledge that was not available to me as a student in Chicago public schools. I had to strike out on my own to access this knowledge, often encountering the doubts and hesitations of my mentors who warned that no one really reads that literature anyway. I had to find an intellectual community and my place in it, always aware that as a comparatist I sought ideas and inspiration from unlikely sources. Like Capó Crucet, my educational and professional trajectory has been one long *contrapunteo*/counterpoint between the heritage culture with which I grew up and the critical distance with which I examine that culture in relation to others. In the embodied economy of U.S. academic institutions, my Latinx Caribbean *cierta manera* is often out of step with the logic of individualism and the demands of solitary labor. Nevertheless, my ongoing effort is to leverage the benefits and privilege I gain individually to create and inhabit spaces where collective labor and collaboration can have a transformative effect at our institutions, so that minoritized subjects can enter fields of power as economic agents and as agents of change. I learned these insights and strategies through my affiliation with the New England Consortium for Latina/o Studies, a grassroots organization that "provides a community-building template for other Latina/o Studies scholars who seek to create a scholarly collective in regions where they are socially and academically isolated yet in relative close proximity to potentially supportive colegas."[6] When I negotiated a retention package at my current institution, I applied what I learned at NECLS and proposed a directorship position that would allow me to create a mentoring and professional development program for pre- and postdoctoral fellows from underrepresented groups who work in Latinx, African American, Native American, and Asian American Studies. One of the objectives of this program is to make explicit and demystify those "unwritten" rules for promotion and tenure; that is, the doxa of collegiality, rigor, and excellence that have become conventional wisdom but are also exclusionary discourses based on access to legitimized forms of social and cultural capital.[7] In another project, I collaborated with my colleague Doug Moody to create an experiential learning course in which Dartmouth students teach ESL to migrant dairy farmworkers in the Upper Valley. So many of our students travel to Latin America and Spain to live and learn in Spanish-speaking countries, yet the migrant farmworkers who live in the area—many from Mexico and Guatemala—are often overlooked as a local Latinx community with much to teach both students and professors alike. These collaborative projects, while small in scale, have contributed to building communities of support and mutual respect. As the title of Capó Crucet's novel suggests, I've survived and succeeded by making my home among strangers. In that way, my *cierta manera* has helped me redirect my upward mobility toward an ethics of creating community cultural wealth while trying to find ways to decolonize my scholarship, my institution, and my own economic agency.

Acknowledgments

There are many colleagues and Latinx / Latin American studies interlocutors who have contributed to the development of this book. I first want to thank those colleagues and mentors who participated in a book manuscript workshop, sponsored by the Leslie Center for the Humanities at Dartmouth College. Professors Rebecca Biron, Donald Pease, Jr., and Eng-Beng Lim from Dartmouth, Emeritus Professor Alberto Sandoval-Sánchez from Mount Holyoke College, and Professor Ricardo Ortiz from Georgetown University all generously provided much-needed feedback and advice on how to improve the arguments and the scope of this project. Also at the Leslie Center, Director of Grants GPS Charlotte Bacon gave me invaluable help with my book proposal and with many other projects.

My colleagues in the Department of Spanish and Portuguese at Dartmouth have always been supportive of my scholarship and teaching: Professors Isabel Lozano-Renieblas, Beatriz Pastor, José del Pino, Txetxu Aguado, Annabel Martín, Noelia Cirnigliaro, Sara Muñoz, Jorge Quintana-Navarrete, and Roberto Rey Agudo. I am especially grateful to Professors Raúl Bueno and Silvia Spitta, who were early readers of this project and have provided key insights in how my analyses can dialogue with Latin American studies. I also greatly appreciate the support of my colleagues in the Latin American, Latino, and Caribbean Studies Program; in particular, Professors Matt García, Desirée García, Mary Coffey, Lisa Baldez, Pamela Voekel, Sebastián Díaz-Dualde, Analola Santana, Keith Walker, Carlos Minchillo, and Rodolfo Franconi have been generous interlocutors, and Librarian Jill Baron helped at several stages of the research for this book. I'm especially grateful to Senior Lecturer and dear friend Douglas Moody, with whom I have collaborated on an experiential learning course and community engagement project with migrant dairy farmworkers in the Upper Valley. Members of the Comparative Literature Program have also engaged with this project either as readers, as interlocutors, or as inspirational colleagues whose own scholarship and teaching have had a great influence on my own work; thanks to Professors Gerd Gemunden, Larry Kritzman, Robert St. Clair, Graziella Parati, Michelle Warren, Dennis Washburn, and Antonio Gómez. I would also like to thank Professor Barbara Will, who provided constant advice and mentorship during her tenure as Associate Dean of the Arts and Humanities.

The members of the New England Consortium of Latina/o Studies have been like an extended family for me over the years, and although some have moved away from the New England area, their mentorship and deep commitment to Latinx studies have helped me stay engaged with the most innovative and interdisciplinary approaches in our field. Special thanks to Professors Marisol Negrón (UMass–Boston), Mari Castañeda (UMass–Amherst), Mérida Rúa (Northwestern University), Ginetta Candelario (Smith College), David Hernández (Mount Holyoke College), Irene Matta (Wellesley College), Stephanie Fetta (UMass–Amherst), Carlos Álamo (Vassar College), Hiram Pérez (Vassar College), Albert Laguna (Yale University), and Jacqueline Hidalgo (Williams College).

I have presented portions of this book project at Latina/o Studies Association and Latin American Studies Association conferences, where co-panelists and session organizers have offered insightful comments and recommendations on how this project engages more broadly with Latinx and Queer Studies. Thanks go to Lázaro Lima (CUNY–Hunter College), Larry La Fountain-Stokes (University of Michigan), Carmen Lamas (University of Virginia), Ylce Irizarry (University of South Florida), Frances Aparicio (emerita, Northwestern University), Efraín Barradas (University of Florida), Lourdes Torres (DePaul University), Arnaldo Cruz-Malavé (Fordham University), William Orchard (Queens College), Ben Sifuentes-Jáuregui (Rutgers University), Carlos Decena (Rutgers University), Salvador Vidal-Ortiz (American University), Arlene Dávila (New York University), Jossiana Arroyo (University of Texas–Austin), Ramón Rivera-Servera (University of Texas–Austin), and Laura. G. Gutiérrez (University of Texas–Austin).

My colleague and cherished friend, Professor Lourdes Gutiérrez-Nájera (Western Washington University) has been a longtime interlocuter and collaborator on many projects, conference sessions, and Latinx studies scholarship.

A special thanks goes to Professor Marc Zimmerman (emeritus, University of Houston) for sharing so much wisdom, support, and our mutual love of my hometown, Chicago.

I also want to thank my lifelong friends Kevin Spaulding, George Payán, and Scott Curry for always having my back and being there when I needed them most.

Of course, many heartfelt thanks go to my family: my dearly departed parents, Anastacio and Margarita; my three sisters Lucy, María, and Haydee; and my brother Mike. Our Zoom calls during the COVID-19 pandemic kept me sane and grounded in what really matters when the world around us is going crazy.

Finally, thanks to my editor, Nicole Solano, for believing in this project. I also appreciate the help I received from Allison Van Deventer with editing my bibliography, from Sergey Lobachev with indexing, and from the Audio Transcription Center with the transcription of the manuscript workshop recording.

Notes

INTRODUCTION

1. See Esther Whitfield, *Cuban Currency: The Dollar and "Special Period" Fiction* (Minneapolis: University of Minnesota Press, 2008).

2. See Lorgia García Peña, *The Borders of Dominicanidad: Race, Nation, and Archives of Contradiction* (Durham, NC: Duke University Press, 2016).

3. See Yarimar Bonilla and Marisol LeBrón, *Aftershocks of Disaster: Puerto Rico Before and After the Storm* (Chicago: Haymarket Books, 2019).

4. Sandra Ruiz, *Ricanness: Enduring Time in Anticolonial Performance* (New York: New York University Press, 2019), 1.

5. Ibid., 9.

6. Omise'eke Natasha Tinsley, "Black Atlantic, Queer Atlantic: Queer Imaginings of the Middle Passage," *GLQ* 14, nos. 2–3 (2008): 197. When discussing the maritime and sexual metaphors in Paul Gilroy's seminal work, *The Black Atlantic: Modernity and Double-Consciousness*, Tinsley writes, "Gilroy's black Atlantic seems equally resistant to victimizing and sexualizing its mariners, as if both impulses were too much part of colonial discourse to warrant sustained attention" (196).

7. See Haseenah Ebrahim, "Sarita and the Revolution: Race and Cuban Cinema," *Revista Europea de Estudios latinoamericanos y del Caribe* 82 (2007): 107–118.

8. See Johan Wedel, *Santería Healing: A Journey into the Afro-Cuban World of Divinities, Spirits, and Sorcery* (Gainesville: University Press of Florida, 2004), 33–46.

9. Rafael Ocasio, "Ethnicity and Cuban Revolutionary Ideology in Sara Gómez's *De cierta manera*," *Polifonía* 6, no. 1 (2016): 127–140, https://www.apsu.edu/polifonia/2016-09-ocasio.pdf.

10. Enrico Mario Santí, "Fernando Ortiz: Counterpoint and Transculturation," in *Ciphers of History: Latin American Readings for a Cultural Age* (New York: Palgrave Macmillan, 2005), 174. Santí cites Esteban Pichardo, *Pichardo Novísimo, o Diccionario provincial casi razonado de vozes y frases cubanas*, ed. Esteban Rodríguez Herrera (1862; Havana: Editorial Selecta, 1953), 204.

11. Ibid., 175.

12. See José Quiroga, *Cuban Palimpsests* (Minneapolis: University of Minnesota Press, 2005), 231n1.

13. Fernando Ortiz, *Cuban Counterpoint: Tobacco and Sugar*, trans. Harriet de Onis (Durham, NC: Duke University Press, 1995); Ángel Rama, *Writing Across Cultures: Narrative Transculturation in Latin America*, ed. and trans. David Frye (Durham, NC: Duke University Press, 2012); Mary Louise Pratt, *Imperial Eyes: Travel Writing and Transculturation* (London: Routledge, 1992); Silvia Spitta, *Between Two Waters: Narratives of Transculturation in Latin America* (Houston: Rice University Press, 1995); Alberto Sandoval-Sánchez and Nancy Saporta-Sternbach, *Stages of Life: Transcultural Performance and Identity in U.S. Latina Theater* (Tucson: University of Arizona Press, 2001); John Beverley, *Subalternity and Representation: Arguments in Cultural Theory* (Durham, NC: Duke University Press, 1999); Gareth Williams, *The Other Side of the Popular: Neoliberalism and Subalternity in Latin America* (Durham, NC: Duke University Press, 2002).

14. See Pratt, *Imperial Eyes*, 4.

15. Fernando Ortiz, *Contrapunteo cubano del tabaco y el azúcar*, ed. Enrico Mario Santí (1940; Madrid: Cátedra, 2002), 260. Ortiz loosely subscribed to the functionalist school of Bronislaw Malinowski, which used an organic analogy of a living body to describe social structures and processes. See Joy Hendry, *An Introduction to Social Anthropology: Other People's Worlds* (New York: Palgrave, 1999), 9–11.

16. Ortiz, *Cuban Counterpoint*, 103.

17. See Aníbal Quijano, "Coloniality of Power, Eurocentrism, and Latin America," *Nepantla: Views from South* 1, no. 2 (2000): 533–580.

18. Enrique S. Pumar, "Economic Sociology and Ortiz's *Counterpoint*," in *Cuban Counterpoints: The Legacy of Fernando Ortiz*, ed. Mauricio A. Font and Alfonso W. Quiroz (Lanham, MD: Lexington Books, 2005), 134. Pumar makes reference to German economist Joseph Schumpeter, who theorized that entrepreneurial innovation and risk taking generate the "creative destruction" that is one of the motive forces of a capitalist economy. See Joseph A. Schumpeter, *Capitalism, Socialism, and Democracy* (New York: Harper, 1950).

19. See Alejandro Portes and Rubén G. Rumbaut, *Immigrant America: A Portrait*, 3rd ed. (Berkeley: University of California Press, 2006); Alejandro Portes, William J. Haller, and Luis Eduardo Guarnizo, "Transnational Entrepreneurs: An Alternative Form of Immigrant Economic Adaptation," *American Sociological Review* 67, no. 2 (2002): 278–298.

20. See Roberto González-Echevarría, "Antonio Benítez-Rojo," *New England Review and Breadloaf Quarterly* 6, no. 4 (1984): 575–578.

21. Gloria Anzaldúa, *Borderlands/La Frontera: The Nueva Mestiza* (San Francisco: Spinster/Aunt Lute, 1987).

22. José David Saldívar, *Border Matters: Remapping American Cultural Studies* (Berkeley: University of California Press, 1997).

23. José Esteban Muñoz, *Disidentifications: Queers of Color and the Performance of Politics* (Minneapolis: University of Minnesota Press, 1999).

24. Alberto Sandoval-Sánchez and Nancy Saporta-Sternbach, *Stages of Life: Transcultural Performance and Identity in U.S. Latina Theater* (Tucson: University of Arizona Press, 2001).

25. Pierre Bourdieu, *Pascalian Meditations*, trans. Richard Nice (Stanford, CA: Stanford University Press, 2000), 141.

26. Leo R. Chávez, *The Latino Threat: Constructing Immigrants, Citizens, and the Nation* (Stanford, CA: Stanford University Press, 2013).

27. Ulrike Hanna Meinhof and Anna Triandafyllidou, "Beyond the Diaspora: Transnational Practices as Transcultural Capital," in *Transcultural Europe: Cultural Policy in a Changing Europe*, ed. Ulrike Hanna Meinhof and Anna Triandafyllidou (Hampshire, UK: Palgrave Macmillan, 2006), 202.

28. Bourdieu's scholarship develops key Marxist critiques of capital and commodity fetishism, but his study of culture did not follow the dominant Marxist politics of postwar France. Bridget Fowler writes, "Bourdieu's attempt to retrieve classical Marxism from routinized banalization has involved an attack on literature and art as ideologies and it is the logic of this attack that his critics have often failed to grasp." Fowler, *Pierre Bourdieu and Cultural Theory: Critical Investigations* (London: Sage, 1997), 7.

29. Quijano writes of the Cartesian mind/body split, "The body was and could be nothing but an object of knowledge. From this point of view the human being is, par excellence, a being gifted with reason, and this gift was conceived as localized exclusively in the soul. Thus, the body, by definition incapable of reason, does not have anything that meets reason/subject. The radical separation produced between reason/subject and body and their relations should be seen only as relations between the human subject/reason and the human body/nature, or between spirit and nature. In this way, in Eurocentric rationality the body was fixed as object of knowledge, outside of the environment of subject/reason." Quijano, "Coloniality of Power," 555.

30. Pierre Bourdieu and Loïc J. D. Wacquant, *An Invitation to Reflexive Sociology* (Chicago: University of Chicago Press, 19992), 20.

31. Ibid., 227. In a footnote, Bourdieu attributes this phrase to the May 1968 French student movement "*il est interdit d'interdire.*" Bourdieu invokes this slogan somewhat ironically, considering that he was highly critical of the intellectuals and academics who supported this movement, in particular Raymond Aron. See David L. Swartz, "In Memoriam: Pierre Bourdieu 1930–2002," in *After Bourdieu: Influence, Critique, Collaboration*, ed. David L. Swartz and Vera L. Zolberg (Dordrecht: Kluwer, 2004), 17–23.

32. See Lillian Guerra, Review of *Cuban Counterpoints: The Legacy of Fernando Ortiz*, edited by Mauricio A. Font and Alfonso W. Quiroz, *Americas Review* 63, no. 4 (2007): 654–656; Caroline Pelletier, "Emancipation, Equality and Education: Rancière's Critique of Bourdieu and the Question of Performativity," *Discourse: Studies in the Cultural Politics of Education* 30, no. 2 (2009): 137–150; Fowler, *Pierre Bourdieu and Cultural Theory*, 5.

33. Bourdieu and Wacquant, *Invitation to Reflexive Sociology*, 238.

34. Bourdieu, *Pascalian Meditations*, 15.

35. Bourdieu, *The Logic of Practice*, trans. Richard Nice (Stanford, CA: Stanford University Press, 1990), 68–69.

36. See Michael Grenfell, ed., *Pierre Bourdieu: Key Concepts*, 2nd ed. (Durham, UK: Acumen, 2012).

37. Antonio Benítez-Rojo, *La isla que se repite: El Caribe y la perspectiva posmoderna* (Hanover, NH: Ediciones del Norte, 1989), xiii.

38. Antonio Benítez-Rojo, *The Repeating Island: The Caribbean and the Postmodern Perspective*, trans. James E. Maraniss (Durham, NC: Duke University Press, 1992), 9.

CHAPTER 1 — A FUTURE FOR CUBAN NOSTALGIA IN PLAYS BY
NILO CRUZ AND EDUARDO MACHADO

1. Fernando Ortiz, *Contrapunteo cubano del tabaco y el azúcar*, ed. Enrico Mario Santí (1940; Madrid: Cátedra, 2002), 137.

2. Fernando Ortiz, *Cuban Counterpoint: Tobacco and Sugar*, trans. Harriet de Onis (Durham, NC: Duke University Press, 1995), 4.

3. Ortiz, *Contrapunteo cubano del tabaco y el azúcar*, 142–143.

4. Ortiz, *Cuban Counterpoint*, 8–9.

5. Ortiz, *Contrapunteo cubano del tabaco y el azúcar*, 296.

6. Ortiz, *Cuban Counterpoint*, 114.

7. Ortiz, *Contrapunteo cubano del tabaco y el azúcar*, 152.

8. Ortiz, *Cuban Counterpoint*, 16.

9. Nilo Cruz, *Anna in the Tropics* (New York: Theatre Communications Group, 2003).

10. Eduardo Machado, *The Cook*, in *Havana Is Waiting and Other Plays* (New York: Theatre Communications Group, 2011), 145–225.

11. Cheryl Hardy, "Hysterisis," in *Pierre Bourdieu: Key Concepts*, ed. Michael Grenfell (Durham, UK: Acumen, 2012), 126–145.

12. José Esteban Muñoz, "The Onus of Seeing Cuba: Nilo Cruz's Cubanía," *South Atlantic Quarterly* 99, no. 2/3 (2000): 455–456.

13. Ricardo Ortiz, *Cultural Erotics in Cuban America* (Minneapolis: University of Minnesota Press, 2007), 159.

14. Pierre Bourdieu, *Outline of a Theory of Practice*, trans. Richard Nice (Cambridge: Cambridge University Press, 1977), 78.

15. See Sebastian Luft, *Subjectivity and Lifeworld in Transcendental Philosophy* (Evanston, IL: Northwestern University Press, 2011).

16. Jon D. Rossini, "Cruz, Tolstoy, and the Pulitzer," *Gestos* 20, no. 40 (2005): 63.

17. Mark F. Peterson, "Leading Cuban-American Entrepreneurs: The Process of Developing Motives, Abilities, and Resources," *Human Relations* 48, no. 10 (1995): 1197.

18. Alejandro Portes, "The Social Origins of the Cuban Enclave Economy of Miami," *Sociological Perspectives* 30, no. 4 (1987): 368.

19. Svetlana Boym, *Future of Nostalgia* (New York: Basic Books, 2001), xviii.

20. Raúl Rubio, "Discourses of/on Nostalgia: Cuban America's Real and Fictional Geographies," *Letras Hispanas* 3, no.1 (2006): 14.

21. Elyse Sommer, "*The Cook*, a CurtainUp Review," *CurtainUp*, 2003, http://curtainup.com/cook.

22. Maya Silver, "Baked Alaska: A Creation Story Shrouded in Mystery," *NPR*, March 29, 2016, https://www.npr.org/sections/thesalt/2016/03/29/469957638/baked-alaska-a-creation-story-shrouded-in-mystery.

23. Ortiz, *Contrapunteo cubano del tabaco y el azúcar*, 162.

24. Ortiz, *Cuban Counterpoint*, 23.

25. Eduardo R. del Río, "Eduardo Machado," in *One Island, Many Voices: Conversations with Cuban-American Writers* (Tucson: University of Arizona Press, 2008), 59.

26. Eduardo Machado, *Tastes Like Cuba: An Exile's Hunger for Home* (New York: Gotham Books, 2007), 307.

27. Del Río, "Eduardo Machado," 64–65.

28. Cruz, *Anna in the Tropics*, 10.

29. Ibid., 10.

30. Ibid., 22.

31. Gerald Poyo, "The Impact of Cuban and Spanish Workers on Labor Organizing in Florida, 1870–1900," *Journal of American Ethnic History* 5, no. 2 (1986): 46–63. Poyo writes, "After several years of bitter debates and confrontations, a prominent Cuban political organizer, José Martí, provided a solution to this apparent incompatibility between social and nationalist perspectives. Martí developed a revolutionary program that called for an independent Cuba based on social justice and racial harmony. His program was successful in persuading Cuban workers—anarchists, socialists, and others—to accept a moderate position on labor management affairs during the 1890s for the benefit of a socially progressive Cuban independence movement that gave workers a voice in its structure" (52).

32. Machado, *The Cook*, 175.

33. See Israel Reyes, "Memory and Culinary Nostalgia in Cuban American Performance and Memoir," in *Des/memorias: Culturas y prácticas mnenónicas en América Latina y el Caribe*, ed. Adriana López Labourdette, Silvia Spitta, and Valeria Wagner (Barcelona: Linkgua, 2017), 193–212.

34. Cruz, *Anna in the Tropics*, 21.

35. Ibid., 21.

36. José Enrique Rodó, *Ariel*, ed. Belén Catro (Madrid: Cátedra, 2000), 139.

37. Ibid., 154–155.

38. Rodó writes, *"Cuando el sentido de la utilidad material y el bienestar domina en el carácter de las sociedades humanas con la energía que tiene en lo presente, los resultados del espíritu estrecho y la cultura unilateral son particularmente funestos a la difusión de aquellas preocupaciones puramente ideales que, siendo objeto de amor para quienes les consagran las energías más nobles y perseverantes de su vida, se convierten en una remota, y quizá no sospechada región, para una inmensa parte de los otros."* Ibid., 157. "When the sense of material utility and comfort dominates societies with the energy now shown, the results of narrow minds and one-sided culture are especially fatal to the growth of purely ideal occupations. From being an object of love to those who nobly and perseveringly cherish them, they change to an unknown land, an unexplored region, whose very existence is unsuspected by an immense multitude of others." José Enrique Rodo, *Ariel*, trans. F. J. Stimson (Boston: Houghton Mifflin, 1922), 32–33.

39. Rodó, *Ariel*, 177–178.

40. Ibid., 201.

41. Stimson, *Ariel*, 99.

42. Rodó, *Ariel*, 202.

43. Stimson, *Ariel*, 101.

44. Rodó's version of Caliban precedes the revolutionary appropriation of this figure that appears in Roberto Fernández Retamar's essay *Calibán*, in which the Cuban poet and critic reimagines Shakespeare's "man-fish" as the conquered and colonized *mestizo* of the Americas. Nevertheless, Fernández Retamar reaffirms Rodó's original critique of U.S. military and economic expansionism, although from the perspective of the subaltern subject (Caliban) rather than from the privileged position of the *criollo* intellectual (Ariel). See Roberto Fernández Retamar, *Calibán y otros ensayos: Nuestra América y el mundo* (Havana: Editorial Arte y Literature, 1979).

45. Rodó, *Ariel*, 165.

46. Stimson, *Ariel*, 46.

47. Rodó, *Ariel*, 228.

48. Cruz, *Anna in the Tropics*, 52–53.

49. Lillian Guerra, "Gender Policing, Homosexuality and the New Patriarchy of the Cuban Revolution, 1965–70," *Social History* 35, no. 3 (2010): 268–289.

50. Machado, *The Cook*, 188–189.

51. Ibid., 197.

52. Ibid., 191, 181.

53. See Ted Henken, "Condemned to Informality: Cuba's Experiments with Self-Employment during the Special Period (The Case of the Bed and Breakfasts)," *Cuban Studies* 33 (2002): 1–29.

54. Ortiz, *Contrapunteo cubano del tabaco y el azúcar*, 119.

55. Ortiz writes, *"Entendemos que el vocablo* transculturación *expresa mejor las diferentes fases del proceso transitivo de una cultura a otra. Porque éste no consiste solamente en adquirir una distinta cultura, que es lo que en rigor indica la voz anglo-americana* aculturation, *sino*

*que el proceso implica también necesariamente la pérdida o desarraigo de una cultura prece-
dente, lo que pudiera decirse una parcial* desculturación, *y, además, significa la consiguiente
creación de nuevos fenómenos culturales que pudieran denominarse de* neoculturación."
Ibid., 96–97.

56. While many *lectores* brought their own literary texts to share with factory workers,
historians and *lectores* attest to the fact that it was usually the workers, themselves, who
requested that certain texts be read. See George E. Pozzetta and Gary R. Mormino, "The
Reader and the Worker: 'Los Lectores' and the Culture of Cigarmaking in Cuba and Florida," *International Labor and Working-Class History* 54 (1998): 1–18 and Louis A. Pérez,
"Reminiscences of a Lector: Cuban Cigar Workers in Tamps," *The Florida Historical
Quarterly* 53, no. 4 (1975): 443–449.

57. Julie Buckler writes, "Tolstoy's novel stages spectacular public scenes such as the
Moscow ball, the steeplechase, Levin's wedding to Kitty, and the provincial nobility elec-
tions, but it also asserts that more intimate episodes are no less theatrical in their under-
lying dramatic structure." Julie Buckler, "Reading Anna: Opera, Tragedy, Melodrama,
Farce," in *Approaches to Teaching Tolstoy's* Anna Karenina, ed. Liza Knapp and Amy
Mandelker (New York: Modern Language Association, 2003), 135.

58. Cruz, *Anna in the Tropics,* 22–23.

59. Ibid., 29–30.

60. Ibid., 30.

61. Ibid., 74.

62. See Mary Helen Kashuba and Manuscher Dareshuri, "Agrarian Issues in Tolstoy's
Anna Karenina as a 'Mirror of the Russian Revolution,'" in Knapp and Mandelker,
Approaches to Teaching Tolstoy's Anna Karenina, 90–94.

63. Cruz, *Anna in the Tropics,* 38.

64. Ibid., 41.

65. Ibid., 53.

66. Pozzetta and Mormino, "Reader and the Worker," 13.

67. Cruz, *Anna in the Tropics,* 36.

68. Machado, *The Cook,* 201.

69. Ibid., 202.

70. Ibid., 203.

71. Ibid., 218.

72. Albert Sergio Laguna, *Diversión: Play and Popular Culture in Cuban America*
(New York: New York University Press, 2017).

73. Pierre Bourdieu, *Pascalian Meditations,* trans. Richard Nice (Stanford, CA: Stanford
University Press, 2000), 61.

74. Machado, *The Cook,* 221.

75. Laguna, *Diversión,* 113.

76. Albert Sergio Laguna, "American Tourists Want to See a Cuba That Cubans Would
Rather Leave Behind," *Washington Post,* March 18, 2016.

77. Fernando Ortiz, "The Human Factors of Cubanidad," trans. João Felipe Gonçalves
and Gregory Duff Morton, *HAU: The Journal of Ethnographic Theory* 4, no. 3 (2014): 460.

CHAPTER 2 — DECOLONIZING QUEER CAMP IN NOVELS
BY EDWIN SÁNCHEZ AND ÁNGEL LOZADA

1. David Graeber, *Debt: The First 5,000 Years* (Brooklyn: Melville House, 2014).

2. Pierre Bourdieu, *Distinction: A Social Critique of the Judgement of Taste,* trans. Richard Nice (London: Routledge, 2010).

3. Edwin Sánchez, *Diary of a Puerto Rican Demigod* (Claryville, NY: Self-published, 2015).

4. Ángel Lozada, *No quiero quedarme sola y vacía* (San Juan, PR: Ediciones Isla Negra, 2006).

5. Maurizio Lazzarato, *Making of the Indebted Man An Essay on the Neoliberal Condition*, trans. Joshua David Jordan (Amsterdam: Semiotext(e), 2012), 30.

6. Tara J. Yosso, "Whose Culture Has Capital? A Critical Race Theory Discussion of Community Cultural Wealth," *Race Ethnicity and Education* 8, no. 1 (2005): 77.

7. See Edwin Sánchez's personal website for a list of his awards and grants: www .edwinsanchez-writer.com.

8. Edwin Sánchez, *Unmerciful Good Fortune* (New York: Broadway, 1996); *Plays by Edwin Sánchez* (New York: Broadway, 1997); *Icarus* (New York: Broadway, 1999); *La Bella Familia* (New York: Broadway, 2018).

9. Ángel Lozada, *La patografía* (Mexico City: Editorial Planeta, 1998); *El libro de la letra A* (Brooklyn: Sangría, 2013).

10. See Jossiana Arroyo, "Historias de familia: Migraciones y escritura homosexual en la literatura puertorriqueña," *Revista Canadiense de Estudios Hispánicos* 26, no. 3 (2002): 361–378.

11. Lawrence La Fountain-Stokes, *Translocas: The Politics of Puerto Rican Drag and Trans Performance* (Ann Arbor: University of Michigan Press, 2021), 13.

12. Piri Thomas, *Down These Mean Streets* (New York: Knopf, 1973); Justin Torres, *We the Animals* (Boston: Houghton Mifflin Harcourt, 2011).

13. Lozada, *No quiero quedarme sola y vacía*, 69.

14. Pierre Bourdieu, *The Rules of Art: Genesis and Structure of the Literary Field*, trans. Richard Nice (Stanford, CA: Stanford University Press, 1996), 224.

15. Ibid., 230.

16. John D'Emilio, "Capitalism and Gay Identity," in *Queer Economics: A Reader*, ed. Joyce Jacobsen and Adam Zeller (London: Routledge, 2008), 181–193.

17. Ann Pellegrini, "Consuming Lifestyle: Capitalisms and Transformations in Gay Identity," in *Queer Globalizations: Citizenship and the Afterlife of Colonialism*, ed. Arnaldo Cruz-Malavé and Martin F. Malanasan IV (New York: New York University Press, 2001), 139.

18. Alexandra Chasin, *Selling Out: The Gay and Lesbian Movement Goes to Market* (New York: St. Martin's, 2000), 14–15.

19. Lozada, *No quiero quedarme sola y vacía*, 73–74.

20. Sánchez, *Diary of a Puerto Rican Demigod*, 8.

21. Ibid., 10–11.

22. Ibid., 25.

23. Ibid., 67.

24. Ibid., 67.

25. Ibid., 68.

26. Ibid., 50.

27. Pierre Bourdieu, "The Forms of Capital," in *Handbook of Theory and Research for the Sociology of Education*, ed. John G. Richardson (New York: Greenwood, 1986), 245–246.

28. Lozada, *No quiero quedarme sola y vacía*, 35.

29. Ibid., 40.

30. Pierre Bourdieu, *Language and Symbolic Power*, trans. Richard Nice (Cambridge, MA: Harvard University Press, 1991), 86.

31. Graeber, *Debt*, 170–171.

32. Pierre Bourdieu, *The Logic of Practice*, trans. Richard Nice (Stanford, CA: Stanford University Press, 1990), 191.

33. Ibid., 176.

34. Graeber's arguments on debt forgiveness became widely popular with the Occupy Wall Street movement after the financial crisis of 2008. For critiques of Graeber's methods and theory, see Julio Huato, "Graeber's *Debt*: When a Wealth of Facts Confronts a Poverty of Theory," *Science & Society* 79, no. 2 (2015): 318–325; Bill Maurer, "David Graeber's Wunderkammer, *Debt: The First 5,000 Years*," *Anthropological Forum* 23, no. 1 (2013): 79–93.

35. Bourdieu, *Logic of Practice*, 120.

36. Sánchez, *Diary of a Puerto Rican Demigod*, 209.

37. Susan Bordo, *Unbearable Weight: Feminism, Western Culture, and the Body* (Berkeley: University of California Press, 2004), 155. The source for Bordo's citation is Hilde Bruch, *The Golden Cage: The Enigma of Anorexia Nervosa* (Cambridge, MA: Harvard University Press, 2001).

38. Charlotte Hooper, "Disembodiment, Embodiment, and the Construction of Hegemonic Masculinity," in *Political Economy, Power and the Body: Global Perspectives*, ed. Gillian Youngs (New York: St. Martin's, 2000), 37.

39. Harrison G. Pope Jr., Katharine A. Phillips, and Roberto Olivardia, *The Adonis Complex: The Secret Crisis of Male Body Obsession* (New York: Free Press, 2000).

40. Sánchez, *Diary of a Puerto Rican Demigod*, 203.

41. Lozada, *No quiero quedarme sola y vacía*, 18–19.

42. Ibid., 54.

43. Michel Foucault, *Technologies of the Self: A Seminar with Michel Foucault*, ed. Luther H. Martin, Huck Gutman, and Patrick H. Hutton (Amherst: University of Massachusetts Press, 1998), 18.

44. Lozada, *La patografía*, 261.

45. Lozada, *No quiero quedarme sola y vacía*, 45.

46. Mikhail Bakhtin, *Rabelais and His World*, trans. Hélène Iswolsky (Bloomington: Indiana University Press, 1984).

47. Lozada, *No quiero quedarme sola y vacía*, 123–124.

48. Julia Kristeva, *The Powers of Horror: An Essay on Abjection*, trans. Leon S. Roudiez (New York: Columbia University Press, 1982).

49. Susan Sontag, "Notes on Camp," in *Camp: Queer Aesthetics and the Performing Subject: A Reader*, ed. Fabio Cleto (Ann Arbor: University of Michigan Press, 1999), 56.

50. Sánchez, *Diary of a Puerto Rican Demigod*, 223.

51. Lawrence La Fountain-Stokes, "Gay Shame, Latina- and Latino-Style: A Critique of White Queer Performativity," in *Gay Latino Studies: A Reader*, ed. Michael Hames-García (Durham, NC: Duke University Press, 2011), 56.

52. Bourdieu, *Distinction*, 55–59.

53. For scholarship on homonationalism and the commoditization of queer embodiments, see Jasbir Puar, *Terrorist Assemblages: Homonationalism in Queer Times* (Durham, NC: Duke University Press, 2007); Lisa Duggan, *The Twilight of Equality? Neoliberalism, Cultural Politics, and the Attack on Democracy* (Boston: Beacon, 2003).

54. Keith Harvey, "Camp Talk and Citationality: A Queer Take on 'Authentic' and 'Represented' Utterance," *Journal of Pragmatics* 34 (2002): 1152.

55. Sánchez, *Diary of a Puerto Rican Demigod*, 27.

56. Ibid., 27.

57. Desireé García, *The Migration of Musical Film: From Ethnic Margins to American Mainstream* (New Brunswick, NJ: Rutgers University Press, 2014), 190–191.

58. Priscilla Peña Ovalle, *Dance and the Hollywood Latina: Race, Sex, and Stardom* (New Brunswick, NJ: Rutgers University Press, 2011), 79. Peña Ovalle cites here a reference in Adrienne L. McLean's *Being Rita Hayworth: Labor, Identity, and Hollywood Stardom* (New Brunswick, NJ: Rutgers University Press, 2004).

59. Sánchez, *Diary of a Puerto Rican Demigod*, 27.

60. Ibid., 27.

61. José Esteban Muñoz, *Disidentifications: Queers of Color and the Performance of Politics* (Minneapolis: University of Minnesota Press, 1999), 32.

62. Sánchez, *Diary of a Puerto Rican Demigod*, 104–105.

63. Ibid., 104–105.

64. Ibid., 103.

65. Bourdieu, *Distinction*, 88–89.

66. Ibid., 88–89.

67. Sánchez, *Diary of a Puerto Rican Demigod*, 107.

68. Andrew Ross, "Uses of Camp," in Cleto, *Camp*, 316.

69. Ibid., 317.

70. Lozada, *No quiero quedarme sola y vacía*, 16.

71. Lazzarato, *Making of the Indebted Man*, 31.

72. Marcel Mauss, *The Gift: Forms and Functions of Exchange in Archaic Societies*, trans. Ian Cunnison (London: Cohen & West, 1966), 35.

73. Bourdieu, *Logic of Practice*, 105.

74. Sánchez, *Diary of a Puerto Rican Demigod*, 32. Perle Mesta (1889–1975) was a wealthy Washington, D.C., socialite known as the "hostess with the mostest" for her A-list parties attended by politicians, businessmen, and celebrities.

75. Sánchez, *Diary of a Puerto Rican Demigod*, 32–33.

76. Lozada, *No quiero quedarme sola y vacía*, 87.

77. Ibid., 77.

78. María Celina Bortolotto, "With the Focus on the I/Eye: Shame and Narcissism in Ángel Lozada's *No quiero quedarme sola y vacía*. 2006," *Centro Journal* 24, no. 1 (2012): 129.

79. Eduardo Subirats, "Conversación entre Eduardo Subirats y Ángel Lozada en 'La Casa del Mofongo' en Washington Heights comiéndonos un 'sanculture,'" in *Escritura y esquizofrenia*, ed. Aureliano Ortega Esquivel and Pascual Gay (Mexico: Universidad de Guanajuato, 2011), 213–243.

80. Carlos Vázquez-Cruz, "Sola y vacía me voy a quedar: La Loca de Ángel Lozada y su sobredosis de Nueva York" (paper, La ciudad en las literaturas hispánicas symposium, Lehman College–CUNY, New York, April 2, 2011).

81. Lozada, *No quiero quedarme sola y vacía*, 20.

82. Ibid., 91.

83. Sánchez, *Diary of a Puerto Rican Demigod*, 106.

84. Muñoz, *Disidentifications*, 120.

85. Carlos Ulises Decena interviews a number of Dominican male respondents who live in the United States and assume a nonconfrontational approach to revealing the "tacit subject" of their sexualities to their families. Nevertheless, in one case the respondent narrates the violent encounter with his father when his homosexuality becomes public knowledge. See *Tacit Subjects: Belonging and Same-Sex Desire among Dominican Immigrant Men* (Durham, NC: Duke University Press, 2011), 31–32.

86. Sánchez, *Diary of a Puerto Rican Demigod*, 183.

87. Ibid., 184.

88. Ibid., 154.

89. Ibid., 145.

90. David Eng, *The Feeling of Kinship: Queer Liberalism and the Racialization of Intimacy* (Durham, NC: Duke University Press, 2010), 14.

91. Sánchez, *Diary of a Puerto Rican Demigod*, 142.

92. Ibid., 143.

93. Ibid., 143.

94. Ibid., 144.

95. Ibid., 149–150.

96. Lozada, *No quiero quedarme sola y vacía*, 23.

97. Ibid., 49.

98. Ibid., 49.

99. Subirats, "Conversación entre Eduardo Subirats y Ángel Lozada," 216.

100. See Arlene Dávila, *Sponsored Identities: Cultural Politics in Puerto Rico* (Philadelphia: Temple University Press, 1997).

CHAPTER 3 — ZERO-SUM GAMES IN FICTION BY
JUNOT DÍAZ AND RITA INDIANA HERNÁNDEZ

1. Rita Indiana Hernández, *Papi* (San Juan, PR: Ediciones Vértigo, 2005); Junot Díaz, *This Is How You Lose Her* (New York: Riverhead Books, 2012).

2. While the main focus of this comparison is on *Papi* and *This Is How You Lose Her* (*TIHYLH*), I also refer to some of Junot Díaz's other fictional works since the recurring narrator and protagonist, Yunior, appears repeatedly throughout.

3. Lorgia García Peña, *The Borders of Dominicanidad: Race, Nation, and Archives of Contradiction* (Durham, NC: Duke University Press, 2016), 155.

4. Maja Horn, *Masculinity after Trujillo: The Politics of Gender in Dominican Literature* (Gainesville: University Press of Florida, 2014). For a theory of social remittances, see Peggy Levitt, "Social Remittances: Migration Driven Local-Level Forms of Cultural Diffusion," *International Migration Review* 32, no. 4 (Winter 1998): 926–948.

5. Juan Flores, *The Diaspora Strikes Back: Caribeño Tales of Learning and Turning* (New York: Routledge, 2004), 5.

6. Jennifer Harford Vargas, "Dictating a Zafa: The Power of Narrative Form as Ruin-Reading," in *Junot Díaz and the Decolonial Imagination*, ed. Monica Hanna, Jennifer Harford Vargas, and José David Saldívar (Durham, NC: Duke University Press, 2016): 201–227.

7. Linda Hutcheon, *The Politics of Postmodernism* (London: Routledge, 1989), 13.

8. Junot Díaz, *The Brief Wondrous Life of Oscar Wao* (New York: Rivermaid Books, 2007), 271.

9. Despite Bourdieu's skepticism of psychoanalysis, his writings on masculine domination and its role in the accumulation of social, cultural, and economic capital integrate key elements of psychoanalytic theory. The intersection between Bourdieu's theory of games and the psychoanalytic notions of (de)negation and misrecognition help elucidate the forms of masculine domination that appear in the fiction of Junot Díaz and Rita Indiana Hernández. Bourdieu's theory of games resists the logic of contemporary game theory, with its emphasis on rational action. See George Steinmetz, "Bourdieu's Disavowal of Lacan: Psychoanalytic Theory and the Concepts of 'Habitus' and 'Symbolic Capital,'" *Constellations* 13, no. 4 (2006): 445–464.

10. Indiana Hernández, *Papi*, 7.

11. Rita Indiana Hernández, *Papi: A Novel*, trans. Achy Obejas (Chicago: University of Chicago Press, 2016), 1.

12. Robin Wood, "The American Nightmare: Horror in the 70s," in *Horror: The Film Reader*, ed. Mark Jancovich (London: Routledge, 2002), 28.

13. Ibid., 28.

14. Carol J. Clover, *Men, Women, and Chainsaws: Gender in the Modern Horror Film* (Princeton: Princeton University Press, 1992), 63.

15. George Steinmetz, "Bourdieu's Disavowal of Lacan: Psychoanalytic Theory and the Concepts of 'Habitus' and 'Symbolic Capital,'" *Constellations* 13, no. 4 (2006): 446.

16. Ibid., 447.

17. In particular, Piñera's "La carne" and "El album" satirize Cuban material and bodily practices as grotesque sociabilities that mitigate conditions of precarity and social disfunction.

18. Indiana Hernández, *Papi*, 10.

19. Ibid., 13.

20. Obejas, *Papi: A Novel*, 7.

21. Antonio Viego refers to the theory of the mirror stage in his analysis of Latino racial subjectivity: "We should keep in mind, however, that as Lacan builds his theory over the years that the mirror stage is meant less to reference a particular historical moment that can be isolated and is meant more as a commentary on the structure of subjectivity itself, which is to say a structure of subjectivity where the subject is precipitated according to a fundamental misrecognition in which she identifies with a point outside herself—with an image of herself." See Viego, *Dead Subjects: Toward a Politics of Loss in Latino Studies* (Durham, NC: Duke University Press, 2007), 95.

22. Jacques Lacan, *Écrits: A Selection*, trans. Alan Sheridan (New York: Norton, 1977), 5.

23. Ibid., 14.

24. E. Antonio de Moya, "Power Games and Totalitarian Masculinity in the Dominican Republic," in *Interrogating Caribbean Masculinities: Theoretical and Empirical Analyses*, ed. Rhoda E. Reddock (Kingston: University of West Indies Press, 2004), 98.

25. Ibid., 73–74.

26. Pierre Bourdieu, *Masculine Domination*, trans. Richard Nice (Stanford, CA: Stanford University Press, 2001), 51.

27. Díaz, *Brief Wondrous Life of Oscar Wao*, 299.

28. Karen Wendling and Paul Viminitz argue that although feminists and egalitarians should not ignore the potential applications of game theory in understanding the morality of choices in relation to social institutions, the more pervasive individualism and calculated rationalism that are associated with game theory tend to perpetuate amoral structures of power and dominance. See Karen Wendling and Paul Viminitz, "Could a Feminist and a Game Theorist Co-parent?," *Canadian Journal of Philosophy* 28, no. 1 (March 1998): 33–50.

29. Frank Moya Pons, *The Dominican Republic: A National History* (Princeton: Markus Wiener, 1998), 427.

30. Horn, *Masculinity after Trujillo*, 130.

31. Wendy Brown, *Undoing the Demos: Neoliberalism's Stealth Revolution* (New York: Zone Books, 2015), 43–44.

32. Indiana Hernández, *Papi*, 13.

33. Obejas, *Papi: A Novel*, 7.

34. Brown, *Undoing the Demos*, 107.

35. Indiana Hernández, *Papi*, 22.

36. Obejas, *Papi: A Novel*, 16.

37. Indiana Hernández, *Papi*, 24.

38. Obejas, *Papi: A Novel*, 18.

39. Bourdieu, *Masculine Domination*, 95.

40. Horn, *Masculinity after Trujillo*, 102–104.

41. John Riofrio, "Situating Latin American Masculinity: Immigration, Empathy, and Emasculation in Junot Díaz's *Drown*," *Athenea* 28, no. 1 (June 2006), 33.

42. Christian Krohn-Hansen, *Political Authoritarianism in the Dominican Republic* (London: Palgrave, 2009), 136.

43. Indiana Hernández, *Papi*, 69–70.

44. Obejas, *Papi: A Novel*, 60.

45. Indiana Hernández, *Papi*, 49.

46. Obejas, *Papi: A Novel*, 41.

47. Indiana Hernández, *Papi*, 52.

48. Obejas, *Papi: A Novel*, 44.

49. Bourdieu, *Masculine Domination*, 35–37.

50. Judith Butler, *Gender Trouble: Feminism and the Subversion of Identity* (New York: Routledge, 1997), 175–178.

51. Pierre Bourdieu, *Pascalian Meditations*, trans. Richard Nice (Stanford, CA: Stanford University Press, 2000), 108.

52. Lois McNay summarizes the Butler/Bourdieu debate and concludes that each makes significant contributions to our understanding of gender identity, yet she emphasizes that while Butler rejects experience as a self-evident form of knowledge, Bourdieu's reflexive sociology offers "a reworked notion of phenomenology that treats experience as a relational entity, rather than as an end in itself," which "can begin to reconnect questions of identity formation to a context of visible and latent power relations." See Lois McNay, "Reflexivity: Freedom or Habit of Gender?," in *Feminism after Bourdieu*, ed. Lisa Adkins and Beverly Skeggs (Oxford: Blackwell, 2004), 188.

53. Indiana Hernández, *Papi*, 16.

54. Obejas, *Papi: A Novel*, 10.

55. There is a similar fetishization of the male clothing in Junot Díaz's *Drown*, when Yunior describes the smell of cigar smoke on his absent father's military uniforms as the only traces he has left behind. See Díaz, "Aguantando," in *Drown* (New York: Riverhead Books, 1996), 70.

56. Indiana Hernández, *Papi*, 18.

57. Obejas, *Papi: A Novel*, 12.

58. Indiana Hernández, *Papi*, 19.

59. Obejas, *Papi: A Novel*, 13.

60. Indiana Hernández, *Papi*, 19.

61. Obejas, *Papi: A Novel*, 13.

62. The scene evokes Lacan's analysis of metaphor and metonymy, which draws from Roman Jacobson's structural linguistics but also resonates with Freud's analysis of the condensation and displacement that occur in dream imagery. See Lacan, *Écrits*, 79–80.

63. Horn, *Masculinity after Trujillo*, 121.

64. Pierre Bourdieu, *Distinction: A Social Critique of the Judgement of Taste*, trans. Richard Nice (London: Routledge, 2010), 171–173.

65. Bourdieu, *Masculine Domination*, 25.

66. Eric Berne, *Games People Play: The Psychology of Human Relationships* (New York: Grove Press, 1964), 15.

67. Díaz, "Aguantando," in *Drown*, 80.

68. Quoted in Brown, *Undoing the Demos*, 80.

69. Ibid., 80.

70. Deborah R. Vargas, "Sucia Love: Losing, Lying, and Leaving in *This Is How You Lose Her*," in Hanna, Harford Vargas, and Saldívar, *Junot Díaz and the Decolonial Imagination*, 352.

71. Ibid., 358.

72. De Moya, "Power Games and Totalitarian Masculinity," 70.

73. Ibid., 82.

74. Bourdieu writes, "The habitus is necessity internalized and converted into a disposition that generates meaningful practices and meaning-giving perceptions." Bourdieu, *Distinction*, 166.

75. Israel Reyes, *Humor and the Eccentric Text in Puerto Rican Literature* (Gainesville: University Press of Florida, 2005).

76. Seymour Chatman outlines various theoretical approaches to narrative structure and the distinction between story—the chain of events—and discourse—the expression, how the story's events are told. See Chatman, *Story and Discourse: Narrative Structure in Fiction and Film* (Ithaca, NY: Cornell University Press, 1978), 19–22.

77. Marianne Hirsch describes a "postmemory" as "the relationship that the 'generation after' bears to the personal, collective, and cultural trauma of those who came before— they 'remember' only by means of the stories, images, and behaviors among which they grew up." See Hirsch, *The Generation of Postmemory: Writing and Visual Culture after the Holocaust* (New York: Columbia University Press, 2012), 5.

78. Carlos Ulises Decena cites Junot Díaz as one of the contemporary Dominican writers and artists who articulate a "diasporic critical assault on traditions of dominicanidad." See Carlos Ulises Decena, *Tacit Subjects: Belonging and Same-Sex Desire among Dominican American Men* (Durham, NC: Duke University Press, 2011), 278.

79. Indiana Hernández, *Papi*, 76.

80. Obejas, *Papi: A Novel*, 66.

81. Indiana Hernández, *Papi*, 82.

82. Obejas, *Papi: A Novel*, 72.

83. Steven Gregory, *The Devil Behind the Mirror: Globalization and Politics in the Dominican Republic* (Berkeley: University of California Press, 2007).

84. Bourdieu, *Masculine Domination*, 9.

85. Ibid., 25–26.

86. Ibid., 43.

87. Ibid., 13.

88. See Virginia Vitzhum, "Junot Díaz's Pro-Woman Agenda," *Elle*, September 8, 2012; Lyta Gold, "Junot Díaz and the Myth of the Male Genius," *Current Affairs: A Magazine of Politics and Culture*, May 8, 2018.

89. See Junot Díaz, "The Silence: The Legacy of Childhood Trauma," *New Yorker*, April 16, 2018; Aisha Beliso de Jesús et al., "Open Letter Against Media Treatment of Junot Díaz," *Chronicle of Higher Education*, May 14, 2018; Colleen Flaherty, "Junot Díaz, Feminism and Ethnicity," *Inside Higher Ed*, May 29, 2018.

90. See Beliso de Jesús et al., "Open Letter Against Media Treatment of Junot Díaz."

91. Yomaira Figueroa-Vázquez, *Decolonizing Diasporas: Radical Mappings of Afro-Atlantic Literature* (Evanston, IL: Northwestern University Press, 2020), 79.

92. Ralph E. Rodríguez, *Latinx Literature Unbound: Undoing Ethnic Expectation* (New York: Fordham University Press, 2018), 15.

93. Jorge Luis Borges, "Borges and I," in *Labyrinths*, trans. James E. Irby (1962; New York: New Directions, 2007), 246.

94. Rodríguez, *Latinx Literature Unbound*, 50.

95. Díaz, "The Sun, the Moon, the Stars," in *TIHYLH*, 9.

96. Ibid., 14.

97. Frantz Fanon, *Black Skins, White Masks*, trans. Charles Lam Markmann (New York: Grove, 1967).

98. Ginetta Candelario, *Black Behind the Ears: Dominican Racial Identity from Museums to Beauty Shops* (Durham, NC: Duke University Press, 2007).

99. Indiana Hernández, *Papi*, 126.

100. Obejas, *Papi: A Novel*, 115.

101. See John S. Strong, *Relics of the Buddha* (Princeton, NJ: Princeton University Press, 2004).

102. Butler writes, "When the phallus is lesbian, then it is and is not a masculinist figure of power; the signifier is significantly split, for it both recalls and displaces the masculinism by which it is impelled. And insofar as it operates at the site of anatomy, the phallus (re)produces the spectre of the penis only to enact its vanishing, to reiterate and exploit its perpetual vanishing as the very occasion of the phallus. This opens up anatomy—and sexual difference—as a site of proliferative resignifications." See Judith Butler, "The Lesbian Phallus," in *Bodies That Matter: On the Discursive Limits of "Sex"* (New York: Routledge, 1993), 89.

103. Indiana Hernández, *Papi*, 141.

104. Obejas, *Papi: A Novel*, 129.

105. Juan Duchesne-Winter, "*Papi*, la profecía. Espectáculo e interrupción en Rita Indiana Hernández," *Revista de Crítica Literaria Latinoamericana* 34, no. 67 (2008): 292.

106. Ibid., 307.

107. Díaz, "The Sun, the Moon, the Stars," 22.

108. Ibid., 24.

109. Alejo Carpentier, *El reino de este mundo* (San Juan, PR: Editorial de la Universidad de Puerto Rico, 1994), 8.

110. Junot Díaz, "Monstro," *New Yorker*, June 2012. See also Sarah Quesada, "A Planetary Warning? The Multi-layered Caribbean Zombie in 'Monstro,'" in Hanna, Harford Vargas, and Saldívar, *Junot Díaz and the Decolonial Imagination*, 291–318.

111. Fanon, *Black Skin, White Masks*, 14.

112. Díaz, "The Sun, the Moon, the Stars," 25.

113. Díaz, "Alma," in *TIHYLH*, 50.

114. Christopher González, *Reading Junot Díaz* (Pittsburgh: University of Pittsburgh Press, 2015), 113–114.

115. Matt DelConte, "Why You Can't Speak: Second-Person Narration, Voice, and a New Model for Understanding Narrative," *Style* 37, no. 2 (2003): 211–212.

116. Marisel Moreno, "Debunking Myths, Destabilizing Identities: A Reading of Junot Díaz's 'How to Date a Browngirl, Blackgirl, Whitegirl, or Halfie,'" *Afro-Hispanic Review* 26, no. 2 (Fall 2007): 106–107.

117. Heidi Marie Rimke, "Governing Citizens through Self-Help Literature," *Cultural Studies* 14, no. 1 (2000): 62.

118. Díaz, "The Cheater's Guide to Love," in *TIHYLH*, 216.

119. Ibid., 216.

120. Bourdieu, *Distinction*, xxviii.

121. Ibid., 4.

122. Linda Hutcheon, *Narcissistic Narratives: The Metafictional Paradox* (Waterloo, ON: Wilfred Laurier University Press, 1980), 7.

CHAPTER 4 — THE GENTRIFICATION OF OUR DREAMS IN
LIN-MANUEL MIRANDA'S MUSICAL THEATER

Lin-Manuel Miranda and Quiara Alegría Hudes, *In the Heights: The Complete Book and Lyrics of the Broadway Musical* (Milwaukee, WI: Applause Theater and Cinema Books, 2006), 19. While Lin-Manuel Miranda wrote the music and lyrics for *In the Heights*, the book or libretto was written by Quiara Alegría Hudes. Hudes has had a successful career as a playwright, and her play *Water by the Spoonful* won the 2012 Pulitzer Prize for drama.

1. Miranda and Hudes, *In the Heights*, 63.

2. Pierre Bourdieu and Loïc J. D. Wacquant, *An Invitation to Reflexive Sociology* (Chicago: University of Chicago Press, 1992), 126–127.

3. Lin-Manuel Miranda and Jeremy McCarter, *Hamilton: The Revolution: Being the Complete Libretto of the Broadway Musical, with a True Account of Its Creation, and Concise Remarks on Hip-Hop, the Power of Stories, and the New America* (New York: Grand Central, 2016), 281.

4. Ron Chernow, *Alexander Hamilton* (New York: Penguin, 2004), 722–731.

5. Richard A. Rogers, "From Cultural Exchange to Transculturation: A Review and Reconceptualization of Cultural Appropriation," *Communication Theory* 16, no. 4 (2006): 477.

6. Ibid., 477.

7. Lyra D. Monteiro, "Race-Conscious Casting and the Erasure of the Black Past in *Hamilton*," in *Historians on Hamilton: How a Blockbuster Musical Is Restaging America's Past*, ed. Renee C. Romano and Claire Bond Potter (New Brunswick, NJ: Rutgers University Press, 2018), 62. Monteiro cites a review by Michael Paulson, "'Hamilton' Heads to Broadway in a Hip-Hop Retelling," *New York Times*, July 12, 2015.

8. Rogers, "From Cultural Exchange to Transculturation," 477.

9. Ibid., 495.

10. Antonio Cornejo Polar, "Mestizaje, transculturación, heterogeneida," *Revista de Crítica Literaria Latinoamericana* 20, no. 40 (1994): 368–371; Ángel Rama, *Transculturación narrative en América Latina* (Mexico: Siglo Veintiuno, 1982).

11. Silvia Spitta, *Between Two Waters: Narratives of Transculturation in Latin America* (Houston: Rice University Press, 1995).

12. Mary Louise Pratt, *Imperial Eyes: Travel Writing and Transculturation* (London: Routledge, 1992), 7.

13. John Beverley, *Subalternity and Representation: Arguments in Cultural Theory* (Durham, NC: Duke University Press, 1999), 47.

14. Rogers, "From Cultural Exchange to Transculturation," 491.

15. Miranda and Hudes, *In the Heights*, 40.

16. Porchlight Music Theater, Chicago, October 27, 2016.

17. See Arlene Dávila, *Barrio Dreams: Puerto Ricans, Latinos, and the Neoliberal City* (Berkeley: University of California Press, 2004); David J. Maurrasse, *Listening to Harlem: Gentrification, Community, and Business* (New York: Routledge, 2006); Russell Leigh Sharman, *The Tenants of East Harlem* (Berkeley: University of California Press, 2006); and Ginetta Candelario, *Black Behind the Ears: Dominican Racial Identity from Museums to Beauty Shops* (Durham, NC: Duke University Press, 2007).

18. Ramona Hernández, Utku Sezgin, and Sarah Marrara, "When a Neighborhood Becomes a Revolving Door for Dominicans: Rising Housing Costs in Washington Heights/Inwood and the Declining Presence of Dominicans" (CUNY Dominican Studies Institute, January 2018), 4.

19. Ibid., 5–6.

20. Miranda and Hudes, *In the Heights*, 106.

21. Ibid., 51.

22. Ibid., 52–53.

23. Tara J. Yosso, "Whose Culture Has Capital? A Critical Race Theory Discussion of Community Cultural Wealth," *Race Ethnicity and Education* 8, no. 1 (2005): 77.

24. Jorge Duany, *Blurred Borders: Transnational Migration between the Hispanic Caribbean and the United States* (Chapel Hill: University of North Carolina Press, 2011), 3.

25. Miranda and Hudes, *In the Heights*, 66.

26. Ibid., 19.

27. Ibid., 19.

28. Ibid., 28.

29. Bourdieu and Wacquant, *Invitation to Reflexive Sociology*, 101.

30. Miranda and Hudes, *In the Heights*, 77.

31. Miranda and McCarter, *Hamilton*, 26.

32. Ibid., 16.

33. Bourdieu and Wacquant, *Invitation to Reflexive Sociology*, 76–77.

34. Miranda and McCarter, *Hamilton*, 121.

35. Lázaro Lima, *Being Brown: Sonia Sotomayor and the Latino Question* (Oakland: University of California Press, 2019), 22.

36. Monteiro, "Race-Conscious Casting," 62.

37. As Ron Chernow notes, it is also ironic that the father of the U.S. financial system should die in debt, leaving his wife and family in a precarious economic position (*Alexander Hamilton*, 724).

38. Pierre Bourdieu, "The Contradictions of Inheritance," In *The Weight of the World: Social Suffering in Contemporary Society*, ed. Pierre Bourdieu et. al., trans. Priscilla Parkhurst Fergusson et. al. (Stanford, CA: Stanford University Press, 1999), 508.

39. Miranda and Hudes, *In the Heights*, 38.

40. In the film version directed by John M. Chu, not only is this scene eliminated but the character of Camila is completely absent from the story, having passed away at some time before the start of the action.

41. Bourdieu has consistently criticized the rational action theory of Gary Becker and his notion of human capital, which he faults for ignoring the role that habitus plays in following the "rules of the game" in social and economic fields. See Pierre Bourdieu, *The Social Structures of the Economy*, trans. Chris Turner (Cambridge: Polity, 2005), 7.

42. Wendy Brown, *Undoing the Demos: Neoliberalism's Stealth Revolution* (Brooklyn, NY: Zone Books, 2015), 32.

43. Miranda and Hudes, *In the Heights*, 65.

44. Ibid., 118.

45. Ibid., 86–94.

46. Ibid., 94.

47. José Luis González, *Todos los cuentos* (México City: Facultad de Filosofía y Letras, Universidad Nacional Autónoma de México, 1992).

48. Juan Flores, *Divided Borders: Essays on Puerto Rican Identity* (Houston: Arte Público Press, 1993), 153.

49. William Orchard, "Brown Bodies on the Great White Way: Latina/o Theater, Pop Culture, and Broadway," in *The Routledge Companion to Latina/o Popular Culture*, ed. Frederick Aldama (New York: Routledge, 2016), 148.

50. Cristina Beltrán, *The Trouble with Unity: Latino Politics and the Creation of Identity* (Oxford: Oxford University Press, 2010).

51. See his interview with Terry Gross on NPR (January 3, 2017).

52. See "Presidente de la UPR lamenta protesta contra Lin-Manuel Miranda," *El Nuevo Día*, November 8, 2018.

53. Although the show was originally slated to be performed at the University of Puerto Rico, Río Piedras Theater, it was relocated to the Centro de Bellas Artes in Santurce due to security concerns. See Jhoni Jackson, "A Breakdown of the Controversy Surrounding Lin-Manuel Miranda and 'Hamilton' in Puerto Rico," *Remezcla*, January 10, 2019, https://remezcla.com/features/culture/lin-manuel-miranda-hamilton-in-puerto-rico-controversy/.

54. Mariela Fullana Acosta, "Emocionante el incio de 'Hamilton' en Puerto Rico," *El Nuevo Día*, January 11, 2019, https://www.elnuevodia.com/entretenimiento/cultura/notas/emocionante-el-inicio-de-hamilton-en-puerto-rico/.

55. According to Bourdieu, "The relationship maintained by producers of symbolic goods with other producers, with the signification available within the cultural field at a given moment and, consequently, with their own work, depends very directly on the position they occupy within the field of production and circulation of symbolic goods." Bourdieu, *The Field of Cultural Production: Essays on Art and Literature*, trans. Randal Johnson (New York: Columbia University Press, 1993), 131. One of the key contributions that Bourdieu makes to analysis of the literary field and cultural production is how notions of taste and distinction function to create cultural and political legitimacy for particular works and their artists. Bourdieu has offered empirically based research on writers and artists such as Flaubert and Manet that has documented and analyzed the various fields, habitus, and species of capital that formed part of these creative artists' historical and biographical lifeworlds. In this scholarship Bourdieu focuses mainly on French and European cultural production, and his distinction between cultural producers and nonproducers seems outdated in the contemporary age of viral YouTube videos and self-publishing on the Internet. Nevertheless, his analyses offer more general insights into how cultural and social capital play a role in establishing the legitimacy of an artist's work.

56. Elizabeth Titrington Craft, "'Is This What It Takes Just to Make It to Broadway?!': Marketing *In the Heights* in the Twenty-First Century," *Studies in Musical Theater* 5, no. 1 (2011): 48–69.

57. Michael Gioia, "Where It All Began: A Conversation with Lin-Manuel Miranda and His Father," *Playbill*, n.d.

58. Ivette Manners, "Lin-Manuel Miranda's Family Takes Center Stage," *New York Lifestyles* 2, no. 5 (May 2016).

59. Jessica Derschowitz, "Lin-Manuel Miranda Remixes *Hamilton* with Hillary Clinton Lyrics at Broadway Benefit," *Entertainment Weekly*, October 18, 2016.

60. Hal Boedecker, "Jennifer López, Lin-Manuel Miranda Deliver," *Orlando Sentinel*, July 5, 2016.

61. Ryan McPhee, "Puerto Rico Engagement of *Hamilton*, Starring Lin-Manuel Miranda, Will Sell $10 Tickets through Lottery and Rush," *Playbill*, August 28, 2018.

62. See Pedro M. Anglada Cordero, "An Open Letter to Lin-Manuel Miranda," *Latino Rebels*, June 10, 2016; Ed Morales, "Why Congress (and John Oliver and Lin-Manuel Miranda) Can't Save Puerto Rico," *80 Grados*, April 26, 2016; Vann R. Newkirk, II, "Congress's Promise to Puerto Rico," *Atlantic*, May 19, 2016.

63. Amy Zimmerman, "Freedom for Oscar López Rivera: Why Lin-Manuel Miranda and Puerto Ricans Are Celebrating Obama's Pardon," *Daily Beast*, January 17, 2017.

64. The exhibition debuted on April 6, 2019 and ran until August 25, 2019. See https://hamiltonexhibition.com.

65. Romano and Potter, *Historians on Hamilton: How a Blockbuster Musical Is Restaging America's Past.*

66. Brian Eugenio Herrera, "Looking at *Hamilton* from Inside the Broadway Bubble," in Romano and Potter, *Historians on Hamilton*, 222–245.

67. See essays in Romano and Potter, *Historians on Hamilton*, by Jim Cullen, "Mind the Gap: Teaching *Hamilton*," 249–259; Michael O'Malley, "'The Ten-Dollar Founding Father': Hamilton, Money, and Federal Power," 119–137; Catherine Allgor, "'Remember . . . I'm Your Man': Masculinity, Marriage, and Gender in *Hamilton*," 94–115; and Leslie M. Harris, "The Greatest City in the World? Slavery in New York in the Age of Hamilton," 71–93.

68. Patricia Herrera, "Reckoning with America's Racial Past, Present, and Future in *Hamilton*," in Romano and Potter, *Historians on Hamilton*, 262.

69. See https://flamboyanartsfund.org.

70. Gerard Alessandrini, *Spamilton: An American Parody* (New York: DRG Records, 2017), 8.

71. Jesse David Fox, "Watching Lin-Manuel Miranda Watch the *Hamilton* Parody, *Spamilton*," *Vulture*, September 16, 2016.

72. Janell Ross, "After Calling Their Votes a 'Whitelash,' Van Jones Finds a New Role Reaching Out to Trump Supporters," *Washington Post*, March 20, 2017, https://www .washingtonpost.com/national/fromwhitelash-to-calling-trumps-speech-an-extraordi nary-moment-in-american-politics-thats-van-jones/2017/03/20/240c4aa4-0287-11e7-a391 -651727e77fc0_story.html.

73. For an analysis of social values and upward mobility in Mexican American and Black literature, film, and television, see *Elda María Román, Race and Upward Mobility: Seeking, Gatekeeping, and Other Class Strategies in Postwar America* (Stanford, CA: Stanford University Press, 2018).

74. Alberto Sandoval-Sánchez, *José Can You See? Latinos On and Off Broadway* (Madison: University of Wisconsin Press, 1999), 103–103.

75. Ibid., 107–108.

76. Broadway Productions, "In the Heights: Finding Home" (2020), https://www.linman uel.com/project/in-the-heights-finding-home/.

77. Cited in Craft, "'Is This What It Takes Just to Make It to Broadway?!,'" 62.

78. Ibid., 64. Titrington Craft writes, "Perhaps the most compelling evidence, though, is from the 2008–2009 Broadway League report The Demographics of the Broadway Audience, the first report to include survey data from In the Heights. 'The 2008–2009 season attracted the highest number of attendances by non-Caucasian theatergoers,' the report discloses. . . . 'Hispanics,' a group including international visitors as well as US residents, jumped from 5.7 per cent of the audience composition in the 2007–2008 season, to an unprecedented 8.6 per cent the following year."

79. Felice León, "Let's Talk about *In the Heights* and the Erasure of Dark-Skinned Afro-Latinx Folks," *The Root*, June 9, 2021, https://www.theroot.com/lets-talk-about-in-the-heights -and-the-erasure-of-dark-1847064126.

80. Maira García et al., "'In the Heights' and Colorism: What Is Lost When Afro-Latinos Are Erased," *New York Times*, June 21, 2021, https://www.nytimes.com/2021/06/21/movies /in-the-heights-colorism.html.

CHAPTER 5 — RACE, SEX, AND ENTERPRISING SPIRITS IN WORKS BY DOLORES PRIDA AND MAYRA SANTOS FEBRES

1. Hortense Spillers, "Mama's Baby, Papa's Maybe: An American Grammar Book," *Diacritics* 7, no. 2 (1987): 67.

2. Gloria Anzaldúa, *Borderlands/La Frontera: The New Mestiza* (San Francisco: Spinster/ Aunt Lute, 1987), 3.

3. Rita de Maesneer and Fernanda Bustamante, "Cuerpos heridos en la narrative de Rita Indiana Hernández, Rey Emmanuel Andújar y Junot Díaz," *Revista Iberoamericana* 79, no. 243 (2013): 395.

4. Alberto Sandoval-Sánchez, *José Can You See? Latinos On and Off Broadway* (Madison: University of Wisconsin Press, 1999), 185–186.

5. Dolores Prida, *Botánica*, in *Beautiful Señoritas & Other Plays*, ed. Judith Weiss (Houston: Arte Público Press, 1991), 147.

6. Sandoval-Sánchez, *José Can You See?*, 185.

7. Dolores Prida, "Dolores dice . . . ¿Habla español?," *Latina*, January 27, 2010.

8. Ibid.

9. Melanie Pérez-Ortiz, "Mayra Santos Febres," in *Palabras encontradas: Antología personal de escritores puertorriqueños de los últimos veinte años. conversaciones* (San Juan, PR: Ediciones Callejón, 2008), 57–59.

10. Ibid., 76.

11. Ernesto Quiñonez, *Chango's Fire: A Novel* (New York: Rayo, 2004). See also Ernesto Quiñonez, *Bodega Dreams* (New York: Vintage, 2000).

12. Angie Cruz, *Soledad* (New York: Simon & Schuster, 2001) and Angie Cruz, *Let It Rain Coffee* (New York: Simon & Schuster, 2005).

13. Loida Maritza Pérez, *Geographies of Home: A Novel* (New York: Viking, 1999).

14. Julia Álvarez, *How the García Girls Lost Their Accent* (New York: Plume, 1992) and Julia Álvarez, *Yo!* (Chapel Hill, NC: Algonquin Books of Chapel Hill, 1997).

15. Cristina García, *Dreaming in Cuban* (New York: Knopf, 1992) and Cristina García, *The Agüero Sisters* (New York: Knopf, 1997).

16. I have not yet attended a staged production of *Botánica*. The only production of a Dolores Prida play I have attended was a 2005 Dartmouth College production of *Coser y Cantar* (1981), directed by Francine A'ness of the Department of Spanish and Portuguese and starring students Aída Gil as Ella and Josefina Guzmán as She.

17. See Augusto Boal, *Games for Actors and Non-Actors*, trans. Adrian Jackson (London: Routledge, 2002), 202. Boal writes, "The ritual image is the image of the body in movement; the kinetic image is the image of the movement of the body." Among these sources she cites María de los Ángeles Acuña León, "Mujeres esclavas en la Costa Rica del siglo XVIII: estrategias frente a la esclavitud," *Diálogos: Revista Electrónica de Historia* 5, nos. 1–2 (2005): n.p. and Jalil Sued Badillo and Ángel López Cantos, *Puerto Rico Negro* (Río Piedras, PR: Editorial Cultural, 1986).

18. In a *Nota de la autora* that appears at the end of the novel, Santos Febres list a number of published sources from which she drew in order to imagine the slave women whose testimonials she then invents.

19. Mayra Santos Febres, *Fe en disfraz* (Doral, FL: Alfaguara, 2009), 16–17.

20. Ibid., 21–22.

21. Prida, *Botánica*, 173.

22. Pierre Bourdieu, *Distinction: A Social Critique of the Judgement of Taste*, trans. Richard Nice (London: Routledge, 2010), 188.

23. Pierre Bourdieu and Loïc Wacquant, "On the Cunning of Imperialist Reason," *Theory, Culture, Society* 16, no. 1 (1999): 44.

24. Ibid., 51.

25. Michael Hanchard, *Orpheus and Power: The Movimento Negro of Rio de Janeiro and São Paulo, 1945–1988* (Princeton, NJ: Princeton University Press, 1994).

26. See John D. French, "The Missteps of Anti-imperialist Reason: Bourdieu, Wacquant and Hanchard's *Orpheus and Power*," *Theory, Culture & Society* 17, no. 1 (2000): 107–128;

George Yúdice, *The Expediency of Culture: Uses of Culture in the Global Era* (Durham, NC: Duke University Press, 2003), 80–81; Kia Lilly Caldwell, *Negras in Brazil: Re-envisioning Black Women, Citizenship, and the Politics of Identity* (New Brunswick, NJ: Rutgers University Press, 2007), xix–xxi.

27. Yúdice, *Expediency of Culture*, 81.

28. See Silvia Spitta, *Misplaced Objects: Migrating Collections and Recollections in Europe and the Americas* (Austin: University of Texas Press, 2009).

29. Black Latinas Know Collective, "The Statement" (2019), https://www.blacklatinasknow .org.

30. Prida, *Botánica*, 173.

31. Prida's play (1991) predates her time as a distinguished visiting professor at Dartmouth College in 1995. See Alberto Sandoval-Sánchez and Nancy Saporta Sternbach, *Puro Teatro: A Latina Anthology* (Tucson: University of Arizona Press, 200), 431. Nevertheless, Millie's description of her hazing ritual is characteristic of the kinds of racist controversies that have plagued student life at this institution for many years. See Andrew Garrod, Robert Kilkenny, and Christina Gómez, *Mi Vida, Mi Voz: Latino College Students Tell Their Life Stories* (Ithaca, NY: Cornell University Press, 2004) and Andrew Lohse, *Confessions of an Ivy League Frat Boy* (New York: Thomas Dunne Books, 2014).

32. Bourdieu argues: "Adolescent revolts often represent symbolic denegation, utopian responses to general social controls that allow you to avoid carrying out a full analysis of the specific historical forms, and especially of the *differential* forms, assumed by the constraints that bear on agents of different milieu, and also of forms of social constraint much more subtle than those that operate through the drilling (*dressage*) of bodies." Pierre Bourdieu and Loïc J. D. Wacquant, *An Invitation to Reflexive Sociology* (Chicago: University of Chicago Press, 1992), 195.

33. René Marqués, *La carreta* (1953; San Juan, PR: Editorial Cultural, 2000), 172. Marqués uses a phonetic spelling of the *jíbaro* accent, which characteristically aspirates terminal "s" and "s" before another consonant.

34. Prida, *Botánica*, 164.

35. Christine Ehren, "Dolores Prida's *Casa Propia*, Winner of Repertorio Espanol's "American Dream" Playwriting Contest," *Playbill*, February 4, 1999.

36. See Viral V. Acharya and Matthew Richardson, "Causes of the Financial Crisis," *Critical Review* 21, nos. 2–3 (2009): 195–210. Acharya and Richardson describe how subprime mortgages were packaged and securitized in such a way that created instability in the mortgage market: "The failure of the likes of Fannie Mae, Freddie Mac, and Lehman Brothers, which invested in the securities created out of these mortgages, led to severe counterparty risk concerns that paralyzed capital markets and thus caused the worldwide recession" (208–209).

37. Pierre Bourdieu, *The Social Structures of the Economy*, trans. Chris Turner (Cambridge: Polity, 2005).

38. Ibid., 12.

39. Ibid., 6.

40. Melvin Delgado, *Latino Small Businesses and the American Dream: Community Social Work Practice and Economic and Social Development* (New York: Columbia University Press, 2011), 173.

41. Bárbara J. Robles, "Wealth Creation in Latino Communities: Latino Families, Community Assets, and Cultural Capital," in *Wealth Accumulation and Communities of Color in the United States: Current Issues*, ed. Jessica Gordon Nembhard and Ngina Chiteji (Ann Arbor: University of Michigan Press, 2006), 261–262.

42. Bourdieu, *Social Structures of the Economy*, 167.

43. Arlene Dávila, *Barrio Dreams: Puerto Ricans, Latinos, and the Neoliberal City* (Berkeley: University California Press, 2004), 105.

44. Prida, *Botánica*, 166.

45. Ibid., 180.

46. Wilma Feliciano, "'I Am a Hyphenated American': Interview with Dolores Prida," *Latin American Theatre Review* 29, no. 1 (1995): 117.

47. Margot Weiss, *Techniques of Pleasure: BDSM and the Circuits of Sexuality* (Durham, NC: Duke University Press, 2012), 102.

48. Patricia Valladares-Ruiz, "El cuerpo sufriente como lugar de memoria en *Fe en disfraz*, de Mayra Santos Febres," *Cuadernos de Literatura* 20, no. 40 (2016): 591.

49. Spillers, "Mama's Baby, Papa's Maybe," 68.

50. Santos Febres, *Fe en disfraz*, 26.

51. See Jean-François Lyotard, *Libidinal Economy*, trans. Iain Hamilton Grant (Bloomington: Indiana University Press, 1993).

52. Weiss, *Techniques of Pleasure*, 154.

53. See Angela Carter, *The Sadeian Woman and the Ideology of Pornography* (New York: Pantheon Books, 1978); Jane Gallop, *Intersections: A Reading of Sade with Bataille, Blanchot, and Kossowski* (Lincoln: University of Nebraska Press, 1981); and Mae G. Henderson, "The Stories of (O)Dessa," in *Speaking in Tongues and Dancing Diaspora: Black Women Writing and Performing* (Oxford: Oxford University Press, 2014), 97–114.

54. Spillers, "Mama's Baby, Papa's Maybe," 67.

55. Alexander G. Weheliye, "Pornotropes," *Journal of Visual Culture* 7, no. 1 (2008): 72.

56. Santos Febres, *Fe en disfraz*, 74.

57. Patricia Valladares-Ruiz, "El cuerpo sufriente," 597–599.

58. Henderson, "Stories of (O)Dessa," 113–114.

59. Jennifer Nash, *The Black Body in Ecstasy: Reading Race, Reading Pornography* (Durham, NC: Duke University Press, 2014), 6.

60. Chrissy B. Arce, "La Fe disfrazada y la complicidad del deseo," in *Lección errante: Mayra Santos Febres y el Caribe contemporáneo*, ed. Nadia V. Celis and Juan Pablo Rivera (San Juan, PR: Isla Negra Editores, 2011), 229.

61. Santos Febres, *Fe en disfraz*, 113.

62. Ibid., 114.

CONCLUSION

1. Nicole Acevedo and Suzanne Ciechalski, "Georgia College Students Burn Latina Author's Book after She Talked about White Privilege," *NBC News*, October 12, 2019, https://www.nbcnews.com/news/latino/georgia-college-students-burn-latina-author-s-book-after-she-n1065396.

2. Jennine Capó Crucet, *My Time among the Whites: Notes from an Unfinished Education* (New York: Picador, 2019), 40.

3. Israel Reyes, *Humor and the Eccentric Text in Puerto Rican Literature* (Gainesville: University Press of Florida, 2005).

4. Pierre Bourdieu, *Distinction: A Social Critique of the Judgement of Taste*, trans. Richard Nice (London: Routledge, 2010), 168.

5. Bridget Fowler describes how Bourdieu proposes reflexivity for sociological study: "Bourdieu has argued for three stages of analysis: first, the objective exposure of invisible (objective) determining relations, of which the agent is often unaware; secondly, the

214 NOTES TO PAGE 190

retrieval of subjective perceptions or experience, including a focus on the active making of collective groups such as classes; and, thirdly, a second-order historical construction of the spaces from which perceptions and perspectives derive." See Fowler, *Pierre Bourdieu and Cultural Theory: Critical Investigations* (London: Sage, 1997), 6.

6. NECLS, "Building Community: The New England Consortium of Latina/o Studies (NECLS)," *Latino Studies* 14, no. 5 (2016): 406.

7. See Patricia A. Matthew, ed., *Written/Unwritten: Diversity and the Hidden Truths of Tenure* (Chapel Hill: University of North Carolina Press, 2016).

Bibliography

Acevedo, Nicole, and Suzanne Ciechalski. "Georgia College Students Burn Latina Author's Book After She Talked about White Privilege." *NBC News*, October 12, 2019. https://www.nbcnews.com/news/latino/georgia-college-students-burn-latina-author-s-book-after-she-n1065396.

Acharya, Viral V., and Matthew Richardson. "Causes of the Financial Crisis." *Critical Review* 21, nos. 2–3 (2009): 195–210.

Acuña León, María de los Ángeles. "Mujeres esclavas en la Costa Rica del siglo XVIII: estrategias frente a la esclavitud." *Diálogos: Revista Electrónica de Historia* 5, nos. 1–2 (2005): n.p.

Alessandrini, Gerard. *Spamilton: An American Parody*. New York: DRG Records, 2017.

Allgor, Catherine. "'Remember . . . I'm Your Man': Masculinity, Marriage, and Gender in *Hamilton*." In Romano and Potter, *Historians on Hamilton*, 94–115.

Álvarez, Julia. *How the García Girls Lost Their Accent*. New York: Plume, 1992.

——. *Yo!* Chapel Hill, NC: Algonquin Books of Chapel Hill, 1997.

Anglada Cordero, Pedro M. "An Open Letter to Lin-Manuel Miranda." *Latino Rebels*, June 10, 2016.

Anzaldúa, Gloria. *Borderlands/La Frontera: The Nueva Mestiza*. San Francisco: Spinster/Aunt Lute, 1987.

Arce, Chrissy B. "La Fe disfrazada y la complicidad del deseo." In *Lección errante: Mayra Santos Febres y el Caribe contemporáneo*, edited by Nadia V. Celis and Juan Pablo Rivera, 226–246. San Juan, PR: Isla Negra Editores, 2011.

Arroyo, Jossiana. "Historias de familia: Migraciones y escritura homosexual en la literatura puertorriqueña." *Revista Canadiense de Estudios Hispánicos* 26, no. 3 (2002): 361–378.

Bakhtin, Mikhail. *Rabelais and His World*. Translated by Hélène Iswolsky. Bloomington: Indiana University Press, 1984.

Beliso de Jesús, Aisha, et al. "Open Letter Against Media Treatment of Junot Díaz." *Chronicle of Higher Education*, May 14, 2018. https://www.chronicle.com/blogs/letters/open-letter-against-media-treatment-of-junot-diaz.

Beltrán, Cristina. *The Trouble with Unity: Latino Politics and the Creation of Identity*. Oxford: Oxford University Press, 2010.

Benítez Rojo, Antonio. *La isla que se repite: El Caribe y la perspectiva posmoderna.* Hanover, NH: Ediciones del Norte, 1989.

———. *The Repeating Island: The Caribbean and the Postmodern Perspective.* Translated by James E. Maraniss. Durham, NC: Duke University Press, 1992.

Berne, Eric. *Games People Play: The Psychology of Human Relationships.* New York: Grove Press, 1964.

Beverley, John. *Subalternity and Representation: Arguments in Cultural Theory.* Durham, NC: Duke University Press, 1999.

Bidet, Jacques. "Bourdieu and Historical Materialism." In *Critical Companion to Contemporary Marxism,* translated by Gregory Elliott, edited by Jacques Bidet and Stathis Kouvelakis, 587–603. Leiden: Brill, 2008.

Black Latinas Know Collective. "The Statement." 2019. https://www.blacklatinasknow.org.

Boal, Augusto. *Games for Actors and Non-Actors.* Translated by Adrian Jackson. London: Routledge, 2002.

Boedecker, Hal. "Jennifer López, Lin-Manuel Miranda Deliver." *Orlando Sentinel,* July 5, 2016.

Bonilla, Yarimar, and Marisol LeBrón. *Aftershocks of Disaster: Puerto Rico Before and After the Storm.* Chicago: Haymarket Books, 2019.

Bordo, Susan. *Unbearable Weight: Feminism, Western Culture, and the Body.* Berkeley: University of California Press, 2004.

Borges, Jorge Luis. "Borges and I." In *Labyrinths,* translated by James E. Irby. 1962. New York: New Directions, 2007.

Bortolotto, María Celina. "With the Focus on the I/Eye: Shame and Narcissism in Ángel Lozada's *No quiero quedarme sola y vacía.* 2006." *Centro Journal* 24, no. 1 (2012): 120–133.

Bourdieu, Pierre. "The Contradictions of Inheritance." In Bourdieu et al., *The Weight of the World,* 507–513.

———. *Distinction: A Social Critique of the Judgement of Taste.* Translated by Richard Nice. London: Routledge, 2010.

———. *The Field of Cultural Production: Essays on Art and Literature.* Translated by Randal Johnson. New York: Columbia University Press, 1993.

———. "The Forms of Capital." In *Handbook of Theory and Research for the Sociology of Education,* edited by John G. Richardson, 241–258. New York: Greenwood, 1986.

———. *Language and Symbolic Power.* Cambridge, MA: Harvard University Press, 1991.

———. *The Logic of Practice.* Translated by Richard Nice. Stanford, CA: Stanford University Press, 1990.

———. *Masculine Domination.* Translated by Richard Nice. Stanford, CA: Stanford University Press, 2001.

———. *Outline of a Theory of Practice.* Translated by Richard Nice. Cambridge: Cambridge University Press, 1977.

———. *Pascalian Meditations.* Translated by Richard Nice. Stanford, CA: Stanford University Press, 2000.

———. *The Rules of Art: Genesis and Structure of the Literary Field.* Translated by Richard Nice. Stanford, CA: Stanford University Press, 1996.

———. "Site Effects." In Bourdieu et al., *The Weight of the World,* 123–129.

———. *The Social Structures of the Economy.* Translated by Chris Turner. Cambridge: Polity, 2005.

Bourdieu, Pierre, Alain Accardo, Gabriel Balasz, Stéphane Beaud, Francois Bonvin, Emmanuel Bourdieu, Philippe Bourgois, et. al., eds. *The Weight of the World: Social Suffering in*

Contemporary Society, translated by Priscilla Parkhurst Ferguson, Susan Emanuel, Joe Johnson, and Shoggy T. Waryn. Stanford, CA: Stanford University Press, 1999.

Bourdieu, Pierre, and Loïc J. D. Wacquant. *An Invitation to Reflexive Sociology.* Chicago: University of Chicago Press, 1992.

———. "On the Cunning of Imperialist Reason." *Theory, Culture, Society* 16, no. 1 (1999): 41–58.

Boym, Svetlana. *The Future of Nostalgia.* New York: Basic Books, 2001.

Broadway Productions. "In the Heights: Finding Home." 2020. https://www.linmanuel.com/project/in-the-heights-finding-home/.

Brown, Wendy. *Undoing the Demos: Neoliberalism's Stealth Revolution.* Brooklyn, NY: Zone Books, 2015.

Bruch, Hilde. *The Golden Cage: The Enigma of Anorexia Nervosa.* Cambridge, MA: Harvard University Press, 2001.

Buckler, Julie. "Reading Anna: Opera, Tragedy, Melodrama, Farce." In Knapp and Mandelker, *Approaches to Teaching Tolstoy's* Anna Karenina, 131–136.

Butler, Judith. *Bodies That Matter: On the Discursive Limits of "Sex."* New York: Routledge, 1993.

———. *Gender Trouble: Feminism and the Subversion of Identity.* New York: Routledge, 1997.

Caldwell, Kia Lilly. *Negras in Brazil: Re-envisioning Black Women, Citizenship, and the Politics of Identity.* New Brunswick, NJ: Rutgers University Press, 2007.

Candelario, Ginetta. *Black Behind the Ears: Dominican Racial Identity from Museums to Beauty Shops.* Durham, NC: Duke University Press, 2007.

Capó Crucet, Jennine. *My Time among the Whites: Notes from an Unfinished Education.* New York: Picador, 2019.

Carpentier, Alejo. *El reino de este mundo.* San Juan, PR: Editorial de la Universidad de Puerto Rico, 1994.

Carter, Angela. *The Sadeian Woman and the Ideology of Pornography.* New York: Pantheon Books, 1978.

Chasin, Alexandra. *Selling Out: The Gay and Lesbian Movement Goes to Market.* New York: St. Martin's, 2000.

Chatman, Seymour. *Story and Discourse: Narrative Structure in Fiction and Film.* Ithaca, NY: Cornell University Press, 1978.

Chávez, Leo R. *The Latino Threat: Constructing Immigrants, Citizens, and the Nation.* Stanford, CA: Stanford University Press, 2013.

Chernow, Ron. *Alexander Hamilton.* New York: Penguin, 2004.

Cleto, Fabio, ed. *Camp: Queer Aesthetics and the Performing Subject: A Reader.* Ann Arbor: University of Michigan Press, 1999.

Clover, Carol J. *Men, Women, and Chainsaws: Gender in the Modern Horror Film.* Princeton, NJ: Princeton University Press, 1992.

Craft, Elizabeth Titrington. "'Is This What It Takes Just to Make It to Broadway?!' Marketing *In the Heights* in the Twenty-First Century." *Studies in Musical Theater* 5, no. 1 (2011): 48–69.

Cruz, Angie. *Let It Rain Coffee.* New York: Simon & Schuster, 2005.

———. *Soledad.* New York: Simon & Schuster, 2001.

Cruz, Nilo. *Anna in the Tropics.* New York: Theatre Communications Group, 2003.

Cullen, Jim. "Mind the Gap: Teaching *Hamilton*." In Romano and Potter, *Historians on Hamilton*, 249–259.

Dávila, Arlene. *Barrio Dreams: Puerto Ricans, Latinos, and the Neoliberal City.* Berkeley: University of California Press, 2004.

———. *Sponsored Identities: Cultural Politics in Puerto Rico*. Philadelphia: Temple University Press, 1997.

Decena, Carlos Ulises. *Tacit Subjects: Belonging and Same-Sex Desire among Dominican Immigrant Men*. Durham, NC: Duke University Press, 2011.

DelConte, Matt. "Why You Can't Speak: Second-Person Narration, Voice, and a New Model for Understanding Narrative." *Style* 37, no. 2 (2003): 204–219.

Delgado, Melvin. *Latino Small Businesses and the American Dream: Community Social Work Practice and Economic and Social Development*. New York: Columbia University Press, 2011.

del Río, Eduardo R. "Eduardo Machado." In *One Island, Many Voices: Conversations with Cuban-American Writers*, 56–66. Tucson: University of Arizona Press, 2008.

D'Emilio, John. "Capitalism and Gay Identity." In *Queer Economics: A Reader*, edited by Joyce Jacobsen and Adam Zeller, 181–193. London: Routledge, 2008.

de Moya, E. Antonio. "Power Games and Totalitarian Masculinity in the Dominican Republic." In *Interrogating Caribbean Masculinities: Theoretical and Empirical Analyses*, edited by Rhoda E. Reddock, 68–102. Kingston: University of West Indies Press, 2004.

Derschowitz, Jessica. "Lin-Manuel Miranda Remixes *Hamilton* with Hillary Clinton Lyrics at Broadway Benefit." *Entertainment Weekly*, October 18, 2016.

Díaz, Junot. "Alma." In *This Is How You Lose Her*, 45–50.

———. *The Brief Wondrous Life of Oscar Wao*. New York: Rivermaid Books, 2007.

———. "The Cheater's Guide to Love." In *This Is How You Lose Her*, 177–217.

———. "Monstro." *New Yorker*, June 2012.

———. "The Silence: The Legacy of Childhood Trauma." *New Yorker*, April 16, 2018.

———. "The Sun, the Moon, the Stars." In *This Is How You Lose Her*, 1–25.

———. *This Is How You Lose Her*. New York: Riverhead Books, 2012.

———. "Ysrael." In *Drown*, 1–20. New York: Riverhead Books, 1996.

Duany, Jorge. *Blurred Borders: Transnational Migration between the Hispanic Caribbean and the United States*. Chapel Hill: University of North Carolina Press, 2011.

Duchesne-Winter, Juan. "*Papi*, la profecía. Espectáculo e interrupción en Rita Indiana Hernández." *Revista de Crítica Literaria Latinoamericana* 34, no. 67 (2008): 289–308.

Duggan, Lisa. *The Twilight of Equality? Neoliberalism, Cultural Politics, and the Attack on Democracy*. Boston: Beacon, 2003.

Ebrahim, Haseenah. "Sarita and the Revolution: Race and Cuban Cinema." *Revista Europea de Estudios latinoamericanos y del Caribe* 82 (2007): 107–118.

Ehren, Christine. "Dolores Prida's *Casa Propia*, Winner of Repertorio Espanol's 'American Dream' Playwriting Contest." *Playbill*, February 4, 1999.

Eng, David. *The Feeling of Kinship: Queer Liberalism and the Racialization of Intimacy*. Durham, NC: Duke University Press, 2010.

Fanon, Frantz. *Black Skin, White Masks*. Translated by Charles Lam Markmann. New York: Grove, 1967.

Feliciano, Wilma. "'I Am a Hyphenated American': Interview with Dolores Prida." *Latin American Theatre Review* 29, no. 1 (1995): 113–118.

Fernández Retamar, Roberto. *Calibán y otros ensayos: Nuestra América y el mundo*. Havana: Editorial Arte y Literature, 1979.

Figueroa-Vázquez, Yomaira. *Decolonizing Diasporas: Radical Mappings of Afro-Atlantic Literature*. Evanston, IL: Northwestern University Press, 2020.

Flaherty, Colleen. "Junot Díaz, Feminism and Ethnicity." *Inside Higher Ed*, May 29, 2018.

Flores, Juan. *The Diaspora Strikes Back: Caribeño Tales of Learning and Turning*. New York: Routledge, 2004.

———. *Divided Borders: Essays on Puerto Rican Identity*. Houston: Arte Público Press, 1993.

Foucault, Michel. *Technologies of the Self: A Seminar with Michel Foucault*. Edited by Luther H. Martin, Huck Gutman, and Patrick H. Hutton. Amherst: University of Massachusetts Press, 1998.

Fowler, Bridget. *Pierre Bourdieu and Cultural Theory: Critical Investigations*. London: Sage, 1997.

Fox, Jesse David. "Watching Lin-Manuel Miranda Watch the *Hamilton* Parody, *Spamilton*." *Vulture*, September 16, 2016.

French, John D. "The Missteps of Anti-imperialist Reason: Bourdieu, Wacquant and Hanchard's *Orpheus and Power*." *Theory, Culture & Society* 17, no. 1 (2000): 107–128.

Freud, Sigmund. *The Standard Edition of the Complete Psychological Works of Sigmund Freud, Vol. XIX*. Translated and edited by James Strachey. New York: Norton, 1989.

Fullana Acosta, Mariela. "Emocionante el incio de 'Hamilton' en Puerto Rico." *El Nuevo Día*, January 11, 2019. https://www.elnuevodia.com/entretenimiento/cultura/notas/emocio nante-el-inicio-de-hamilton-en-puerto-rico/.

Gallop, Jane. *Intersections: A Reading of Sade with Bataille, Blanchot, and Kossowski*. Lincoln: University of Nebraska Press, 1981.

García, Cristina. *The Agüero Sisters*. New York: Knopf, 1997.

———. *Dreaming in Cuban*. New York: Knopf, 1992.

García, Desirée. *The Migration of Musical Film: From Ethnic Margins to American Mainstream*. New Brunswick, NJ: Rutgers University Press, 2014.

García, Maira, Sandra E. Garcia, Isabelia Herrera, Concepción de León, Maya Phillips, and A.O. Scott. "'In the Heights' and Colorism: What Is Lost When Afro-Latinos Are Erased." *New York Times*, June 21, 2021. https://www.nytimes.com/2021/06/21/movies /in-the-heights-colorism.html.

García Peña, Lorgia. *The Borders of Dominicanidad: Race, Nation, and Archives of Contradiction*. Durham, NC: Duke University Press, 2016.

Garrod, Andrew, Robert Kilkenny, and Christina Gómez. *Mi Vida, Mi Voz: Latino College Students Tell Their Life Stories*. Ithaca, NY: Cornell University Press, 2004.

Gioia, Michael. "Where It All Began: A Conversation with Lin-Manuel Miranda and His Father." *Playbill*, n.d.

Gold, Lyta. "Junot Díaz and the Myth of the Male Genius." *Current Affairs: A Magazine of Politics and Culture*, May 8, 2018.

González, Christopher. *Reading Junot Díaz*. Pittsburgh: University of Pittsburgh Press, 2015.

González, José Luis. *Todos los cuentos*. México City: Facultad de Filosofía y Letras, Universidad Nacional Autónoma de México, 1992.

González-Echevarría, Roberto. "Antonio Benítez-Rojo." *New England Review and Breadloaf Quarterly* 6, no. 4 (1984): 575–578.

Graeber, David. *Debt: The First 5,000 Years*. Brooklyn: Melville House, 2014.

Grasmuck, Sherri, and Patricia R. Pessar. *Between Two Islands: Dominican International Migration*. Berkeley: University of California Press, 1991.

Gregory, Steven. *The Devil Behind the Mirror: Globalization and Politics in the Dominican Republic*. Berkeley: University of California Press, 2007.

Grenfell, Michael. *Language, Ethnography, and Education: Bridging New Literacy Studies and Bourdieu*. New York: Routledge, 2012.

———, ed. *Pierre Bourdieu: Key Concepts*. 2nd ed. Durham, UK: Acumen, 2012.

Guerra, Lillian. "Gender Policing, Homosexuality and the New Patriarchy of the Cuban Revolution, 1965–70." *Social History* 35, no. 3 (2010): 268–289.

———. Review of *Cuban Counterpoints: The Legacy of Fernando Ortiz*. Edited by Mauricio A. Font and Alfonso W. Quiroz. *Americas Review* 63, no. 4 (2007): 654–656.

"'Hamilton' Heads to Broadway in a Hip-Hop Retelling." *New York Times*, July 12, 2015.

Hanchard, Michael. *Orpheus and Power: The Movimento Negro of Rio de Janeiro and São Paulo, 1945–1988*. Princeton, NJ: Princeton University Press, 1994.

Hanna, Monica, Jennifer Harford Vargas, and José David Saldívar, eds. *Junot Díaz and the Decolonial Imagination*. Durham, NC: Duke University Press, 2016.

Hardy, Cheryl. "Hysterisis." In *Pierre Bourdieu: Key Concepts*, edited by Michael Grenfell, 126–145. Durham, UK: Acumen, 2012.

Harford Vargas, Jennifer. "Dictating a Zafa: The Power of Narrative Form as Ruin-Reading." In *Junot Díaz and the Decolonial Imagination*, edited by Monica Hanna, Jennifer Harford Vargas, and José David Saldívar, 201–227. Durham, NC: Duke University Press, 2016.

Harris, Leslie M. "The Greatest City in the World? Slavery in New York in the Age of Hamilton." In Romano and Potter, *Historians on Hamilton*, 71–93.

Harvey, Keith. "Camp Talk and Citationality: A Queer Take on 'Authentic' and 'Represented' Utterance." *Journal of Pragmatics* 34 (2002): 1145–1165.

Henderson, Mae G. "The Stories of (O)Dessa." In *Speaking in Tongues and Dancing Diaspora: Black Women Writing and Performing*, 97–114. Oxford: Oxford University Press, 2014.

Hendry, Joy. *An Introduction to Social Anthropology: Other People's Worlds*. New York: Palgrave, 1999.

Henken, Ted. "Condemned to Informality: Cuba's Experiments with Self-Employment during the Special Period (The Case of the Bed and Breakfasts)." *Cuban Studies* 33 (2002): 1–29.

Hernández, Ramona, Utku Sezgin, and Sarah Marrara. "When a Neighborhood Becomes a Revolving Door for Dominicans: Rising Housing Costs in Washington Heights/Inwood and the Declining Presence of Dominicans." CUNY Dominican Studies Institute, January 2018.

Herrera, Brian Eugenio. "Looking at *Hamilton* from Inside the Broadway Bubble." In Romano and Potter, *Historians on Hamilton*, 222–245.

Herrera, Patricia. "Reckoning with America's Racial Past, Present, and Future in *Hamilton*." In Romano and Potter, *Historians on Hamilton*, 262.

Hilgers, Mathieu, and Éric Mangez. *Bourdieu's Theory of Social Fields: Concepts and Applications*. New York: Routledge, 2015.

Hirsch, Marianne. *The Generation of Postmemory: Writing and Visual Culture after the Holocaust*. New York: Columbia University Press, 2012.

Hooper, Charlotte. "Disembodiment, Embodiment, and the Construction of Hegemonic Masculinity." In *Political Economy, Power and the Body: Global Perspectives*, edited by Gillian Youngs, 31–58. New York: St. Martin's, 2000.

Horn, Maja. *Masculinity after Trujillo: The Politics of Gender in Dominican Literature*. Gainesville: University Press of Florida, 2014.

Huato, Julio. "Graeber's *Debt*: When a Wealth of Facts Confronts a Poverty of Theory." *Science & Society* 79, no. 2 (2015): 318–325.

Hutcheon, Linda. *Narcissistic Narratives: The Metafictional Paradox*. Waterloo, ON: Wilfred Laurier University Press, 1980.

———. *The Politics of Postmodernism*. London: Routledge, 1989.

Indiana Hernández, Rita. *Papi*. San Juan, PR: Ediciones Vértigo, 2005.

———. *Papi: A Novel*. Translated by Achy Obejas. Chicago: University of Chicago Press, 2016.

Jackson, Jhoni. "A Breakdown of the Controversy Surrounding Lin-Manuel Miranda and 'Hamilton' in Puerto Rico." *Remezcla*, January 10, 2019. https://remezcla.com/features /culture/lin-manuel-miranda-hamilton-in-puerto-rico-controversy/.

Jameson, Fredric. "How Not to Historicize Theory." *Critical Inquiry* 34, no. 3 (2008): 563–582.

Kashuba, Mary Helen, and Manuscher Dareshuri. "Agrarian Issues in Tolstoy's *Anna Karenina* as a 'Mirror of the Russian Revolution.'" In Knapp and Mandelker, *Approaches to Teaching Tolstoy's* Anna Karenina, 90–94.

Knapp, Liza, and Amy Mandelker, eds. *Approaches to Teaching Tolstoy's* Anna Karenina. New York: Modern Language Association, 2003.

Kristeva, Julia. *The Powers of Horror: An Essay on Abjection.* Translated by Leon S. Roudiez. New York: Columbia University Press, 1982.

Krohn-Hansen, Christian. *Political Authoritarianism in the Dominican Republic.* London: Palgrave, 2009.

Lacan, Jacques. *Écrits: A Selection.* Translated by Alan Sheridan. New York: Norton, 1977.

La Fountain-Stokes, Lawrence. "Gay Shame, Latina- and Latino-Style: A Critique of White Queer Performativity." In *Gay Latino Studies: A Critical Reader,* edited by Michael Hames-García, 58–80. Durham, NC: Duke University Press, 2011.

———. *Translocas: The Politics of Puerto Rican Drag and Trans Performance.* Ann Arbor: University of Michigan Press, 2021.

Laguna, Albert Sergio. "American Tourists Want to See a Cuba That Cubans Would Rather Leave Behind." *Washington Post*, March 18, 2016.

———. *Diversión: Play and Popular Culture in Cuban America.* New York: New York University Press, 2017.

Lazzarato, Maurizio. *The Making of the Indebted Man: An Essay on the Neoliberal Condition.* Translated by Joshua David Jordan. Amsterdam: Semiotext(e), 2012.

León, Felice. "Let's Talk about *In the Heights* and the Erasure of Dark-Skinned Afro-Latinx Folks." *The Root*, June 9, 2021. https://www.theroot.com/lets-talk-about-in-the -heights-and-the-erasure-of-dark-1847064126.

Lester, Richard, et al. *The Ritz.* Burbank, CA: Warner Bros., 1976.

Levitt, Peggy. "Social Remittances: Migration Driven Local-Level Forms of Cultural Diffusion." *International Migration Review* 32, no. 4 (Winter 1998): 926–948.

Lima, Lázaro. *Being Brown: Sonia Sotomayor and the Latino Question.* Oakland: University of California Press, 2019.

Lohse, Andrew. *Confessions of an Ivy League Frat Boy.* New York: Thomas Dunne Books, 2014.

López, Gustavo, and Eileen Patten. *Hispanics of Puerto Rican Origin in the United States, 2013.* Washington, DC: Pew Research Center, 2015.

Lozada, Ángel. *El libro de la letra A.* Brooklyn: Sangría, 2013.

———. *La patografía.* Mexico City: Editorial Planeta, 1998

———. *No quiero quedarme sola y vacía.* San Juan, PR: Ediciones Isla Negra, 2006.

Luft, Sebastian. *Subjectivity and Lifeworld in Transcendental Philosophy.* Evanston, IL: Northwestern University Press, 2011.

Lyotard, Jean-François. *Libidinal Economy.* Translated by Iain Hamilton Grant. Bloomington: Indiana University Press, 1993.

Machado, Eduardo. *The Cook.* In *Havana Is Waiting and Other Plays,* 145–225. New York: Theatre Communications Group, 2011.

———. *Tastes Like Cuba: An Exile's Hunger for Home.* New York: Gotham Books, 2007.

Maesneer, Rita de, and Fernanda Bustamante. "Cuerpos heridos en la narrative de Rita Indiana Hernández, Rey Emmanuel Andújar y Junot Díaz." *Revista Iberoamericana* 79, no. 243 (2013): 395–414.

Manners, Ivette. "Lin-Manuel Miranda's Family Takes Center Stage." *New York Lifestyles* 2, no. 5 (May 2016).

Marqués, René. *La carreta*. 1953. San Juan, PR: Editorial Cultural, 2000.

Marx, Karl. *Capital: A Critique of Political Economy. Volume I*. Translated by Ben Fowkes. London: Penguin, 1990.

Matthew, Patricia A., ed. *Written/Unwritten: Diversity and the Hidden Truths of Tenure*. Chapel Hill: University of North Carolina Press, 2016.

Maurer, Bill. "David Graeber's Wunderkammer, *Debt: The First 5,000 Years*." *Anthropological Forum* 23, no. 1 (2013): 79–93.

Maurrasse, David J. *Listening to Harlem: Gentrification, Community, and Business*. New York: Routledge, 2006.

Mauss, Marcel. *The Gift: Forms and Functions of Exchange in Archaic Societies*. Translated by Ian Cunnison. London: Cohen & West, 1966.

McLean, Adrienne L. *Being Rita Hayworth: Labor, Identity, and Hollywood Stardom*. New Brunswick, NJ: Rutgers University Press, 2004.

McNay, Lois. "Reflexivity: Freedom or Habit of Gender?" In *Feminism after Bourdieu*, edited by Lisa Adkins and Beverly Skeggs, 191–209. Oxford: Blackwell, 2004.

McPhee, Ryan. "Puerto Rico Engagement of *Hamilton*, Starring Lin-Manuel Miranda, Will Sell $10 Tickets through Lottery and Rush." *Playbill*, August 28, 2018.

Meinhof, Ulrike Hanna, and Anna Triandafyllidou, eds. *Transcultural Europe: Cultural Policy in a Changing Europe*. Hampshire, UK: Palgrave Macmillan, 2006.

Miranda, Lin-Manuel, and Quiara Alegría Hudes. *In the Heights: The Complete Book and Lyrics of the Broadway Musical*. Milwaukee, WI: Applause Theater and Cinema Books, 2006.

Miranda, Lin-Manuel, and Jeremy McCarter. *Hamilton: The Revolution: Being the Complete Libretto of the Broadway Musical, with a True Account of Its Creation, and Concise Remarks on Hip-Hop, the Power of Stories, and the New America*. New York: Grand Central, 2016.

Monteiro, Lyra D. "Race-Conscious Casting and the Erasure of the Black Past in *Hamilton*." In Romano and Potter, *Historians on Hamilton*, 58–70.

Moore, Rob. "Capital." In *Pierre Bourdieu: Key Concepts*, edited by Michael Grenfell, 98–113. Durham, UK: Acumen, 2012.

Morales, Ed. "Why Congress (and John Oliver and Lin-Manuel Miranda) Can't Save Puerto Rico." *80 Grados*, April 26, 2016.

Moraña, Mabel. *Bourdieu en la periferia: Capital simbólico y campo cultural en América Latina*. Santiago de Chile: Editorial Cuarto Propio, 2014.

Moreno, Marisel. "Debunking Myths, Destabilizing Identities: A Reading of Junot Díaz's 'How to Date a Browngirl, Blackgirl, Whitegirl, or Halfie.'" *Afro-Hispanic Review* 26, no. 2 (Fall 2007): 106–107.

Moya Pons, Frank. *The Dominican Republic: A National History*. Princeton, NJ: Markus Wiener, 1998.

Muñoz, José Esteban. *Disidentifications: Queers of Color and the Performance of Politics*. Minneapolis: University of Minnesota Press, 1999.

———. "The Onus of Seeing Cuba: Nilo Cruz's Cubanía." *South Atlantic Quarterly* 99, no. 2/3 (2000): 455–459.

Nash, Jennifer. *The Black Body in Ecstasy: Reading Race, Reading Pornography*. Durham, NC: Duke University Press, 2014.

NECLS. "Building Community: The New England Consortium of Latina/o Studies (NECLS)." *Latino Studies* 14, no. 5 (2016): 406–412.

Newkirk, Vann R., II. "Congress's Promise to Puerto Rico." *Atlantic*, May 19, 2016.

Ocasio, Rafael. "Ethnicity and Cuban Revolutionary Ideology in Sara Gómez's *De cierta manera*." *Polifonía* 6, no. 1 (2016): 127–140. https://www.apsu.edu/polifonia/2016-09-ocasio.pdf.

O'Malley, Michael. "'The Ten-Dollar Founding Father': Hamilton, Money, and Federal Power." In Romano and Potter, *Historians on Hamilton*, 119–137.

Orchard, William. "Brown Bodies on the Great White Way: Latina/o Theater, Pop Culture, and Broadway." In *The Routledge Companion to Latina/o Popular Culture*, edited by Frederick Aldama, 142–150. New York: Routledge, 2016.

Ortiz, Fernando. *Contrapunteo cubano del tabaco y el azúcar*. Edited by Enrico Mario Santí. 1940. Madrid: Cátedra, 2002.

———. *Cuban Counterpoint: Tobacco and Sugar*. Translated by Harriet de Onis. Durham, NC: Duke University Press, 1995.

———. "The Human Factors of Cubanidad." Translated by João Felipe Gonçalves and Gregory Duff Morton. *HAU: The Journal of Ethnographic Theory* 4, no. 3 (2014): 445–480.

Ortiz, Ricardo. *Cultural Erotics in Cuban America*. Minneapolis: University of Minnesota Press, 2007.

Ortiz Miranda, Carlos. "Haiti and the United States During the 1980s and 1990s: Refugees, Immigration, and Foreign Policy." *San Diego Law Review* 32, no. 673 (1995): 680–693.

Pellegrini, Ann. "Consuming Lifestyle: Capitalisms and Transformations in Gay Identity." In *Queer Globalizations: Citizenship and the Afterlife of Colonialism*, edited by Arnaldo Cruz-Malavé and Martin F. Malanasan IV, 134–146. New York: New York University Press, 2001.

Pelletier, Caroline. "Emancipation, Equality and Education: Rancière's Critique of Bourdieu and the Question of Performativity." *Discourse: Studies in the Cultural Politics of Education*. 30, no. 2 (2009): 137–150.

Peña Ovalle, Priscilla. *Dance and the Hollywood Latina: Race, Sex, and Stardom*. New Brunswick, NJ: Rutgers University Press, 2011.

Pérez, Loida Maritza. *Geographies of Home: A Novel*. New York: Viking, 1999.

Pérez, Louis A. "Reminiscences of a Lector: Cuban Cigar Workers in Tampa." *Florida Historical Quarterly* 53, no. 4 (1975): 443–449.

Pérez-Ortiz, Melanie. "Mayra Santos Febres." In *Palabras encontradas: Antología personal de escritores puertorriqueños de los últimos veinte años. conversaciones*, 51–85. San Juan, PR: Ediciones Callejón, 2008.

Peterson, Mark F. "Leading Cuban-American Entrepreneurs: The Process of Developing Motives, Abilities, and Resources." *Human Relations* 48, no. 10 (1995): 1193–1215.

Pietri, Pedro. "El Puerto Rican MANIFESTO." *El Puerto Rican Embassy*, artistic director Adál Maldonado. http://www.elpuertoricanembassy.org/home.html.

Polar, Antonio Cornejo. "Mestizaje, transculturación, heterogeneida." *Revista de Crítica Literaria Latinoamericana* 20, no. 40 (1994): 368–371.

Pope, Harrison G., Jr., Katharine A. Phillips, and Roberto Olivardia. *The Adonis Complex: The Secret Crisis of Male Body Obsession*. New York: Free Press, 2000.

Portes, Alejandro. "The Social Origins of the Cuban Enclave Economy of Miami." *Sociological Perspectives* 30, no. 4 (1987): 340–372.

Portes, Alejandro, William J. Haller, and Luis Eduardo Guarnizo. "Transnational Entrepreneurs: An Alternative Form of Immigrant Economic Adaptation." *American Sociological Review* 67, no. 2 (2002): 278–298.

Portes, Alejandro, and Rubén G. Rumbaut. *Immigrant America: A Portrait*. 3rd ed. Berkeley: University of California Press, 2006.

Poyo, Gerald. "The Impact of Cuban and Spanish Workers on Labor Organizing in Florida, 1870–1900." *Journal of American Ethnic History* 5, no. 2 (1986): 46–63.

Pozzetta, George E., and Gary R. Mormino. "The Reader and the Worker: 'Los Lectores' and the Culture of Cigarmaking in Cuba and Florida." *International Labor and Working-Class History* 54 (1998): 1–18.

Pratt, Mary Louise. *Imperial Eyes: Travel Writing and Transculturation*. London: Routledge, 1992.

Prida, Dolores. *Botánica*. In *Beautiful Señoritas & Other Plays*, edited by Judith Weiss, 141–180. Houston: Arte Público Press, 1991.

———. "Dolores dice . . . ¿Habla español?" *Latina*, January 27, 2010.

Puar, Jasbir. *Terrorist Assemblages: Homonationalism in Queer Times*. Durham, NC: Duke University Press, 2007.

Pumar, Enrique S. "Economic Sociology and Ortiz's *Counterpoint*." In *Cuban Counterpoints: The Legacy of Fernando Ortiz*, edited by Mauricio A. Font and Alfonso W. Quiroz, 127–138. Lanham, MD: Lexington Books, 2005.

Quesada, Sarah. "A Planetary Warning? The Multi-layered Caribbean Zombie in 'Monstro.'" In *Junot Díaz and the Decolonial Imagination*, edited by Monica Hanna, Harford Vargas, and José David Saldívar, 291–318. Durham, NC: Duke University Press, 2016.

Quijano, Aníbal. "Coloniality of Power, Eurocentrism, and Latin America." *Nepantla: Views from South* 1, no. 2 (2000): 533–580.

Quiñonez, Ernesto. *Bodega Dreams*. New York: Vintage, 2000.

———. *Chango's Fire: A Novel*. New York: Rayo, 2004.

Quiroga, José. *Cuban Palimpsests*. Minneapolis: University of Minnesota Press, 2005.

Rama, Ángel. *Transculturación narrative en América Latina*. Mexico: Siglo Veintiuno, 1982.

———. *Writing Across Cultures: Narrative Transculturation in Latin America*. Edited and translated by David Frye. Durham, NC: Duke University Press, 2012.

Rancière, Jacques. *The Philosopher and His Poor*. Translated by Andrew Parker. Durham, NC: Duke University Press, 2004.

Reyes, Israel. *Humor and the Eccentric Text in Puerto Rican Literature*. Gainesville: University Press of Florida, 2005.

———. "Memory and Culinary Nostalgia in Cuban American Performance and Memoir." In *Des/memorias: Culturas y prácticas mnenónicas en América Latina y el Caribe*, edited by Adriana López Labourdette, Silvia Spitta, and Valeria Wagner, 193–212. Barcelona: Linkgua, 2017.

Rimke, Heidi Marie. "Governing Citizens through Self-Help Literature." *Cultural Studies* 14, no. 1 (2000): 61–78.

Riofrio, John. "Situating Latin American Masculinity: Immigration, Empathy, and Emasculation in Junot Díaz's *Drown*." *Athenea* 28, no. 1 (June 2006): 23–36.

Robles, Bárbara J. "Wealth Creation in Latino Communities: Latino Families, Community Assets, and Cultural Capital." In *Wealth Accumulation and Communities of Color in the United States: Current Issues*, edited by Jessica Gordon Nembhard and Ngina Chiteji, 241–266. Ann Arbor: University of Michigan Press, 2006.

Rodó, José Enrique. *Ariel*. Edited by Belén Catro. Madrid: Cátedra, 2000.

———. *Ariel*. Translated by F. J. Stimson. Boston: Houghton Mifflin, 1922.

Rodríguez, Ralph E. *Latinx Literature Unbound: Undoing Ethnic Expectations*. New York: Fordham University Press, 2018.

Rogers, Richard A. "From Cultural Exchange to Transculturation: A Review and Reconceptualization of Cultural Appropriation." *Communication Theory* 16, no. 4 (2006): 474–503.

Román, Elda María. *Race and Upward Mobility: Seeking, Gatekeeping, and Other Class Strategies in Postwar America*. Stanford, CA: Stanford University Press, 2018.

Romano, Renee C., and Claire Bond Potter, eds. *Historians on Hamilton: How a Blockbuster Musical Is Restaging America's Past*. New Brunswick, NJ: Rutgers University Press, 2018.

Ross, Andrew. "Uses of Camp." In Cleto, *Camp*, 308–329.

Ross, Janell. "After Calling Their Votes a 'Whitelash,' Van Jones Finds a New Role Reaching Out to Trump Supporters." *Washington Post*, March 20, 2017. https://www.washingtonpost.com/national/fromwhitelash-to-calling-trumps-speech-an-extraordinary-moment-in-american-politics-thats-van-jones/2017/03/20/240c4aa4-0287-11e7-a391-651727e77fc0_story.html.

Rossini, Jon D. "Cruz, Tolstoy, and the Pulitzer." *Gestos* 20, no. 40 (2005): 63–77.

Rubio, Raúl. "Discourses of/on Nostalgia: Cuban America's Real and Fictional Geographies." *Letras Hispanas* 3, no. 1 (2006): 13–24.

Ruiz, Sandra. *Ricanness: Enduring Time in Anticolonial Performance*. New York: New York University Press, 2019.

Saldívar, José David. *Border Matters: Remapping American Cultural Studies*. Berkeley: University of California Press, 1997.

Sánchez, Edwin. *Diary of a Puerto Rican Demigod*. Claryville, NY: Self-published, 2015.

———. *Icarus*. New York: Broadway, 1999.

———. *La Bella Familia*. New York: Broadway, 2018.

———. *Plays by Edwin Sánchez*. New York: Broadway, 1997.

———. *Unmerciful Good Fortune*. New York: Broadway, 1996.

Sandoval-Sánchez, Alberto. *José Can You See? Latinos On and Off Broadway*. Madison: University of Wisconsin Press, 1999.

Sandoval-Sánchez, Alberto, and Nancy Saporta Sternbach. *Puro Teatro: A Latina Anthology*. Tucson: University of Arizona Press, 2000.

———. *Stages of Life: Transcultural Performance and Identity in U.S. Latina Theater*. Tucson: University of Arizona Press, 2001.

Santí, Enrico Mario. *Ciphers of History: Latin American Readings for a Cultural Age*. New York: Palgrave Macmillan, 2005.

Santiago, Esmeralda. *When I Was Puerto Rican*. New York: Vintage, 1993.

Santos Febres, Mayra. *Fe en disfraz*. Doral, FL: Alfaguara, 2009.

Schulman, Sarah. *The Gentrification of the Mind: Witness to a Lost Imagination*. Berkeley: University of California Press, 2012.

Schumpeter, Joseph A. *Capitalism, Socialism, and Democracy*. New York: Harper, 1950.

Sharman, Russell Leigh. *The Tenants of East Harlem*. Berkeley: University of California Press, 2006.

Silver, Maya. "Baked Alaska: A Creation Story Shrouded in Mystery." *NPR*, March 29, 2016. https://www.npr.org/sections/thesalt/2016/03/29/469957638/baked-alaska-a-creation-story-shrouded-in-mystery.

Skop, Emily H. "Race and Place in the Adaptation of Mariel Exiles." *International Migration Review* 35, no. 2 (2001): 449–450.

Sommer, Elyse. "*The Cook*, a *CurtainUp* Review." *CurtainUp*, November 15, 2003. http://curtainup.com/cook.html.

Sontag, Susan. "Notes on Camp." In Cleto, *Camp*, 53–65.

Spillers, Hortense. "Mama's Baby, Papa's Maybe: An American Grammar Book." *Diacritics* 7, no. 2 (1987): 64–81.

Spitta, Silvia. *Between Two Waters: Narratives of Transculturation in Latin America*. Houston: Rice University Press, 1995.

———. *Misplaced Objects: Migrating Collections and Recollections in Europe and the Americas*. Austin: University of Texas Press, 2009.

Steinmetz, George. "Bourdieu, Historicity, and Historical Sociology." *Cultural Sociology* 5, no. 1 (2011): 45–66.

———. "Bourdieu's Disavowal of Lacan: Psychoanalytic Theory and the Concepts of 'Habitus' and 'Symbolic Capital.'" *Constellations* 13, no. 4 (2006): 445–464.

Strong, John S. *Relics of the Buddha*. Princeton, NJ: Princeton University Press, 2004.

Subirats, Eduardo. "Conversación entre Eduardo Subirats y Ángel Lozada en 'La Casa del Mofongo' en Washington Heights comiéndonos un 'sanculture.'" In *Escritura y esquizofrenia*, edited by Aureliano Ortega Esquivel and Pascual Gay, 213–243. Mexico: Universidad de Guanajuato, 2011.

Sued Badillo, Jalil, and Ángel López Cantos. *Puerto Rico Negro*. Río Piedras, PR: Editorial Cultural, 1986.

Swartz, David L. "In Memoriam: Pierre Bourdieu 1930–2002." In *After Bourdieu: Influence, Critique, Collaboration*, edited by David L. Swartz and Vera L. Zolberg, 17–23. Dordrecht: Kluwer, 2004.

Thomas, Piri. *Down These Mean Streets*. New York: Knopf, 1973.

Tinsley, Omise'eke Natasha. "Black Atlantic, Queer Atlantic: Queer Imaginings of the Middle Passage." *GLQ* 14, nos. 2–3 (2008): 191–215.

Titrington Craft, Elizabeth. "'Is This What It Takes Just to Make It to Broadway?!' Marketing *In the Heights* in the Twenty-First Century." *Studies in Musical Theater* 5, no. 1 (2011): 49–69.

Torres, Justin. *We the Animals*. Boston: Houghton Mifflin Harcourt, 2011.

Valladares-Ruiz, Patricia. "El cuerpo sufriente como lugar de memoria en *Fen en disfraz*, de Mayra Santos Febres." *Cuadernos de Literatura* 20, no. 40 (2016): 583–604.

Vargas, Deborah R. "Sucia Love: Losing, Lying, and Leaving in *This Is How You Lose Her*." In *Junot Díaz and the Decolonial Imagination*, edited by Monica Hanna, Jennifer Harford Vargas, and José David Saldívar, 351–375. Durham, NC: Duke University Press, 2016.

Vázquez-Cruz, Carlos. "Sola y vacía me voy a quedar: La Loca de Ángel Lozada y su sobredosis de Nueva York." Paper presented at the La ciudad en las literaturas hispánicas symposium, Lehman College–CUNY, New York, April 2, 2011.

Vega, Ana Lydia. "Encancaranublado." In *Encancaranublado y otros cuentos de naufragio*, 11–20. San Juan, PR: Editorial Antillana, 1982.

Vélez, Diana L. "We Are (Not) in This Together: The Caribbean Imaginary in 'Encancaruanublado' by Ana Lydia Vega." *Callaloo* 13, no. 3 (1994): 826–833.

Viego, Antonio. *Dead Subjects: Toward a Politics of Loss in Latino Studies*. Durham, NC: Duke University Press, 2007.

Vitzhum, Virginia. "Junot Díaz's Pro-Woman Agenda." *Elle*, September 8, 2012.

Wedel, Johan. *Santería Healing: A Journey into the Afro-Cuban World of Divinities, Spirits, and Sorcery*. Gainesville: University Press of Florida, 2004.

Weheliye, Alexander G. "Pornotropes." *Journal of Visual Culture* 7, no. 1 (2008): 65–81.

Weiss, Margot. *Techniques of Pleasure: BDSM and the Circuits of Sexuality*. Durham, NC: Duke University Press, 2012.

Wendling, Karen, and Paul Viminitz. "Could a Feminist and a Game Theorist Co-parent?" *Canadian Journal of Philosophy* 28, no. 1 (March 1998): 33–50.

Whitfield, Esther. *Cuban Currency: The Dollar and "Special Period" Fiction.* Minneapolis: University of Minnesota Press, 2008.

Williams, Gareth. *The Other Side of the Popular: Neoliberalism and Subalternity in Latin America.* Durham, NC: Duke University Press, 2002.

Wood, Robin. "The American Nightmare: Horror in the 70s." In *Horror: The Film Reader,* edited by Mark Jancovich, 25–32. London: Routledge, 2002.

Yosso, Tara J. "Whose Culture Has Capital? A Critical Race Theory Discussion of Community Cultural Wealth." *Race Ethnicity and Education* 8, no. 1 (2005): 69–91.

Yúdice, George. *The Expediency of Culture: Uses of Culture in the Global Era.* Durham, NC: Duke University Press, 2003.

Zimmerman, Amy. "Freedom for Oscar López Rivera: Why Lin-Manuel Miranda and Puerto Ricans Are Celebrating Obama's Pardon." *Daily Beast,* January 17, 2017.

Index

About the Author

ISRAEL REYES is an associate professor of Spanish and Portuguese at Dartmouth College. He received his BA in creative writing and English from the University of Illinois–Chicago and his PhD in comparative literature from the University of Iowa. He teaches and conducts research on Latin American, Puerto Rican, and U.S. Latinx literatures and cultures. His publications include *Humor and the Eccentric Text in Puerto Rican Literature* and scholarly articles on Judith Ortiz Cofer, Lalo Alcaraz, Nemesio Canales, Cristina García, Ana Lydia Vega, and Manuel Ramos Otero, among others.

Available titles in the Latinidad: Transnational Cultures in the United States series

Catherine S. Ramírez, Sylvanna M. Falcón, Juan Poblete, Steven C. McKay, and Felicity Amaya Schaeffer, eds., *Precarity and Belonging: Labor, Migration, and Noncitizenship*

Israel Reyes, *Embodied Economies: Diaspora and Transcultural Capital in Latinx Caribbean Fiction and Theater*

Cecilia M. Rivas, *Salvadoran Imaginaries: Mediated Identities and Cultures of Consumption*

Jayson Gonzales Sae-Saue, *Southwest Asia: The Transpacific Geographies of Chicana/o Literature*

Mario Jimenez Sifuentez, *Of Forest and Fields: Mexican Labor in the Pacific Northwest*

Maya Socolovsky, *Troubling Nationhood in U.S. Latina Literature: Explorations of Place and Belonging*

Susan Thananopavarn, *LatinAsian Cartographies*

Melissa Villa-Nicholas, *Latinas on the Line: Invisible Information Workers in Telecommunications*